Contemporary Music in Europe:

A Comprehensive Survey

Contemporary Music in Europe:

A Comprehensive Survey

Edited by
Paul Henry Lang and
Nathan Broder

G. Schirmer, Inc./ *New York*
W. W. Norton & Company, Inc./ *Distributor to the Book Trade*

These essays were written for the Fiftieth Anniversary
issue of *The Musical Quarterly*, January 1965.

CONTENTS

Introduction   3
    PAUL HENRY LANG

Some New British Composers   12
    ANDREW PORTER

French Music Since 1945   22
    ANTOINE GOLÉA

Music in Portugal Today   38
    FRANCIS D. PERKINS

Contemporary Music in Spain   44
    ARTHUR CUSTER

The New Music in Italy   61
    MARIO BORTOLOTTO

On Swiss Musical Composition of the Present   78
    WILLI REICH

Belgium from 1914 to 1964   92
    ALBERT VANDER LINDEN

Dutch Music in the 20th Century   97
    JOS WOUTERS

Scandinavian Music After the Second World War   111
    BO WALLNER

Entr'acte: "Formal" or "Informal" Music?   144
    DANIEL CHARLES

The Variety of Trends in Modern German Music   166
    WOLF-EBERHARD VON LEWINSKI

Contemporary Music in Austria   180
    RUDOLF KLEIN

Problems of Style in 20th-Century Czech Music   191
    JAN RACEK and JIŘÍ VYSLOUŽIL

Modern Hungarian Music   205
    IMRE FÁBIÁN

Music in Yugoslavia   215
    EVERETT HELM

New Music in Greece   225
    NICOLAS SLONIMSKY

Modern Composition in Rumania   236
    NICOLAS SLONIMSKY

Polish Music After World War II   244
    STEFAN JAROCINSKI

Soviet Music Since the Second World War   259
    BORIS SCHWARZ

Musical Composition in Modern Israel   282
    ALEXANDER L. RINGER

Index   299

ILLUSTRATIONS

Between pp. 152 and 153

France

Pierre Boulez

Olivier Messiaen

Italy

Bruno Maderna and Luciano Berio in the electronic studio in Milan

From Sylvano Bussotti's *Five Piano Pieces for David Tudor*

Czechoslovakia

Alois Hába at a quarter-tone piano

France

Pierre Henry

Austria

Sketch by Casper Neher for Alban Berg's *Lulu* (Theater an der Wien, 1962, 1963)

Switzerland

Wladimir Vogel

Yugoslavia

Milo Cipra

Sweden

Ingvar Lidholm

Holland

Scene from Hendrik Andriessen's opera *Philomela*

Switzerland

A page from the large orchestra version of Frank Martin's *Symphonie concertante* in the composer's handwriting

Israel
> Josef Tal in the electronic studio in Jerusalem

Spain
> Ramon Barce, Arthur Custer, Luis de Pablo, Gerardo Gombau

Germany
> Scene from Giselher Klebe's opera *Alkmene* (Berlin, Deutsche Oper)

Norway
> Scene from Arne Nordheim's ballet *Katharsis,* décor by Guy Krogh after Hieronymus Bosch (Oslo, 1962)

Belgium
> Jean Absil

Italy
> Luigi Nono

Poland
> Boleslaw Woytowicz
> Zygmunt Mycielski

Czechoslovakia
> Scene from Bohuslav Martinu's *Julietta, or The Key to Dreams* (Prague, 1963)

Greece
> Jani Christou
> Iannis Xenakis

Soviet Union
> Scene from Prokofiev's ballet *The Stone Flower* (Bolshoi)

Yugoslavia
> Scene from Milko Kelemen's ballet *Appassionata*

Contemporary Music in Europe:

A Comprehensive Survey

INTRODUCTION

By PAUL HENRY LANG

LIKE the poets, few living composers are honored as highly as their predecessors, dead and gone. But we of the 20th century may at least claim that our attitude towards contemporary art is more liberal and enlightened than that of our 19th-century forebears. To be sure, we must face the eternal corollary of artistic change and development: a new style and idiom of music is as repellent to some cultivated minds as it is attractive to others, and it is as natural to youth to see nothing in age but decay as it is to proclaim its own exuberance. In addition, however, today we must count on an unholy confusion in the mind not only of the layman but of many musicians as to what constitutes "modern" music. There is nothing that more disturbs the picture than the acceptance of the composer's dates as a criterion. Rachmaninov was a "20th-century composer," yet he had nothing in common with such leaders of the times as Bartók or Stravinsky. On the other hand, dissonance alone does not make music modern. We must also admit

that the opponents of contemporary music can point to many inconsistencies and weak points on the part of its proponents. In the first
place, they are given to understand that geniuses are crowding the
approaches to Olympus, the only thing standing in the way being the
callous and cynical hostility of public and press. Geniuses have always
been few, but fine musicians deserving of a hearing are numerous.
Among them are many who in the face of the prevailing trends retain
their own artistic convictions. For their integrity these composers suffer
from both the scorn of the avant-garde and the neglect of the public.
Then there are those who imitate without conviction or ability. Somehow they are often the ones who get performed, providing the occasion
for the opponents of advancing art to point out with justice the short-
comings of "modern music." The case of the great converts is perhaps
the most baffling to the spectator who sees the visionaries turn into
prophets by decree. *Le Sacre du printemps* was still a naturalist's vision,
but a vision that was also a bit of judgment, justice pronounced over
an artistic society. Gradually the contours of a promised paradise become
visible and the prophet appears in full stature. With *Threni* Stravinsky
became the bane of the "traditionalists" and the idol of the "progres-
sives." In contradistinction, a Carl Orff could become the internationally
acclaimed popular hero of contemporary music on the basis of a
clever and effective theatrical scheme that is half idyll, half orgy. He
convinced even some astute critics that he was the head of a new
conquering sect. But *Carmina burana* and its companions show only
a substratum of fantasy under a veneer of realism, and it is the non-
musical realism that protects the fantasy.

Now the time is perhaps appropriate for some sort of reckoning;
not a final reckoning, for posterity will have its say, but for the verdict
of this age. The critic writing at the moment must try to assist the
jury to find that verdict, not as an advocate for or against — they have
both been heard at length — but so far as he can and dares as a judge
summing up. Art should be considered on the plane of life in general,
for the subject of art is precisely life. But not life "in general." Art
delimits, particularizes, formalizes; therefore it would perhaps be better
to postpone the judge's summation until we hear a few more witnesses.
The depositions of the witnesses gathered in this anthology deal with the
period that straddles the esthetic, philosophical, and political revolution
separating the post-war years from the first half of our century by a
gulf of turmoil, conflicting passions, destruction, and new idealism.
Every anthology must be, in greater or lesser degree, an affair of

personal predilection; we cull those flowers we like. But let it be said at once that in this case such limitation could not be maintained beyond a modest degree, for this anthology represents not so much an attack on the central problems as a series of reconnaissances from different directions. The discipline of an enforced blueprint would have brought more penalties than rewards, and requiring the contributors to restrict themselves to an exact tracing of the ideas behind the trends could have resulted in a general impression of strained urgency. Therefore we asked each contributor to give us his version of the state of music in his country, requesting him to concentrate on the post-war years but otherwise leaving him free to keep somewhere near the boundary of the inherently relevant.[1] This makes for variety and for a middle ground between dry recitation and lofty philosophizing. The reader will find that most of the collaborators possess the proper appreciation, discrimination, sympathy, and intelligence needed to deal with music whose proportions, values, and motives seem novel, as though projected on a new system of coordinates. The length of the individual articles varies. The Scandinavian report is long because it thoroughly covers four countries, but some others are brief simply because there was very little to report, or because imagination failed to step in to complete what speculation had begun. We limited the inquiry to Europe, since the aim was to acquaint the American reader with the developments whose repercussions he sees around him; but Israel was included because most of her composers are of European origin and training. Daniel Charles's article was placed in the middle. Since it is both an examination of the ideological premises upon which the music of the vanguard is based and also a profession of faith, we trust that it will serve not only as an intermezzo but as a focal point to which ideas and phenomena only touched upon by the chroniclers can be referred.

There are a few scenes performed in this musical amphitheater that we should like to comment upon. Pierre Boulez detects a fundamental difference between the European and the American musical procedures. "Poetry," which still imbues the European composer, he finds missing in the American. This curious judgment seems to be based solely on John Cage, whose works, according to Daniel Charles, "are only known

---

[1] In some cases native reporters were replaced by Americans conversant with the local situation. This was due partly to our inability to find a contributor, partly, as in the case of Russia, to the impossibility of obtaining an article reasonably free from political restraints.

imperfectly, but their reputation appears to be established." We do not intend to question Cage's contribution to contemporary art, but he — and even more some of his followers — do little to convince us that at least some of their contributions are not deliberately induced mental aberrations of common clinical occurrence, and it is rather interesting to observe that as practicing artists they turn their musical collage and frottage to good commercial ends. They seem deliberately to foster an acute and irremovable prejudice in the public. However, they must know that the purely destructive, febrile, nihilistic program of the Dada movement earlier in the century attracted a certain amount of public interest, mostly by its ability to scandalize. We find it inadmissible to make such a sweeping statement as Boulez's on such slender — and outré — evidence. There are a number of excellent American composers living in a despised state of musical respectability whom we would consider far more poetically inclined than many of their European colleagues, not to mention the present-day Stravinsky. If those among our composers who have altogether embraced serialism seem — or indeed are — "less poetic" than their European brethren of the same communion, it is probably owing to the nature of the movement. Since the United States joined the camp with a considerable time lag, what was a process of gradual transformation in Vienna became a revolution in this country. Revolutions are notoriously unpoetic in enforcing their tenet.

This presence or absence of poetry is the very point upon which the future of music hinges, for indeed the intellectual interests of many a total serialist, though genuine, are very carefully limited so as not to cause the least spiritual disturbance. Theirs is an astonishing world with most of the troublesome humanity left out; it is therefore not only bleak — for that in some composers can be a positive quality — but it is dull. And dull not merely by reason of a deficient imagination of humanity, but because of the very thing Boulez lays at our doorstep: lack of poetic intensity. One can observe how this spirit has taken possession of the aged Stravinsky, the most notable convert to serialism. He has become a composer of felicitously ordered surfaces rather than of concentrated depths, a human being designed to run with extraordinary efficiency at low temperature.

Neo-Classicism was too self-conscious to reassert successfully that reaction from Romantic to Classical ideals which was uppermost in the minds of composers in the early 'thirties. Nor was its musical diction, so aptly called a vehicle for sewing-machine counterpoint, adequate to human behavior. We are struck by the contrast between its lucidity of utterance and the suppression of any feeling, the result being all movement and no substance. Then came dodecaphony. Schoenberg was possessed by his idea, and his idea was the most necessary idea of his time. The conception of the "historical necessity" of an idea assuredly needs a thorough examination, but Schoenberg was certainly conscious of it, and it was the servant of an interest beyond the personal. But since dodecaphony was an invented academicism it, too, soon ran its course and was presently succeeded by total serialism in the hope of lending new life or revealing new resources to an exhausted art. The total serialists present a loose confederacy of disparate tribal elements, knit together by a common weal and woe round a small nucleus. It is a quasi-feudal system, with hierarchy and authority, which seems to exert a strong attraction on young composers. Again and again one is struck when studying their music by the intrusion of intellectual problems that are extraneous to art because they are not esthetically resolved. Few are the composers in whose hands such music does not appear more notable for its accomplished technique than for creativeness, and most of the time it becomes monotonous and featureless, as the baffled intellectual is entangled in self-created mental fantasies. Antoine Goléa says that "the music that appears to be the most 'mathematical,' the most 'intellectual,' is precisely that in which the freedom of the composer is the greatest." But what freedom? Is it not Goléa himself who declares that those who "abjured" serialism do not deserve a place among the coryphees? To his great credit, and unlike most others, Goléa is not hostile to these infidels and renegades and does not dispute their value, but it is the doctrine that counts, which of course negates "freedom."

Serialism is ideally placed for the reception of derivative virtue, if we may use that word in its esthetic sense, and the habits of mental fabrication and of self-conscious fluency often join in the gamboling; the participants in this dance can hardly be told apart. Survival value, after all, depends on the personality behind a work of art, however old-fashioned the statement appears. Webern created a province in music that is inalienably his and remains fascinating precisely because of that. It is not there for imitation, nor does it lend itself to comparisons. Opinions pass, the personality remains. These articles speak of "the crisis of serialism" and refer to "classical" serialism (that is, a style on the way to the museum) as well as to "neo-serial" music. Yet, to dismiss serialists because of their lack of humor and of the power of self-criticism, and because of their fluency is to ignore a valid intellectual experience. The conclusion is nevertheless inescapable that serial music

to gain its place in the world's respect must preserve the spiritual autonomy of music. It can do so only by refusing to become swamped by
a featureless conformity that reduces music to a system of clever con-
trivances, a merely ingenious musical machinery with springs, wheels,
and pulleys.

In Boulez's eyes "it would be inconceivable for the creator to descend
from his pedestal," and if he surrenders many of his prerogatives to the
performer he is fairly in the act of leaving his exalted height. The
eternal comparisons with Baroque music are no more relevant than the
serialists' belief in essential kinship with medieval music. It is claimed
that aleatory participation was designed to "strengthen the bonds between the composer and the performer, between the performer and the
work, between the performer and the public." All these are altogether
new notions, unknown in the Baroque era. The bonds between the
composer and the performer did not have to be strengthened for the
simple reason that the two were usually one and the same, therefore
the first two categories cited fall away. Since there was no "public" in
the 18th century, only *Kenner und Liebhaber*, both thoroughly in-
doctrinated in the prevailing style, in contrast to our mass concertgoing
public carefully nurtured on the products of the "good old days," the
third category is also voided. But the most important point is even more
fallacious. "Chance by inadvertence" could never have occurred to
a Baroque performer; he ornamented, filled in, and varied, but essentially
carried out a well and minutely planned musical structure. That there
is danger in this aleatory improvisation is recognized by a number of
composers and by Boulez himself, who appears to frown upon allowing
the interpreter too much liberty in meddling with the composer's scheme.
We shall not even discuss the other argument that insists that the
"chance" of the present-day composer corresponds to the "unexpected"
in traditional, written music; its logic is palpably askew. But we should
like to quote Pope's lines: :

> True ease in writing comes from art, not chance;
> As those move easiest who have learned to dance.

In a work of art the creative artist is an esthetic necessity that cannot
be replaced by reliance on the machine and on chance configurations.
It may be, of course, that the only fault of our electronic composers is
that the machine is ahead of them, that their use of it is before their
time. Their mistake, then, would be in taking the thought of the age too
confidently at its own value. The immense advance of scientific knowledge and technology has given impetus to faith in the "inevitability of

progress." This idea is of course old as the hills, but the belief that this progress will be carried out by the machine, that man can turn to the machine to serve him in all facets of life, including arts and letters, is new. Needless to say, we have no quarrel with the machine as the generator of new musical *resources;* our concern is with the dumb god to whom prayers might be offered but from whom no words could come.

The electronic composers live in the laboratory. The moment they leave its magic switches and circuits they become as unsubstantial as were the ghosts in the *Odyssey* till they had drunk of the blood that restored their speech. The pronouncements issuing from these laboratories are truly bewildering, especially when they venture into regions where both the scientist and the philosopher would tread with wariness. The electronic composers both invoke and deny science, as for instance when they variously assert and reject the presence of the "laws of nature" in physics and music. But the originators of this type of music, from which all its subsequent variants have grown, were neither musicians, nor philosophers, nor scientists, but engineers. And we might add that among Pierre Schaeffer's pioneer crew in the adventure of *musique concrète* there was not one of those pragmatic Americans who would be expected to hit upon such an unpoetic idea, though subsequently our gadgeteer's blood asserted itself with a vengeance. While the electronic party seems to deny the "laws of nature" (whatever they mean by that), they do follow certain laws, albeit laws as unspecified as those of nature. One wonders what is meant when Pierre Henry's electronic composition is declared to be "rigorously constructed according to laws of form and structure specified down to the smallest detail." The old and bald *logos* must be having a difficult time in such vague company. However, things are not really so forbidding as they appear to be. With certain characteristics disproportionately emphasized and with those associated with conventional beauty eschewed to the point, now and then, of obtrusion of the barbarously ugly, the connections of electronic music with our musical language are still to a considerable extent its outlets to the wider world. While the electronic composers synthesize sounds, they also record those produced by "conventional" instruments, they combine live music with electronic means, and in their spare time most of them teach "traditional" music in our universities. Thus like cats, the electronic composers lead a double life. The sleekest and most comfortable Persian, curled upon silken cushions by the living-room fire, can have a nocturnal career at which his human associates can only guess.

We are still linked in the bond of common citizenship with the electronic musician, therefore his artistic achievements cannot be a matter of indifference to us. One wonders, though, whether eventually we shall not be forced to turn to the security and comfort of the machine. The way the difficulties of execution are growing no human hand or larynx will be able to cope with them. The loss would be tremendous, the distinguishing character of the machine being that while it lends itself to the realization of mental operations, it breaks the continuity with nervous impulses, as a musical instrument manipulated by hand does not. There is a chance, however, that we may escape this melancholy future. T. W. Adorno promises a solution that would really do away with all the problems we are struggling with. "A silent, imaginative reading of music could make the sonorous performance superfluous, just as reading the written word suppresses the spoken word." Thus the chief ideologist of the party. While his logic could be challenged by a child, we cannot refrain from delighting in the idea of silent, unheard, and non-existent aleatory musings while reading a score comfortably seated in an armchair.

Finally, a word about the literary aspects of contemporary music. We have arrived at the age of the philosophical composer in the sense that he is not content, as a creator, with musical expression but feels compelled to present his music as an illustration of philosophical ideas. In so doing he often appears like a surgeon who performs a painful but salutary operation without being personally interested in the patient. These philosophical ideas are presented in a manner so diffuse and abstract that it is only for a handful of initiates that they will have a message. The long, very careful, pedantic, rather dry, and strikingly unattractive discourses of Adorno have even infected the French, heretofore immune to vaporous literary expression. Many of these philosophers are deliberately doing violence to the language, bringing no delighted astonishment in return. It is profoundly perverse, so profoundly that we cannot help respecting it and regarding it not as a perversion but as a reversal, as it were, an intentional severance of all links to common experience. Reading the best of them is like trying to watch an interesting scene when someone has his head in the way.

The conventional point of view, often put forward by writers on recent music, has been that the principles of dodecaphony, proclaimed to the world almost two generations ago, have swept away the past. Or, as one of our contributors to this volume says, we are dealing with "the total dismantling of music and its total reconstruction under new laws." *Ecraser l'infâme* is the watchword of the more intransigent of the avant-garde.

To them the "traditionalist" seems very much as the defender of religion in any form seems to the Marxists: a traitor. But beneath all this there is a purpose that is historically understandable and defensible: to weaken the stranglehold of tradition on the present-day composer's freedom. With the ardent champions of this movement objective truth is inevitably a secondary consideration, hence their inability (or a deliberate and perhaps reluctant refusal) to believe in any kind of "other world." Composers who are aware of the existence of other possible worlds are likely to be accused of latent Romanticism, of running away from reality. They are blamed for yielding to the unwholesome habit of relying on purely musical imagination, for being unwilling to stay out in the wind, for taking refuge in a thicket of musical dreams. But the reader will find that a careful reading of *all* the articles will not support this view. Even those perusers who are inclined to flinch from what is undoubtedly a complicated chain of reasoning, will find, if they are brave and open-minded, many things to cheer them on their way. The inquiring mind may linger with the products of a strenuous new generation and speculate upon its symbolism, its line and rhythm, and its conception of the poetic function altogether. Whatever is to be the fate of the individual works, the totality is a distinct experience and deserves to be studied with care.

SOME NEW BRITISH COMPOSERS

By ANDREW PORTER

HOW much easier it is, in London, to produce a tidy, schematic account of French, German, or Czech contemporary music, based firmly on the main works of the main composers, and untroubled by the knowledge of scores and performances that daily, for the English writer, amplify and alter details in his picture of the English contemporary scene. I can generalize confidently about, say, Hans Werner Henze; the moment I do so about, say, Alexander Goehr I realize how reckless the generalizations are. Knowing at any rate the external circumstances that prompted and to some degree determined most of Goehr's works, knowing their initial receptions and subsequent careers, I must reck these factors. And so before passing to the composers I consider the public. If this article has a thesis, it is that the interaction of public welcome and private vision has produced, from a new generation of British composers, an extraordinarily healthy and vital corpus of "central" music, neither reactionary nor avant-garde — though each epithet has been used of it, by people whose standpoint is described by the opposite one.

The wide British musical public has no taste for contemporary music. In the opera house it goes regularly to a handful of works from Mozart to Puccini, in the concert hall from Bach to early Stravinsky. It has no national pride, and when a composer dies he is forgotten (last year there was but a single performance of a Vaughan Williams symphony in London's Festival Hall). This is the steady background; foreground figures come and go, for as Delius remarked in 1912, "the English like vogues for this and that. Now it's Sibelius, and when they're tired of him they'll boost up Bruckner and Mahler." In fact it took about fifty years (and Sibelius's death) for Bruckner and Mahler to oust Sibelius from the public's favor — and then the ousting was complete. This "vogue" aspect of English musical life (which involves performers too) is an important, distasteful, and often unhealthy feature of English musical life. Its movements are unpredictable. Interest does not endure. In the early 'sixties, for example, a trio of contemporary S's came up to challenge the three popular B's (who in England at that time were Beethoven, . Berlioz, and Bruckner); but the vogue for Shostakovich, Stravinsky, and Schoenberg did not, with the big public, last long. At the moment of writing, a rediscovered Elgar is the "smart" composer. One living composer alone draws the crowds, and he with only one work, the *War Requiem.* Yet already the reaction against the paeans that greeted it initially has set in. Of Benjamin Britten's other works, only the *Young Person's Guide* has established itself in popular repertory.

Britten dominates the musical scene. I do not propose to discuss him here; his achievements — however differently rated — are known the world over. And after him, not the older "established" composers — Walton, Tippett, Berkeley, Rawsthorne — but a group of seven younger ones: Alexander Goehr (born 1932), Peter Maxwell Davies (born 1934), and Harrison Birtwistle (born 1934); Richard Rodney Bennett (born 1936) and Nicholas Maw (born 1936); Thea Musgrave (born 1928); Malcolm Williamson (born 1931). All of them are offered more commissions than they can fulfill. Their compositions are published. Up and down the country, festival committees, university authorities, schools, seek works from them. Come to London any week and you are likely to hear a first performance, or at least a first London performance, of a composition by one, perhaps two of them. They were thrown into prominence by a beneficent vogue — the 1960 vogue for "new music" — and they have remained prominent by merit.

One man, William Glock, cut through British musical conservatism and opened the door to "new music." Born in 1908, Glock at first pursued a twin career as pianist (he was a pupil of Schnabel at the Berlin Hochschule, 1930-33) and critic. In 1948 he founded the Bryanston, later Dartington, Summer School of Music, and here he fertilized an inner circle of musicians with his ideas. Men like Stefan Wolpe, Elliott Carter, Nono, Berio, and Maderna came to teach there. Carter brought with him records, among them Schoenberg's Orchestra Variations, and people who attended the early years of the School still recall the excitement among a group of young musicians, including Peter Maxwell Davies, clustering round to hear this work for the first time. In 1959 Glock was appointed Controller of Music to the British Broadcasting Corporation, the largest patron and performer of music in the world, and boldly seized this chance of putting his ideas before the widest public. Before this, most of us still had to learn our Schoenberg and Webern, heard hitherto only in isolated performances, often by performers unversed in the idiom. They became Glock's repertory. The latest products of Donaueschingen and Darmstadt reached England without delay. Young English composers were encouraged. Glock summoned to his staff men like Hans Keller, Schoenberg's most fervent champion in this country; David Drew, probably the most perceptive of younger critics; the composer Alexander Goehr. BBC music was transformed.

At just about the same time most of England's older critics were superseded by enthusiastic young ones, as recorded in a footnote of Stravinsky's *Expositions and Developments* (1962): "The open-door policy to new music in England in the last few years was made possible to a large extent by the accession of an intelligent younger generation in the musical press. In consequence, London has become a great capital of contemporary music." That "in consequence" may be overstating the case, but certainly the critics played their part in changing, for a while, the climate of musical taste. The BBC's Thursday Invitation Concerts of chamber music and their public symphony concerts received praise and publicity. Audiences went. Other concert-giving organizations followed suit. The whole thing snowballed, and for a while London could fairly be called "a great capital of contemporary music." It was a little shrill, a little unnatural. The old guard — and not only the old guard — were dismayed when *The Times,* formerly a repository of accepted opinion, cried that we should hear less Beethoven, more Berio, or, after *Sul ponte di Hiroshima,* that Luigi Nono was the Verdi of our day. The vogue aspect also meant that all this bore hardly on good composers — Rawsthorne, Rubbra — who did not write in one of the fashionable idioms of the time.

One episode from those years, the "Zak Incident," deserves recall, for it was significant, and encouraging. The BBC itself decided to test how much element of bluff there was in the delighted approval that had greeted such works as Stockhausen's *Zyklus.* Hans Keller and Susan Bradshaw went into the studio where the *Zyklus* battery was set out, and "bashed out" a spoof composition on the spur of the moment, also simulating electronic noises into a microphone linked to an echo chamber. On June 5, 1961 a tape drawn from this was broadcast with due solemnity, in a chamber concert with Nono's *Polifonica-Monodia-Ritmica,* Webern's Six Songs Op. 14, Petrassi's *Serenata* and Mozart's

Serenade for thirteen winds. The new work purported to be Piotr Zak's *Mobile* for electronic tape and two partially improvising percussion players, while a parody program-note referred to "strictly measurable quantities-frequency ratios, velocity graphs and decibel indexes." The percussionists were "specially brought over from the Continent" (as a Cologne player had been for *Zyklus*). The work was played twice. The critics gave Zak's *Mobile* their critical attention — in such a context they were bound to. And the result could be deemed a triumph for Stockhausen, a rebuff for those who had declared that the new critics would not be able to tell a hoax from a seriously intentioned composition, or that any old notes would do. To the extent that "Zak" was treated as if he existed, the critics were "taken in"; but not in respect of musical merit: "The BBC's policy of giving the musical avant garde a hearing needs no justification, but there are bound to be occasional lapses; Piotr Zak's *Mobile* sounded like one of them . . . such recognizably musical events as did occur seemed trivial" (*The Times*); "A *farce d'atelier* which has no possible claim to be considered as music" (*The Listener*); "wholly unrewarding . . . non-musical origins" (*The Telegraph*). London is center of Britain's music-making, but fashion reaches out to the provinces. In May 1961 for example there was a packed house in Glasgow for the British premières of Stockhausen's *Gruppen,* Gunther Schuller's *Spectra,* and Thea Musgrave's *Obliques.*

But the vogue for new music did not last. In 1963 London concert audiences fell off; programs became more conventional. Building operations at the Festival Hall, which made it more difficult and less attractive of access, may have had something to do with it; but it was noticeable that the BBC Invitation Concerts became less adventurous, and received less attention. The opposite of a snowballing process began. The critics quickly grew older, steadier: responsibility brings with it conservatism. Glock's programs became less committedly avant-garde. The first intoxication had passed. But the legacy of those years is a public that has had at any rate some first-hand experience of Boulez, Berio, Stockhausen, Nono; several solo performers and ensembles accustomed to working in post-Webern idioms; a steady if small audience who support the recitals of our several progressive concert-series; and a continuing stream of new commissions for the young composers who were thrown to the fore by the 1960-61 wave.

Some generalizations about the seven named above may now be risked. They are all much of an age. All are familiar with what might be called the Darmstadt experience. None of them shows much continuity with the English symphonic school, dominant well into the 'fifties, and still active. Five of them studied in Paris. All of them, when younger, have flirted with fashion, and in recent years striven for a new clarity and communicativeness. None has an ivory-tower attitude. All of them have welcomed, in an almost 18th-century way, commissions that have set strict limits to means, and in varying degrees to idiom. At the moment at least six of them are engaged in the form that most openly bids for public acceptance: opera.

The first three, Alexander Goehr, Peter Maxwell Davies, and Harrison Birtwistle, constitute the "Manchester Group," linked initially by their being students in Manchester at the same time and forming in 1953, with the pianist John Ogdon, an actual Group that brought its music to London in 1956; re-linked subsequently (after each had pursued a rather different path) in their organizing a Summer School at Wardour Castle, Dorset, in 1964. Goehr[1] is the son of the late Walter Goehr, who was a Schoenberg pupil at the Berlin Hochschule, and a conductor of modern music. An early work, the Fantasias for clarinet and piano Op. 3 (1951-52), shows him fluent, while still in England, in the international, anonymous, avant-garde style of the day. The Fantasia for orchestra Op. 4 (1954) was performed at Darmstadt. In 1955-56 came his year at the Paris Conservatoire — Messiaen's composition classes, strict discipline with Yvonne Loriod. The record of subsequent works shows that most of them, according to current English practice, were first heard at festivals, written to their commission, and that many of them have had only occasional, and some of them no, performances since.

Goehr's is one of the toughest and most vigorous musical minds working in England today. To define his special quality is difficult. One might put it like this: that each composition is not a piece of self-expression, nor an experiment, but an object created by him, created for us, and bearing a definite relation to, even making a statement about, all other music. Many modern works seem to find their starting-point in

[1] See Hugh Wood, *The Music of Alexander Goehr,* in *Musical Times,* May 1962. *Grove* will be consulted in vain for details of these composers. Readers must forgive the apparent immodesty of my citing so often articles in the paper I edit; these articles were deliberately planned to provide the biographical information and list of works omitted in our conservative reference-books. Each issue also contains a composition by the composer in question, which had to be short, to an English text, and technically accessible to an amateur S.A.T.B. choir. Some, as a consequence, are uncharacteristic; Goehr's happens to be a fine, if small-scale, example of his musical thinking.

what has gone immediately before; a new technique is developed a stage further, or applied to a different kind of material; this is true of most of the ephemeral pieces that turn up annually at the ISCM Festivals. One feels that Goehr, on the other hand, has embraced as his heritage the whole of music. Each composition has a visionary origin; in setting down that vision as a sequence of sounds in time, what Beethoven might have done is as relevant as what might Boulez; either, or both, might influence what Goehr actually does.

So Goehr, a serialist, belongs to no school. His first major piece, the cantata *The Deluge* (1957-58), combines violent, picturesque imagery with a firmly constructed formal scheme; the fragmented instrumental texture reveals its date. The long cantata *Sutter's Gold,* commissioned by the Leeds Festival in 1961 (where Sullivan's *Martyr of Antioch,* Dvořák's *St. Ludmila,* Walton's *Belshazzar's Feast* were among earlier commissions), brought him up against executants — and an audience — of limited comprehension. He overrated their abilities; *Sutter's Gold* still awaits a satisfactory performance. But in later works — notably several unaccompanied choral pieces, the Violin Concerto, and the *Little Symphony* — Goehr has judged his means more surely and — without compromise — produced music that requires no special sympathies or affinities for its comprehension. He does not scorn aurally perceptible repetition; and his forms grow increasingly clear.

Peter Maxwell Davies,[2] after an exuberant avant-garde start, turned to contemplation of medieval music; his intricate musings on both its material and its methods produced intricate, fragmented compositions which only on repeated hearings revealed the lyrical thought that underlay them. His *St. Michael Sonata* for seventeen winds (with basic material derived from the chants of the Requiem Mass) gave rise, at the Cheltenham Festival of 1959, to a repetition of the old story about the clarinetist who used the wrong instrument — and no one noticed. In his case, the simplification began on his appointment as director of music at Cirencester Grammar School. He composed two works within the capabilities of children (*O magnum mysterium* and *Te lucis ante terminum,* both cycles of carols with instrumental sonatas) which were widely heard; adults were almost shamed into comprehending what children had responded to so readily. Maxwell Davies's work at Cirencester spread out to influence musical education generally in this country; it influenced his own "grown-up" compositions in the direction of a new simplicity. His latest compositions have a curiously timeless quality; the only "pro-

[2] See Robert Henderson, *Peter Maxwell Davies,* in *Musical Times,* October 1961.

cedures" seem to be those that have been known since early times: progression from pitch to pitch, consonance and dissonance, imitation, variation and difference, degrees of loud and soft, short and long.

Harrison Birtwistle[3] is, so far, a composer on a smaller scale than Goehr or Maxwell Davies, with a very delicate ear. Where Goehr creates, so to speak, a "public" work, Birtwistle invites his listeners to withdraw into a private, enchanted world. His music suggests the cliché-word "haunting." His feeling for individual notes and timbres and his gentle, open textures suggest at first sight the international avant-garde style of the late 'fifties. The serial thought is stringent; the tones of the individual voice are unemphatic, lyrical. Music of the utmost precision is set down with a quiet fastidiousness. Birtwistle teaches at two preparatory schools.

Simultaneously with the "Manchester Group" there emerged at the Royal Academy of Music, London, a group of brilliant young students eager (as their teachers were not) to discover what the rest of the world had been discovering. The most brilliant was Richard Rodney Bennett,[4] amazingly fluent, able to assimilate anything. There are delightful early works that show late-Romantic ideas, Bartók influence, and Darmstadt decoration in well-judged and attractive proportions. 1957-58 brought two years of study with Boulez, and an easy command of total serialization. Since 1959 there has been a steady flow of pieces, all of them attractive in sound, effortless in technique, cunningly written. Bennett, it seems, can do anything. Ever since 1955 (when he was nineteen) there has been a by-product of two or three film scores a year from him. It is easy, but it would be wrong, to make this immensely gifted musician sound merely facile. It is true that his music never shows any signs of struggle with the material. He has a *glückliche Hand*. But his natural mastery of techniques and effects is applied to ideas of distinction.

One of the Royal Academy group events still remembered with something like awe was a performance by Bennett and Cornelius Cardew of Boulez's *Structures*. Cardew (born 1936) should be the subject of a brief diversion. After the Academy he went to Cologne, worked with Stockhausen on *Carré*.[5] In international avant-garde circles he is probably a more familiar figure than any of the seven young "central" composers here considered; his music is performed frequently at their concerts —

[3] See Robert Henderson, *Harrison Birtwistle*, in *Musical Times*, March 1964.

[4] See Nicholas Maw, *Richard Rodney Bennett*, in *Musical Times*, February 1962.

[5] See Cornelius Cardew, *Report on "Carré*," in *Musical Times*, October-November 1961.

and in the ordinary run of British concert life, hardly at all. He is our only significant composer who has worked with graphic or other experimental notation, with indeterminate or only partially determined composition. His work is thoughtful, and the emphasis is on choice rather than chance.

Nicholas Maw,[6] another Berkeley pupil at the Academy, is the most traditional of the composers so far considered. His first avowed work, *Eight Chinese Lyrics* (1956), is a serial composition with a vocal line far more traditionally "singable" than serial vocal lines usually are. His tonal *Nocturne,* composed in 1958, before Britten's, but first heard after it, won him comparisons with the older composer; only examination of the score revealed the intricate technical procedures beneath its easily enjoyed lyricism. Maw came back from a year in Paris (study with Boulanger, and more consistently Max Deutsch) with some Boulez sounds in his head. Soon they were assimilated. The comparison with Britten was not inept. Maw has the same quality of using "learned" techniques in a popular way.

Thea Musgrave,[7] a Scottish composer, started slightly earlier than the others. There is a vein of clear common sense in her musical personality. For four years she worked in Paris with Boulanger. It is as if she has regarded each new discovery of our times with a coolly appraising eye, and then taken possession of such elements of it as can enhance her already considerable skills. Her intentions are always clear, her line is direct. A characteristic piece is the *Triptych* for tenor and orchestra (1959), which conceals none of its debt to Britten (in the matter of melodic shapes), nor to Boulez (in pretty instrumentation), and yet has a decisive, personal tone.

Malcolm Williamson,[8] Australian-born, stands apart from the other six. He studied at the Sydney Conservatorium with Eugene Goossens, came to Europe to work with Elisabeth Lutyens, encountered Boulez, returned in 1953 for further study with Lutyens and the Schoenberg pupil Erwin Stein. He is in manners an eclectic, a virtuoso in a dozen different styles ranging from austere serialism to pop tunes modelled on Richard Rodgers. Often different Williamsons jostle together disconcertingly — night-club pianist and the pious Catholic organist; music pours from both. The key work is *English Eccentrics* (1964), an

[6] See Susan Bradshaw, *Nicholas Maw,* in *Musical Times,* September 1962; Anthony Payne, *The Music of Nicholas Maw,* in *Tempo,* Spring 1964.

[7] See Susan Bradshaw, *Thea Musgrave,* in *Musical Times,* December 1963.

[8] See Colin Mason, *The Music of Malcolm Williamson,* in *Musical Times,* November 1962.

episodic opera-diversion in which Williamson's many strains — witty, exuberant, high-spirited, melancholy, devout, visionary — are balanced within a structure that calls for all of them.

Seven composers cannot stand for a scene that extends from the latest symphony by Havergal Brian (born 1876) to the latest piece of indeterminacy by Roger Smalley (born 1943). The traditional symphonists — Walton, Rawsthorne, Rubbra — are still active, and in the climate of today are being listened to more attentively than they were a few years ago (o fashion! — it is now avant-garde not to be too avant-garde). Berkeley, for so long labelled "miniaturist," "Boulanger pupil," has lately begun to work on a larger scale; the Second Symphony (1958), Violin Concerto (1962), and *Ronsard Sonnets* (1963 — at once a song-cycle and a symphony) show a new strength and grandeur of manner. Tippett with the opera *King Priam* (1962), the Second Piano Sonata (1962), and Concerto for Orchestra (1963) entered a "mosaic" period; his intensely contrapuntal earlier style yielded to a succession of direct, contrasting statements — vivid and personal, as all his music has been. Britten remains all-conquering. His latest opera, *Curlew River* (1964), incorporates random elements; his Cello Symphony (1963) has a severe, uncompromising character very different from the instant eloquence of the *War Requiem*.

Wilfrid Mellers discussed these composers, and others, in an article twelve years ago.[9] He mentioned only two who worked then with the twelve-tone technique: Humphrey Searle and Elisabeth Lutyens. He predicted that "the tendency towards a highly sophisticated stylization, more European and international than local, is likely to continue. A stringent discipline, rather than a rhapsodic utterance, will probably be encouraged." But within a decade there had arisen a group of young British composers who accepted serialism, not in any doctrinaire fashion, nor as a "discipline," but as one of the many facts of musical life. I have mentioned the most prominent,[10] though there were several others. They owed little to their immediate predecessors, were English mainly in their steadiness, and powers of assimilation. They kept in close touch with the rest of Europe, but the annual swings of avant-garde fashion found little reflection here. The mode for clarity of texture, for chamber ensembles including the "pretty" instruments — guitar, mandolin, fancy

[9] *Recent Trends in British Music*, in *The Musical Quarterly*, April 1952.

[10] If the names of Peter Racine Fricker and Iain Hamilton are absent from this study it is for two not unrelated reasons: my relative ignorance of their later music, and the fact that neither of them figures so largely on the musical scene as once he promised to do. But through ignorance I am probably doing them an injustice.

percussion — probably had the most lasting effect. There is in this country no electronic music nor *musique concrète* of any significance. Total serialization and aleatory techniques were Darmstadt fashions never acclimatized. All very conservative, if you like.

But — because of Glock, and because of the vogue that threw their names before the public — our young "central" composers who have the general (as opposed to inner circles') ear are far *less* conservative than those in most European countries. That "general" needs qualification. British concert life, with its emphasis on the 19th-century repertory, remains unhealthy. New works are commissioned frequently, heard once or twice by large audiences who like them, and then not heard again. But the music that is being written for them is healthy indeed.

FRENCH MUSIC SINCE 1945

By ANTOINE GOLÉA

EVERYTHING in Western music has been put into question since 1910: the foundations of harmonic writing, the significance and the role of those constituent elements of music that we call rhythm, timbre, and dynamics; even the deepest wellsprings of music, the sources of sound itself, have undergone revolutionary mutations.

In this upheaval French music has played and continues to play an essential role; first, at the beginning of the century with the appearance of the striking genius of Claude Debussy; from 1941 on, with the teaching and creative work of Olivier Messiaen; since 1945, with the brilliant manifestation of the inventive and creative powers of Pierre Boulez.

The genius of Debussy is the starting point of the revolution in the musical language of our time. His activity ran parallel with that of Schoenberg. In 1902, when Debussy's *Pelléas et Mélisande* was presented in Paris, Schoenberg in Vienna was composing a symphonic poem of the same name; from that time on, one can discern in the two composers a similar evolution in the domain of harmonic writing, rhythm, and instrumentation.

Debussy turned his back on the strait jacket of tonality in which music had lived for two hundred years. He had recourse to the modes of Gregorian chant and of the Orient. To these he added modes without any previous regular existence and unknown from the treatises, like the scale in whole tones that appears in the first measures of *Pelléas*. In those measures Debussy inaugurated the "suspension of tonality" in Western music, six years before Schoenberg.

On the rhythmic level Debussy abolished the tyranny of the barline. Originally the barline had nothing to do with rhythm; born with polyphony, it was simply meant to facilitate its coherence and synchronization. But in the 18th and 19th centuries the barline became more and more associated with the "strong beat" of the rhythmic units, which resulted in a marked rhythmic impoverishment. Turning towards the ancient modes, Debussy naturally turned also towards the richness and diversity of the ancient rhythmic structures. He returned the barline to its original function of "guidepost" or "guard-rail" in polyphonic song, nothing more.

Lastly, as concerns timbre, with the flute in his *Faun* Debussy gave the starting signal to a whole evolution that has ended with the establishment of a sort of dictatorship of timbre over all the other elements in music. In pre-Classic music timbre played no part in musical expression; what mattered to a Bach was the musical "idea" in its pure state, not in its incarnation. Certainly there were exceptions, especially in French music. In the refinement of his timbres Debussy also drew subtle lessons from the predominantly sensual art of Couperin and Rameau. But above all he precipitated an evolution, in which Berlioz played a large role and which ended in a complete reversal of values, timbre "in itself" being raised today to first place among the means of musical expression.

Debussy's role as a precursor in the invention of new musical forms, in breaking the shackles of the sonata form, would merit a close study all to itself. Twenty years after Debussy's death, Messiaen, in the first phase of his creative activity, had only incomparably enlarged and systematized Debussy's gains. Messiaen went on to universalize Debussy's modal message; to systematize and enlarge the use of Gregorian modes and the modes of the Orient; to them he would add modes of his own invention, which answered to the most precise definitions, but did not however prevent the flowering of one of the most abundant melodic inspirations of our century.

In the field of rhythm Messiaen was also Debussy's successor, enlarging and systematizing in the same way. His great innovation was the systematic use of the rhythms of India, which he made completely independent of the unfolding of melody and harmony. But in doing this Messiaen took a step that was decisive in another way, and that would lead him straight to the musical language of Pierre Boulez and his fellow-thinkers. This forward leap of Messiaen's was in the domain of timbre; here too, regions of autonomy were established that led directly to the musical world of the post-war composers.

However, before the decisive *Etudes de rythme* of 1949, it was not the music of Messiaen that influenced the younger generation, seduced as it was from 1946 on by serial writing, which meant at that time the "classic" dodecaphony of Schoenberg, especially as it appeared in Webern's subtle sonorous enigmas. The twenty-year-old Boulez (he was born in 1925) detested the *Visions de l'Amen,* the *Trois petites liturgies de la présence divine,* and the *Vingt Regards sur l'Enfant Jésus,* all works of Messiaen from the war years. He detested them because of their sonorous abundance and because of their theoretically modal composition, which did not however preclude a most sensuous and alluring voluptuousness of tone. But from this time on, Messiaen's teaching put its mark on the young generation. This teaching, which had only a very partial connection with what Messiaen was composing between 1942 and 1945, constituted and continues to constitute the most original, the most paradoxical, the most fecund phenomenon of French and international musical life of the past twenty years.

In 1942, a newly liberated prisoner of war, Messiaen was named professor of harmony at the Paris Conservatory. In 1947 Claude Delvincourt, the Conservatory's audacious director, created for him a class in analysis, esthetics, and rhythm, which was in reality nothing less than a camouflaged class in composition. This camouflage was necessary, for to have openly named Messiaen professor of composition would have caused an insurrection in official musical circles. Actually, for the past twenty years, Messiaen has been the only professor at the Paris Conservatory to inspire numerous composers and to contribute heavily to the creation of the decisive current in contemporary music.

In the midst of the war, in the midst of the Nazi occupation, Messiaen introduced his students to certain works of Schoenberg and of Berg. But he did not limit himself to the composers of the Viennese School; the most famous and the most fruitful of his analyses, by reason of the horizons they opened and the influence they exercised, remain those of the *Sacre du printemps* of Stravinsky and the *Pelléas* of Debussy.

Serial or non-serial, the works analyzed by Messiaen for his students were always examined at the deepest level of their formal structure; and when he analyzed his own works, he proceeded in the same scholarly manner, bringing to light especially the rhythmic structure employed. Pierre Boulez, the prototype and guiding light of his whole generation, even before initiating himself into the workings of the twelve-tone system as taught in France since 1945 by René Leibowitz, had received from Messiaen the decisive shock of his "inquiétude rythmique," of which the latter spoke freely; a shock provoked by the revelation of the possibility of using rhythmic structures independent of sonorous structures. This revelation may be considered to be the source of the "totally" serial music of the marching wing of French music since 1945, far more than its apprenticeship to the Schoenbergian twelve-tone rules.

Boulez and other students of Messiaen, like Michel Fano, Jean-Louis Martinet, Serge Nigg, André Hodeir, Jean Barraqué, Maurice Le Roux, Gilbert Amy, instructed in rhythm by Messiaen and initiated, with or without direct contact with Leibowitz, into the rules of classic twelve-tone composition, at first combined Messiaen's teachings with the revelation of the style and esthetics of dodecaphonism, especially Webernian dodecaphonism, boldly clearing the ground for total serialism.

But in this work of ground-clearing, after temporary divergences, after some resounding quarrels and terrible verbal battles, all the younger generation in France again found Messiaen on their road.

It was in fact in 1949 that Messiaen published his *Quatre études de rythme* of which the second, entitled *Mode de valeur et d'intensités,* was to be the first musical work embodying the principle of the integral organization of the world of sound. With the numerous variants that have appeared since, this remains the principle of the most recent music. This organization, in Messiaen's étude, is not yet serial, merely modal, as its title indicates. Let us see how the two organizations differ, but also how one leads inevitably to the other.

Messiaen's piano étude employs:

1) a melodic mode of thirty-six sounds, all different, the same sounds never being repeated from one octave to another;

2) a mode of twenty-four "durations" or different rhythmic values;

3) a mode of seven different intensities;

4) a mode of twelve different keyboard attacks, these attacks being to the piano what the timbres of the different instruments are to the orchestra.

These four modes are utilized so that each sound always appears with the same rhythmic duration, the same intensity, and the same attack. Furthermore, the entire piece evolves in a triple canon, the first voice of the canon using the sounds of the high octave and the smallest note values, the second voice of the canon the sounds of the middle octave and intermediate note values, the third voice of the canon the sounds of the low octave and the longest note values. The imperious logic of the construction results in an unfolding and a superposition of absolute variety and extraordinary differentiation of sound.

What is typically modal in the étude is the immobility of its elements taken in themselves. Here the musical world is already complete and self-contained. This étude is one of the first "musical happenings" of contemporary music. The constituent elements of this event revolve around each other, modifying at each instant the appearance of the entire event; but they never change in their own constitution, neither in length, timbre, nor intensity.

In totally serial music, on the other hand, of the type established in Boulez's *Structures* for two pianos, not only the entire musical event but each of its smallest parts undergoes a perpetual transformation.

Boulez built the first of his *Structures* on the first of the three fragments of the mode of thirty-six pitch levels of Messiaen's étude. But Messiaen's modal fixity is transmuted by Boulez into a varied and incessant movement, each pitch level in principle appearing in turn in each attack in the series of attacks, in each intensity in the series of intensities, in each note value in the series of durations. This means that for a particular pitch value the same attack, the same intensity, and the same duration will never recur.

Vertigo must seize anyone who reflects on the multiplicity of possible combinations, a vertigo not unlike that brought on by contemplating infinity. One sees that in totally serial music the organic necessity of choice stands at the center of the creative effort. Can one form an idea of the length of a work that used all the permutations and combinations possible under the laws of serial music? But in saying limitation one says choice, and he who says choice says freedom.

The music that appears to be the most "mathematical," the most "intellectual," is precisely that in which the freedom of the composer is greatest. It is under the banner of this freedom that all French serial music since about 1948 has been born.

I have already named the most widely known of Messiaen's students who after 1945 launched first into the writing of twelve-tone music and subsequently of serial music. They have not all persisted in the direction first chosen; several of them have even "abjured" the serial faith in a rather spectacular way. Today these composers are among the upholders of tradition, though they have arrived there by other routes and for other reasons than those that have constrained and guided the habitual disciples of official teaching.

Their works, serial or not, have been far from negligible. But in spite of the value their serial works may have, their "abjuration" denies them any place beside those who have pushed the experience, the discipline, and the style of serial music to its farthest conclusions.

There are also the purely "classical" serial composers, students of René Leibowitz alone, who have limited their writing and their style to the rules established by Schoenberg. Leibowitz himself is of this number but his creative personality has never been strong. Among his "classical serial" students we must cite Antoine Duhamel and André Casanova; the latter especially, after a period of twelve-tone stagnation rather discouraging because of its underlying academicism, seems to have succeeded in raising himself to a level that commands respect, as is shown by his orchestral work *Anamorphoses*.

In the circle around Boulez, who himself soon abandoned the classical teaching of Leibowitz for "totally" serial composition, we must not forget those of his contemporaries who have advanced as far as possible down the same road. Jean Barraqué and Maurice Le Roux are to be considered here above all.

Barraqué, enigmatic, secretive, difficult, the enemy, it must be said to his credit, of all acclaim, composes very little; and, it would seem, with so many reservations and scruples that most of what he puts to paper becomes the prey of a deep-seated discontent and finally, one supposes, of a rage of destruction like that which in the past consigned to the fire so many works of Duparc and Dukas.

We call attention to his Sonata for Piano, one of the most important works for this instrument in recent French music alongside the sonatas of Boulez. Similar in spirit to this sonata and linked organically to it by the serial raw material of its structure, a *Séquence pour voix et instruments* on a fragment of text from Nietzsche attests a temperament of uncommon lyric richness.

It is possible and eminently to be desired that Barraqué, released from certain inhibiting obsessions, will assert himself as one of the most interesting and positive personalities of his generation. According to his friends he has been working for some years on a composition of vast proportions, set to a text by the Austrian writer Hermann Broch. One fragment of this work, entitled . . . *Au delà du hasard,* for four instrumental groups and one vocal group, has just been presented to the public.

Maurice Le Roux's apprenticeship was similar to that of Boulez. Messiaen was his master and Leibowitz initiated him into the classic serial technique. In addition to songs on poems by Henri Michaux and psalms for five-part chorus *a cappella* on texts by Patrice de la Tour du Pin, his main work to date, *Le Cercle des métamorphoses* for orchestra, seemed to destine him to a career parallel to that of Boulez in the exploration of serial music. This work shows him to be as convinced as Boulez of the great expressive power of serial music; and his personality is revealed to be strong and original enough to occupy an important place at Boulez's side.

Unfortunately this work, which dates from ten years ago, has not yet been followed by another of comparable importance. Le Roux has meanwhile pursued two new objectives. He plunged initially into film music, where he was the first composer who dared to write serial music. This was the case in the film *Bitter Victory,* taken from the novel by René Hardy.

In the same spirit, concerned to give music a functional role without however falling into the too facile or the vulgar, he composed the music for a ballet inspired by Saint-Exupéry's *Le petit prince.* This music of a gossamer delicacy and a rare sensibility perfectly complements Saint-Exupéry's story as narrated by Gerard Philipe and is preserved on a recording that belongs in the anthologies. In similar works Le Roux has resolved the painful problem of functional music in our time with a rigor equal to that of Boulez, composing the incidental music for Jean-Louis Barrault's production of the *Orestes* trilogy of Aeschylus.

In addition, Le Roux boldly took up the career of orchestra conductor, where he has especially distinguished himself by the originality of his programs, devoted in large part to contemporary music. All this is necessary in the musical life of today, in order to open the way to a wide and direct contact between the general public and the new music. But one may be permitted to regret that Le Roux's real activity as a composer has been impeded, interrupted perhaps forever.

Boulez's activity as a practicing musician has also been far from negligible. But up to now — one can still say this in spite of certain mildly disquieting signs that might lead one to suppose the contrary — this activity has not prevented him from pursuing his purely creative work.

Boulez has been for ten years director of music for the Renaud-Barrault theatrical company, has traveled the world over in this capacity, has furnished a considerable body of work as adapter, director, or composer of scores for the theater. With the generous aid of the directors of the company, he has founded the famous "Concerts Marigny." Two years after their foundation in 1953 these concerts had taken the definitive form of that "Domaine Musical" which for the past nine years, in spite of errors in the choice of certain works that might better have been avoided, has been the center, the crucible, the brain of avant-garde French music.

Finally, in the past four years, Boulez, like Le Roux, has shown himself to be a conductor particularly well qualified in the interpretation of modern music; and he has already attacked, with varying success, certain masterpieces of the repertory.

But his creative work remains central to Boulez's life. It is to be hoped that the present tense of the preceding sentence will never have to be changed to the past tense. The disturbing fact is that for the past three years, if one excepts a short fragment presented at Basel in January 1964, Boulez has produced nothing, even though, in compensation, he has directed more and more.

From 1946 to 1961 Boulez's works arrange themselves in a splendid pyramid whose base seems to grow ever wider so that the peak may rise ever higher. As he composes new works, his earlier ones are established in an ever wider historical perspective, permitting the most recent to mount the assault of new conquests.

The Sonatina for Flute and Piano of 1946 is still a homage to Schoenberg, composed as it is in the form of the First Chamber Symphony of the Austrian master and in classic serial style. It succeeded the *Three Psalmodies* for piano, which have remained unpublished by will of the author; these pieces are still charged with the influence of Messiaen, the Messiaen of before the *Études de rythmes,* but already full of that "serial presentiment" that haunted Boulez ever since he became thoroughly acquainted with two works, obviously major, of Schoenberg's atonal period: the Three Piano Pieces, Opus 11 and *Pierrot lunaire.*

In that same year of 1946 Boulez published two other works: the First Sonata for piano and the cantata, *Visage nuptial,* in its first version for two solo voices and orchestra, on a cycle of poems by René Char.

In these works we find, added to the classic serial structure, rhythmic and sonorous structures that turn their back on the primitive series of twelve tones, new structures for which, however, the Sonatina for Flute had already furnished some indications. The works of Boulez, like those of all true creators, are linked organically one to the other, each bringing new gains in style to put at the side of the former gains, which disappear only little by little as the new ones impose ever more on the mind of the composer.

And Boulez's works continue on their course: in 1948, *Le Soleil des eaux,* a cantata also composed on poems by Char, and the Second

Sonata for piano; in 1950-51 the *Polyphonie X* for seventeen solo instruments, in which timbral serial structure comes to join already existing structures of pitch and rhythm; at almost the same time, after the publication of Messiaen's *Mode de valeur et d'intensités,* Boulez's *Structures* for two pianos is presented, in which the series of attacks comes to take its place in the construction of a music recovering little by little the totality of sonorous space from the rigor of its parameters.

And finally in 1954 — its first public performance was in Baden-Baden in 1955 — appears *Le Marteau sans maître,* a cantata for one contralto voice and a small instrumental ensemble, again on poems by René Char. It is with this work that Boulez definitively conquers the integrality of sonorous space, and for the first time obtains a large international audience.

After this epitome of totally serial music, Boulez, whose spirit cannot bear any stagnation, had to push ahead, always seeking to widen and deepen the domain of his art. Following certain experiments by Karlheinz Stockhausen and John Cage, Boulez introduced into contemporary music the revolutionary notion of the "aléa," or chance, in his Third Sonata for piano and the two *Improvisations sur Mallarmé.*

Here it is a question of a new suppleness in the writing, which goes so far as to concede to an interpreter and even a group of interpreters certain opportunities of choice and improvisation in the course of performing a work. Thus in the Third Sonata Boulez, within the framework of the most rigorous serial construction, indicates nevertheless several possibilities of interpretation and even of order of execution, presenting the different sections among which the interpreter may choose at the moment of performance.

Boulez's fundamental idea was to achieve a certain aeration of serial writing, an *aleatory* fantasy designed to strengthen the bonds between the composer and the performer, between the performer and the work, between the work and the public.

Improvisation has always existed in music, from the time of the troubadours to the cadenzas, the realizations of figured bass, the various ornamentations on melodic themes common from the 16th to the 18th centuries; but these improvisations have always evolved in a general framework of strict rules impossible to transgress.

This concern to enclose improvisation in a rigorously defined framework is shared by Boulez, who has violently spoken out, and with reason, against certain excesses of his close associates who "compose" only sketches of works, which carry only a certain number of very loose "general directions" and leave the interpreter an absolute license.

This kind of music, where all the most shameless forms of amateurism are displayed, can only lead to the impasse of anarchy. Boulez has always been perfectly aware of this danger and has done his best to avoid it, strictly limiting the aleatory parts of his works and reserving for himself, the composer, the final word.

The *Improvisations sur Mallarmé* have been enlarged into a great work for soprano solo and orchestra in five parts, entitled *Pli selon pli, hommage à Mallarmé*. Before completing this, Boulez had composed *Poésie pour pouvoir,* a work inspired by a poem by Henri Michaux. This piece, for the first time in Boulez's work, presents, in alternation and simultaneously, passages for ordinary instruments and fragments produced by electronic means.

Boulez's style in all his works is that of the most violent Expressionism. This style is far from the "sonorous mathematics" of which the adversaries of serial music are wont to speak. This music, this technique, in the hand of an authentic composer, is a cry from the depths, the unanimous protest of our age against the overwhelming cruelty of our condition.

To write, in the atomic age, atomic music may seem to be pretentious; but there is certainly a measure of truth in this relationship. The total dismantling of music and its total reconstruction under new laws, that and nothing else is what contemporary serialists are undertaking. The music of Boulez and his associates who have something real to say is just that. And in that, they are doing nothing more than transposing into music the terrible disorder of the world we live in.

That this music has its imitators, its second-raters, its commercializers who are beginning to exploit what looks to be a profitable style will surprise no one. There are fewer of these in France than in a country like Germany, for example, where serial conformism plays the same role today as classical conformism under the Nazis. In France people generally have the courage of their convictions, which must be respected, even when their opinions seem to be in error. There are in France certain serial composers without talent, and also some "traditionalists" who have something to say and who would not dream of changing sides to follow the fashion.

Among Boulez's successors, Michel Fano seemed to promise much, but he has not yet fulfilled his promises. However Gilbert Amy has shown himself to be one of the most interesting of the serial composers. He was at first a student of Darius Milhaud, who recognized his talent and encouraged him with all his might, even after he realized how far Amy's road diverged from his own, Amy's first published works being in the "total" serial technique.

His temperament is the opposite of Boulez's; he is a person of gentleness and suavity, his passion being contained, not explosive. His music as it appears in the *Movements* for chamber orchestra, or in the *Epigrams* for piano, where the serial technique is relaxed by findings from the aleatory domain, is very sure of form, absolutely transparent in style, and of winning charm and clarity. It is the music of a young man who, instead of expressing his terror of life as it is offered, finds in himself the resources to tap the springs of joy, innocence, and freshness. Amy has known how to find in the refinement of the most modern technique the means of expressing his most intimate aspirations.

Jean-Claude Eloy, now twenty-five years old, also shows great promise. He was a student of Boulez when the latter taught at the Conservatory of Basel. In 1963 his *Equivalences* was presented at the "Domaine Musical"; this work for eighteen solo instruments showed him to be endowed with a great imagination for sound, a sensibility truly surprising for his age, and a firm command of his craft. Although he has not studied under Messiaen, the latter's influence is to be seen in this work; and here I speak not of the Messiaen of the *Études de rythme* but of the scintillating, colorful, luminous Messiaen of the *Oiseaux exotiques* and the *Catalogue des oiseaux*.

Among the composers who place themselves outside of serial music, there are those who were formerly serialists but who have turned away from this technique and would now willingly burn what they formerly embraced. The best-known of these are Jean-Louis Martinet and Serge Nigg.

Of the band of Messiaen's students from the war years, Martinet is by a dozen years the oldest of his comrades. Soon after the war he made a remarkable start with two vast symphonic triptychs, *Orpheus* and *Prometheus*. These two works reveal the combined, but perfectly assimilated and individualized influences of Debussy, Stravinsky, and Bartók. A broad and ample imagination for sound exalts an inexhaustible rhythmic invention, and an authentic talent gives to these vast ensembles a life of singular acuteness.

Harmonically, they are modal, completely sheltered from all convention, Messiaen's influence in this respect having been as completely assimilated as that of the masters cited above.

After acquaintance with Boulez and in accordance with Leibowitz's teaching, Martinet became a serial composer. An admirable Suite for string quartet attests this evolution, leading one to expect that Martinet would become a brilliant representative of the new serial school.

But he has evolved in another direction. Is it because of political marching orders, or is it simply because, like many others, he became frightened of the "totally" serial technique that began to sprout about him, and because he saw in it the negation of the human element in music? The fact is that the musician who could compose certain songs to poems by Char, among which are to be found, not by chance, texts from the time of the Resistance, could still deliver, even after abandoning the serial technique, an authentic message of life and truth. But this was no longer the case for the author of certain *Symphonic Movements* written in a conventional style that denied not only his own serial works but, unfortunately, his admirable symphonic poems *Orpheus* and *Prometheus.*

Serge Nigg, who is the same age as Boulez, after passing a period of his youth under the sign of Bartók, Stravinsky, and Messiaen, adopted the serial technique and justified this adoption with impeccable logic: "It is a new cycle to undertake, or rather to continue; since for almost thirty years the serial technique has permitted the composition of works of genius, which have proved its value and incontestable reach."

For the East Berlin Radio, to which he was drawn by political sympathies, Nigg composed around 1950 a work in the Schoenbergian serial style, a challenging work that has not yet been presented in public. Entitled *Le Fusillé inconnu,* it is a vast oratorio on a text by a poet friend; from all the evidence, the "martyr" is meant to be a parallel to the Unknown Soldier of the two World Wars. Radio East Berlin did not accept this work, simply because it was serial and therefore contravened the official esthetic code of Soviet Russia. Nigg made a swift examination of his conscience and set himself to compose music capable of being "understood by all the world," with the result that his personality has undergone perceptible changes more and more damaging to his creative work. However, in spite of such ridiculous watchwords as "clear, simple, and primitive rhythms," "melodies that can be learned by heart," Nigg has succeeded in composing a symphonic poem, *Pour un poète captif,* which apart from every consideration of style, is a work of a sure and authentic expressive power. One can say the same thing of a very recent piece, created for the Strasbourg Festival of 1964, *Fils résorbé,* on a text by Mallarmé, for reciter, baritone, and orchestra.

Certainly the situation of composers who have never set themselves the problems that Martinet and Nigg have set appears more simple,

clear-cut, and comfortable. There are the composers of the older generation, who have continued to write according to the esthetics and technique of their youth, sometimes evolving in a very interesting way:
among them Milhaud, Poulenc, Auric, Sauguet. Works like the *Sacred
Service* of the first, the opera *Voix humaine* of the second, who died in
January 1963, the ballets *Peintre et son modèle, Phèdre,* and *Chemin
de lumière* of the third, the Second String Quartet and the ballets
Les Forains, Les Mirages, La Rencontre of the fourth are the fruit of
sincere and authentic talents and carry the indelible mark of the personality of their composers.

Then there are the composers of Martinet's generation (he was
born in 1914) who have always composed works of value outside of
the serial technique. Three of them merit special mention: Maurice
Ohana, of Spanish descent, author of admirable oratorios based on the
poems of Lorca, like the *Plainte pour Ignacio Sanchez Mejiaz;* Marcel
Landowski, author of operas like *Le Rire de Nils Halerius* and *Le Fou,*
whose librettos, by the composer himself, pose with insight and generosity
the essential problems of the modern world, caught up in the vertiginous
folly of its self-destruction; Henri Dutilleux, author of two symphonies
of powerful expressive originality, in a style (especially in the Second
Symphony) that decisively removes the author from the beaten paths
of the Prix de Rome winners, of whom he is one. The same Dutilleux
is the composer of *Loup,* a ballet score among the best since the war,
and a lovely Sonata for piano. In the development of his musical ideas
he shows a tendency towards a severity and a concentration that link
him with the "stripped-down" school of French music represented by
Roussel, and in the generation between, by such perfect musicians as
Henri Barraud and Jean Rivier.

These two in their most recent works show themselves to be at the
peak of their creative power. Barraud's symphonic poem *Offrande à
une ombre,* his oratorio *Le Martyr des Saints Innocents,* his opera
Numance, a symphony, and symphonic poems like the *Rapsodie carté-
sienne* and the *Rapsodie dionysienne* are works of a truly overwhelming
lyricism, which spring from the depths of a tormented soul of striking
nobility.

Rivier's Sixth Symphony shows to what an extent its author is
capable of self-renewal in the direction of an ever-growing concentration
on the means of expression, which is exactly the direction of the
tendencies of the newest music. The same thing is manifest in Barraud's
Rapsodie dionysienne, with its strong thematic unity and bold rhythmic

innovations.

In the same generation Emmanuel Bondeville is the author of symphonic works, of songs, and also of the opera *Madame Bovary*, which continues and renews the liveliest tradition of French opera, achieving a bold synthesis between the lyrical language of Massenet and that of Debussy, with a personal note of warmth and an extremely attractive sensuousness.

As an opera composer Henri Tomasi must be mentioned, with his *Don Juan de Manara* and, in the comic category, *Le Testament du Père Gaucher*. He is a traditional, tonal composer with a great freedom of expression who often borrows very successfully from folklore and who has a sure sense of dramatic effect that crowns his lyric outbursts with a fine glow and a great clarity of expression.

Manuel Rosenthal, a conductor known internationally for his devotion to the cause of contemporary music, is the composer not only of a masterpiece of modern oratorio, *Saint François d'Assise,* but also of two operas, *Les Femmes au tombeau* and *Hop! Signor . . .* In all these works this pupil of Ravel displays an originality and an independence of thought and of writing, a refined art of orchestration, and finally a wealth of ideas that make him one of the most remarkable of those musicians who, outside of isms and theories, succeed in opening the "narrow gate" through which modern music may find the road towards a public thirsting, as always, for beauty and truth.

And finally there is André Jolivet, that *franc-tireur* of the music of our time, whose works since 1945 are numerous and significant enough to assign him an exceptional place alongside those holding to the extremist tendencies of our music, though he has not yet, at least in any systematic way, used the serial technique.

But his First Piano Sonata, his Concerto for Ondes Martenot and Orchestra, his Piano Concerto, his three symphonies, his concertos for the trumpet, his brilliant Cello Concerto, are manifestations of a musical temperament as exceptional as that of Messiaen or Boulez. Jolivet has remained in essence the modal composer he has always been; but like Messiaen, and perhaps even more than Messiaen, he has pressed the exploration of modes to the ends of the earth, and has included them in his music — Asiatic modes and African modes, as a living testimony to the direct and magical communication man has always had with the visible and invisible forces of the universe. And like his modal language, his rhythmic and orchestral language responds to the same deep need to preserve for music its essential role of mystic incantation.

Alongside Messiaen, to whom he owes a great deal, alongside Boulez and the Italian, Nono, André Jolivet represents and incarnates one of the strongest creative forces of contemporary music.

Jolivet was one of the first French composers to use the Ondes Martenot. This instrument played its part as a precursor of that revolution which has provided music with new sources of sound, perhaps the most fundamental of all the revolutions contemplated in the course of this study.

It was in 1949 that the music called "concrète" began to appear in Paris. Its first step was aimed at the fabrication of "musical happenings." Its inventor, Pierre Schaeffer, with his staff of technicians from Radio Française, began by recording, first on a flexible disc and soon on magnetic tape, the most diverse sounds and noises of animate and inanimate nature. These recordings, once made, could then be manipulated according to processes that have been continuously perfected, leading to the creation of "complex sounds" which recall less and less the original sounds and noises. These manipulations are essentially the acceleration or deceleration of the speed at which the tape is played, the inversion of the original line, its precise fragmentation by means of simple snips of the scissors into bits whose length — and therefore whose duration — can be exactly calculated, and finally, the making of a closed circuit by gluing the two ends together and passing the tape over an apparatus called the "phonogène" by its inventor, Pierre Schaeffer. It is evident that this closed circuit can be made to undergo various transformations, can be superposed on other circuits of the same kind, at which moment one leaves the simple fabrication of musical events and proceeds to the composition of true works of *musique concrète*.

Through the channel of Karlheinz Stockhausen, who worked with Schaeffer in Paris, experiments in *musique concrète* have given rise in Germany to electronic music, which differs from *musique concrète* only in that the sounds in the musical events are electronically generated. The sounds therefore are musically pure, instead of the transformable noises of *musique concrète*. Except for that, the aims and methods of electronic music are the same as those of *musique concrète*.

Since this double birth, and the rivalries and conflicts have often been violent between the two groups, there has been a movement of rapprochement; *musique concrète* has renounced more and more the use of noises for the use of regular musical sounds, either instrumental or vocal; and electronic music makes more and more use of sounds "concretely" produced, in addition to those electronically produced. In a general way, in the last seven years the distinction between the former *musique concrète* and the former electronic music has tended to disappear; all the works of the last few years have been "electronic," employing indifferently the two techniques as originally constituted.

Among the French works in the electronic category we must cite, in addition to the classic *Symphonie pour un homme seul* by Pierre Schaeffer and Pierre Henry, *Le Voile d'Orphée* by Pierre Henry, a work of great inspiration, rigorously constructed according to laws of form and structure specified down to the smallest details.

One has a feeling, furthermore, that the new techniques have tempted the serial composers, and for several reasons: first, the difficulties of instrumental and vocal execution of the new music go on growing, and the composers, confronted with more and more unsatisfactory interpretations, confide with a sort of somber joy their more complicated inventions in sound and rhythm to the security of the machine.

Serial composers in some sort call the machine to their aid, for the fixation of sonorous and rhythmic structures is facilitated for the composer, apart from any idea of interpretation, by the technical means at his disposal.

Finally, with the introduction of the principle of chance, the latest developments of serial music find allies of unlimited fantasy in the researches into timbre conducted by the electronic technique; for in seeking new timbres, even when one knows theoretically the frequency one wishes to arrive at, one very often winds up with unexpected results, especially when one proceeds to the combination of already constituted "musical happenings," or to researches into timbre deductible by inference.

It is certainly true that chance plays a part in the construction of all the recent works of electronic music. One can say that chance corresponds, in this technique, to the element of the "unexpected" and the "aléas" of inspiration in traditional music, in written music.

I have already cited Boulez's *Poésie pour pouvoir* as one of the first great works employing the electronic technique side by side with the normal instrumental technique. Many other works have been born under the same banner, although we can in no sense yet speak of masterpieces; for in this domain, experimentation still rules, and the flight of creative thought is far from having reached its maximum curve.

(Translated by Lucile H. Brockway)

MUSIC IN PORTUGAL TODAY

By FRANCIS D. PERKINS

PORTUGUESE composition during the last few decades has been
in a transitional phase, aiming at the development of individual
and national styles in which foreign influences will be absorbed rather
than echoed. The Italian influence, which had been dominant since
early in the 18th century, began to wane late in the 19th. The turn of
the century also brought an increasing search towards the expression
of nationalism based upon folk music. Meanwhile German 19th-century
music, from Beethoven on, became a major influencing force; later
this was rivalled and even outstripped by French music ranging from
Franck and Fauré to Debussy and Ravel. France and Germany still
provide the principal foreign trends in Portuguese music; many of the
Portuguese composers who study abroad do so in Paris; others go to
Berlin and other German cities.

Few if any influences come from Portugal's larger neighbor, Spain;
the Portuguese, on the whole, have a traditional dislike for the Spaniards,
in spite of the frequent official manifestations of inter-Iberian friendship
and solidarity, and the sympathy between the two ruling regimes. A
foreign listener to many of the Portuguese works of recent years may
find them more or less conservative, even in terms of the 1920s. This
impression is also noticeable in Portuguese painting. Some composers,
however, show an awareness of Stravinsky, Hindemith, Bartók, and
Schoenberg; a few experiment with twelve-tone music and two or three
with electronic methods.

Portuguese composers of today face certain handicaps. Bounded only
by Spain and the Atlantic Ocean, Portugal is relatively remote from
major cultural centers elsewhere in Europe. It is a small country, 335
miles long and, on an average, 125 miles wide, with a population of
about twelve million, not counting the islands and colonies. A million

38

or more of its inhabitants live in the area of Lisbon, the capital; about 400,000 live in Porto and its neighborhood. No other cities reach the 50,000 figure. This means that the country's musical life is centered mainly in Lisbon and Porto, the only two cities that have symphony orchestras, and limits the stimulus to composers and outlets for their works.

On the other hand, the Portuguese Government provides considerable encouragement to native composers by giving their works countrywide hearings over the National Radio and in providing fellowships for study at home and abroad. The Government also supports the National Conservatory of Music in Lisbon, while the Porto Conservatory is supported by the city.

Joaquím de Silva Pereira, the director of the Porto Conservatory, has described the National Radio (Emissora Nacional) as the principal factor in the renaissance of Portuguese music in recent years. The supply of music over the radio includes all-Portuguese programs of various kinds, while the National Radio's orchestra devotes a respectable portion of its live and recorded concerts to Portuguese music.

An annual music festival is held in various parts of the country. Judging by the programs, the 1964 festival's aim seemed to be the presentation of a wide range of past and present European music to Portuguese audiences rather than to focus attention upon Portuguese works. But home-grown music and musicians were far from neglected. Two of the eight conductors and seven of the thirty-four soloists and recitalists were Portuguese. Modern Portuguese offerings included Fernando Lopes Graça's *Canto de Amor e de Morte* (*Song of Love and Death*) for orchestra, *Para uma Criança que vai nascer* (*For a Child About to Be Born*) for chamber orchestra, and Joly Braga Santos's *Requiem to the Memory of Pedro Freitas Branco* for chorus and orchestra, along with earlier works by F. A. A. Almeida and Marcos Portugal.

The regular major winter and spring opera season at the Teatro de San Carlos in Lisbon includes one Portuguese work; the rest of the season is devoted to Italian, French, and German operas sung in their original languages by artists specially assembled for each production. The Companhia Portuguesa de Opera, with headquarters at the Trindade Theater in Lisbon, operates on a simpler scale but with a wider range, appearing in Porto, Aveiro, Coimbra, and Figueira da Foz as well as in the capital, and also visiting the islands. Along with familiar Italian works, its repertory includes operas by Joly Braga Santos, Ruy

Coelho, and other contemporary and earlier Portuguese composers. It
has also staged Gershwin's *Porgy and Bess*.

Portugal's principal concert-giving organization is the Círculo de
Cultura Musical, founded in Lisbon by Elisa de Sousa Pedroso in 1935.
The Porto branch was formed two years later, and there are other
branches at Coimbra, Braga, Evora, and Setúbal in metropolitan
Portugal and also in Angola and Moçambique in Africa and Macao
in the Far East. There are local musical societies and instrumental and
vocal groups in the other principal cities and towns, which give
Portuguese music a fair amount of representation. On the whole, however, the principal societies seem to aim more at pleasing their subscribers than widening the outlets for Portuguese composers, but this
can also be said of concert courses in the United States.

About fifteen living or recently deceased composers can be regarded
as nationally known although, with the possible exception of Brazil,
little of their music is known abroad. This is one of the reasons why
the many foreign musicians who come to Portugal each year perform
few Portuguese works, while some local musicians prefer to cultivate
the standard cosmopolitan repertory to pushing their compatriots' music.
No Portuguese composers of serious music can afford to devote all their
time to composition; they are also teachers, critics, musicologists, authors,
conductors, and instrumentalists. But this is a condition that holds true
in many other countries.

The late José Viana da Mota, who was born in 1868, is considered
to be one of the fathers of modern Portuguese music. He was one of
the first to look at his country's musical folklore as a basis for its more
sophisticated music, and German composers also influenced his style.
Among the composers of the next generation Luís de Freitas Branco
(1890-1955) had a marked influence upon the trends and development
of the Portuguese music of his time. Long associated with the National
Conservatory in his native Lisbon, he studied composition there with
Tomás Borba and later went abroad to continue his studies with Gabriel
Grovlez in Paris and Engelbert Humperdinck in Berlin. He had already
become acquainted with Vincent d'Indy's musical theories.

According to João José Cochofel, writing in the *Dicionario de
Música* edited by Borba and Graça, Freitas Branco's influence upon
Portuguese music dates from 1915. Some of his early works shook
local conformist ideas through their affiliation with the dominating
European currents of the time, including French Impressionism in
particular and, up to a certain point, Schoenbergian atonality. His First

Symphony (1924) marked an important date in the history of Portuguese orchestral music, and also introduced a new trend in a style that had begun to include neo-Classicism on a diatonic and modal base. In general, Freitas Branco is credited with raising Portuguese musical standards. His brother, Pedro, was a prominent conductor, and his son, João, who writes for *O Seculo* of Lisbon, is one of Portugal's principal critics.

Claudio Carneyro (1895-1963), son of the painter Antonio Carneyro, was Porto's best-known composer. Except for visits abroad, he pursued his career mainly in his native city, where he was associated with its Conservatory for more than thirty years as a teacher and as director. Originally planning to be a violinist, he began to concentrate upon composition during his stay in Paris (1919-22), studying with Widor. In 1935, on a grant from the Instituto de Alta Cultura, he returned to Paris for further study with Dukas.

Although he lived in the United States for two years late in the 1920s, his style shows no American influences. It is described as inclined towards a classicism prompted by the inspiration of folklore, but also including the inspiration of modern techniques. This modern influence is most advanced in his *Khroma* for viola and orchestra, in which there are hints of the twelve-tone system and of Schoenberg and his disciples, but his most characteristic style is conservative and best illustrated in his more intimate works and those based upon or inspired by folk music.

Like most of his fellow composers, Ruy Coelho (b. 1892) has written music in many forms, but he is best known for his many operas and seven ballet scores. Born at Alcacer do Sal, he studied in Lisbon at the National Conservatory before going to Berlin for five years' study with Humperdinck. He had no competitor in the field of opera during the first half of the 20th century, but his artistic personality has been the subject of prolonged controversy. His works have been animated by a renovating spirit from the start, but his style has not yet won freedom from 19th-century Italian models. But, in spite of this hybridity of style and defects in vocal writing, prosody, and dramatic expression, Coelho's contributions to Portugal's stage music should not be underestimated.

Ivo Cruz (b. 1901), who was born in Brazil, studied at the National Conservatory in Lisbon and later in Munich, and succeeded Viana da Mota as the conservatory's director in 1938. He is also the conductor of the Lisbon Philharmonic, and has held various musical and official positions, including membership in Lisbon's Camara (City Council).

Cruz's music is on an amateur plane, but he has made cultural contributions through his other activities, including research into early Portuguese music and increasing local acquaintance with major classic and other choral works.

Frederico de Freitas, born at Lisbon in 1902, had his training at the National Conservatory and later in Paris. He also visited Brazil, Holland, and Italy before becoming a conductor of the Emissora Nacional in 1935. His music shows a combination of various styles and influences; some of his works have Romantic and Impressionistic derivations and others illustrate more recent styles and trends, but his compositions also show an aim to contribute to a type of music that will also be individual in language and style. His ballet music is regarded as significant in its field and, as a conductor, he is sympathetic towards modern Portuguese music.

Fernando Lopes Graça (b. 1906) is one of the most often performed present-day composers. He was a pianist in a movie theater in his home town, Tomar, before he came to Lisbon in 1924 to study at the National Conservatory with Borba as his teacher of composition. Without private or official backing he went in 1937 to Paris, where Charles Koechlin was one of his advisers. He has been active as a musicologist, teacher, writer, and lecturer, with cultural and political ideas not always in accord with those locally in vogue. Vocal music is one of his principal interests, and he has arranged many Portuguese folksongs.

Portuguese traditional music is an important element in Graça's mature style which, like Freitas's, aims at combining nationalism with individuality. Some earlier works illustrated various contemporary influences, including those of Stravinsky, Schoenberg, and Bartók, but he now draws upon contemporary foreign music more selectively in a style primarily lyric.

Armando José Fernandes, born at Lisbon in 1906, was a pupil of Freitas Branco at the National Conservatory. Later, on a scholarship, he studied for three years in Paris with Nadia Boulanger and Roger-Ducasse. His style exhibits occasional national influences, but is mainly cosmopolitan in a modern way with some hints of Hindemith.

Jorge Croner de Vasconcelos (b. 1910) also studied with Freitas Branco at the National Conservatory and later, on an official fellowship, went to Paris to study with Dukas, Nadia Boulanger, Roger-Ducasse, and others. Most of his works are short, but exhibit him as an accomplished composer.

Joly Manuel Braga Santos, born in Lisbon in 1924, is regarded as an emerging composer who has something definite to say. His works continue tendencies shown in those of Freitas Branco, with whom he studied privately after leaving the National Conservatory in 1945.

Among the younger modernists Filipe Pires, a twelve-tone devotee, is studying in Germany on a government grant. Jorge Peixinho, who is influenced by Stockhausen, is interested in electronic methods. Others who can be described as members of the Portuguese musical left wing are Alvaro Cassuto, who is gaining in prominence; Fernando Correia Oliveira, who has developed a scale of his own based upon mathematical formulas, and Victor Macedo Pinto.

In the early stages of an acquaintance with contemporary Portuguese music, a foreign listener is likely to find its derivative elements most prominent in his impressions. But modern Portugal has a good number of talented composers who are expert craftsmen, although it has not yet produced an internationally well-known creative musician. Meanwhile local appreciation of native music is increasing, and the emergence of such a musician can be expected in the not distant future.

CONTEMPORARY MUSIC IN SPAIN*

By ARTHUR CUSTER

C URRENT musical practice in Spain finds its focus in a concern
for the "universalization" of Spanish music. Since 1958, the year
of the formation of the Grupo Nueva Música, this ideal has been
manifested in a militant rejection of folkloric elements, those superficial
trappings that have enabled Russians and Frenchmen to compose very
convincing Spanish music.

Spanish musicians today strive for "liberation from explicit nationalism," in an attempt to speak a universal musical language. Their syntax
is serialism. Their activities center around the recently formed Aula
de Música in the venerable Ateneo de Madrid, the traditional spring-
board for significant movements in arts and letters in the capital.

Fortuitously for the aims of the Grupo Nueva Música, the directorship of the new *aula* was assigned to Fernando Ruiz Coca, a man whose
interests were clearly in line with their views. Ruiz Coca possessed
a complete conservatory education, in addition to having studied
in the Faculty of Philosophy and Letters of the University of
Madrid. As co-founder of the Juventudes Musicales Españolas and
as music critic for the daily *El Alcazar,* he was known as an
informed and self-acknowledged champion of contemporary music.
Furthermore, he had a first-hand acquaintance with musical trends in
Central Europe, having represented his country at several international
congresses in France, Germany, and Luxembourg.

Aware that most post-Schoenbergian music was virtually unknown
in Spain, Ruiz Coca quickly set about filling the gap. Since the
inauguration of the Aula de Música in January 1959, frequent lecture-
recitals on different aspects of serial and post-serial music have attracted

* This is a revised version of an essay that appeared in the January 1962 issue
of *The Musical Quarterly.*

eager audiences, and overflow crowds have jammed the Ateneo auditorium to listen, seriously and critically, to everything from Schoenberg's
Opus 11 to Stockhausen's *Zeitmasse,* and beyond.[1] Highlights of the
first complete season were the cycle of five *conferencias* on electronic
music given by Gyorgy Ligeti and the series entitled *Algunos com-
positores serialistas españoles ante su obra.*

Eight years ago the very idea of a series of distinguished lectures
featuring Spanish composers discussing and playing their own serial
compositions would have been unimaginable. That it actually took
place was a clear indication of the readiness and eagerness of many
young Spanish composers to place their art in the mainstream of
contemporary Western music, and a thorough vindication of Ruiz
Coca's forthright challenge to history. As concert followed *conferencia,*
the regressive effects of Spain's twenty-five-year cultural isolation began
to vanish, and for the first time since 1936 musicians in Madrid could
begin to evaluate their creative efforts in terms of contemporary production across the frontier.

The bulk of the study, analysis, and performance of the Aula's
workload was capably and diligently executed by a handful of musicians
who must be counted among the most important musical figures in
Spain today: Cristóbal Halffter, Luis de Pablo, Ramón Barce, Manuel
Carra, Gerardo Gombau, and Enrique Franco.

Cristóbal Halffter is perhaps the best known among the composers
of the younger generation. Although only thirty-four, Halffter already
has an impressive catalogue of widely accepted works behind him, in
styles ranging from the "neo-Classic" Sonata for piano (1951) to
Espejos (*Mirrors*) for four percussionists and tape recorder (1963).
An extreme stylistic diversity has in fact characterized Halffter's production until very recently. A sensitive musician, Halffter has responded
readily in his own work to influences from many quarters.

Among his major scores it is possible to cite the unmistakably
Bartókian *Dos movimientos* for timpani and string orchestra, Op. 12
(the recipient of the UNESCO prize in 1956), and the Stravinsky-

---

[1] Many of the works included in these concerts were performed for the first
time in Spain. Among the more important premières of the first two seasons were
the Septet, Octet, and *Canticum Sacrum* of Stravinsky, Schoenberg's Fantasy, Op.
47, Webern's Concerto, Op. 24, Messiaen's *Visions de l'Amen,* the *Contrasts* of
Bartók, Berg's *Frühe Lieder* (1907), Pousseur's *Trois chants sacrés,* the *Mutazione* of
Berio, and Evangelisti's *Proiezioni sonore.*

inspired *Misa ducal*, Op. 10, written in the same year on commission by the present Duke of Alba.

Nor has he ignored his special Spanish heritage as the nephew of the brothers Ernesto and Rudolfo Halffter. In his first major work, *Antífona pascual*, Op. 4, for soloists, chorus, and orchestra, he pays stylistic tribute to the Falla of the Harpsichord Concerto period, while at the same time bowing to the Scarlattian ambit of his uncles. Halffter feels a philosophical as well as a familial kinship with the two older men, in that he considers himself an heir to both the spontaneity of Ernesto and the more cerebral quality of Rudolfo.

In a recent reminiscence,[2] Halffter stated that he was attracted to the music of Ernesto in terms of its "original treatment of Spanish folklore," but that it was the "decisive influence" of Rudolfo's polytonality that led him ultimately to write atonally. Among his pre-twelve-tone atonal works, the most successful are perhaps the *Concierto* for piano and orchestra, Op. 6, which won the National Music Prize in 1953, and the ballet *Saeta*, Op. 11, written for the Marques de Cuevas company.

Since 1956 Halffter has been more and more attracted to dodecaphony. His first serial work was the *Tres piezas* for string quartet, Op. 9, which he has subsequently rewritten for string orchestra and which appears in the catalogue of his works as the Concertino, Op. 13. Since then he has refined and codified his serial technique in such works as *Introdución, fuga y final* for piano, Op. 15 (1957), *Tres piezas* for solo flute, Op. 18 (1959), and Sonata for solo violin, Op. 20 (1959).

In an interview published in the *Estafeta Literaria* of February 15, 1960, Halffter said, "I started young; now I consider that that youth has passed. I would like now to have my works considered by the public not as promises, but as realities." In the same interview he stated that his greatest aspiration was to "Latinize serialism." With the writing of his *Cinco microformas* for orchestra (1960), Halffter went a long way towards the fulfillment of these wishes.

The "microforms" are a set of five variations on a twelve-tone series that is exposed in the first four measures (see Ex. 1). According to the composer, each variation represents a "completely closed form whose constructive value makes it independent from the others." The first, in which "intensities play a fundamental role," is only twenty-eight measures in length, and employs a texture that might be described as

2 In an interview with Otto Mayer-Serra published in the Mexican journal *Audiomúsica* of July 10, 1961.

"group pointillism," the "points" generally being chord groups rather than soloistic fragments.

Ex. 1

The second variation, which is based upon the retrograde form of the series, is marked "Two Counterpoints," and is constructed upon two free contrapuntal lines, each of which is fragmented and distributed among a particular instrumental group.[3] At the mid-point, each line is subjected to retrograde treatment (which is strict in the intervals only) while at the same time the instrumental groups are interchanged. The third variation, "Vertical and Horizontal Structures," begins with a series of chords, after which a succession of short melodic lines proceeds over sustained tones which are prolongations of the initial chords. This leads to a union of both textural elements in which each proceeds in retrograde form.

The fourth variation, "Rhythms Without Definite Pitch," is written for percussion only, and is constructed on four rhythmic elements whose conjunction, juxtaposition, and combination conspire to make this perhaps the most exciting movement. Although the series is quoted from time to time, the pitch-producing instruments of the percussion section are used primarily in such a manner that the pitches they produce have no value as such. In the scheme of the movement, their importance lies exclusively in their timbre.

As in the fourth variation, rhythm is the dominant element in the fifth, although here there is a greater richness of rhythmic components. Two sections of five measures each function as the structure upon which the movement is based. The last three measures state the "theme" of

[3] For this purpose the orchestra is divided as follows: *Group 1:* piccolo, oboes, bass clarinet, contrabassoon, horns, trumpets, harp. *Group 2:* clarinets, English horn, trombones, tuba, strings.

the work in its retrograde form.

In his subsequent music, Halffter's hand has been directed by the esthetic and technical ambience of the *Microformas*. His *Formantes* for two pianos, Op. 26, was produced in an atmosphere of intense activity in the spring of 1961. Between two guest-conducting assignments, he served as Spain's representative to the UNESCO contemporary music conference in Tokyo, supervised the recording of his orchestral setting of Albéniz's *Rapsódia española,* and read the proofs of the *Microformas,* which have since been published by Universal Edition. In July of the same year he conducted the National Symphony Orchestra of Mexico in a performance of the *Microformas* during a Festival of Contemporary Music held in Mexico City.

The *Formantes* represents Halffter's first essay, albeit a tentative one, into the realm of aleatory music. Subtitled *Móvil,* the work has the following structure:

Formante I — A-B-C-D-E-F — *Formante* VIII

The composer considers the first and last sections "pillars" in the design, and hence they must form the beginning and the ending of the piece. The aleatoric aspect derives from the fact that sections A through F may be played in whatever sequence the two performers have decided upon. In the bases for performance established by the composer, there is the additional liberty of repeating one (but only one) of the six middle sections. The piece lasts about eight minutes, and is played without pause. Halffter prefers that, in performance, the work be repeated as a kind of second movement to itself, with a different ordering of the internal sections.

Halffter's *Espejos* for four percussionists and tape recorder (1963) possesses a highly unified structure, and unfolds with a cumulative impact, despite the diversity of its elements, which range from free improvisation to a carefully controlled rhythmic pulse. An unseen member of the ensemble is the recording engineer, who records the first section of the composition and, on cue from the conductor, plays that portion back through a brace of speakers on both sides of the auditorium, while the percussion group on stage continues playing a dazzling and dizzying counterpoint to itself.

Except for his *Codex No. 1* for solo guitar, written for Narciso Yepes and yet to be performed, Halffter's most recent work is his *Sinfonía para tres grupos instrumentales.* This music was commissioned by the Southwest German Radio, and first played under the direction of Ernest Bour at the 1963 Donaueschingen Festival by the Southwest

German Radio Orchestra. For Claude Rostand, writing in *Figaro Littéraire* of November 2, 1963, Halffter's symphony and Castiglioni's *A Solemn Music* seemed the only bright spots in an otherwise unexciting landscape of avant-garde musical activity. Citing the "brilliant orchestration" and "vigorous, dramatic dynamism" of the Halffter work, Rostand termed it "one of the best scores to come out of Spain in many years."

This "symphony," which has more the character of a concerto grosso, is scored for the following instrumental groups:

Orchestra A: strings "a soli," woodwinds in pairs, trumpet, horn

Orchestra B: 13 percussion instruments, piano

Orchestra C: Piccolo, English horn, bass clarinet, contrabassoon, trumpet, horn, standard string section.

The physical configuration of the percussion group thus functions as a mediating influence between "ripieno" (Orchestra A) and "grosso" (Orchestra C) ensembles. The different groups play sometimes alone and sometimes in combination as the work unfolds in five uninterrupted sections which the composer calls *formantes*. The use of this term bespeaks a philosophical, if not a technical link with the piece for two pianos described above. Nor should one fail to observe that certain features of the *Microformas* (note the title) have more fully realized counterparts in the *Sinfonía:* the five-movement structure, the division of the orchestra into groups, the prominent and soloistic use of percussion instruments, and the manner in which the materials are related in the different movements.

One might observe that Halffter's formative and derivative periods are now behind him. In his development, he listened to a host of other voices in his search for his own musical language. In *Microformas, Espejos,* and in the *Sinfonía* for three instrumental groups, he speaks with his own tongue, and his utterance is strong, exciting, and personal.

As in the case of Halffter, the music of Luis de Pablo has passed through several phases. He had responded, successively, to the influence of Mompou, Falla of the later period, and to musical Expressionism. Since 1955, however, he has evidenced a definite and specific inclination towards a pure Webernian idiom at first, and then an extended and imaginative post-serialism.

De Pablo completed his first serial work, *Cinco invenciones* for flute or violin and piano, in 1957, and negating all his previous works (which included his prize-winning *Elegia* for orchestra), he assigned Opus 1 to the new piece. From that moment de Pablo's music has reflected the central European post-Webern evolution, with the same general sound and posture as that of Boulez, Nilsson, and the Italian school.

One finds in de Pablo's music a serious preoccupation with rhythm, which he considers an essential feature of each of his works. He has said that although his approach to rhythm is different from piece to piece, a possible common denominator might be what he calls "constant variation," which implies that there is no absolute symmetrical repetition in any of his compositions. He employs, in some works, a "regularized rhythm" in which each sound appears with a determined value, while others are constructed according to an "irrational forming," in which a rhythmic figure undergoes unlimited transformation.

In the first category are the *Coral,* Op. 2, for mixed chorus or wind septet, in which the rhythm is treated serially, and the Piano Sonata, Op. 3, which employs as a basis a palindromic rhythmic figure which is, consequently, not subject to retrograde treatment. Among his works in the second category, those whose rhythmic character is based upon free, almost rhapsodic variants, one may cite the *Comentarios,* Op. 6, for mezzo-soprano, piccolo, vibraphone, and double bass. In his work as a whole de Pablo has tried to achieve the "maximum flexibility of texture in the musical development, which becomes a rationalization, to the limit, of a greater immediacy and a greater plasticity of the sonorous material."

De Pablo's Opus 5, *Cuatro invenciones* for orchestra, was the last of his works based upon "orthodox" twelve-tone procedures. Since then he has greatly extended his serial techniques in order to achieve a greater linear flexibility. In his *Móvil,* Op. 7, for prepared piano, he serializes not only the intervals, but also the "set" of pre-determined sonorities, and *Progressus,* Op. 8, for two pianos, is constructed according to two series, one determining the linear direction of the work, the other controlling the dynamics.

One of de Pablo's most interesting and successful scores is his *Radial,* Op. 9, for twenty-four instruments. Performed at the 1961 Palermo Festival conducted by the Gruppo Universitario Nuova Musica (of which de Pablo is the Spanish representative), *Radial* is a kind of *música abierta,* in which the material is given to eight groups of three instruments, each of which, depending upon the manner of performance, may play notes outside its own group at the discretion of the performer.

Ex. 2

A more determined attempt to draw the performer more integrally into the creation of the work is found in de Pablo's Opus 11, *Libro para el pianista,* which was performed by the brilliant young Spanish pianist Pedro Espinosa at the 1961 Darmstadt Festival. In the manner of Stockhausen's *Klavierstück XI,* the *Libro* provides for the performer what de Pablo calls "sonorous objects" whose ordering is largely a matter of free choice. Given certain ground rules for the performance of each of the three movements (de Pablo plans the addition of a fourth), the pianist is allowed great liberty in the choice and sequence of the material. Perhaps the most striking movement is the third, which is played from a twelve-page manuscript in which the staves are divided by a narrow wooden ridge, making it possible for the performer to play, for example, the top staff of page one with the bottom staff of page three, or any of the 254 possible combinations.[4]

In the last three years, de Pablo's music has attracted an ever wider, if specialized, audience outside of Spain, principally in the European festivals that have come to be identified with the "newest" music. His *Polar* (1961) for violin (with all strings tuned a major second higher), soprano saxophone, bass clarinet, and large percussion group received its first performance at the 1962 Darmstadt Festival, with Bruno Maderna conducting the Kranichsteiner Musikensemble.[5] For the composer, *Polar* "presents an accumulation of possibilities

[4] In the 1961 Darmstadt performance the following sequence of page combinations was employed:

1 2 3 4 5 6 8 7 9 10 11
1 2 3 5 6 7 6 9 8 11 10

[5] This work, like most of de Pablo's music, is available from the Darmstadt publishing firm, Tonos Verlag.

of formation, always controlled, which proceed from nothing to a climax. It is a study in the polarization of the sonorous material."

De Pablo's friendship with the Italian flutist Severino Gazzelloni has resulted in two compositions for that instrument: *Condicionado,* for solo alto flute, written in Darmstadt in 1962, and dedicated to Gazzelloni, who has performed it frequently following the première in Warsaw; and *Recíproco* for piccolo, flute, alto flute, "jazz flute," piano, and percussion, commissioned by the Venice Festival and first performed there in 1963, again with Gazzelloni. Between the writing of these two chamber works, de Pablo brought to completion an orchestral composition of immense proportions, *Tombeau,* dedicated to the memory of Dr. Wolfgang Steinecke, founder and director of the Darmstadt Festival.

De Pablo's most recent composition is *Cesuras* for flute, oboe, clarinet, violin, viola, and cello. As in the works that immediately preceded it, the technical orientation of *Cesuras* involves a superposition of free and controlled elements. Here he juxtaposes an "inexactness in the duration of the notes and a new statistical approach to the number of sonorous events."

In his book *La Historia de la música española contemporanea* (Madrid, 1958), the Spanish critic and historian Federico Sopeña called de Pablo the "most intellectual" of the younger group, an appellation that appears thoroughly justified in the light of his technical procedures, which are always based upon a firm rationale. The intellectualization of music, for the sake of intellectualization, can of course be a dangerous and wholly inartistic procedure, but one has the feeling that de Pablo, in his indisputable sincerity, permits his rationalization to serve the cause of art as he sees it, and one can respond to his music, not for its novelty, but for its musical properties, its logic, and its sonority. Procedures aside, it appears that de Pablo represents the most complete embodiment to date of the quest for a more "universal" Spanish music, and it is evident that his stature grows with each new work.

Ramón Barce, like de Pablo, is completely self-taught in composition. Unlike both de Pablo and Halffter, however, Barce embraced atonality from the very beginning of his creative career, and although he has been the most enthusiastic spokesman and propagandist for new directions in Spanish music, he has remained until recently the most conservative of the group. Up until 1962 most of his music, although completely atonal and dodecaphonic, has a relatively traditional sound owing to its rather heavy contrapuntal texture, and it might be said that whereas de Pablo followed Webern, Barce's stylistic point of departure was Schoenberg.

One sees a progressive technical and artistic maturity throughout Barce's twenty-some works to date, and in the more recent twelve-tone pieces he demonstrates a technical skill more consistent with his high artistic purpose. Particularly worthy of mention are two works for soprano and instrumental ensemble, *Canciones de la ciudad*, Op. 13, and *Soledad primera*, Op. 20. Commissioned by the Aula de Música in celebration of the 400th anniversary of the birth of the Spanish poet Góngora,[6] the five songs of *Soledad* are fused into a tightly knit structural unit in which Barce demonstrates a facility and control greater than those found in any of his previous compositions. The piece shows a preoccupation with linear elements, and the thickness found in such works as the String Quartet, Op. 10, is here replaced by a lucidity and transparency wholly befitting the Góngora text.

Barce was silent for more than a year following *Soledad,* and when his Op. 21 finally appeared in September 1962, it was clear that he had undergone a rather rigorous self-analysis. *Estudio de sonoridades,* Op. 21, No. 1, and subsequent works demonstrate an evolution towards what Barce himself terms an "extreme vanguardism." The *Estudio* is the first in a projected collection of ten piano pieces, which bears the general title *Estudios seriales.* Subsequent works in the sequence will be devoted to different aspects of contemporary keyboard techniques as related to serial composition, and *Estudio de sonoridades,* as its title indicates, is concerned almost exclusively with timbre. A rhythmic germ serves as a generator for the entire piece, and its manipulation exploits all manner of sonorous effects such as are found in much virtuoso piano writing of the past decade.

Ex. 3

[6] Other composers commissioned for the *Homenaje a Góngora* concert: Manuel Castillo, Gerardo Gombau, Luis de Pablo, Antón Garcia Abril, and the Argentinian Isidro Maiztegui.

Example 3 shows a passage from *Estudios* in "time notation," in which durations are given relative values as suggested by the length of the "notes." Barce explains that the breath marks indicate definite breaks in the sound, that the small notes have no absolute time value, and that the glissandos are executed as a "continuous line," not as a chromatic scale. The "chords" are performed with the entire hand, or the forearm if necessary. The performer is cautioned that in this passage continuity is more important than precision, since the subject matter is timbre, not rhythm.

Barce's most recent works are *Parábola,* Op. 22, for woodwind quintet, *Objetos sonoros,* Op. 23, for twelve instrumentalists, and *Concierto de Lizara* for three soloists (oboe, trumpet, percussion) and string orchestra *a* 6. Written in the past two years, these works manifest the composer's growing preoccupation with instrumental timbre, projecting a quality of transparency almost totally absent in his previous production. One senses a certain self-consciousness in this new posture, and there is some question as to whether Barce's quest for "melodic values" will find ultimate fulfillment in this direction.

Whatever the intrinsic worth of these recent compositions may be, they do externalize Barce's search for a personal idiom, and reveal the same sensitivity to the musical world around him found in his steady stream of essays, articles, editions, and translations, and in the material he prepared for a two-hundred-broadcast series devoted to contemporary music heard over Radio Nacional during the past two years.

In Federico Sopeña's *Historia,* cited above, the author acknowledges the plight of the young performers who, "called upon to defend the musical language of the present, sacrifice great possibilities in the field of creation." He goes on to say that "this is the case with Manuel Carra, upon whose shoulders rests the music of Schoenberg, Bartók, and the young Spaniards." The case is well stated, and although it is too soon to offer a judgment of Carra as a composer, one has the feeling that were he to allow himself more time for it, his creative contribution to the work of the young Spanish group would be as considerable and as important as his activities as a performer and commentator. Highly intelligent, Carra is endowed with keen musical acumen, which manifests itself in all aspects of his art, and there is no doubt that he is one of the best pianists in Spain today.

Carra's *Cuatro piezas breves* (1960)[7] comprise a brilliant, eminently pianistic work. The first, marked Prestissimo, is a highly compressed

[7] Published by Union Musical Española, Madrid.

three-part structure whose textural and dynamic treatment is reminiscent of many pages of Webern. The second (Presto) is freely based upon a figure that is palindromic rhythmically, dynamically, and texturally.

Ex. 4

The third piece is a strict canon which has the appearance of a wide-ranging rhapsodic Lento, while the fourth is an extremely brilliant *perpetuum mobile*-like Prestissimo, essentially two-part in texture, in which Carra employs, most effectively, a kind of hocket technique. The forward movement is checked at three points (which define the structure) and a short coda serves to decelerate the work and bring it to an end.

A fascinating feature of the *Cuatro piezas* is the manner in which Carra has treated the climax in each movement. In spite of the great diversity of elements in the piece as a whole, there exists, on the expressive plane, a remarkable cohesiveness and inevitability. In the first piece the climax is represented, a little more than halfway through, by a carefully prepared twelve-tone *fortissimo* chord, while in the second it is achieved by means of a single accented note. In the third movement the climax occurs early, in a three-note *fortissimo* chord that spans six octaves, and in the fourth, a series of closely spaced accented notes leaps out of the figuration, creating a climax that is at once dynamic and linear.

Among the composers of the Madrid group whose activities center about the Ateneo, Gerardo Gombau occupies a singular position. His relation to the others is, in fact, something of a conundrum, since he is twenty years older than they, and a full professor at the traditionally traditional Madrid Conservatory as well. The puzzle is that instead of settling into his historically appropriate role as a musical reactionary, Gombau exhibits even more inquietude than some of his younger colleagues.

Expressing his views on the relationship of the older generation to the younger, Gombau said that "music, and in general all the arts in Spain have recently 'taken real flights.' The young artists of today are passionately involved in that which before could be considered only a novelty, and in general they have surpassed the previous generation, which has been somewhat frightened to see the direction Spanish music is taking. This phenomenon has never occurred before in Spain." Gombau went on to say that "today some composers who are older than fifty are trying to incorporate themselves into the movement of those who are thirty. I have much hope for this movement, which is of great value and interest for Spain, and I am grateful to be associated with it."

It can readily be observed that among the younger composers Gombau's gratefulness is fully reciprocated. A complete and respected musician, Gombau has assumed a positive and varied role in the activities of the Madrid group. Firmly believing that true Spanish music is not a matter of tambourines and *toros,* but simply music written by Spaniards, Gombau challenges the artistic validity of conscious nationalism, preferring to align himself with the movement towards an eclectic universalism. Although manifesting itself in music that has changed its point of view through the years, this conviction has served as an orientation for Gombau since his student days at the Madrid Conservatory with Conrado del Campo. As in the case of Halffter, one finds in Gombau evidence of a restless search that makes each new score appear as a transitional work.

Gombau's most efficacious serial composition is his *No son todos ruiseñores,* another of the works commissioned by the Ateneo for the Góngora program already mentioned. Written for soprano, clarinet, viola, and guitar, this is a highly polyrhythmic piece in which the voice is employed in a *concertato* manner, and although given longer lines, plays an approximately equal part with the instruments. In spite of the "modernity" of the sonorities, Gombau has not yet relinquished certain traditional procedures. The poem being strophic, he has chosen to repeat the rhythm of the strophe on its first return, and on the last to repeat literally ten measures from the original statement. In the composition can be found also many features of Gombau's earlier production, including characteristic repeated notes and octaves in the vocal part and a wide-ranging ostinato figure in the guitar. Its rather active texture and rhythmic color give *No son todos ruiseñores* an on-going quality that is its real charm.

Although Enrique Franco has composed music for radio (*El Bur-*

lador de Sevilla), the theater (*La Hidalga del valle*), and films (*Cuerda de presos*), in addition to many songs, his importance in contemporary Spanish musical life lies principally in other areas. An intelligent and perceptive critic-historian, he has become the most ardent and influential spokesman and commentator for the new artistic movement. It is impossible to measure the effectiveness of his presence, but it is fair to say that the initial impetus towards a stylistic and ethical reform in Spanish music was largely due to his encouragement and influence, which was felt in Madrid and elsewhere long before the formation of the Grupo Nueva Música in 1958.

In his double capacity as music critic for the Madrid daily *Arriba* and chief of the music section of the Spanish National Radio, Franco has enjoyed, since 1952, the opportunity to travel frequently to the musical capitals of Europe, where he has witnessed, studied, and been attracted by the evolving serialist panorama. His reports written for his newspaper have been widely read, and composers who are not completely shackled to the traditional Hispanic formulas have been quick to investigate the possibilities that serialism might afford. Franco went further by opening up the programming for the Radio Nacional to include more contemporary music. As an influential figure embodying traditional training, avant-garde ideas and tastes, and the historical perspective to make the two reconcilable, he was sought out by the younger group, and when the Grupo Nueva Música was formed, the then thirty-eight-year-old Franco was cast in the role of patriarch. Since then he has been one of the permanent fixtures at the Ateneo, where he has personally accounted for at least one *conferencia* in each of the important cycles given since January 1959.

Enrique Franco's interest, enthusiasm, and encouragement have indeed been decisive in the development of a new orientation in Spanish music — an esthetic environment that has been so favorable to many young composers that Franco was able to predict in 1961 that "within a few years one will be able to speak of a Spanish 'manner' ('school' is a risky term) of serial composition . . . Spanish music will then have achieved — again — its universal moment.[8]

It was inevitable that the roots put down by these men around Ruiz Coca's program at the Ateneo would spread to other quarters. During the 1960-61 season, presumably influenced by the awakened interest in *la música vanguardia* created by the activities of the Aula's

[8] Quoted from *Serialismo en España*, in *Panorama*, a feature section of the *Arriba* of June 11, 1961.

second year, Madrid was alive with contemporary music. Among the various concert societies, Cantar y Tañer offered several special programs devoted exclusively to contemporary music, and the concerts of the Juventudes Musicales boasted more premières of Spanish works than ever before. The same spirit was reflected in the bi-weekly programs of the Sociedad de Música de Cámara (which is identified with the excellent State-supported Agrupación Nacional de Música de Cámara, a string quartet) and in the concerts of the Orquesta Filarmonica de Madrid.

In the same year, encouraged by what was perhaps the most favorable climate in Spanish musical history for such a project, Luis de Pablo mounted a series of five concerts under the banner *Tiempo y Música*. Apart from the excellence and modernity of its programs, the significant feature of this novel enterprise was that it was financially underwritten by the Sindicato Español Universitario, an unmistakable acknowledgment on the part of Spanish officialdom of the need for a greater public cognizance of contemporary developments in music. The *Tiempo y Música* concerts have since brought to the public for the first time live performances of such works as Bo Nilsson's *Zwanzig Gruppen*, Bruno Maderna's *Serenata*, the *Improvisations sur Mallarmé* and the Sonatina of Pierre Boulez, and Franco Evangelisti's *Ordini*, in addition to several compositions by Spanish serialists.

An interesting aspect of these programs has been the presentation of works by Catalan composers. Serialism in Barcelona has a much longer history than in Madrid, and there has evolved, from the lineage of Joaquin Homs (who studied briefly with Schoenberg and Roberto Gerhard), a rather loosely knit movement that today is concentrated in the music of four young composers (all in their thirties) who struggle for recognition in a tradition-bound city whose artistic climate is anathema to those interested in pursuing current tendencies. Although these composers, José Cercós, José Maria Mestres, Juan Hidalgo, and Xavier Benguerel, have recently been able to find an outlet for their music in concerts given in Barcelona under the title *Música Abierta*, their inclusion in the *Tiempo y Música* programs has provided a rare opportunity to hear music that deserves wider recognition. Mestres and Cercós adhere closely to the post-serial ambit as represented by Boulez, while Benguerel makes a Stravinskyan use of ostinato techniques and tonal goals, within a serial framework. Hidalgo is the most avant-garde of the Catalans, favoring a species of *música abierta à la* John Cage.

Two other composers, who have only recently begun to make their presence felt in Spain, are Carmelo Alonso Bernaola and Miguel Angel Coria. The works of both men reveal an esthetic kinship with the specific ideals of de Pablo, and one senses the emergence of a fraternal triumvirate within the general movement. Bernaola, who is thirty-five, won the Prix de Rome following a brilliant career at the Madrid Conservatory. He has studied with Petrassi, Tansman, Maderna, Jolivet, and Messiaen, receiving the Spanish Premio Nacional de Música in 1962. His recent works include *Cuarteto, Constantes, Sinfonietta progresiva, Espacios variados,* and *Permutado. Superficie No. 3,* completed in March 1963, is scored for piccolo, alto saxophone, xylophone, and bongos, and is a "summary of the author's experiences in 'flexible music'." As in most music of its type, "the instrumental mixtures and superpositions are realized with the greatest care and precision."

Miguel Angel Coria, whom de Pablo cites as "a new worthy," is the youngest composer in Spain's youthful musical society. Like Bernaola, the twenty-seven-year-old Coria was a prize-winning student at the Madrid Conservatory. His *Juegos de densidades* for piano has been performed in Mexico and recorded at Radio Cologne. *Imágenes* for flute, oboe, violin, viola, and vibraphone, according to the composer, "is written for various clearly delimited *formantes.* A strict, though not integral, organization controls the succession or interruption of punctuating and variable forms, forms in groups, etc." *Imágenes* was first performed in December 1963 in a première-laden Madrid concert sponsored jointly by the German Institute and the Juventudes Musicales.

Apart from the serial realm, which indeed is the most vital and positive force in the Spanish musical consciousness today, it is necessary to consider briefly certain other figures among the younger generation whose work is important for its own sake. In Barcelona, Manuel Valls and José Casanovas, both long-time members of the Círculo Manuel de Falla (which convened every Saturday during the decade 1948-1958), continue to write, in a free atonal manner, well-constructed music of considerable beauty. The *Sevillano* Manuel Castillo, perhaps the only important composer outside the Madrid-Barcelona orbit, is considered a valuable creative personality by the Madrid group. His composition *Al nacimiento de Nuestro Señor* demonstrates an expressiveness and delicacy all but lacking in much of the music of his colleagues.

Antón Garcia Abril and Alberto Blancafort are two composers of the Madrid New Music Group whose chose not to follow the dodeca-phonic route to the Ateneo when that group dispersed in 1959. Abril has since occupied himself almost exclusively with composition for films, but from time to time he produces well-made and convincing scores in a tonally oriented atonal idiom. Significantly however, he has lately begun study with Petrassi, and it will be interesting to watch his development in the light of this experience.

Blancafort, one of the best-trained of the younger Spanish com-posers, has unfortunately all but renounced a creative career. The son of a composer-father and a violinist-mother, Blancafort, who is now thirty-six, has been immersed in music since childhood. His early train-ing at home and in the Schola Cantorum of the Jesuit school he attended was complete in every respect, and when his first mature work was given its première by Carlos Surinach at Barcelona in 1950, he was offered a one-year scholarship by the Count of Cartagena to study in Paris, the same grant that sent Falla northward many years earlier. Like Falla, Blancafort stayed not one year, but seven. His teacher for six of these was Nadia Boulanger.

Returning to Spain in 1957, Blancafort settled in Madrid, and after studying one season with Joaquin Rodrigo, he assumed the directorship of the chorus of the National Radio, a move that, coupled with his subsequent assumption of the musical direction of the sixty-station Cadena Azul (Blue Network) de Radio Difusión, virtually terminated his compositional activity.

The world is familiar with the "Generation of 1910," and those acquainted with Gilbert Chase's excellent book *The Music of Spain* are aware of the tragic dispersal, to all parts of the earth, of the promis-ing "middle group." What has been reported here, then, is more than a mere segment of present musical activity. In effect, this *is* Spanish music today. Reflecting upon the greatness of this country's cultural heritage, one wonders whether this delayed flowering of vigorous and worthy activity may not signal the beginning of a new renaissance in Spanish music.

THE NEW MUSIC IN ITALY

By MARIO BORTOLOTTO

VIENNESE compositional ideas and practices began to penetrate into Italy only after the Second World War. There are only two exceptions to this statement: Luigi Dallapiccola, whose interest in Schoenberg began years before the war, and Camillo Togni, who composed the first serial score in Italy in 1941-42.

It was, however, primarily the teaching of Bruno Maderna that, directly and indirectly, brought musical Expressionism into the mainstream of Italian music. This Venetian composer, who was among the earliest participants in the celebrated *Ferienkurse* at Darmstadt, exerted in his roles as composer, performer, and teacher an incomparable influence on young Italian musicians. This influence can be seen above all in the works of Luigi Nono, to whom (as Heinz-Klaus Metzger has pointed out) we owe the first interesting composition of the European post-war years: *Polifonia-Monodia-Ritmica*.

Anybody today who studies the latest of Nono's compositions will find much to reconsider and correct in previous discussions of Nono's music. Since the days of his earliest group of compositions (*Variazioni* for orchestra on a row by Schoenberg, 1950; the first *Composizione* for orchestra, 1951; *Due espressioni*, 1953; as well as the above-mentioned work) Nono has shown himself to be far from a *pur Weberien*, as Antoine Goléa has somewhat too hastily categorized him. It is true that since the early 1950s Nono has been very careful to assimilate some of the structural principles of the Viennese masters. However, the cold fire of his instrumental writing, which harbors an incandescent purity, the torrid violence of certain of his percussive explosions, and the singular outpouring of isolated sounds that push towards an aggressive resolution are quite alien to the introspection and song-like intimacy that characterize the works of Webern.

His early compositions certainly once and for all led him from the road of rigid musical abstraction. His three-part *Epitaffio per Federico García Lorca* (1952-53) was already a study in so-called *poésie engagée*. As a consequence it includes in the Webern-like spatial conception such heterogeneous elements as derivations from folksong, semi-liturgical melodic lines, and such provocative sounds as those of castanets, etc.

In the Italian musical tradition, the works of Nono, with their ruggedness and their lack of feeling, are an isolated case — so much so that one cannot even find any relationships between this music and that of the "anti-gracefulness" of the futurists and followers of Casella. Nono considers art a lenitive and in Schoenberg he no longer seeks Pierrots or transfigured nights, but the reality of the social trauma.

The results of Nono's attitude are most evident and immediate in his two orchestral compositions *Incontri* and *Diario Polacco,* the latter of which displays a certain lack of invention and strains for effects in its rudimentary use of percussion. Nono's "unpleasant" philosophy is even more apparent in his three choral works entitled *Il Canto sospeso, La Terra e la campagna,* and *Cori di Didone,* whose texts are taken from letters of condemned anti-Fascists, from lyrics of Cesare Pavese, and, finally, from certain poems of Ungaretti. Nono's choral writing is also quite different from Schoenberg's, as the latter is exemplified in the marvelous chorus of the burning bush from *Moses und Aron.* Nono's almost constant superimposition of all twelve tones negates any perception of openness and creates a great mass of pure white sound. However, in those sections where the soloists enter (e.g. the entrance of the tenor in *La Terra* and the soprano solo at No. 7 in the *Canto*), an exceptional melodic sensibility displays itself with vibrant intensity.

Unfortunately the delicate equilibrium between musical reasoning and political ideology could not be maintained for a long period. In two recent small vocal pieces, *Sarà dolce tacere* (again on a text by Pavese) and *Ha venido* (text by Machado), Nono's passion for madrigalism induces the composer to a belated repentance leading to some fastidious tonal polarity.

The new cantata, *Sul ponte di Hiroshima,* happily ignores the solutions of the new music: the lesson of Webern becomes the aphasia of an orchestra that doesn't know how to overcome isolated sound, except when it bursts forth in explosive sections in the percussion. The vocal line occasionally displays original curves and bits of melody within the limits of Expressionistic vocalism; it manifests certain diatonic tendencies and begins to wander within the space of an octave. The relationship

between the vocal parts and the orchestra is that of ornamental subordi-
nation of the latter to the former. Bad literature, we are told by **Gide**,
is conceived above all with the best of intentions. Nono today appears
to fear precisely what we most admire him for — his lyrical gifts, as
the best parts of his opera *Intolleranza 1960* decisively demonstrate.
He feels himself alienated from precisely what he is best able to do.

Berio's evolution, when compared with Nono's, has shown itself
to be more judicious. Aided by an exceptional craft and an excellent
knowledge of the traditional musical repertory, Berio rarely ignores the
exigencies of the ear, though he sometimes fails to satisfy those of the
mind. His music springs from Stravinsky's sphere of influence, as does
much other present-day Italian music, and this force is still quite
evident in his *Magnificat*. But Berio, early in his career, consciously
sought to work out his own style. Though *Nones*, for orchestra, still
displays a debatable tonal "polarity," in the *Allelujah's* (1 and 2) the
composer incorporates musical materials that are decidedly panchro-
matic. The essential merits of *Allelujah* lie in the clarity and facility with
which such materials are presented and in their immediate compre-
hensibility. It would be difficult to find in any other contemporary
European music a comparable physical expression of *musizieren*. In
Allelujah no problems are presented that are not immediately solved
in the fabric of the music itself as it is presented in an incomparably
full orchestral sonority.

Berio has achieved equally felicitous results in his String Quartet,
a composition that, in its extreme precision of sounds, could be the work
of a watchmaker (to use an old *boutade* of Stravinsky). The same can
be said of his by-now-celebrated *Sequenza*, for flute solo, a work liberated
from Webern influences. *Circles*, for voice and percussion, on a text
of Cummings, presents us with a score of singular precision and happy
inventiveness, although at times the voice does not blend well with
the arid percussion sounds. For example, in the finale the voice ends
by touching upon a pathos that does not integrate with the rest of
the ensemble.

This pathetic vein has come to the fore especially in Berio's most
recent compositions: the two stage works presented in 1963, of which
the second, *Passaggio*, is a true opera. In this work certain Expressionistic traits reappear, traits one had hoped Berio had abandoned: e. g.
the notable lack of balance between the dry orchestral sonorities, the
marvelous choral passages, and a kind of spoken chorus on the one
hand, and, on the other, the voice of the soprano (an "honest whore"

for a change, in the manner of the Elizabethan theater!).

Berio, however, is a musician of inexhaustible vitality as well as of great talent. For this reason it would be well to await his future works to see if he will overcome this undeniable artistic impasse.

The position of Niccolò Castiglioni is completely different. His early works were quite eclectic, but before long he began to develop an individual style mostly concerned with color. If there is any composer in Italy who has followed to the letter the line from Debussy through Webern and Boulez, it is this young musician.

If we study only one fragment of his *Aprèslude*,[1] the analysis will easily introduce us to his style. Measure 20 of the fourth movement alone demonstrates the following techniques:

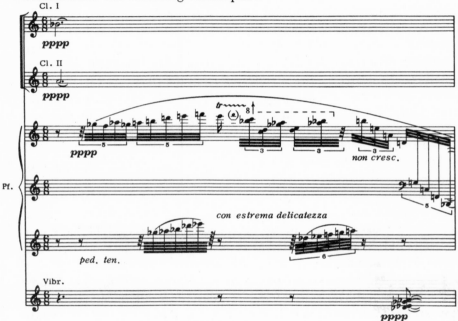

1) the series of black keys (dear to all pianists who have studied Chopin's Etude, Op. 10, No. 5) counterposed to the white keys;
2) the succession of whole tones (D♭, E♭, F, G, A, B) which marks the resumption of the hexatonic scale;
3) successions of perfect fifths;
4) light clashes of major seconds;
5) the superimposition of various rhythmic values in order to avoid any rhythmical regularity;

[1] Examples copyright © 1960 by Edizioni Suvini Zerboni, Milan.

and, further on (mm. 24-25):

6) the insistent repetition of F which develops into a trill on a minor second (F-G♭);
7) repetition of the tritone (A-D♯);
8) trill on a major second (G♭-A♭);
9) alternation of major and minor thirds in an evocative manner (according to the French tradition dating from the celebrated

Ex. 2 Castiglioni, mm. 24-25

study by Saint-Saëns);

10) blocks of minor seconds followed by major seconds;

11) a fragment of the chromatic scale which evaporates into nothing-
ness.

We venture to say that anyone who, by accident, were to know only
these few measures by Castiglioni would be able, intuitively, to divine
the whole score. One will notice that none of these techniques is in

itself very advanced, but the composer's conviction tends to change their significance when they are taken together as part of his style. It is a fact that, at least until his very recent works, Castiglioni has demonstrated an incontestable precision and capacity for synthesis. Derivations from Debussy (and perhaps even Chopin), Messiaen, Webern, and Cage in his compositions, because they all are a part of Castiglioni's sure compositional techniques, are not important in themselves. These things are merely a matter of vocabulary, a vocabulary the composer employs, feeling secure in the thought that he can use it in new and original ways. Castiglioni's *Inizio di movimento*, for piano solo, the *Movimento continuato* for piano and small ensemble, the *Tropi*, the *Impromptus I-IV* for full orchestra, at the very least, are proof of his compositional abilities. At times, e.g. in the *Impromptus*, his orchestral means can be minimal. These pieces might have been entitled more accurately, in the manner of Schubert, *Moments musicaux*. Here, as in the famous Viennese examples (the two cycles for orchestra by the young Webern), nothing is predetermined: in their short duration, the composer presents fleeting ideas, intent to *noter l'inexprimable* or to *fixer des vertiges*. The desired result is achieved; and the extreme delicacy of the texture and the sensitive blending of colors recall the enchantment conjured up by the *tachistes*. Above all, in the fourth piece, the presentation of a chord (the *Mutterakkord*), as in Schoenberg's *Farben*, achieves a maximum of emotional coloristic intensity balanced by a minimum of formal dialectic. Variation and contrast are provided by the continuously changing colors. At intervals during the piece the piano becomes the protagonist and the composer makes the most of the part, providing it with jewel-like decorative patterns and *agréments*. Here he follows in the tradition begun by Couperin, which in our century has been echoed in the *Feux d'artifice* and in the constellations of sound found in the sonatas of Boulez. If this search for sweet and luminous sounds, for a suspended spatiality, for a gravity-defying fluidity has brought about some of the most poetic moments in the works of Castiglioni, it has also approached, at times, a dangerous stagnation. The early *Cangianti*, for piano solo, was already marred by a certain coquettishness and even Castiglioni's latest scores are filled with like compromises. In the opera *Gyro* (based on a cosmic biblical text) the use of hissing choruses, anemic sonorities, and pseudo-orientalism are, frankly, insupportable. Castiglioni's problem is that he must learn to add weight and vigor to his music without diminishing the lightness of its texture: in a word, it is the problem of incorporating sounds louder than *mezzo forte.*

Franco Evangelisti, a Roman, has few musical connections with the past. Even his earliest works reflect the spirit of the *neue Musik.* An early piece of his for violin and piano and another for piano solo served merely as preparatory works. But with his first orchestral work, *Ordini,* the composer rose to a level probably not since attained by any other piece of Italian music. *Ordini* is indeed a masterful work, in which one is at a loss whether to admire more the bold, expressive progression towards transcendental goals or the crystalline elegance of the writing. Its intransigent violence never descends to mere noise, but is always precisely measured and clean-sounding. This work abandons pan-serial techniques and proceeds according to several dynamically related systems, called by the composer "orders" [*ordini*].

One can delineate two basic principles that permeate all of Evangelisti's music: 1) an extremely acute sense of silence, which isolates single notes or groups of notes, and 2) a tendency towards the deformation of sound which weakens an awareness of the individual instruments.

Spazio a cinque, for taped voices and percussion, appeared soon after *Ordini.* This work reveals an even greater elegance of writing, though the percussion parts are not nearly so inventive as the absolutely spontaneous vocal writing. The percussion is nevertheless employed in a delicate, but virtuoso, manner. In *Random or not Random,* for orchestra, Evangelisti's style becomes ever purer and more distilled. Silence is important and the lines of orchestral color are never exteriorized, never become too impressionistic, but remain firm and precise as in a fine line drawing. If one were to compare this work with a Chinese drawing, he could not but recall Mallarmé's lines — *au coeur limpide et fin.* Evangelisti is in the tradition of Varèse with his precise attention to the genesis of sounds. He seems to conclude, with the extreme sonorities of his music, a complete historical movement. One might also mention his piece for flute solo, a delicate thread of extraordinary color, which incorporates simultaneous-sounding tones through the use of harmonics. One should also mention his electronic work, *Incontri di fascie sonore,* which is doubtless one of the few happy essays in this questionable medium. The most recent piece by Evangelisti, yet to be published, is a scenic work, *Die Schachtel,* which is an ironic commentary on the destiny of the human race. We maintain, however, that the best of Evangelisti is to be found in one of his less intense works: the string quartet entitled *Aleatorio,* which is a precious and disarming gem.

There is no preciosity, but a precise constructivism, in the works of Aldo Clementi — once he broke from Stravinskyan influences. Even when he followed in Stravinsky's footsteps, he was not a mere formal imitator. His study of *Oedipus* and the symphonies was eminently abstract and outside the boundaries of Stravinsky's esthetics. "Abstraction" is a general and equivocal word, especially when one borrows its usage from the realm of the visual arts and applies it to a composer. It is possible to use "abstraction" as a convenient term, to define it as a total lack (psychologically, narratively, and illustratively) of that *expression* which according to Hanslick could not be found in any serious music. In the music of Clementi, interior time, the time of experience (the *Erlebniszeit*) is consistently eliminated, and the music, bound as it is to the insurmountable limits of clock time, tends to disperse itself by spatial expansion. Individual phrases, or "episodes," as Clementi calls them, are not opposed in the classical manner, nor are they recalled by analogy. They are juxtaposed, are brought together by means of a technique of fusion, or to use an artistic term, by "collage," a technique that can also be applied to much modern European poetry. Pointing out that the absence of duration (*durée*) is the chief characteristic of such a manner of composing, recalls the classical formulations of absence in the piercing words of Mallarmé.

After some rather uncertain attempts, even though these proceeded along clear and decisive lines, Clementi produced three instrumental works: *Episodi* for orchestra, *Ideograms No. I* for sixteen instruments, and *No. 2* for solo flute and seventeen instruments. In these three works one can find the essence of his style. This style avoids all serial principles; its basic element becomes intervallic logic, which, by means of the systematic employment of "disassociative" or "aggregate" intervals, avoids the formation of any traditional harmonic or melodic figures and removes the necessity of using any of the classical serial principles. Clementi's abandonment of serialism is accomplished by these few very simple principles. This method is one of great freedom, which arrives at the same results as do the more calculated serial scores, but at the same time leaves a freedom that Schoenberg did not allow and also avoids introducing any of the traditional clichés — e.g. melodic figurations, rhythms, and musical phrases. Let us look at one of Clementi's works, *Ideogrammi I,* mm. 91-92 (Ex. 3).[2]

It contains:

in the E-flat clarinet   minor 6th

[2] Example copyright © 1960 by Edizioni Suvini Zerboni, Milan.

Ex. 3

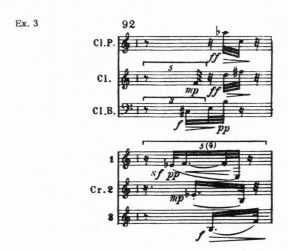

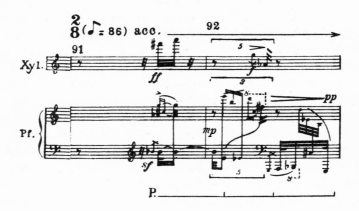

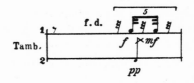

in the clarinet	major 6th; major 3rd
in the bass clarinet	minor 3rd; perfect 5th
in the 1st horn	major 2nd; minor 9th
in the 2nd horn	diminished 4th
in the 3rd horn	diminished 5th
in the xylophone	minor 3rd; major 7th
in the piano	diminished 5th, aug. 3rd, 4th, aug. 5th, then an octave, maj. 9th, aug. 4th, maj. 2nd, min. 2nd, aug. 2nd, then an octave, aug. 4th; and in the ornamentation of the right hand a maj. 7th, dim. 3rd, maj. 2nd.

One can, then, find all the intervals in a very short space, as well as all of the sounds. This is similar to the panintervallic series (*Allintervallreihe*) in Webern. Analogous situations exist on the horizontal plane where there are many encounters of notes. They are carefully regulated, within the maximum of an octave, never to form chords or simple consonances in the classical sense. In this way the well-knit *Tabulatur,* the primitive system of twelve tones, is replaced in a manner characterized by clarity and elementary simplicity. One must keep in mind that, within these defined limits, a boundless number of combinations are possible. The few basic principles of this system guarantee, *a priori,* coherence within the defined boundaries.

The episodes here firmly individuated can be compared to the individual heavenly bodies. Thus the Webern image, saturated with Viennese song, becomes a symbol of a nameless reality. Here the sound is as extremely precise and as little diffused as one could imagine. And if the title, *Ideogramma,* seems hyperbolic, since a title describes the *limits* of a work, one must keep in mind that it also points up the non-human chill of this work, which deprives all hedonism of its right to existence. Silence, as in Webern, is the basic event in the music of Clementi, and into silence the individual sounds cry to be swallowed up. The *horror pleni* presents itself in the works of Clementi as a lack of faith in logic: the music does not develop nor is there repetition; it simply occurs, always different, always the same, as with the coincidence of opposites.

Clementi, working with ever more restricted means, has limited himself to a few instruments, e.g. flute, oboe, and clarinet, in his *Triplum.* And, in his *Intavolatura,* he reaches, with surprising virtuosity, the logical conclusion of this trend by writing for only one instrument, the harpsichord. In this work sounds are frozen in the limited context. Clementi also has concerned himself with "de-creation," with anti-materials, as can be seen in his ballet *Collage*. In his most recent works, the three *Informels,* the sound is undeniably larger, but the immobility is more decisive. In fact No. 3 is made up of 43 rhythmic units, to each one of which one sound is assigned. There are 72 parts in this counterpoint *alla fiamminga.* The constant density that would result from this is varied, however, by a process of cancellation, obtained by irregular curves traced in the score. All the notes encompassed by these curves disappear in performance and are not sounded. The number of versions of this work, theoretically infinite, is fixed at eight. There results an identity of variation, each of which repeats certain of the constructive principles essential to the ideas of the composer. Clementi's next composition, *Variante,* will make use of these compositional principles in a choral composition on the text of the Mass.

Camillo Togni, in his most recent compositions, has also made use of these abstract, "de-humanizing" constructive principles. His *Rondeaux* (on texts by Charles d'Orléans) confine the vocal soloist, a coloratura soprano, to the outer limits of her register, thus avoiding any warm, human sounds. Accompanying her, the harpsichord weaves coldly exquisite patterns. Now, however, Togni is working on a theatrical piece based on a marionette play by Trakl. In this work, his recent theories, which have removed him from the sphere of classical serial composition, will have a chance to be expanded.

The music of Sylvano Bussotti contrasts greatly with that of Togni, in that Bussotti has incorporated the ideas of Cage as a point of departure. Whoever has heard Cage's *Pieces for David Tudor,* where even the most radical piano techniques are expanded, will realize how much Bussotti's music owes to these sounds, performance techniques, and even the conception of the work. In line with this Bussotti explored and amplified the possibilities of the voice in *Due voci,* in which the soprano soloist delivers a paradoxical and fascinating reading of a fragment from La Fontaine. Bussotti's extravagant use of sound is not merely for display. Even where he indulges himself in his virtuosity, and there are many instances of this, he never fails to convince the listener that nothing is in the score for merely decorative purposes. If anything, the danger lies in another direction: that of imbuing the undeniable violence of his music with a sentimental and pathetic sense which recalls musical *verismo.* In these instances the shade of Puccini is present in an embarrassing proximity to Cage and Boulez. This has occurred especially in the cantata *Memoria* and in certain sections of *Torso*. In Bussotti's instrumental works, however, he has managed to overcome such temptations. *Pour clavier* is a fine work that displays an almost terrifying musical invention. One need only cite the by-now-celebrated page 7, where the sound of fingernails on the keyboard is not merely an intentional "gesture," but an integral part of the counterpoint, a technique used by Cage in *The Wonderful Widow of Eighteen Springs*. Bussotti also furiously explores aleatory principles in *Fragmentation pour un joueur de harpes*. There is a second harp, tuned according to a system designated by the composer; this harp echoes, interrupts, and underlines the music of the principal harp, extemporaneously. By this implementation of density it is easy to imagine how great the distance is between what is written on the page and what actually is heard. In *Phrase,* for string trio, inspired by the *petite phrase* in a famous passage from Proust, the instruments continuously discover new musical patterns in the enigmatically drawn notation (Ex. 4).[3]

In *Mit einem gewissen sprechenden Ausdruck* (a title that appears to be the manifesto of Bussotti's Expressionistic revolution) the performers must read different types of notation, passing from sectors to normal writing to typical action script, which can be realized only within certain specified limits. Thus in a work such as *Pearson Piece,* for baritone and piano, an unlimited number of songs can be constructed from the lines in the score. In the *Siciliano* (from *Memoria*), for *a cappella* male chorus, the art of choral writing is carried to an extreme. Even in the more dubious areas of his writing, that which is never absent is the knowledge of reality, where even sensuality is clarified through the consciousness, as in the 18th century. It is not surprising that Bussotti loves the writings of de Sade, in fact at the moment he is planning a huge cantata to be entitled *Passion selon Sade*. A preview of parts of this work has already appeared, called *Tableaux vivants,* for two pianos. These are once again examples of Bussotti's mastery of the piano idiom. Aside from Boulez and a few pieces by Cardew, we know of no present-day composer who makes such radical use of the resources of the piano.

And finally *Torso,* in spite of all its weaknesses, is worthy of mention because of its richness of color, which seems to be summarized in the voluptuous use of percussion, and especially the glass chimes.

Bussotti is baroque and decadent, and he never ceases to surprise us. We are in opposition to his interpretation of Cage with respect to formal

---

[3] Reproduced with the kind permission of Universal Edition, Milano.

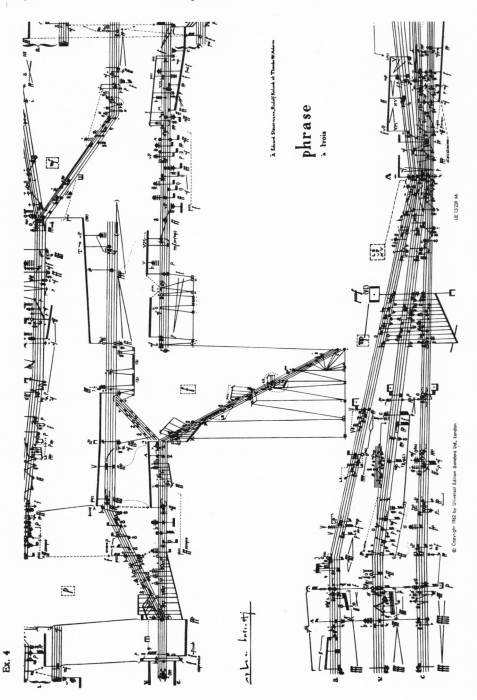

phrase
à trois

à Eduard Steuermann, Rudolf Kolisch et Theodor W. Adorno

Ex. 4

UE 13239 Mi

flexibility and we feel that the essential path of the new music should lead towards the abolition of *all* formal predisposition. "This way lies, no doubt, a revelation," says Cage.

Franco Donatoni has undoubtedly followed this path. He has not come from any particular school of composition, especially not that of Stravinsky, which is so influential in present-day Italy. Donatoni has shown us indisputably in his published works that among the many contemporary roads to the new music, the flowery one certainly has a place — so much so that the critic who studies his early works will learn little or nothing of his present style. Those works, though written well enough, were nothing more than disarming pieces à la Bartók. But certain aspects of the new music infiltrated even into them and, finally, in the Second Quartet for strings they were adopted wholeheartedly. Donatoni went even further in *Movimento* for piano, harpsichord, and nine instruments and in the divertimento *For Grilly* for three winds, three strings, and percussion. Finally the whole development reached a new brilliance, under the influence of Stockhausen, in *Doubles* for harpsichord solo. This spirited work is a series of variations (in the sense of integral variation) or *esercizi* wherein the impetuosity of Scarlatti becomes frozen in a most sophisticated manner. Furthermore another, more destructive facet exists in the work of Donatoni. This shows itself in the huge, violent symphonic works: *Strophes, Sezioni, Per orchestra,* and in a singular piece entitled à la Kleist, *Puppenspiel,* which ironically plays with Romantic notions. Finally, in his most interesting and recent works, Donatoni has completely discarded any structural conventions — a move towards the essential innovations of the new music in the '60s.

With Donatoni it seems that the concept of Utopia, which has always interested the traditional avant-garde, has lost its view of future practicability, whether in time (Adorno) or beyond time (Benjamin). Instead it descends intransigently into the work and, indeed, into all musical activity as such. If such music is still a composition and this musician is still a composer, it is only, as the saying goes, an enigma seen in a mirror, but we venture to say that it is more mirror than it is enigma. For, the aboriginal tradition (which Romanticism rediscovered emanating from the inner man) handed down to us as the sign of man (and therefore also of music) is with respect to the macrocosm, to nature, exactly the reverse, mirror-like. The connection of signs, of graphic symbols, is no longer established by means of historical classification. The meaning of this music does not correspond to what is written down, but can be understood only as a point of departure for the interpreter. But this does not eradicate, as might be supposed, the immediate reality of the music itself. Its precariousness and its concession to the ephemeral are certainly characteristics of industry at its zenith. But one can never assert that this music has worth in the social sense that money has, because even a (possibly) beautiful performance can never be repeated. And besides, the concepts of money are changed by historical and geographical considerations, while the new music of today is aimed in a direction that is anything but one of exchange. The choice of materials in Donatoni's Fourth Quartet is on a smaller scale than in his preceding works, and the concept of playing a game is evident, even in its notation. There is no score, only individual parts. In these are notated three circuits, or series of instrumental modalities: upon these, chance techniques operate by means of the silent reading of a newspaper. This, therefore, gives it the literal appearance of a game. The past of the composer, the influences and techniques here descend to mere materials. If appearance, form, is unreality (in the Hegelian sense), it follows that the negation of style happens through necessity by means of style. Anyone who would deny this would take a positive, affirmative position, and then the whole question would become superfluous. That which changes, then, and less in Donatoni than in others, is not style abstractly considered, but its function. Thus it happens that what is heard can be new, additional materials, such as non-musical sounds, or things very carefully notated, but completely disfigured by a gratuitous, improvised view of them, thus forming another "reality." This is certainly "dizzy music" in the broad sense of Emily Dickinson. The most recent piece by Donatoni is for harpsichord: *Babei*. The title contains an implicit homage to the art of Borges. This piece is a reworking of the *Doubles* of 1961. In fact a few pages of the original version are repeated in this new piece, giving us (analogously with the *Pandorasbox* of Kagel) a demonstration of the existence of a rigorous structuralism outside that of rigorous intervallic fixation.

This reworking by Donatoni requires a new manual technique: under the keyboard is attached a contraption connecting the harpsichord with "glissatori" (thin, long pieces of wood, first conceived by Clementi, and applicable to various types of keyboards): at times the performer's fingers are to be replaced by these rigid prongs, according to carefully planned technical procedures. The composer has indicated 84 of them and these range from the most simple to the very limits of instrumental style. It is curious how, for works such as this, the term "exercise" comes to mind: an ascetic word if there ever was one. With these circuits of Donatoni, the investigation of musical thought reaches a breach that is in no way reducible solely to stylistic considerations. An analogous solution is being sought by musicians in America; the first name that comes to mind is that of Christian Wolff.

Any reverential attachment to a venerable work is no longer allowed, and there is beginning to appear a certain frivolous quality in all the formal variability. The elements imagined within a determined technique, structuralism, remained, in the final instance, only particles of style. One thinks of eliminating (and this would be the sublime form of Utopia descended into a work) all rapports of style so that the work would have value solely for itself: forcing out metaphors (the millennium of metaphors that music is) in order to have a basis, or support, for a presence that can be evoked in no other way. The *modus operandi* of the new music, the opening of the way to negations or liberations, is that *actio non agens:* an impassive gesture solicitously open to anyone.

It is undeniable that the perfect anonymity has not yet been allowed to our techniques in their present stage of development. If "we want the world's end," the problem, then, is to acquire it. The partial and necessary failure of many enterprises is today the only necessary and decent solution. All the internal circuits, the immanent uprisings, must be investigated. One must not concede *ignoratio elenchi.*

". . . And yet more hundreds of astronomes will distinguish and reckon more thousands of new yet unseen stars, mapping them, and giving each one its name. When we see them all, then will be no night in heaven." (Lawrence)

As of now it seems to us that, with more resolute music, the new Italian composers have reached a point of reflection. It is obvious that one cannot speak here of the very youngest musicians. We shall, however, make two exceptions: Ivan Vandor, whose String Quartet, awarded a prize by the ISCM, has revealed a musician of talent and rich in ideas; and the upcoming Marcello Panni, whose orchestral piece demonstrates a sure technique and genuine poetic qualities.

(Translated by William C. Holmes)

ON SWISS MUSICAL COMPOSITION
OF THE PRESENT

By WILLI REICH

AT PRESENT the pace of cultural evolution in other — and larger — countries is so rapid that the achievements of the past are quickly left behind; Switzerland, however, is far more strongly tied to old traditions. Hence, a reasonably careful examination of the creative output of Swiss composers in our time requires, more than a survey of other countries would, a synopsis of earlier times.

The role of music in Switzerland, like that of any of its cultural manifestations, is distinguished by the extraordinary variety of regions and peoples that is a main characteristic of the small country. Above all, the German, French, and Italian language areas, co-existing peaceably, have significantly determined the evolution of Swiss culture.

Especially favorable for the development of musical individualities were the many towns that, despite their relatively small size, enjoyed rapid economic progress. Situated in areas usually defined and encompassed by mountains, they formed independent, idiosyncratic centers of culture, being always concerned with the maintenance of their own well-trained orchestral and theatrical personnel. The healthy cultural competition among the towns and cities has greatly spurred art in general and music in particular. Since the 19th century many Swiss towns have, as it were, assumed the role of patrons, elsewhere exercised by rulers and aristocrats. The most important urban centers of music in Switzerland are Zurich, Basel, Berne, Lucerne, Winterthur, St. Gall in the German area; Geneva, Lausanne, Fribourg, Bienne, and Neuchâtel in the French area; and Locarno and Lugano in the Italian area.

Characteristic of the general musical life in Switzerland is the magnificent and vital tradition of choral singing, especially the men's choruses.

Even small places often have excellent choral societies; they compete annually in great singing festivals that often present truly magnificent musical achievements. It should be mentioned in this context that the founding of the first musical organization in Switzerland is intimately connected with the active tradition of choral singing. This was the Schweizerische Musikgesellschaft, brought into being in 1808 by Beethoven's friend, Hans Georg Nägeli (1773-1836), who defined its truly national and democratic ideal as the quality of a "noble communality [*edle Popularität*], presenting the public spectacle, so delightful to the lover of mankind, of art not being restricted to the few favored by fortune, but exercised — and properly — by the many as their attribute, with the result that their united efforts can raise art to a state where it becomes the precious property of an entire nation."

This idealistic declaration is well designed to bring into relief the fundamental cultural feature that characterizes all artistic life in Switzerland: the decided democratization which, in conjunction with the excellent Swiss educational system, has during the past decades produced a large number of creative and performing artists, especially in music. Their achievements are far above average, as regards solidity and skill in invention and execution, though manifestations of universally valid genius are relatively rare. Achievements of the latter sort may be said to have come during the most recent years only from the pens of two men already deceased — Arthur Honegger (1892-1955) and Othmar Schoeck (1886-1957) — and one living composer — Frank Martin (born 1890).

It is important to observe that even these three composers, though men of indisputable genius, by no means belonged to the "avant-garde," as that term is generally understood, but, consciously rooted in the main traditions, contributed in very individual ways to the further evolution of those traditions. The case of these leading musicians is a potent example of the powerful hold that tradition has on the Swiss generally. This feature is the necessary guideline for our subsequent discussion of contemporary Swiss composers.

In this respect the artistic development of Frank Martin is an instructive example. Probably the Swiss composer who has achieved the greatest renown in our day, he was born in Geneva into a Huguenot family of French origin. While his beginnings as a composer are generally seen in connection with French music of the turn of the century, his early supporter, the great Swiss conductor Ernest Ansermet, has proved convincingly that with respect to harmony and the technique of thematic development Martin's first works belong to the German late Romantic tradition, save for occasional utilizations of French folk tunes. Only after 1920 did he begin to be significantly influenced by French Impressionism and the rhythmic experiments of Emile Jaques-Dalcroze; for a long time he also was a teacher at the latter's institute in Geneva. In 1946 he moved to Holland, his wife's native country, where he now lives as a free-lance composer.

The decisive event in Martin's artistic development occurred in 1930 when he came to grips with a number of twelve-tone works of Arnold Schoenberg. Martin himself has confessed that they helped him considerably, though his whole musical feeling rebelled against them. Significantly, he did not publish the works he composed under the immediate influence of this encounter. He felt the necessity to refashion Schoenberg's twelve-tone system in a manner commensurate with his individuality; as a result, he uses twelve-tone rows only melodically, while otherwise proceeding freely in accordance with his strongly developed sense of tonality. Once having worked out this idiom, he returned to the composition of larger works, of which the first major one is *Le Vin herbé* (1938-41) after Joseph Bedier's novel *Tristan et Iseut*. With this work Martin, by then fifty years old, established his mature personal style, in which he relatively rapidly produced the compositions on which his renown is founded.

In 1943 he completed *Der Cornet,* a cycle for alto and small orchestra, based on Rainer Maria Rilke's early masterpiece *Die Weise von Liebe und Tod des Cornets Christoph Rilke,* and settings for baritone and piano, orchestrated six years later, of six monologues from Hugo von Hofmannsthal's mystery play *Jedermann.* In general approach *Der Cornet* is related to *Le Vin herbé* inasmuch as both works are based on the idea of the text being recited by the poet or a representative, while music provides the story with adjuncts in the form of visions in sound; under the circumstances, "musical form is determined by literary form," as Martin has put it. Martin admirably solved the problem, considered insoluble by Rilke himself, of musically enhancing a text that already often hovers on the edge of music. No less admirable is the clear and forceful cogency of the rhythmic idiom, by means of which he musically interpreted Hofmannsthal's compact language, seemingly popular, though actually fashioned with great artistic sophistication. Both works attest Martin's remarkable knowledge and creative insight into recent German literature, which is an exceptional attribute for a composer belonging to the French orbit.

Two large religious works completed in 1944 and 1948 are indicative of Martin's striving for the creation of a new sacred style commensurate with modern attitudes. One of these, commissioned by Radio Geneva, is the oratorio *In terra pax,* based on biblical texts and composed for the Armistice Day of World War II; the other, stimulated by an etching of Rembrandt, is the Passion composition *Golgotha,* on texts from the Gospels and the writings of St. Augustine. For both works Martin consciously fashioned music of vivid immediacy, since he considered the modern public, unlike the contemporaries of Bach and Handel, incapable of active religious empathy.

Of Martin's instrumental masterpieces from this period the following are often performed in concert halls throughout the world: *Petite Symphonie concertante* for harpsichord, harp, and double string orchestra (1945), Concerto for seven wind instruments, timpani, and string orchestra (1949), Five Etudes for string orchestra (1956), and his Violin Concerto (1951). Mood and thematic content of the last-named work relate it closely to his opera *Der Sturm* (1954), based on Shakespeare's play.

Martin's most recent large-scale compositions are the powerful Christmas oratorio *Le Mystère de la Nativité* (1959), based on a text by Arnoul Gréban, and his recently (1963) completed opera *Monsieur de Pourceaugnac,* based on Molière's comedy.

Since Frank Martin, the only living Swiss composer of world-wide renown, conceives it as his artistic mission to acquaint many strata of society with the sublimated idiom of modern music by means of immediately intelligible works, a citation of his musical credo dating from 1943, which precisely defines his view of the relation of the modern composer to his public, is of basic importance.

The passionate search for the absolute in art is extraordinarily dangerous, because it brings about impotence. It is the exact counterpart to the religious search with the aid of a magic formula, so as to gain Paradise without creative effort. No matter how high one may esteem such passive gratification, it can never bestow the same true joy that results from a real effort . . . Why, then, do contemporary composers often give their works so tumultuous a character at the expense of calm beauty? Admittedly, these composers are in a difficult position, being constantly confronted by two cliffs, the two contrary demands for originality and for perfection. These demands come not only from the public, but also from composers. Indeed, are these not also part of the public? Both demands spring from an attitude that, being familiar and pleased with the works of all earlier epochs, at once discovers in each new work every similarity with past manifestations; such similarity troubles us. Thus it is only through novelty, through originality that contemporary music can find its justification. However, since we have the fullest knowledge of the bliss and awareness of perfection afforded us by classical works, we expect no less of the new works that are presented to us. Never before has so much been expected of composers, nor did composers ever make such demands of themselves. For the majority, if not all of them, this is very bad! It is all too easy to lapse into a search for originality at any cost or into the other extreme, i.e. the cult of banality to the detriment of creativity. Doubtless a truly genuine attitude would cause a composer to create only what he would truly love to produce. Today — let us admit it — only a few do so, and, all the contrary appearances notwithstanding, it is the most difficult task to accomplish. Especially, it requires much courage; for fashion is both puissant and enticing, and whoever believes himself independent of her often obeys her against his will. At any rate, in view of such extreme and contrary demands, a work of art reflecting creative serenity will be achieved only rarely and with great difficulty. Rather, it will reflect struggle, struggle within, with the public, and, above all, with those inordinate and contradictory demands. But unquestionably the composer is at the same time powerfully stimulated by this situation, for in his heart the hope springs eternal to reconcile or encompass those two opposites, i.e. originality and fierce turbulence on the one hand and calm beauty and serenity on the other. Then, too, the hope keeps recurring that the mirage of a responsive public will turn into reality, that in other words, the composer will finally present it with the new *and* classic work that it expects. How wondrous and how impossible!

Not only does this extensive quotation of Frank Martin's personal credo constitute a most authentic presentation of his thinking and his character — ruthlessly honest towards himself and others — but, because of his seniority and international standing, it also serves to point up paradigmatically the general problems that so intensively engross a large part of Switzerland's creative musicians and have already given rise to a number of beautiful and convincing solutions. Brief characterizations of their authors, in order of age, will constitute the remainder of this essay.

A composer of considerable international repute is Wladimir Vogel (born 1896 in Moscow), who immigrated into Switzerland in 1933, became a Swiss citizen some time ago, and created his most important works in this country. With respect to the fundamental significance of his confrontation with the *oeuvre* of Arnold Schoenberg, Vogel's case is not unlike that of Frank Martin. Two aspects of Vogel's music are due to this influence. As early as 1920, having become familiar with Schoenberg's *Pierrot lunaire* melodramas, he felt impelled to experiment with "speech-melodies." But with his oratorio *Wagadus Untergang durch die Eitelkeit* (1930), based on old Berber minstrel stories, he went far beyond Schoenberg's handling of the *Sprechstimme* device by combining *Sprechmelodien* polyphonically. He was able to develop this procedure further in Switzerland, since a special "Sprechchor," existing primarily for the performance of his works, was available to him. His chief opus in this category is the two-part oratorio *Thyl Claes* (1937-1945), based on Charles de Coster's *Legende von Ulenspiegel;* this powerful confessional composition is dedicated to the victims of the resistance movement. While in the *Wagadu* oratorio the *Sprechchor,* apart from purely musical and musico-dramatic functions, was employed above all for the purpose of illuminating the salient points of the story and for certain refrain-like turns, its use in *Thyl Claes,* which calls for a large orchestra also, is much more comprehensive. The mingling of instrumental, vocal, and spoken music primarily served Vogel's striving for meaningful emphasis of the most important words and for a particular coloristic mold achieved by crisp prosody of the individual syllables and willful repetition of sentences. The individual orchestral instruments not only take up but reshape and recolor the word rhythms, thus completely unifying the musical utterances. This procedure is even more apparent in the oratorio *Jona ging doch nach Ninive* (1959).

With his *Arpiade* for soprano, *Sprechchor,* and five instruments (1954) Vogel added the *Sprechchor* to the field of chamber music. The work is based on surrealist poetry by Hans Arp, which assumes purely musical, supralingual character because of the musical devices applied to it, e.g. verbal ostinatos, canonic shifts, syncopation of word accents, etc. In addition, strictly phonetic devices, such as varying shades of individual vowels and rhymes of vowel colors, serve the same purpose. *Sprechchor* technique reached its peak in the setting of Schiller's *Lied von der Glocke* for *Sprechchor* a cappella (1959); the resultant *Gestalt* is a sonorous abstraction that has provoked vehement controversies with every performance.

The second achievement that Vogel owes to his involvement with the art of Arnold Schoenberg is the sovereign virtuosity and striking originality with which he handles the twelve-tone technique. The first instance is the scherzo of his four-movement Violin Concerto (1937); its main theme, given to the solo violin, is a manifestation of a twelve-tone row, whose four forms, in ever-varying instrumentation, turn out to be the sole substance of the movement. His next work, *Epitaffio per Alban Berg* (1938), represents a further and particular development of twelve-tone technique. This piano piece honors the memory of the Viennese composer, for whom Vogel has a specially high regard, by deriving a tone-row from the applicable letters in the words "Alban Berg aufs Grab Friede!" and developing this "soggetto cavato" in the manner of a passacaglia. Since this row continuously appears in one or another of the voices, unity is guaranteed regardless of the bold figurations in the remaining parts. As is always the case with Vogel's compositions, the expressive elements are plainly prominent in performance, in spite of the almost mathematically strict structure of this work.

One of Vogel's most recent pieces, completed in 1962, strikes one as a synthesis of his entire previous output and particularly of his passionate striving for new combinations of words and tones. His *Worte* for two female *Sprechstimmen* and string orchestra uses texts by Hans Arp, whose recondite inner meaning Vogel illuminates by turning them into apprehensible symbols through artful declamation by the solo voices and instrumental interpretation using twelve-tone technique. Many a product, both surprising and convincing in effectiveness of invention and boldness of structure, may still be expected of Wladimir Vogel's artistry; ceaselessly searching, it unites combinatorial ingenuity and elemental musicality.

A composer whose output is strongly beholden to older influences is Albert Moeschinger (born 1897 in Basel). His nearly one hundred larger works of all types reflect the strict polyphony of Baroque music and the differentiated harmonic idiom of late Romanticism and Impressionism. Most characteristic seem the shorter instrumental pieces, in which freshness of thematic invention is often paired with witty, humorous, and ironic passages. Moeschinger's numerous chamber works with their themes reflecting native folklore are likewise very significant.

Walther Geiser (born 1897 in Zofingen), who studied in Berlin with Ferruccio Busoni, represents pronounced neo-Classic tendencies. Especially his sacred works for voices and his concertante pieces excel through artful contrapuntal technique and strictness of form.

One of the most prolific composers of French Switzerland is Roger Vuataz (born 1898 in Geneva), whose more than 500 works frequently exhibit a melodic style influenced by the psalm tunes of the Reformation. His feeling for musical dramaturgy and his considerable radio experience account for his outstanding musical contributions to the legitimate stage and to radio plays, which effectively show off his gift for plastic acoustic utterance.

A man of earthy musical temperament held in check by extraordinarily disciplined concepts of form and profound historical knowledge is Paul Müller (born 1898 in Zurich), who is also an especially talented musical pedagogue. Particularly noteworthy among his numerous vocal and instrumental works are his vocal compositions for patriotic festivals and his symphonies, playful and a joy to perform. While his entire output evinces strong ties with the masters of the past, his works are no epigonous compromises, but fresh and original elaborations of a stylistic heritage in the spirit of the old masters.

Similar observations apply to Walter Müller von Kulm (born 1899 in Kulm in the Aargau). His creativity, however, is centered in sacred choral works of large dimensions, among which a setting of the *Pater noster* for a large apparatus (solos, mixed chorus, children's chorus, organ, and orchestra) and his oratorio *Petrus* stand out. He, too, has considerable didactic talent, which since 1947 he has put to use in his capacity as director of the Basel Musik-Akademie.

Hans Haug (born 1900 in Basel) is a musician who excels equally as composer and conductor. His creative temperament attracts him especially to the comic musical stage. Of his numerous musical settings for stage and radio his two operas based on Molière, *Der eingebildete Kranke* (1934) and *Tartuffe* (1937), deserve special mention. His classicistic style, which also obtains in many of his instrumental works, is individualized by his special gift for the humorous and the grotesque.

While his numerous compositions for films — both feature and documentary — have given a special aspect to Robert Blum's (born 1900 in Zurich) output, he has also attracted significant attention with five symphonies and with large-scale choral works. His earlier instrumental pieces show the neo-Classic influence of his teacher Busoni, but lately he has successfully taken up the more recent technical achievements and has applied them in individual ways.

Since from 1925 to 1933 Conrad Beck (born 1901 in Lohn, near Schaffhausen) made his home in Paris, where he was closely acquainted with Albert Roussel, Jacques Ibert, and Arthur Honegger, his early output, especially in the field of chamber music, in every way evinces modern French influences. After his return to Switzerland he cultivated larger forms, producing several symphonies and concertos, as well as some larger choral works, of which the dirge *Der Tod zu Basel* (1953) is the most important. Beck's style, in which austere sonorities are frequent, in many ways indicates his predominant concern with unification of the French and German types of musicality.

Adolf Brunner (born 1901 in Zurich) is mainly concerned with sacred music and, more particularly, with a modern renewal of Protestant church music, though the nature of his religiosity is general enough to account for his setting of a number of Latin texts of the Catholic liturgy, as, for example, in his *Missa a cappella* (1935), a work of large dimensions. In some of his Protestant music he has also shown skill and originality in using the form of the "sacred concerto."

One of the most gifted composers in the French area of Switzerland is André-François Marescotti (born 1902 in Carouge near Geneva). The rhythmic vigor of his style is well exemplified by a number of orchestral and chamber works in the spirit of the old suite, which revive such dances as the sarabande, musette, gigue, etc. His most important works in this regard are the two *Concerts carougeois* of 1942 and 1959.

Neo-Classicism is clearly the determining influence in the works of Peter Mieg (born 1906 in Lenzburg), a student of Frank Martin. Mieg, who is also strongly gifted as a painter, has attracted attention with a number of *concertante* works for chamber orchestra and solo instruments, which in their linearity and rhythmic idiom occasionally recall Stravinsky's classicistic period.

That Heinrich Sutermeister (born 1910 in Feuerthalen near Schaffhausen) is known far beyond the Swiss borders is due mainly to his stage works, in which unusually felicitous musical invention is paired with outstanding insight into the musical stage. The following statement, dating from 1955, is a kind of credo that attests to the clarity of his view of today's operatic problems.

When the Classic-Romantic opera theater came into being, it filled a fundamental social and economic need. At best, the large popular public that filled the opera houses in those days has today migrated to the cinema; but above all people go to the sports arenas, and what remains of their power of absorption is about to wither away because of television. I am absolutely convinced, therefore, that the modern opera composer must also devote his attention to the fields of broadcasting and cinema; he has much to learn there. Only then can he gain clarity about his position in the culture of today. The situation is not hopeless, once he realizes that today's public must be stirred and shocked with means radically different from those of earlier times. The musical idiom may certainly be as modern as possible, as long as there is tangible evidence of a will of almost "evangelistic" fervor to be harsh and uncompromising in showing up the eternal relations to which we are subject and to say yes or no.

It is in the light of these tenets that we must view the considerable string of operas Sutermeister has had performed on the stage, generally with good success; some were also done in radio studios, with appropriate revisions. Here is a list of the works: *Romeo und Julia* (1939, two acts, derived from Shakespeare); *Die Zauberinsel* (1942, based on Shakespeare's *Tempest*); *Niobe* (1945, monodrama in two acts for soprano, double chorus, ballet, and orchestra; text by Peter Sutermeister); *Raskolnikoff* (1947, after Dostoevsky); *Der rote Stiefel* (1951, based on a fairy tale by Wilhelm Hauff); *Titus Feuerfuchs* (1958, after Johann Nestroy).

In addition he created numerous vocal and instrumental works, notably a *Missa da Requiem* (1952), a cello concerto (1955), and three piano concertos (1942, 1954, 1962).

Sutermeister's contemporary Rolf Liebermann (born 1910 in Zurich) is likewise primarily devoted to opera. Its regeneration involved him creatively from 1950 to 1962 and actively, in his role as director of the Hamburg Staatsoper, from 1962 on. It is interesting that he expects the libretto to spark the solution of the crisis of contemporary opera.

It seems high time [he said in 1954] that all of us opera composers finally take cognizance of the developments that have occurred in the dramatic field during the last three decades. While authors like Bert Brecht, Thornton Wilder, and Jean Giraudoux have revolutionized the drama, all the librettists seem to have been hit by a sleep so deep as to recall Sleeping Beauty; as a result of their ossified concepts of story and stage we get clichés and conventions. The composer, on the other hand, is up-to-date and aggressive; he belongs to the avant-garde and deals with yesterday's problems in tomorrow's language. If we manage to regenerate the musical stage by way of the scenic concept, i.e. the libretto, if we achieve congruence of libretto and music in content and expression, and if, finally, we have the courage to bring up problems of our time in opera and to quit the esthetes' beloved ivory tower, then we shall surely have made decisive contributions towards the solution of the crisis.

Two of Liebermann's operas were written in this spirit, *Leonore 40/45* (1952) and *Penelope* (1954). The composer and his librettist (Heinrich Strobel) have subtitled each work *opera semiseria,* thereby indicating the operas' dual character. Both deal with problems caused by world wars and requiring for their solution profound empathy and true humanity. The serious aspects are always counterbalanced by satiric episodes, which produce strong contrasts giving sharp definition to the role played by music. Moreover, they enable the authors to maintain a sovereign detachment from the complex stage events, which permits an ultimate reconciliation of the contrasts within strictly defined musical forms. Liebermann's third work for the musical stage — *Die Schule der Frauen,* based on Molière's comedy — received its première in December 1955 in Louisville, Kentucky, as the result of a commission; shortly thereafter the one-act opera was expanded into three acts. Here, too, the libretto is marked by a novel ironic twist, since Molière himself joins the action, which thus proceeds on a second level. In all three works Liebermann's musico-dramatic approach is characterized by the consistent use of purely musical means (tonal, polytonal, and atonal harmonies, changes in timbre, old forms, etc.) to symbolize and represent the dramatic conflicts.

Three of Liebermann's instrumental works deserve specific mention. Two of them incorporate elements of jazz: his *Concerto für Jazzband und Symphonieorchester* (1954) and the *Geigy Festival Concerto* for

Basel drum and orchestra (1958). The third, entitled *Les Echanges,* is a composition for electronically activated office machines, which in 1964 was performed several times daily in one of the industrial pavilions of the Swiss Exposition Nationale in Lausanne. The artfully structured piece takes all of three minutes to perform! This recent occasional work is further proof of Liebermann's enormous talent in compositional technique; it is to be hoped that he will continue to contribute significant works to Swiss music, as soon as he has given up his administrative post in Hamburg.

Armin Schibler's (born 1920 in Kreuzlingen) music has universal, almost too universal character. This highly impressionable artist, a man of considerable musical and literary education, has intensively soaked up all conceivable external stimuli and has utilized them creatively in his works. Successively he produced pieces in neo-Baroque style, works with late Romantic and Expressionistic sound belonging to the world of Gustav Mahler and Arnold Schoenberg, pieces in the radical twelve-tone style, compositions reminiscent of early Stravinsky, works of pure dance character, etc. They all attest to his mastery of technique; that most of them are nonetheless not entirely convincing is probably due to the listener's feeling that what he hears are products of a "composition virtuoso," whose manner of musical utterance is determined more by his phenomenal technical ability than by sheer inner necessity. It must be pointed out, though, that Schibler's search is by no means disingenuous; he himself is clearly aware of the unsatisfying aspects of his output and has not minced words in the several critical statements that he has publicized. It is exactly this attitude as well as the high level of his general musical talent that justify the hope for a true musical masterwork from his pen.

So far only those Swiss composers have been discussed whose works somehow evince a connection with past traditions. Finally, a few words about several artists who have consciously cut the threads to the past.

A completely isolated case is that of Constantin Regamey (born 1907 in Kiev), son of a Swiss father and a Russian mother. Regamey is a philologist and university teacher by profession, who as a musical autodidact composes purely for the love of it. He is therefore artistically independent, a state he prizes greatly, since it allows him to indulge in stylistic and formal experiments, by most of which the general concert public is vehemently affronted. The few works he has published so far, mostly in the vein of chamber music, are especially interesting for their singular sonorities, which quite often have an "exotic" flavor. A good example of the originality of his structural thinking is the construction of his most recent *concertante* piece (1963), which carries the curious title *4 x 5*. It is a concerto for four quintets — woodwinds, brasses, strings, and percussion (including piano and harp) — with each of its five movements fashioned according to a different stylistic precept, indicated by the following Italian designations: *Pérotinamente* (linear counterpoint in parallel motion [!]; *Quasi una monodia* (monophony with varying timbres); *Condensazioni in moto* ("mobiles" of chord clusters); *Mosaica e Corale* (a kind of mosaic of sonorities, produced by the pointillistic use of the individual quintets); *Concertando* (in the manner of a concerto grosso, with the various quintets taking turns in functioning as concertino).

While Regamey is an independent autodidact pursuing individual paths, the remaining composers to be mentioned briefly may be regarded as more or less belonging to the Darmstadt group; their international musical idiom therefore betrays a certain relationship with the musical language of Anton Webern or Pierre Boulez. (Since the latter for a time taught composition at the Basel conservatory, he has, of course, exercised a direct influence as well.) The following composers may be singled out:

Robert Suter (born 1919 in St. Gall) has primarily presented chamber works so far, which, their daring harmonies and rhythms notwithstanding, in some ways reveal formal concepts that are still reminiscent of older models. Some of his compositions are notable for a strong leaning towards jazz.

Having studied with Wladimir Vogel for several years, Jacques Wildberger (born 1922 in Basel) became coach at the Basel opera, where he gained experience in the world of the theater. So far his works, written mainly for chamber ensembles, reflect his bent for experiments in sonorities. Great originality marks his *Epitaphe pour Evariste Galois* (1962), where he builds acoustic structures with documents — and pertinent commentaries — from the life of the great French mathematician, which are given sounding reality by two solo singers, *Sprechchor,* loudspeaker, orchestra, and tape recorders.

Klaus Huber's (born 1924 in Berne) concern is to treat sacred texts with the newest devices of serial music. A composer with an unusually discriminating ear for sonorities, he has completed some works that handle this aspect very persuasively, particularly his *Soliloquia* (1960-62) for solo voices, chorus, and orchestra, on words by Aurelius Augustinus.

In addition to being a composer concerned with regeneration of concepts of sonority and form, Rudolf Kelterborn (born 1931 in Basel) not only functions as teacher and conductor, but as a writer on music also strives intensively for a penetrating view of the new compositional problems. A singular work is his three-part opera *Die Errettung Thebens* (1962) on a libretto by the composer himself.

Having first (1959) attracted attention as an outstanding oboist, Heinz Holliger (born 1939 in Langenthal) then revealed himself as a

composer; so far he has given us a few chamber works, often with voice, which clearly characterize him as a follower of Webern. This is quite plain in the above excerpt, the end of his cantata *Himmel und Erde* (1961) for tenor, flute, violin, viola, cello, and harp, based on texts by Alexander Xaver Gewerder.[1]

It is obvious that in the brief synopsis offered in these pages only those few artists could be considered who for some reason are particularly prominent. Their ranks are joined by hundreds of thoroughly trained composers who for their service to society, in whatever capacity, receive the recognition they so richly merit. All of them are solid craftsmen of a genuinely artistic disposition who, with the exception of the radicals of the group discussed in the preceding paragraphs, consciously make use of their ties to the great traditions of the Classic and Romantic periods. In general, it seems to me that Switzerland's mission in the realm of contemporary composition is the amalgamation of the tried-and-true trends of the past with open-minded striving for music that both reflects new creative processes and has an immediate appeal for a significant number of the groups comprising the audience of today.

(Translated by Ernest Sanders)

---

[1] Used by kind permission of B. Schott's Söhne, Mainz.

BELGIUM FROM 1914 TO 1964

By ALBERT VANDER LINDEN

I F ONE considers the regions of Belgium today, compressed as they are between the North Sea and the legendary Ardennes forest, one must accept the fact that this "compass dial," which launched the dominant musical currents of the 15th and 16th centuries, has turned its pointers inward upon itself; one seeks in vain for a Roland de Lassus, a Philippe de Monte, a Grétry, or even a César Franck. These composers could once demand of the world that it pay attention to a tiny country, whose dual streams of cultural and artistic development, like its two major rivers, meet, confront, and blend with one another there.

If one pauses momentarily at the outset of the First World War, one sees a musical evolution closely resembling that of the principal countries of Western Europe: after weathering the chromaticisms of César Franck and Richard Wagner, Belgian composers exacerbated their Romanticism by employing the orchestral palette of Richard Strauss; or, they discovered Italian *verismo* or were seduced by French Impressionism.

This was the situation in 1914 with such Franckian composers (most of whom were pupils at the Schola Cantorum in Paris) as Victor Vreuls (1876-1944), Théo Ysaye (1865-1918), Armand Marsick (1877-1959), Léon Delcroix (1880-1938), Jean Rogister (1879-1964), Eugène Guillaume (1882-1955), and Joseph Jongen (1873-1953), whose "Franckism" was already refined by the elegance of his melodic language.

But, at this time the Flemish school, descended from Peter Benoit, had its lineage represented by Paul Gilson (1865-1942) and Auguste De Boeck (1865-1937). Both possess a distinctly Flemish temperament, characterized by dense and solid writing; both, after having come under the tyrannical influence of Richard Wagner, combined it with that of the Russian "Five." But this receptivity to external influences rarely creates individuality — and such is the case with the majority of Belgian composers, of whose art *impersonality* (if one may use the word) is the salient feature. In fact, it would be no paradox to affirm that the Flemish school was a flash in the pan limited to a single individual, Peter Benoit (1834-1901). The latter's intentions were to create a peculiarly Flemish musical language. However, to isolate Flanders from international developments and reduce its speech to quaint picturesqueness, is to rob it of its natural advantages, its central international position, and to force it into narrow provincialism.

In reality, the nationalist theories of Peter Benoit resulted merely in the creation of a heady musical atmosphere in Antwerp, and *not* in the establishment of a school of Flemish composers giving more than lip service to his precepts. Undoubtedly, one will no longer find Flemish musicians, after Benoit, entirely enslaved by French esthetics, if only because they prefer to submit to the pervasive omnipotence of German Romanticism.

If one considers objectively the evolution of the music of post-Benoit Flemings, one must conclude that the latter have found, individually, conditions ideal for their development along lines that conform to their native abilities and temperament. Thus, side by side with Gilson and De Boeck, a Lodewijk Mortelmans (1868-1952), justly named the "Flemish Brahms," and a Joseph Ryelandt (b. 1870) seem the most refined and delicate of purists when contrasted to the rough-hewn and truculent style of a Flor Alpaerts (1876-1954) or of a Jef Van Hoof (1886-1959).

The reactionary attitude is not solely the province of the Flemings; Walloon composers remained faithful for a long time to the esthetics of César Franck's disciples. This is true of most of the composers listed above (from Vreuls to Jongen).

But Belgium's position as the "crossroads of the West" makes it susceptible to all external influences: the rhythmic power of Stravinsky, the polytonality of Milhaud, the "musique concrète" of Pierre Schaeffer, and, of course, electronic music; all participate in the elaboration of a language in continual evolution and subjected equally to innovations as to backward glances.

The result of this confrontation, of this diversity, of these occasionally contradictory currents is evidently a tower of Babel, where only real talents stand out in any relief from the mass of eclectics all behaving like little Stravinskys, Alban Bergs, Bartóks, Hindemiths, Boulezes, or Stockhausens. It is evident that the hundreds of musical styles and the multiple languages that co-inhabit Belgium bear witness, not to the existence of a Belgian music, but to the co-existence of all tendencies, be they subtly reactionary or audaciously modern.

Among the principal names, one must cite Jean Absil (b. 1893), Raymond Chevreuille (b. 1901), Marcel Poot (b. 1901), Marcel Quinet (b. 1915), Victor Legley (b. 1915), André Souris (b. 1899), and Henri Pousseur (b. 1929). The novel language of Jean Absil does not shrink from the application of the subtle rhythms of Rumanian folklore, but its coherence and poise derive from an authentic talent, a bold inspiration, and a superbly variegated artistry. A very personal musician, Raymond Chevreuille presents simple ideas tinged with fantasy and mystery and so expressed as to engender feelings of intense joy or powerful anguish. In contrast, Marcel Poot successfully exploits a facile lyricism, full of verve, which, though occasionally superficial, is decidedly and winningly popular. Two disciples of Jean Absil, Marcel Quinet and Victor Legley, starting from the world of atonality, have each conceived a very personal language, measured and sensitive and with perfect control of their expressive means. As for André Souris, after having disowned Debussy and Stravinsky, he turned towards Schoenberg. He not only composed robust works whose character might be described as lean and direct, simple and convincing (notably in functional music for films), but he enjoys discovering new talents and knows how to excite their interest in the creative activity of our time. He was responsible for stimulating many young composers to try their hand at writing dodecaphonic music, notably Pierre Froidebise (1914-62), whose style moved from that of Absil to Webern before entering upon unconstrained personal audacities, and Henri Pousseur, who was the first Belgian to work with electronic music and who remains in the foreground of recent developments.

Aside from these names, there are dozens and dozens of others. All have attempted to create an original language or to make their mark with a personal style without managing to achieve more than earnest outbursts that are fused, more or less readily, within the framework of a heterogeneous musical output.

New musical trends in Belgium would exhaust themselves rapidly were it not for the possibility of getting works performed. Obviously, their reception depends on the sophistication of the audience. The latter has profited from the increase in concert halls (notably the Palais des Beaux-Arts in Brussels, established 1929-30), the democratization of concert life (e.g. the "Concerts de Midi" at Brussels, Liège, Antwerp, and Mons, where ticket costs are minimal), the creation of the Jeunesses Musicales movement (1940), the establishment of the Orchestre National de Belgique (1936), the growth of concerts of the "éducation populaire" type, subsidized since 1949 by the National Ministry of Education and Culture. But it is, above all, to the radio and the recording industry that one owes this non- (and post-) scholastic musical education, which is at the root of a veritable transformation in the musical life of Belgium.

The national radio supports hundreds of public concerts and daily offers its listeners many hours of orchestral and chamber music. As for recordings, especially since the advent of long-playing discs, they are sold in the thousands. Furthermore, the renting out of records has been possible since 1953, the date of the establishment of Belgium's Discothèque Nationale, which has branches in many provincial cities.

Musical life, moreover, is studded with festivals; formerly quite rare, their present multiplicity robs them of their character of unusual events. Lastly, the public has an ardent interest in the Concours International Reine Elisabeth, devoted alternately to violin, piano, and composition. This formidable tourney, which attracts contestants from the entire world, has already launched many a talented virtuoso.

To be complete, the musical picture of Belgium must not fail to include that branch of science which studies music in all of its aspects: musicology. It was only around 1920 that musicology made its timid entry into the university, but by the beginning of the Second World War, it was granted equal status with its sister disciplines. The Société Belge de Musicologie was founded in 1946 under the presidency of Charles van den Borren, whose ninetieth birthday last year reminds us of a long and fertile career, boundless in its erudition and dedicated to all periods of history, despite a predilection for the 15th and 16th centuries.

The society publishes the *Revue belge de musicologie,* dealing with all branches of musicology, including ethnomusicology; the latters' most active champion is Paul Collaer (b. 1891), prime mover of the "Colloques de Wégimont" as well as one of the most enlightened explorers of the contemporary sonorous world.

Thus, having lost a supremacy earned in the past by the genius of its composers, and unable to regain it today even by the exceptional talents of performers like Arthur De Greef (1862-1940), the "carillonneur" Jef Denijn (1862-1941), the Pro Arte Quartet (1912-40), the violinist Arthur Grumiaux (b. 1921), the clavecinist Aimée van de Wiele (b. 1907), the organist Flor Peeters (b. 1903), or the conductor, now a French citizen, André Cluytens (b. 1905), Belgium represents, in the variety of its esthetic preoccupations and the diversity of styles practiced by its composers, the microcosm of a widespread situation; no one can predict its evolutionary or revolutionary future.

(Translated by Barry S. Brook)

DUTCH MUSIC IN THE 20TH CENTURY

By JOS WOUTERS

IT IS a notable fact that the majority of Dutch composers whose works form part and parcel of the present Dutch repertory have been pupils of Willem Pijper. It was in fact primarily Pijper who determined the nature of Dutch music in the years between the two World Wars and who at the same time succeeded in giving it a place in the musical life of Europe.

Musical life in the Netherlands began to flourish again around the beginning of the 20th century after a long period of no more than local significance. The movement that began in about 1880 to arouse indigenous Dutch culture and to give it new life started in the field of literature, but rapidly had its effects on architecture and painting as well. It was also to be of great importance for Dutch music. The founding of the Concertgebouw Orchestra in Amsterdam in 1888 was of immense significance in this respect. This orchestra very soon became an ensemble with a worldwide reputation and at the same time exerted a decisive influence on the whole of Dutch musical life. Through the impressive performances that took place principally under the baton of Willem Mengelberg, who conducted the orchestra for almost fifty years, there developed a feeling of self-confidence concerning the musical potentialities of the Dutch. Previously, music and music-making had been regarded as rather an unimportant and, to a certain extent, un-Dutch activity. A certain self-confidence also developed in the field of composition and gradually a creative existence emerged. This is shown most clearly in the first decades of the 20th century in the compositions of Alphons Diepenbrock, whose work not only contained numerous promises of a national and independent school of composition, but whose best compositions already represented a fulfillment of those promises. His music to Sophocles's drama *Electra* (from which Eduard Reeser has

97

compiled a suite for concert use), his overture *The Birds* (from the incidental music to Aristophanes's comedy of the same name), his Te Deum for soloists, chorus, and orchestra, together with various of his songs form a permanent monument to his position in the renaissance of Dutch music. His significance in the general cultural revival of the Netherlands in the late 19th and early 20th centuries emerges from the extensive *Letters and Documents* collected and annotated by the Utrecht professor and expert on Diepenbrock, namely Eduard Reeser. The first volume of these was published in 1962 by the Society for the History of Music in the Netherlands.

Two influences in the work of Diepenbrock have to a greater or lesser extent remained typical of Dutch music in the 20th century. There is on the one hand the influence of German music — in the case of Diepenbrock particularly that of Gustav Mahler, for whose work so much propaganda was made in the Netherlands by Willem Mengelberg — and on the other the influence of French music, particularly that of Debussy. This influence from a Germanic and Romance side can perhaps be explained by the geographical and cultural position of a small country such as the Netherlands in relation to its neighbors.

This flourishing of musical life in the Netherlands had its direct consequences on the generation following that of Diepenbrock, that is to say that born between 1880 and 1890. Compared with previous periods, the number of composers of importance that now emerged was strikingly large and although their significance was generally more national than international, they undoubtedly contributed to raising the esteem in which Dutch music was held. This group included both composers who remained close to traditional movements, such as Bernard van den Sigtenhorst Meijer (1888-1953), for whom the reproduction through music of impressions of nature turned out to be an important source of inspiration, these being both from the East (including the piano works *Ancient China, Six Views of Fuji,* and the *Songs of the Nile*) and the Dutch landscape (*The Meuse, Ancient Castles,* and *Dead Cities*), and the very progressive personality of Daniël Ruyneman (1886-1963), whose experiments in sound from the 'twenties appear as a herald of what the young generation of composers of today is engaged in. A further member of this older generation is Matthijs Vermeulen (born 1888), a composer with an extremely personal outlook whose compositions are characterized by a strict use of polymelodic techniques. It is notable that only in the last ten years or so has more attention been paid to his work and the performance of his compositions (including six symphonies). Of great importance in those years, both in the field of composition and that of organization and teaching, was Sem Dresden (1881-1957), who exerted a marked influence on the young generation of musicians as director of the Amsterdam Conservatory from 1924 to 1937 and then till 1949 (with a break during the war years) as director of the Royal Conservatory in The Hague. He was also a pioneer in various other fields of musical life in the Netherlands. His efforts on behalf of newer music of his own time as well as for the vocal music of the earlier Dutch composers, whose works began to be republished in those years through the efforts of several musicologists, including the Utrecht professor Albert Smijers, exerted a very considerable influence. Dresden's early compositions showed a pronounced preference for chamber music, in particular his Sonata for Flute and Harp dating from 1918. During his later years he wrote choral works and a number of solo concertos, while the most important compositions from his last years included the orchestral work *Dance Flashes,* the oratorio *Saint Antoine,* and the opera *François Villon.* Dresden's compositions are characterized mainly by very clear instrumentation, mobility of rhythm, and a colorful use of harmonic devices.

If we now look back — forty years after — on the period between 1920 and 1940, all the names of composers in the Netherlands are overshadowed by that of the man who succeeded in conferring international repute on Dutch music and who was the leader in composition in the Netherlands, namely Willem Pijper.

We find in Pijper's work also the two spheres of influence that characterize Dutch music. During his youthful years he was influenced by Mahler, and this is very evident from his First Symphony (1919), and also in the orchestral timbre and instrumentation of his Second Symphony (1921). There is the influence of a French Impressionistic sound in certain of his songs for soprano and orchestra (*Romance sans paroles, Fêtes galantes*) and in a chamber work such as the first violin sonata. Pijper found his personal style in about 1920, and it was not long before he could be counted among the most advanced of European composers. His compositions attracted attention in the circle of the International Society for Contemporary Music of those years and various foreign publishers showed interest in his work. The characteristic element in Pijper's music is the play of essential musical forces, the thematic material being derived from the most primary form of musical source of energy, namely the germ cell. There is, in his compositions written after 1921, hardly any further use of extensive thematic material. A short motif or one given chord functions as the starting-point, as the source or germ cell from which the whole composition develops in an organized manner, being directed by the composer's technical skill. Pijper used this "germ cell theory" with great intelligence and a deep sense of musical feeling. His compositions consequently show both a highly constructive and strongly musical character. Each melodic, harmonic, or rhythmic element is laden with its own energy, which pursues its own path when developed in polyphonic construction from the germ cell. Polytonal and polyrhythmic elements are essential features in his technique of composition, while his works are also characterized by an extreme sense of tension and a high degree of concentration. The basic musical elements continually offer Pijper new aspects and he tried in every work, as he said himself, "to bring the various problems nearer their solution." The idea of the germ cell and the process of growth developing from it dominated Pijper's world of musical thought. As his pupil Bertus van Lier once said, he saw in it "the symbol of the everlasting principle of which all that is transitory is an aspect." Among his most characteristic works based on the germ cell principle we have his Third Symphony (1926), dedicated to Pierre Monteux, who did much to make the work popular both in the Netherlands and abroad, the Piano Concerto (1927), and the *Symphonic Epigrams,* written in 1928 on the occasion of the fortieth anniversary of the founding of the Concertgebouw Orchestra of Amsterdam, together with various chamber works such as the third, fourth, and fifth string quartets (composed in 1923, 1928, and 1946 respectively), the wind quintet (1929), and the Sonata for Flute and Piano (1925). Also of importance is the incidental music he wrote to various Greek dramas, such as to Euripides's *Bacchae* and *Cyclops* and Sophocles's tragedy *Antigone,* above the score of which Pijper wrote "In memoriam Alphons Diepenbrock." Through his symphonic drama *Halewijn* Pijper also made a valuable contribution to the Dutch repertory in the field of music drama. Pijper wrote his most representative works between 1920 and 1940. The violence of the war years, from 1940 to 1945, weakened a large part of his musical inspiration and after the liberation of his country he was not granted many years in which to continue his work. He died in fact in March 1947. Through the original way in which Willem Pijper approached music as a phenomenon, he opened the way for many new possibilities in Dutch music.

As a teacher — from 1925 to 1930 he taught at the Amsterdam

Conservatory and from 1930 until his death he was director of the Conservatory in Rotterdam — he trained a large number of the generation of composers born in the first decades of the 20th century. In his teaching, along with his fiery idealism there was the strictness of a highly logical way of thinking and clarity of expression. His teaching was however always directed towards making his pupils think musically in an independent and personal way, and although many of them willingly conformed to his principles of composition, he considered it absolutely necessary to leave each of them free in processing the musical material. Pijper's starting-point as a teacher was the discovery of one's own personality and the development of one's own particular manner of musical expression. This principle is in no small way the explanation of the extremely varied nature of musical expression among contemporary Dutch composers.

This variety is also increased by the products of a contemporary of Pijper whose works show a completely different musical personality, namely Hendrik Andriessen (born 1892), who also succeeded in finding his own form of musical expression, very far from Pijper's ideas, which accounts for an important aspect of Dutch music. Most of Andriessen's orchestral works form part of the regular repertory of various Dutch orchestras and enjoy a firm reputation with the concert public. As an organist Andriessen grew up in the practice of Catholic church music and quite a large number of his compositions were consequently inspired by and intended for Catholic services. He carried out pioneering work in this field and opened up new paths for church music. His music avoids any emotional exaggeration and strives for a sound of mystical simplicity which is borne by a contemplative consideration of the liturgical text. A characteristic trait is a juxtaposing of widely separated harmonies which sometimes suggest the changes in organ registers and a use of vaulted melismatic effects with a melodic outline that is conceived modally rather than chromatically. His numerous works for organ are by preference in a contemplative mood, making full use of the rich possibilities of the instrument that the composer loves so much. Although liturgical and organ works occupy a large place in the output of Hendrik Andriessen, he has also shown himself to be a composer of importance in his numerous orchestral and chamber works. In addition to four symphonies, he has written various short orchestral works (Capriccio, Ricercare, *Symphonic Study,* Variations and Fugue on a Theme by Joh. Kuhnau, *Mascherata*), chamber music, and the opera *Philomela*. The most typical features of the writing of this poetic and contemplative composer are a broadly flowing sense of melody, often based on modal scales, and a very personal use of harmonic sound effects, in which there is usually a tonal basis, coupled with colorful instrumentation which often betrays the organist in him.

A strange combination of typically French and Dutch stylistic features is evident in the work of Alexander Voormolen (born 1895), a composer whose name often appeared on programs of Dutch orchestras in the years preceding World War II. Little has been heard of him in the post-war years, however, and his work has become forgotten to a greater and greater extent. His first works clearly bore the influence of the French Impressionistic school and, after he had studied under Roussel and Ravel in Paris, this tendency was further intensified. There was a stylistic change after 1930, embodying an effort towards more intense expression with the melodic and rhythmic elements more in the foreground. The element of humor forms an important constituent of his works. Amongst his best compositions are the Concerto for Two Oboes and Orchestra, the *Baron Hop Suite,* and the Chaconne and Fugue for orchestra.

When, after the war years, in 1945 Dutch musical life began to revive and greater attention began to be paid to local music because of a new cultural policy, it turned out to be mainly the pupils of Willem Pijper who began to put their mark on Dutch music.

An outstanding place among them was taken by Guillaume Landré (born 1905). He had already attracted attention prior to the war with his first Symphony (1932), Suite for string orchestra and piano (1936), and his short opera *The Pike* (1937). After the war years he blossomed into one of the most important Dutch composers. His early works are still very much under the influence of his teacher, but this influence gradually became restricted to a strict discipline concerning the nature and possibilities of the musical material. Instead of working with the short, concentrated, germ-cell-like motifs characteristic of Pijper's style, Landré expresses himself preferably in broadly sung, chromatically constructed melodies, which were for quite a time characterized by a somber timbre. Many of his works have a certain resigned and elegiac mood, such as the *Piae Memoriae pro Patria Mortuorum,* written in memory of those who fell in the war, the *Sinfonia Sacra in memoriam patris,* and the Third Symphony, dedicated to the memory of a friend who had died. We recognize the pupil of Pijper in the manner of derivation of all melodic and rhythmic material from one basic thought; in works dating from later years, including the orchestral pieces *Kaleidoscopio,*

Permutationi sinfoniche, and *Anagrams*, a dodecaphonic structure is perceptible, without there being any question however of a strictly consistent use of the twelve-tone technique. Many of Landré's works have also gained fame outside the Netherlands and have secured him a good reputation in international circles.

Henk Badings (born 1907) also studied for a short time under Pijper, but was, in contrast to most pupils of Pijper, in the end only very slightly influenced by him. Badings regards himself rather as one who was self-taught and whose musical imagination developed completely from his own studies. Endowed with a sharp intelligence, he succeeded in acquiring a knowledge of composition in addition to his studies in engineering at the Technical University at Delft. His skill as a composer was greeted with general admiration when, in 1930, the First Symphony of this then still completely unknown composer was awarded a prize. We can regard his manner of writing in broad outline as a continuation of the line Brahms-Reger-Hindemith. He has in common with them a sense of form, counterpoint, and full-sounding harmonies. His early works, i.e. those written up to about 1940, often have a decidedly somber character with elegiac melodies, a darkly colored, sometimes very complicated harmonic structure, and penetrating rhythmic figures, such as can be found in his Third Symphony (1935) and the Symphonic Variations (1936), these being two of the best works written in the Netherlands in those years. His later works are often lighter in tone, more playful in atmosphere, and more transparent as regards instrumentation. Important elements in his compositions are counterpoint and a very personal use of the chromatically tonal possibilities of harmony, which find their starting-point on the one hand in a development of octophonic scales, consisting of symmetrical eight-note successions of alternating intervals of a minor and major second and which are, on the other hand, caused by a combination of several modal series. Although his music often shows bitonal and pluritonal aspects, the tonal center is seldom completely obliterated. In his technique of instrumentation Badings shows his thorough knowledge in the field of acoustics and often creates outstanding images in sound, while his compositions are frequently also characterized by interesting rhythmic details. Badings is extremely versatile, having written notable works in practically every form of musical expression. He also shows himself to be a master of all conceivable problems of composition. Apart from numerous chamber works, varying from the solo sonata via the trio and quartet to the octet, he has written orchestral works, including twelve symphonies and many smaller orchestral pieces, concertos for piano, violin, cello, saxophone, flute, and a very successful one for two violins, works for chorus and orchestra, such as the *Symphony of Psalms* and the oratorio *Apocalypse,* four operas, and various radiophonic and electronic compositions. As far as composing with the help of electronic sources of sound is concerned, the unique combination of composer and engineer shown in one person stamps Badings as a composer who appears predestined to use new findings in the sciences for the purposes of musical expression.

The pupils of Willem Pijper also include the composers Rudolf Escher, Hans Henkemans, Oscar van Hemel, and Kees van Baaren. They have each gone their own way and have thus contributed to the varied picture shown by Dutch music today. Rudolf Escher (born 1913) first attracted wide attention through his orchestral work *Musique pour l'esprit en deuil,* which was inspired by the war and was awarded the music prize of the city of Amsterdam in 1946. One of the characteristics of Escher's compositions is a polymelodic style which influences both harmony and counterpoint as well as the orchestral sound. He uses this technique in such a way that melismatic figures, motifs, and themes can be extended to form vertical fields of sound which can then lead to a form of group polyphony. Most of his works are dominated by an extended tonality, which provides the composer with the whole chromatic scale while retaining a tonal center as the pole of attraction. This tendency is found not only in the *Musique pour l'esprit en deuil,* but also in later compositions, such as the *Hymne du grand Meaulnes* (inspired by Alain Fournier's description of the deserted landscape of Sologne in France and that strange atmosphere of happiness revealed in his novel *Le grand Meaulnes*), the Second Symphony, and his chamber work *Le Tombeau de Ravel.* All these compositions also reveal the composer's attachment to French culture, which likewise found a strong echo in the choral work *Le vrai visage de la Paix,* an impressive musical setting of the poem by Paul Eluard, in which Escher also shows a strong feeling for the new possibilities of sound in his vocal expression. Escher's musical output is so far not particularly large, he is a very conscientious worker who considers thoroughly the musical possibilities of each new work and always adopts a critical attitude towards his compositions. There is however no question of his great talent from the works he has already written. They occupy a very special place in contemporary Dutch music.

The works of Pijper's oldest pupil, namely Oscar van Hemel (born

1892), are of a very different nature. He became Pijper's pupil quite late in life and he was already over forty when he attracted attention in 1933 with a violin sonata. It has been mainly in the post-war years that he has developed as a productive composer, writing outstanding works in various fields of musical production. Characteristic of his work is a decided "musicantesque" liveliness and energy, coupled with a sensitive lyricism, evident in clearly delineated melodic structures. His compositions have remained traditional as regards both musical form and sound structure, although he also has an open ear for what is new in sound techniques. Within the limits of what has grown historically, his musical fantasy seeks paths that enable him to give expression to his original thoughts and musical élan. In addition to his orchestral works, including four symphonies and concertos for violin, oboe, and viola, his chamber music, particularly his Fourth and Fifth String Quartets and the Clarinet Quintet, is of importance. Many of his choral works form part of the repertory of various Dutch and international choral societies.

Pijper had a great influence on the training of Hans Henkemans (born 1913) as a composer, though the influence did not set its direct stamp on Henkemans's compositions. He was one of Pijper's last pupils, having studied under him from 1933 to 1938, at the same time as he was studying medicine at the University of Utrecht. After graduating as a doctor, Henkemans nevertheless devoted himself completely to music and has built up a career as pianist and composer. He has won international fame as a pianist mainly through his interpretations of Mozart and Debussy. As a composer, he has made his name with a number of concertos and certain orchestral works. In common with his teacher, he is very interested in the autonomous energy of the basic musical material. It is always his aim to process this material in its most varied possibilities. Although polytonal sound complexes occur repeatedly in his compositions, Henkemans adheres in principle to the concepts of tonality — even if they be greatly extended — the physical and psychological values of which are of major significance to him. His music is also characterized by nervously sensitive melody formation, often complicated form, and a use of the possibilities of the interpreting media which is conditioned by his high degree of intelligence. Henkemans has been particularly attracted to the solo concerto. Apart from the Passacaglia and Gigue for piano and orchestra — the work through which he first attracted attention beyond the Netherlands — he has written a flute concerto, a violin concerto, a concerto for viola, and one for harp. Although the orchestral part in these works is conceived very symphonically, the compositional trend is nevertheless clearly ruled by the sound properties of the solo instrument, while a notable unity is achieved in the whole score through a colorful and finely balanced harmony between the solo instrument and the orchestra. Outstanding works from recent years include the Partita for orchestra (1960) and the Wind Quintet (1962), two compositions that are each characterized in its own way by melodic forces that evoke tension and an effort towards equilibrium between a spontaneous and extremely sensitive passion for music-making and a form that is transparent and well considered in spite of its complicated nature.

Although he was not one of Pijper's pupils, Marius Flothuis (born 1914) has been clearly influenced by the master's compositions and particularly by his highly intelligent thoughts on music. Since 1955 Flothuis has held the responsible and demanding post of artistic director of the Concertgebouw Orchestra. He is also a composer who feels himself bound to tonality and for whom experimenting with sound as such has little personal appeal, although new paths in the way of technique fascinate him. Amongst his most important works are a Fantasy for harp and chamber orchestra, a Capriccio for string orchestra, a Sonata for Flute and Harp, a String Quartet, the *Symphonic Music* for orchestra — one of the best orchestral works composed in the Netherlands in recent years—and *Canti e giuochi,* a concerto for five wind instruments and string orchestra completed in the summer months of 1964. His works are in general characterized by a very poetic and artistically high degree of musical expression which is not devoid of a tendency towards lyricism and romanticism.

It is an essential feature of most composers who have determined the picture of Dutch music in the post-war years that they have adhered to tradition, although this certainly does not mean that they have become lost in certain epigonal tendencies. A general characteristic is rather a search for a synthesis between forces proceeding from tradition and new elements. It is not their desire to be original at any price and their efforts are directed more — to use Arthur Honegger's words — to playing the old game in a new way. Their artistic line of thought avoids both aggressive excessive complication and forced experiments with sound as well as a more or less pointless repetition of traditional formulas that retain no really creative artistic force.

A notable exception in the above-mentioned generation is however Kees van Baaren (born 1906), a pupil of Willem Pijper and since 1957 the director of the Royal Conservatory in The Hague. He is the only composer of his generation using twelve-tone and serial techniques and, as an advocate of this method of composition, is an outstanding phenomenon among his contemporaries. Van Baaren is not a particularly productive composer, but the works he has written so far bear witness to a striking musical personality. His method of writing is a continuous development in the sense that he is always seeking new possibilities for reaching that form of expression through the technique of music which is in accordance with his personality. It is not his intention to engage in an experimental and speculative venture, but rather he deliberately seeks new formations of musical material which develop to a personal utterance in sharply considered and controlled sound structures. His rich fantasy, coupled with extraordinary skill, enables him to make the technique of composition subservient to the artistic result. Among his most important compositions are the cantata for chorus and orchestra (written in 1948) *The Hollow Men* to a text by T. S. Eliot; a Septet for concertante violin with flute, oboe, clarinet, bassoon, horn, and double bass, a work that occupies a very special place in the Dutch chamber repertory; and the *Variazioni per orchestra* (composed in 1959), a score whose main feature is a sound image clearly and simply within the serial structure, coupled with a sharply delineated characteristic for each variation which also illuminates a separate facet of the technique of composition. The variations treat successively vertical tone groupings, interval relationships, variable groupings as regards meter and length of notes. His most recent works are a string quartet and a quintet for winds, which the composer called *Sovraposizione I* and *Sovraposizione II* respectively. Both works contain sections in which the pitch components are fixed by a placing above one another (*sovraposizione*) of six twelve-tone series, while both works also contain sections in which completely independent tempos and structures of different character simultaneously overlap. The aleatory principle is also used to a very limited extent in these works. Both the *Variazioni* and the two chamber-music works are among the most striking compositions in serial and post-serial techniques to be written in the Netherlands.

In addition to being a composer, Kees van Baaren also occupies a foremost place in contemporary Dutch musical life as a teacher. In the same way in which formerly Willem Pijper was the leading personality for a large group of younger composers, the younger talents now collect around Kees van Baaren. The new musical thought first initiated in the Netherlands by Pijper and the search for new possibilities have been fully developed by van Baaren. It is the younger composers of the moment who are reaping the fruits of this process of growth. As in many European countries, in the Netherlands too it is the generation born after 1920 that desires to free itself from preceding generations. Its members want to seek their own way in a new relationship to the material. Among the eldest in this group are the composers Ton de Leeuw and Hans Kox. Neither of them belongs to the group of van Baaren's pupils. Ton de Leeuw (born 1926) intended to study under Pijper when the latter died in 1947. His path then passed via Henk Badings to Olivier Messiaen in Paris. In many ways however he has had to seek his own path as a composer, a path that was in the greatest agreement with his musical personality. In many of Ton de Leeuw's works, the line of composition is dominated principally by rhythmic problems and those of sound structure, as, for example, in his most successful work so far, the *Mouvements rétrogrades* (1957). His first String Quartet (1958) is strongly influenced by the serial manner of writing. In it the composer strives for maximum simplicity and transparency of form. In his *Antiphony* (1958), for wind quintet and four sound-tracks, he makes well-considered use of the electronic sources of sound. Great attachment to the esthetic world of thought of the East is evident in his latest compositions, the orchestral works *Ombres* and *Nritta* and particularly in the opera *The Dream* and the *Haiku* songs. The lack of any causality and the stressing of a high degree of objectivity are the most striking features of his music. He is undoubtedly one of the most outstanding talents among the younger Dutch composers. Also of importance is the new notation, differing from the traditional one, that de Leeuw has used in his latest works. In order to avoid numerous complicated rhythmic figures, he has developed a proportional notation in which the temporal distances are reproduced visually in their mutual relationships. The duration of the note is shown by the distances between the various notes on the paper. In order to show clearly these distances and their mutual relationships, use is made of a grid of equally spaced vertical lines. It is possible by this system to reproduce a virtually unlimited scale of note values, depending on the distances apart of the note heads on the paper. An important point here is that the interpreter no longer "counts" but "measures" in units of time. Ton de Leeuw first used this notation in his Symphony for Wind Instruments composed in 1963 on a commission from the Pittsburgh Wind Symphony Orchestra.

Considerably less complicated, as regards both sound and musical structures, is the work of de Leeuw's contemporary Hans Kox, one of Henk Badings's most promising pupils. He is a very versatile composer who has written a number of chamber works and vocal compositions, including the remarkable *Chansons cruelles* (1957), incidental music for the stage, and orchestral pieces. His Symphony (1956), Piano Concerto (1962), *Concertante Music* for horn, trumpet, trombone, and orchestra, commissioned by the Concertgebouw Orchestra in 1956, the Violin Concerto (1963), and the Concerto for Two Violins and Orchestra (1964) are all to be regarded as expressions of a healthy musical personality for whom the main aim in composing is a maximum balance between harmonic, melodic, and rhythmic elements and who at the same time does not feel himself bound to any specific technique of composition.

Finally, we come to the youngest generation of composers, which is for the most part represented by the pupils of Kees van Baaren. A notable figure in that group is Peter Schat (born 1935), who has already shown his undeniably great talent in various works. He is a familiar figure in international circles of new music. Through his Septet (1957), *Mosaics* for orchestra (1959), *Entelechy* for five groups of instruments (1961), and *Signalement* for six percussion instruments and three double basses (1962) he has drawn the attention of the avant-garde to himself at the International Society for Contemporary Music, the Donaueschinger Musiktage, the Domaine Musical in Paris and the Gaudeamus Foundation at Bilthoven in the Netherlands. In his *Improvisations and Symphonies,* written for wind quintet in 1960, he uses aleatory and improvisational elements, and in his new composition *Labyrinth,* he sets out to create a form of musical theater in which a number of "happenings" occur alongside the real story and in which a form of interaction between the stage and the body of the hall is evoked. An instrumental section from this work, the *Dances from Labyrinth,* has been conducted by Pierre Boulez, with whom Schat studied for a period after his years of training with Kees van Baaren. In addition to van Baaren and Boulez, it is certain that John Cage has also been of influence on his musical thought.

Otto Ketting is of the same age, but as a composer is less extreme and wishes to follow the path laid out by Alban Berg and Anton Webern. One of his most successful works is the *Due Canzoni,* written for five woodwind instruments, four brass instruments, harp, celesta, and percussion in 1958. Partly as a result of his special knowledge of wind instruments — he was for some years a trumpet-player in the Hague

Philharmonic Orchestra — he has written a few works for brass instruments in which his feeling for timbre has led to effective results. He has also written certain chamber pieces and a notable Concertino for orchestra and jazz quintet.

Also born in 1935 was Jan van Vlijmen, who has attracted attention in particular through certain chamber works, including *Constructione* for two pianos (1959) and a Sextet for winds and piano (1961). His orchestral work *Gruppi* (1962) is a definite pinnacle among avant-garde music in the Netherlands.

At the beginning of his career as a composer is the twenty-six-year-old Louis Andriessen, the youngest son of Hendrik Andriessen, who has had the Italian Luciano Berio as a teacher in addition to his father and Kees van Baaren. He has aroused high expectations with his Nocturnes for orchestra and soprano solo and the *Itrospezione* I and II. The hopes and expectations for the future of Dutch music in general are fixed upon him and his colleagues and those of similar mind.

SCANDINAVIAN MUSIC AFTER THE SECOND WORLD WAR*

By BO WALLNER

T HE following is an attempt at a short description of the renewal in Scandinavian music after 1945.

Immediately following the armistice and for some years thereafter, it was Danish music that drew the greatest interest. During the 'fifties, on the other hand, Swedish composers dominated. Thus far into the 'sixties, where radical musical creation is concerned one can perceive common tendencies in all the Scandinavian countries.

The modest position assumed by Norwegian music is a noteworthy feature in the picture. True, right after the war Fartein Valen (1887-1952) established his position, and then Klaus Egge (b. 1906) wrote some of his most important works: among them, the Violin Concerto of 1953 and his Third Symphony (1957) — both removed from folk music. Also, Harald Saeverud (b. 1897) cultivated his increasingly mannered means of expression in several long works. But, at the same time, there was a dearth of talent among the younger generation. A similar situation prevailed in Finland.

Danish music of the 'forties was dominated by the triumvirate Herman D. Koppel, Vagn Holmboe, and Niels Viggo Bentzon.

During the 'thirties Koppel (b. 1908) had created a long succession of works that varied greatly in form and character. He spent some of the war years in Sweden — and at the same period experienced a need to deepen his expression. "My wish to write music immediately deriving from knowledge of evil done to others was very strong," he remarked in his introduction to a group of choral works based on biblical texts, first among them *Three Psalms of David,* for mixed chorus, boy's choir, tenor, and orchestra (1949). Here as in his Fourth Symphony (1946)

*Regrettably, Iceland is not included, since the source material necessary for such a study has been unavailable.

he definitely turned his back on music of a merely diverting kind. His music lacks markedly personal traits. But when one points out that Koppel's music can be conveniently described with reference to Nielsen, Bartók, and Prokofiev, perhaps also to Shostakovich and Britten, it is not to characterize him as a successor to such composers. He writes tonally — though with many and far-reaching extensions. He builds on traditional formal patterns, albeit taking certain liberties with them; and he prefers virile, motoric rhythms. While orchestral color abounds, purely coloristic traits are not allowed to dominate. Moreover, his formal solutions are convincing. His Third Piano Concerto (1948) occupies a leading place in the Scandinavian repertory. The composer stresses color and lyricism more in his Fourth Piano Concerto (1961); and the intense outbursts can also be regarded as a broadening of his emotional range.

Like Koppel, Vagn Holmboe (b. 1909) succeeded in establishing himself as a composer before World War II, though not to the same extent. Thus far, his most personal and inspired period seems to have been the middle and later 'forties. He then produced his Fifth, Sixth, and Seventh Symphonies, his first three string quartets, and his symphonic piano suite *Suono da bardo*. In these he appears as a follower of Nielsen and the generation of the 'twenties; indeed, he seems to complete what they began.

By means of his works and also as a teacher, Holmboe has been of extreme importance to Danish music and of some importance to music in the rest of Scandinavia. The following lines from his article on *Symfoni, koncert og nutidens musik (Symphony, Concerto, and Contemporary Music)*, published by *Dansk Musiktidskrift* in 1944 (pp. 233-38), throw light on his esthetic position:

> The so-called "neue Sachlichkeit" of the 'twenties treated problems in a consistent if somewhat rough manner, and with an eagerness that came close to eliminating music itself. But the amateur wind-instrument movement of the 'twenties had its significance, and already at the beginning of the 'thirties the scene cleared considerably. It is not easy to distinguish cause from effect, but in any case today one can perceive a general and widespread sense of balance and wish to achieve balance in the artistic objective; at the same time, one observes in many composers a gift for writing well-rounded works of art, using simple and artistically certain means.

Thus, Holmboe favored the classic ideals. But the two sides of his talent were to lead him further, past music of diverting and casual quality, to deeply serious individuality. His intellectual disposition was constructive, and his studies of folk music in Rumania, in 1933-34, put him in direct contact with ethnic musical material of rhythmic and melodic vitality. Moreover, his understanding of Bartók was thereby deepened.

This folkloric connection — which in Holmboe's case lacks any national content — is particularly noticeable in his lively orchestral movements from the late 'forties (there manifested first of all in powerful rhythms and a glaring coloration). An effective earlier example is the Second Chamber Concerto (1940), for violin, flute, celesta, percussion, and strings.

But a trait more evident in Holmboe's musical expression than the folkloristic strain is thematic variation. In his earlier work this has been given the form of variation chains broken up in a traditional way — as may be seen in some of the twelve chamber concertos (1939-50) which along with his symphonies and string quartets, form the most important part of his large production. However, for a long time Holmboe visualized a continuously increasing transformation: the metamorphosis. He has told of this in his study *Three Symphonies* (in *Modern nordisk musik,* pp. 152-66). He remarks: "The metamorphosic development — whether it takes place in stages or in a single unbroken chain — must be marked by the strictest musical logic, so that each link in the process of transformation appears as an inescapable necessity and points, to an ever-increasing degree, towards the final transformation." Holmboe developed fully his metamorphosic technique first in *Suono da bardo* (1949) and his Seventh Symphony (1950); and he applied it on the highest level of complication in his Eighth Symphony, of 1952-53.

Holmboe definitely rejects Impressionism, atonality, and twelve-tone technique. But at the same time one could claim that the continuous variation of a basic material is a common denominator of both the metamorphosic technique and serial composition in its different forms — a connection valid at least if one compares Holmboe's musical ideas with the variations, in twelve-tone technique but bound to tonality, that were to become characteristic of young Swedish music at the beginning of the 'fifties.

Not infrequently, Holmboe's later symphonies acquire a trace of Bruckner's monumental quality — and, as this implies, at the same time there is moral elevation in the musical expression. One notes also a tendency to asceticism and later towards an ethereal refinement, for instance, in the Sixth (thus far, the last) String Quartet — of 1961.

Though Vagn Holmboe speaks of the metamorphosic technique as his personal form of expression, Niels Viggo Bentzon (b. 1919) takes a quite different view in his contribution to *Modern nordisk musik*. Bentzon holds that the technique constitutes "the form of our times": he draws a parallel with the fugue in the Baroque era and with the sonata during Viennese Classicism and under Romanticism; moreover, he finds metamorphosis prefigured in the great Romantic works — of Brahms, for example, when he uses variation technique. Bentzon's way of putting the matter would be justified on two conditions: if he included serial procedure (which he does not do, any more than Holmboe himself), or if Danish music during the 'forties and 'fifties had played the same role in general musical developments as the Viennese School of Schoenberg and Webern had done. Assuredly, Danish music did nothing of the kind. Nevertheless, it can be said that the metamorphosic technique was "the form of our times" where Danish composition was concerned. A long line of both contemporary and younger composers followed in the footsteps of Holmboe and Bentzon. This is easily understandable when one considers that both Carl Nielsen and Bartók can be related to the technique. (So can a composer to whom less concentrated interest was given: Sibelius — especially in his later symphonies.)

Most of the Danish metamorphosic works are distinguished by a variation in expression and construction which reveals eloquently that the technique afforded each composer room to move about. This applies in the case of Bentzon — though in most things he is the opposite to Holmboe.

In Bentzon's article — the central work discussed is the Fourth Symphony (1949), subtitled *Metamorphoses* — the sections dealing with orchestral techniques are of special interest. Holmboe can be said to "register" the scores of his later symphonies, thus giving prominence to the thematic and polyphonic play. Bentzon, on the other hand, often works with sonorous and coloristic means; he himself declares that at the end of the 'forties he passed under the influence of Schoenberg and Britten. The orchestral effect has not always been clear and shimmering; on the contrary, his scores suffer rather often from a heavy block impression related to Brahms. This seems to derive from a very specific trait in his temperament: inspiration of a wildly upflaming sort. He has a great talent for swift improvisation, but this leaves him no time to balance delicately or to work out in detail. His output seems already to be considerably greater even than Hilding Rosenberg's; only a small number of his works meet the high demands that, especially

in Denmark, are placed on his talent. Few of them are carried through
in an altogether satisfactory way.

In 1950 Bentzon published a textbook on twelve-tone technique.
His presentation of this deserves respect, coming in Scandinavia when
it did — even if it is based on too little experience and too limited
belief in the possibilities involved. What he emphasizes concerning
Schoenberg (in his article on the Fourth Symphony, not in the textbook)
is instead the *emotional effect* of his music. A strongly emotional
attitude towards music and concentration on giving an emotional effect
in his own music are characteristic of Bentzon. He believes that the
Fourth Symphony is a "key work" in his production (at least before
1957), and that he there found a balance between his material and his
development of it.

But the question of which is Bentzon's central work may be examined from two entirely different aspects; and the listener may claim
that the style of the Partita for piano makes it Bentzon's most original
contribution to Danish composition. (One encounters the same style
in two other piano works: the Passacaglia, of 1944, and the Third
Piano Sonata, of 1946-47.) The opening passages of the Partita, for
instance (Ex. 1), exhibit powerfully the emotional expressiveness so
rare in Danish music. Their genuinely pianistic structure recalls Bentzon's
great talent as a pianist.

Ex. 1 *Praeambulum*

Such titles as Partita, Passacaglia, and Toccata bear witness to the young Bentzon's interest in the neo-Baroque. This interest is evident in his effective Chamber Concerto for Eleven Instruments, of 1948: three of the instruments are solo pianos, and Bentzon uses soloistic trumpets, as in Bach's second *Brandenburg Concerto*. This attachment to older models forms the background to the technique, new for him, of the Fourth Symphony. But during recent years one finds other works of interest in his unremitting and variegated production. There is the virtuoso Solo Sonata for Cello (1956), with its guitar-like pizzicato movement and slow cantilena of which the euphonious and long-curved melodies have few equivalents in modern Danish music. There is the Chamber Symphony, of 1962, influenced by Alban Berg. There is (also of 1962) the cantata for chorus and orchestra, *Bonjour Max Ernst,* of which the "Exorcism" movement can best be described as an uncontrolled and desperate howl. There is *Propostae novae,* for two pianos, to which Bentzon was inspired by Schoenberg's Opus 16 and whose first two movements are of expressive and resonant refinement.

Both Holmboe and Bentzon took mainly a traditional German line to begin with. Another line, followed in the 'twenties by Knudage Riisager in particular, was that of neo-Classical French music. His interest was taken up by Jörgen Jersild (b. 1913; a pupil of Albert Roussel) and, somewhat later, by Poul Rovsing Olsen (b. 1922; a pupil of Boulanger). Though Jersild has cultivated somewhat thin but always clear and well-formulated phrasing, one finds greater expressiveness in his *Trois pièces en concert* for piano (1945) and in his *Three Six-Part Madrigals,* of 1957. Rovsing Olsen is a musical ethnologist, and, especially in the last years of the 'fifties, he used rhythmic and melodic material derived from other continents than Europe. But one may note that in his song-cycle of 1953, *Schicksalslieder* — with text by Hölderlin — a synthesis of neo-Classicism and Impressionism still dominated. Of relevance here, too, is the earlier work of Bernhard Lewkowitch, especially his four piano sonatas from 1949-51, strongly influenced by Niels Viggo Bentzon and Prokofiev.

In the middle 'forties, Bartók, Hindemith, and Stravinsky were still little known in Sweden, and masters of the Viennese School were scarcely more than names in a chapter of musical history entitled "Götterdämmerung." The only modern composer who attracted considerable attention was Shostakovich. In the circumstances, it is surprising that Hilding Rosenberg succeeded in gaining general acceptance.

He was helped by the radio, which, being state-financed, can disregard the size of audiences and their caprices. Where music was concerned, the cultural life of Stockholm remained deeply conservative. It must be said, however, that Stockholm provided — in spite of prevailing conventions — a wonderful field for radical young musicians with bold ideas and an unobstructed will to work.

There were such young people. In the middle of the 'forties a group appeared consisting of composers (primarily, Karl-Birger Blomdahl, Sven-Erik Bäck, and Ingvar Lidholm), instrumentalists (in first place, the pianist Hans Leygraf), and musicologists (notably, Ingmar Bengtsson). The group had a chamber orchestra at its disposal, and also a chorus directed by the eminent choir-leader Eric Ericson. (At one time or another, whether as soloists or members, this contained such singers of international repute today as Elisabeth Söderström, Kerstin Meyer, Nicolai Gedda, and Erik Saedén.) Somewhat later, Sixten Ehrling and the Kyndal Quartet, among others, joined in the interests of the group. One may, without exaggeration, speak of a youthful and talented élite gathered together to serve new music.

The composers involved — who, because they met weekly on that day to discuss their ideas, were known as "the Monday Group" — had not acquired their training in composition at the Academy of Music in Stockholm, the only Swedish institution giving higher musical education. Instead, they studied privately under Rosenberg, whose idealistic and progressive view of musical developments directed their own. They got stimulation and a sense of competition through their contacts with composers and musicians in Copenhagen (first of all, with Holmboe and Bentzon), by making journeys on scholarships to France, Italy, and Switzerland, and through their participation in the yearly festivals of ISCM. The most important of these festivals from the Scandinavian viewpoint was naturally that of 1947 in Copenhagen; attention was directed for the first time upon Bentzon, who played his Partita, and on Blomdahl, who had his String Trio performed. Another aspect of the group is worth observing: its interest in the musical development from Bach and backwards in time. During the war, Mogens Wöldike, the well-known Danish conductor of Baroque music, sojourned in Stockholm; a number of the young studied under him then, notably Bäck and Bengtsson, and later members of the group deepened their understanding of such music at the Schola Cantorum in Basel and under Handschin at the university there. Their studies led to music of Landini, Machaut, Dufay, Josquin, Monteverdi, and others being performed probably for the first time in Sweden in the years around 1950.

The group worked with the central idea of reaching the resources and using the experience of existing concert institutions in order to expand. A first move in this direction was the taking over of "Fylkingen," the orchestral society. Its personnel joined forces in the autumn of 1950 with the Swedish section of ISCM; thereupon the society devoted itself exclusively to music of our time and of increasingly radical tendencies. (This may be judged from the fact that in the autumn of 1964 Cage and Tudor made their visit to Stockholm — their third — under the society's auspices, and there collaborated with the choreographer Merce Cunningham and the "pop" artist Rauschenberg.) A special series of orchestral concerts, with the name *Nutida musik*, was inaugurated in 1954; at first, the Philharmonic Society of Stockholm and Radio Sweden were jointly responsible for these concerts, but in the autumn of 1962 the radio took over the society entirely. As was indicated above, Swedish radio services and television are state enterprises without commercial competition, and are thus in the fortunate situation of being able to cater to advanced tastes. The radio has done so during the past decade by having music especially composed, through its pedagogical series, reports from different parts of the world, productions of new drama and ballet, also by distributing gramophone records and publishing the periodical *Nutida musik* — of which the first number was for 1957-58. In consequence of the radio's efforts, the attitude towards modern music became constructive and forward-looking, and during the 'fifties it became an established part of Swedish musical life. A further contribution of the radio should be mentioned: it is now constructing an electronic studio — the first in Scandinavia — under the artistic leadership of Knut Wiggen.

That new music had established itself was confirmed by productions — in some cases initial ones — at the Stockholm Opera: *Wozzeck* in 1956, *Aniara* in 1959, *The Rake's Progress* in 1961, and a number of ballets with music by, among others, Rosenberg, Blomdahl, Lidholm, and Bäck. An important part in the establishment has been played by a seminar founded at the Academy of Music in Stockholm for the study of composition. Here Ligeti and Lutoslawski have been guest professors, and lecturers have included Pousseur, Kagel, and Koenig. Blomdahl became professor of composition in 1960, and Lidholm takes over in 1965.

The picture would be incomplete without mention of the critics. Swedish musicians are much less interested than Danes in public debate;

but, after several skirmishes, open conflict concerning new music broke
out at Christmas-time of 1956, and battle was waged in the larger
newspapers until into the spring of 1957. The contributions involved
can be studied in a "white book" published by Yngve Flyckt and Bengt
Holmqvist under the title *Erkänn musiken!* (*Recognize the Music!,*
Stockholm, 1957). The incendiary spark was not a matter of importance: in his oratorio inspired by Saint-John Perse's *Anabase,*
Blomdahl used the original French text. Debate quickly flowed into
channels of greater significance: the international versus the national,
such models as Schoenberg, Webern, Varèse, and the Darmstadt composers opposed to Bartók, Shostakovich, and Britten, the composer's
responsibility in gaining contact with the public against the pedagogue's
often negative and dilettantish attitude. The result of all this was that
the conservative faction lost its balance — an occurrence that is not
really to be regarded as desirable. The demand from protagonists of
new music for younger music critics could not be met because there
were so few younger writers on musical subjects. By offering them much
stimulating work, the radio drew off talented young people.

To return to the 1940s, the melodic style inspired by the Bach-
Hindemith line and the contrapuntally thorough technique that characterizes most of the youthful works of Blomdahl (b. 1916) and Bäck
(b. 1919) were regarded by the musical public in Sweden as radical —
though a considerable amount of Rosenberg's and Nystroem's work was
not less advanced. Meanwhile, in certain artistic and literary circles it
was thought too academic, too much the property of a clique and
backward-looking. But support came from the highly cultivated and
literary Göte Carlid (1920-53), who shared the newly aroused interest
in the Schoenberg circle. And a decisive effect in bringing about an
esthetic change was made by the composers' contact with modern
Swedish poetry — that of Ekelöf, Lindegren, Vennberg, Oswald, and
so on, which is to say a poetry rooted in surrealism and related to that
of Pound, Eliot, Eluard, etc.

One cannot say that the change came unannounced. It was presaged
in the restful chords and rich atmosphere of Sven-Erik Bäck's Second
String Quartet (1947), which reflects the Christian mysticism pervading
so much of his production; and Lidholm had already in his first
orchestral work (1945) placed a toccata influenced by Hindemith
beside a poetic, intimate *canto*. With a deeper experience of life and
ears attuned to stylistic changes in continental Europe, the composers
now began — each, so to speak, in his own room — industriously to

study Bartók's quartets (which thus acquired their great stylistic importance in Swedish music), also Stravinsky's later work, Alban Berg, and, not least, the twelve-tone technique. Krenek and Leibowitz, through their writings, served as intermediaries. Expressiveness, emotional intensity, refinement of color had become positive and valuable qualities.

All this served as a general background to the almost explosive development in Swedish composition during the 'fifties — a development unparalleled since the years about 1900, and one that quickly carried the young composers to a leading position in Scandinavian music. Eventually, they would gain international attention rare for Swedes.

In spite of great differences in the music of individual composers, one can speak of certain common structural characteristics.

One of these is *tonally oriented use of the twelve-tone technique.* Another is a striving — very evident in Blomdahl's case — to combine structural influence from Bartók (from his Fourth String Quartet, to begin with) and from Schoenberg (the influence here being not at all of a psychological kind). The result can be studied in the work that established Blomdahl internationally, his Third Symphony, or *Facetter* (1950). The strong will and virile basic quality to be found in the composer's works in the 'forties have here been tremendously magnified. At points of culmination the polyphonic weave achieves a closeness and a degree of complication unprecedented in Swedish music, and with no trace of mechanical emptiness. On the contrary, the musical expression is dominated by *joie de vivre,* with subjugating dance-like or march-like rhythms (Ex. 2). There is an evident connection with the concerto grosso, and in the spun-out string movement an elegiac expressiveness unusual in Swedish composition.

The tonal twelve-tone technique can be studied also in Bäck's Chamber Symphony of 1954. Here again the rhythmic element is important. But one must speak of two temperaments divided in spirit and manner of expression. While Blomdahl outlines his motifs with alternating accents and syncopations combined by melodic mobility, Bäck devotes himself to frenetic ostinato rhythms. In every phrase of his symphony Blomdahl builds architecturally, but Bäck is more of an impulsive improviser; he adds short homophonic episodes to one another.

Turning to a work by another of Rosenberg's pupils, Ingvar Lidholm's *Ritornell* (1955) — which, like *Facetter,* won international attention — one perceives that the composer stands nearer to atonality. One can find there no equivalent to the hard resonance in Blomdahl's

Ex. 2

orchestration, not even in the ecstatic final passages. Rather, there is a poetic shimmer; and the pointillistic dissolutions are colored in a manner unequivocally influenced by Webern.

This leads us to an important point when describing the three pupils of Rosenberg: the progressively refined orchestration, reaching its culmination in Lidholm's two orchestral pieces: *Motus-Colores* (1960) and especially *Poesis* (1963). Here there are fireworks of sound with partly new instrumental effects; melody is almost entirely eliminated, and dynamic alternations are allowed to replace rhythm as the power that holds a work together.

This development is connected with a rather complicated net of influences. That of Webern has been mentioned. Stravinsky undoubtedly is among the masters of these composers — whose interest shifts noticeably from the Germanic to the Gallic. Debussy, Ravel, Dallapiccola, later Boulez and the "neo-Impressionist" Hungarian, Ligeti, should be named. One may observe in passing that new possibilities of expression offered by percussion instruments were exploited in, among other works, Bäck's *Favola* (1962) — there in combination with solo clarinet.

Yet another point concerning this generation of composers: their interest in the relation between music and word.

At first it seemed surprising, that after their radical processes, they turned to vocal music. But one explanation has already appeared here: the liberating effect of contact with new poetry. Another explanation has to do with tone color: the human voice is an instrument that produces not only musical pitches but also an endlessly variable scale of coloristic nuances, not least on the phonological plane. There are indications of the work that lay ahead in a choral piece by Blomdahl and the poet Lindegren *I speglarna sal* (*In the Mirror Room,* 1951-52), where the composer was the first in Sweden to write a completely pointillistic vocal movement; his technique was further developed in his oratorio after St. John Perse's *Anabase* (1956), which he built up in a more mosaic-like manner. In accord with its more popular subject, vocal parts in the opera *Aniara* received a simpler and more traditional form.

But it is in Lidholm's production that change in the vocal means employed can most clearly be seen. His rather extensive *a cappella* works gave new life to the choral poem, which had not flourished to such a degree since Romanticism. In the earliest of his pieces in the genre, *Laudi,* the stylistic starting-point is almost a synthesis of the Palestrina tradition and Stravinsky. A stage of his development is represented by the *Four Choruses* of 1953; here the earlier polyphonic manner of writing is replaced by a more harmonic expressiveness. The most important stage thus far — his third and still uncompleted one — is that of his *A Cappella Book.* This work, begun in 1956, is built up using a common tonal series and incessantly alternating techniques and effects; and it is crowned by the movement after Ezra Pound's *Canto LXXXI,* where the pointillistically broken structure seems a vocal pendant to *Ritornell.* In yet another phase of his development, that of the choral episodes in *Nausikaa ensam* (*Nausicaa, Alone,* 1963), Lidholm works with wordless effects, one of these being a murmur that suggests the wind (Ex. 3).

Bäck, too, has produced a considerable number of vocal works, especially of a dramatic type. A common denominator is proximity to certain historical models: 16th-century vocal polyphony is used in a long series in *Choral Motets* (begun 1960); Gregorian recitative style and melismatic melody appear in, for example, the admired chamber opera *Tranfjädrarna* (*The Crane Feathers,* 1956).

The progressive movement in Swedish music of the 'fifties soon found an heir in Bengt Hambraeus (b. 1928). However, rather than

Ex. 3

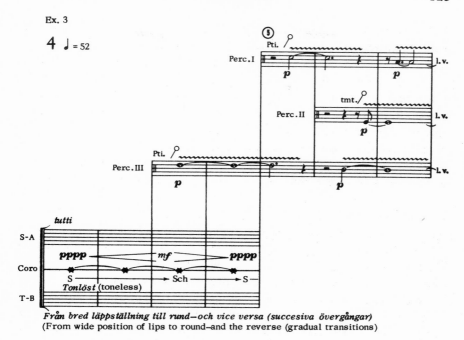

Från bred läppställning till rund—och vice versa (succesiva övergångar)
(From wide position of lips to round–and the reverse (gradual transitions))

by the three composers described here, Hambraeus was influenced by
his scholarly studies, primarily of medieval and non-European music,
and by his work as an organist (he was the first in Sweden to take up
Messiaen), also by his participation in the Darmstadt courses, beginning
in 1951. These courses allowed Hambraeus to immerse himself at an
early stage in the work of Webern, Stockhausen, and Boulez, as well as
in taped and electronic sound. He was the first in a Scandinavian
country to compose an electronic work, *Doppelrohr II* (1955), produced
in the Cologne studio. As in the production of Blomdahl, Bäck, and
Lidholm, color plays a very important part in that of Hambraeus; one
may notice this in, for example, the clock sounds worked out as motifs
in *Introduzione — Sequenze-Coda* (1959) or in such electronically
transformed organ music as the series *Konstellationer* (1960-62) —
No. 1 for organ only, No. 2 recorded for tape, No. 3 a combination
of No. 2 and "natural" organ but based on No. 1. There are two
points where Hambraeus's work differs radically from that of his
predecessors: the passage of time is usually not marked by any pulse
beat, and instead one can speak of a floating continuity; and the form
is not laid out with traditionally well-marked divisions — as it is in
Blomdahl's case, especially. Hambraeus's dependence on the German-

Italian avant-garde movement of the 'fifties is evident. *Rota* (1956-62), with mixtures of orchestral sound (three instrumental groups) and taped sound, can be regarded as a summing up of experience gained.

In the middle 'fifties Hambraeus was of great — though for the most part concealed — importance to the wonder-boy in Swedish composition, Bo Nilsson (b. 1937). That this was so bears witness to the notable part that radio and gramophone records have had in Scandinavian musical life. During most of his career Nilsson has lived in Malmberget, which lies in the northernmost part of Sweden and is a wilderness from the musical point of view. His first compositions — which came after he had spent some years as a jazz musician — may be associated with such names as Boulez and Stockhausen. Before he was twenty years old he attracted much attention — not yet in Sweden, but in Germany, and especially in Darmstadt — with a number of smaller chamber works. The best known of these is *Frequensen;* all are characterized by a refined and in many ways unusual manner of instrumentation, and by an exquisite feeling for aphoristic form. In a large cycle of works based on poems by Gösta Oswald (*Briefe an Gösta Oswald,* 1958-59, as well as in revised versions of *Mädchentotenlieder, Ein irrender Sohn,* and *Und die Zeiger seiner Augen*), and in such orchestral pieces as *Entrée* (1962) and *Szene III* (1961), there is an excessive force at some places in his range of expression. The basic character is, however, still ethereal, slightly "oriental" sound from the ensemble. The speculative trait that can be found in the work of the Darmstadt group reappears in Nilsson, but with him it is only a playful attitude. In his heart and soul, he is an extemporizing musician of spontaneously flowing imagination.

Ever since the last phase of Romanticism, there had been a surprising stylistic reserve in each generation of Swedish composers. But this was broken by composers who made their first appearance in the 'fifties. Hambraeus and Bo Nilsson represent the progressive wing of the movement then; those on the opposite side, who look back to neo-Classicism and admire the idyllic, include a group of Lars-Eric Larsson's pupils. Foremost among them are Jan Carlstedt (b. 1926) and Hans Edlund and Maurice Karkoff, who are a year younger.

Carlstedt's work is oriented towards Shostakovich and Prokofiev. Edlund's considerably larger production is also influenced by the Russians, but it contains an atmospheric expressiveness rooted in the Scandinavian tradition. Though Karkoff is also a pupil of Larsson, he has studied with Blomdahl, Dallapiccola, Jersild, Wladimir Vogel, Max

Deutsch, and others; and his production is as variegated as that list might suggest. It is characteristic of him that he swings between such a "ball-dribbling" piano piece as his *Capriccio on Football* (1960) and his Fourth Symphony (1963), a heavy, rhythmically intricate work with certain rhythmic motifs taken from Israeli folk dance and tragic accents.

Another composer born in 1927, Gunnar Bucht, seems a more isolated figure. Like Hambraeus, he is a musicologist as well as a composer. In his earlier work, he composed under the influence of Nielsen, Sibelius, Bartók, and Blomdahl; his style, diatonically constructive in principle (Bucht finds nothing negative in the epithet "academic"), has been manifested in his Fourth Symphony (1957-58) and in the choral work *La Fine della diaspora* (1958; text by Quasimodo). In 1961-62 Bucht stayed in Paris and studied with Max Deutsch, a pupil of Schoenberg. The result has been an increased range of expression and greater structural elaboration, which can be witnessed in the Sixth Symphony — called *Sinfonia encyclopedica* by the composer. Elaboration may have been carried too far here, but the richness of the material places it among the most important works composed thus far by his generation.

Four other composers deserve mention. Hans Holewa — who was born in 1905 in Vienna and received his schooling there — seems to be closest to the Alban Berg tradition. Allan Pettersson (b. 1911) was once called "the most naked heart in Swedish music"; he has written four large "confessional" symphonies. Though a pupil of Blomdahl and Leibowitz, he is not a dodecaphonist. Carl-Olof Anderberg (b. 1910, and from Skåne) appears to seek in his work for personal grounds in relation to stylistic developments in the 'fifties. Sten Broman (b. 1902) is well known as a supporter of ISCM. After producing only some small chamber pieces, he fell into silence as a composer. But then he surprised the entire musical world of Sweden by writing two large-scale symphonies — 1962 and 1963 — where the effective orchestral technique comes closest to that of Blomdahl and Lidholm.

What, it may be asked, has the Swedish march forward during the 'fifties meant to composition in other Scandinavian countries?

This question is difficult to answer. There are works — by, for example, Erik Bergman and the Norwegian Arne Nordheim — strikingly connected in style with those of Blomdahl and, especially, of Lidholm. But is the connection direct or does the similarity derive only from intense study of international stylistic development by all the composers involved? Swedish composers are not alone in freeing themselves increasingly from the Scandinavian tradition since World War II; the greater number of Finnish musicians and, particularly, Danish ones have done the same.

This is one of the reasons why Scandinavian composition has long walked on crutches. True, forms of collaboration between the countries are many. "Scandinavian Music Days," devoted to new music, are held every other year in different capitals; there are foundations, scholarships, concert tours, and so on. But for the most part the collaboration is kept alive by artificial respiration. Prestige and ambition maintain the activity, but do not create a living, stimulating interest. There has been a shining exception to this during recent years, however; Scandinavian Conservatory Festivals have established contacts among the youngest composers and induced a desire to work together in the future. Then, too, young Swedes have got into touch with the phalanx of radical composers in Finland; Norwegians study at the Academy of Music in Stockholm; and so on.

Though it is seldom spoken of openly, musical competition exists among the Scandinavian capitals. And here one can speak with certainty of Swedish influence. The activity of the associations Fylkingen and Nutida Musik, and also of the radio, in support of modern music has had a stimulating effect — and at the same time applied pressure — on similar but more conservative institutions in Copenhagen, Oslo, and Helsinki.

Swedish influence is especially marked in Norway, where, as was mentioned earlier, few composers now in their forties and fifties exist to give inspiration to a younger crop of composers. One may note that, although radio stations elsewhere have done much on behalf of modern music, in Norway the policy of the radio has been stingy and conservative — in spite of well-informed and at times very aggressive criticism in the Norwegian press.

Since 1938, support of new music has been unified by the music society Ny Musikk, which is the Norwegian section of ISCM. Pauline Hall (b. 1890), a composer and music-critic, was chairman of it until 1961. The world festival of 1953 in Oslo had an undeniable artistic success. But it is characteristic of the severe musical climate prevailing in Norway that the festival did not notably improve the situation of modern music there.

In the years around 1960, however, a decisive step was taken: two talented young instrumentalists — the pianist Kjell Baekkelund and the flutist Alf Andersen — and a new generation of composers, foremost among them Arne Nordheim, Finn Mortensen, and Egil Hovland (born in 1931, 1922, and 1924), joined together to advance an active musical policy involving series of concerts, radio and television performances, etc. They associated themselves with two older composers: Gunnar Sönstevold (b. 1912), who was a pupil of Rosenberg and is the first Norwegian to occupy himself with electronic music, and Knut Nystedt (b. 1916), a pupil of Copland and well known as a choir leader and church musician. A third composer comes into the picture here, though he has since disappeared from it: Edvard Fliflet Braein (b. 1924), who at the beginning of the 'fifties drew attention with a number of orchestral works in neo-Classical style.

In general, the composers mentioned above have developed in the same direction as those in the rest of the Scandinavian countries: from a somewhat classical attitude, with music built on modern diatonic counterpoint, towards a more or less personal use of the twelve-tone technique, then towards a serial or non-serial technique dominated by vertical and coloristic means of expression. (The folkloristic element has practically disappeared.) This progression is most evident in Mortensen's case. The first attitude is represented by a Wind Quartet (1954; ISCM 1956) and a long but unfinished symphony; the twelve-tone stage was reached in a Fantasy and Fugue for piano (1958; ISCM 1960), and the next one in two relatively short works: *Evolution,* for orchestra (1961) and a Piano Concerto (1963). The most interesting of these works is *Evolution*. In it Mortensen begins with violently hammering chords; meanwhile and throughout there is a faint c^4 - c^5 in the violins; the melodic element is pushed entirely to the background. In an article on Mortensen's work, Nordheim asks: "Can one speak of eruptivity as part of compositional technique?" The question arises frequently in modern composition and not only in the case of Mortensen, but he has gone farthest in the use of eruption as contrast — even though it may be debated whether the result is convincing. In an article on Mortensen by Sverre Lind, he is said to lack "an environmental background and contact with living musical life. He lost contact through his isolation." Though this pronouncement was made in the middle of the 'fifties, it has probably a certain application still and may be connected with an absence of organic flow in Mortensen's music. Generalizing about the Norwegian situation, one might perhaps find a drawback in the lack of an established progressive and radical movement.

While Mortensen is a "cerebral" musician, Nordheim possesses more of poetic mood. He is hypersensitive to the nuances of sound; consequently, color is the most personal element in his music — in his settings, for soprano and chamber ensemble, of the Pär Lagerkvist poems *Aftonland* (*Evening Country,* 1957-58) and in his orchestral pieces *Canzona* (1960) and *Epitaffio* (1963). The last has taped episodes inlaid and electronically transformed effects. Like Mortensen, Nordheim balances the shimmering and the eruptive; he does so most evidently and effectively in his music to the Hieronymus Bosch ballet *Katharsis* (1962, with choreography by Ivo Cramér and décor by Guy Krogh).

Egil Hovland is more dextrous in technique than Mortensen or Nordheim, but at the same time less personal in musical expression. Hovland studied with Holmboe, Copland, and Dallapiccola. As in Mortensen's case, his development has been from the classically schematic to more open and imaginative structures. Among his most important works are *Music for Ten Instruments* (1957), a Second Symphony (1956), and *The Song of Songs,* for flute, piano, and percussion (1963). And one may mention two other composers. Though the music of Finn Arnestad (b. 1915) is more introverted, it has something of the same lyrical expressiveness as can be found in that of Saeverud and Bäck. Edvard Hagerup Bull (b. 1922) has written *Trois mouvements symphoniques,* which blend the Saeverud tradition with the humor of a Parisian street urchin.

In Finland as in Norway, a decade after World War II new musical trends had not received much recognition. Even interest in Bartók, Stravinsky, and Shostakovich was scorned in certain circles as cultural Bolshevism.

Many of the new composers wrote in a style that derived wholly or partly from the past. For example, Tauno Pylkkänen (b. 1918) did so. He gained attention when still in his teens, and was attracted at an early stage by musical drama; Puccini fascinated him. Veikko Helasvuo has described Pylkkänen's *Mare ja hänen poikansa* (*Mare and Her Son,* 1945) and *Suden morsian* (*The Wolf Bride*) as a kind of "Finnish verismo." Ahti Sonninen (b. 1914) is more uneven but of more personal imagination. Among the works he is known for are *Pessi ja Ilussia* (1952) and the song cycle *El Amor paza* (1953; ISCM 1956).

Perhaps it was not accidental that renewal came through three composers in the Swedish-language group; for linguistic reasons they had greater contact with Scandinavia. Of the three, Nils-Eric Fougstedt

(1910-63) was the first to take up twelve-tone technique. He synthesized this with a rather heavy symphonic style, and used it primarily in the polyphonically elaborated outer movements of *Trittico sinfonico* (1958; ISCM 1959). Another of the three, Einar Englund (b. 1916), has turned in a different direction: the melodic stream and resonant orchestral motion in his Second Symphony (1948) disclose the influence of Prokofiev and Shostakovich; and in a piano concerto of 1951 he balances teasingly the serious and the entertaining. (Earlier, Englund was one of Finland's most appreciated jazz pianists, and he still gives a considerable part of his time to lighter music.) Throughout his work, Englund reveals a vital musical temperament, not very unlike Uuno Klami's (1906-61). Regrettably, he became silent at a time when the esthetic ideal in Finnish music either grew intellectualized or rather coarsely radical — with "happenings," collage techniques, and so on as a result.

At the end of the 'forties, Englund belonged to the group who struggled eagerly for a wider musical perspective that brought Continental modernism into view. Aims of the group were furthered first by the Finnish section of ISCM, called Nykymusikki. And here the third Swedish-language composer referred to, Erik Bergman (b. 1911), played a role by giving concentration to the progressive musical view. Since 1963, he has been professor of composition at the Sibelius Academy — which is to say, the Finnish Academy of Music.

Bergman's musical expression is very unlike Englund's. While Englund seems to proceed along main lines, Bergman works more from without; he gives more detail to his motifs. And he elaborates his scores with a thoroughness unusual in Finnish music; they bear witness to a broad experience of music and advanced technique. But one must look elsewhere for the traits that enabled him to awaken the musical conscience of the younger generation. Though there is a striving towards expressiveness in his early production — of song cycles, piano music, and some smaller orchestral pieces (most notably *Burla*, 1948) — this is not closely connected with new techniques. But a change appears in his music from the middle of the 'fifties. Bergman took up his studies again, this time under Wladimir Vogel in Ascona, and he acquired a deeper knowledge of twelve-tone technique; he also studied oriental music — which he approached from an oriental aspect. And a large production emerged from this crucible, expressed by means that have few precedents in Finnish music. One can follow his development towards an increasingly complicated serial technique in his *Tre aspetti d'una seria dodecafonica* (1957), *Simbolo* (1960), and *Concerto da camera* (1960). It is the coloristic element that interests most in *Aubade* (1958), where there are a number of similarities to Lidholm's *Ritornell* and Nordheim's *Canzona*. Bergman is most personal in his choral work; with his *Rubáiyát* for male choir and instrumental ensemble (including percussion and guitar, 1953) he broke out from narrower tonality and stricter formation of motifs. But his main work from those years is *Aton* — i.e. Echnaton's hymn to the sun — composed for baritone, mixed choir, and orchestra, with recitations spoken by a chorus (1959). Here Bergman makes use of all his broad vocal-melodic range; and the recitation is often of high tension. He returns frequently to spoken choruses, especially in his pieces for male choirs. For a long time he has been leader of two such choirs in Helsinki, one of them composed of Swedish-language students; and he has presented a repertory rendered very unconventional by the element of new music. One might mention his fondness for mingling the sound of male voices with that of instruments, also that he brings cluster technique into such pieces as *Fåglarna* (*The Birds,* 1962; ISCM 1964; to a text by Solveig von Schoultz; see Ex. 4).

There is in Bergman's work, for all the mixture of styles, a certain conformity. For example, one finds a shrewd, often aggressive, astringency in the quick movements. But one cannot easily discover anything so consistent in works of the other great seeker in modern Finnish music, Einojuhani Rautavaara (b. 1928).

The piece that established Rautavaara was *Requiem in Our Time,* for wind ensemble (1954). It is most similar in style to Stravinsky and Prokofiev, with sharp dissonances. A fuller chordal sound, of a character recalling Messiaen, dominated his piano cycle *Icons;* and in the orchestral piece *Previata* (ISCM 1957) the means of expression were turned radically towards the pointillistic. Also during 1958, he completed his Second String Quartet: here the compositional premise is a strictly carried out twelve-tone technique. But at the same time Rautavaara looked backwards; he wrote in a commentary that the Quartet implies "moving a distance from pointillistic influences." He noted having given "less attention to the soloistic possibilities of the different instruments than to the smooth blending of string sound, in the same spirit as, for example, Schoenberg does in *Verklärte Nacht* or Bruckner in the Quintet." During the years that followed, Rautavaara composed a number of works — among them the song cycles *Die Liebende* and *Sonette an Orpheus* — influenced by Schoenberg, or perhaps rather

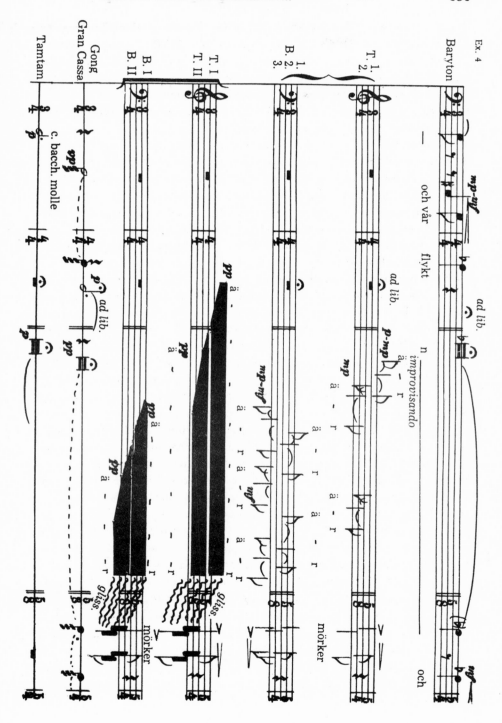

by the early Alban Berg. One can even speak of Bruckner strains in his Third Symphony (1961-62). His opera *Kaivos* (*The Mine*, 1958-60) has the same basis. Nor has the composer stopped there. In his orchestral work *Arabescata* (1962; ISCM 1963) he takes up current problems of form. The second movement is a series of "graphic variations," and in the outer movements everything begins with the number eleven: tonal height, time value, color, and dynamics.

The wavering among styles in Finnish music has of course been a matter of temperament and experience. But, as with new Norwegian music, one must take into account that poor information about developments elsewhere can have caused a disturbing cleavage. As a background to the struggle for renewal, tradition in compositional training has its importance and presents a problem — one that Rautavaara attempted to solve during the 'fifties by studies abroad, both in Europe and America.[1]

In comparison to Rautavaara's work, the stylistic stability in that of Joonas Kokkonen (b. 1920) is great. Kokkonen was Bergman's predecessor as professor of composition, and he now holds the position at the Academy of Finland that was earlier Yrjö Kilpinen's (1892-1959) and Klami's. His production is still relatively small, consisting in the first place of two chamber pieces, *Music for String Orchestra* (1957) and *Sinfonia da camera* (1962), of two symphonies (1960, 1961), and of an *a cappella* Mass. All are characterized by sound contrapuntal technique; the expressive value of the details is subordinate, at least in the symphonies, to architectural force and line. But it must be admitted that people in other Scandinavian countries have found it difficult to understand Kokkonen's central position in Finland. Perhaps the matter must be regarded from a specifically Finnish point of view. In the first place, a melodic purity in his compositional technique and a harsh, even heavy, classicism (which at certain points recall Bartók) can have been regarded as a cleansing of the often rather porous — for all its sonority — Finnish compositional tradition. And in the second place, one finds an introverted poetic feeling in the symphonies, especially, and a strain of nature mysticism (but not nature painting) that may bring Sibelius to mind.

Erkki Salmenhaara is another Finnish composer who has drawn attention in recent years with a symphonic work that recalls Sibelius. The relation of his Second Symphony (1963) to Sibelius was dis-

---

[1] He had then almost as many teachers as Karkoff: Aarre Merikanto in Helsinki, Wladimir Vogel, Sessions, Copland, Persichetti, etc.

cussed in *Helsingin Sanomat* by a Sibelius specialist and professor of musicology, Erik Tawaststjerna. The work was placed closer than any other in Finnish composition to Sibelius's Fourth Symphony — though Salmenhaara employs a technique with cluster-like sound, and he does not supply what is customarily regarded as organic symphonic development. Tawaststjerna, too, brought up that "distant landscape." To an outsider, it seems that he may have fallen victim to a certain national suggestion. But his remarks on the Sibelian tradition in general were more important:

> Actually, no deep, essential influence of Sibelius has as yet been found, either in Finnish or in any other music, with the possible exception of Vaughan Williams's work. It has been enough to repeat some harmonic and melodic turns of musical phrase, which when used by the master have a Sibelian charm, but which belong to the outer layer of his nature. His regenerating symphonic thought, his integration of large forms and an organically growing texture have not been continued by anyone because such a symphonic line has not been touched by the musical impulsions current during the first half of the 20th century.

As for Salmenhaara, he wrote his symphony after occupying himself in recent works with aleatory and electronic devices. But, even when one takes these pieces into consideration, among young Finnish musicians Salmenhaara is one of those most conscious of tradition and best schooled in composition.

The group to which he belongs have not chosen to hide their lamps under bushels; they have displayed them in the marketplace with an engaging impudence. Their number includes, along with Salmenhaara, Henrik Otto Donner (b. 1913), who is active also as a jazz musician, Kari Rydman (b. 1936), a music pedagogue and writer, Reijo Jyrki-äinen (b. 1934), who is a music technician at Radio Finland, and Ilkka Kuusisto (b. 1935). A music critic, Kaj Chydenius (b. 1939), serves as particular spokesman of the group.

The Norwegian-Finnish number of *Nutida musik* contains (pp. 47-52) a contribution from Chydenius where the young Finnish composers speak for themselves. The following statements will give an idea of their esthetic and way of working.

Donner: Ken Dewey [a theater man from San Francisco who occupies himself with "happenings"] has taught me to perceive the importance of traveling a great deal, of proceeding from — and adapting oneself to — various situations in different countries, of working efficiently in the surroundings where a piece of music will be realized . . . For me music does not exist in absolute form, but only in combination with other forms of communication . . . European music means relatively little to me. The United States and Russia are highly topical

. . . In Charles Ives I have experienced a composer who has not locked himself into any ostensible logic or any system . . . The Soviet Union is about equally interesting. There are Russian composers who write oratorios in praise of work, to the welfare of astronauts, etc. — which is to say that they write music organically connected to society and, what may be more important, music that has a public.

Jyrkiäinen: In contrast to my colleagues in Finland, I believe that the Darmstadt courses have lost much of their original significance . . . Above all, I appreciate the series of analyses made by Pierre Boulez and György Ligeti; they are among the most important ones in the study of modern music.

Kuusisto: A "church-like organ style" is a lie. The only possibility of a living organ tradition lies in music that has contact with other compositional currents of the time. At present, I receive scarcely any stimuli either from Finnish colleagues or from foreign injectors of ideas. I am still waiting for a very simple music; after the extreme complexity of recent times, such music ought soon to have its day.

Rydman: For me music is only an acoustical form of art, nothing more. Thus far, I have no interest in mastering the whole "apparatus" that can be regarded as having influence on the experience of music.

The last pronouncement should probably be considered a criticism of such forms as "happenings" and of attempts to blast away the boundaries of music by improvising combinations of speech, music, scenic action, and so on. Differences of opinion among these young composers seem to be relatively great. And the young Finns must be still more widely ranged when one takes into consideration three who write in traditional style. Paavo Heinninen (b. 1938) was a pupil of the Juilliard School. In such works as *Petite symphonie joyeuse* (1962) he reveals a rather splintered compositional style. Usko Meriläinen (b. 1930) was a pupil of Vogel. He writes effective instrumental music — for example, in his ballet *Cortège of the Reed-Pipe* (1961) and in a Chamber Concerto for Violin (1962). Aulis Sallinen (b. 1935) has the most personal and expressive style of the three, as may be judged from his *Mauermusik* (1962), inspired by the Berlin crisis.

Among those works from the radical group that deserve special mention are the Sonata II by Rydman, an unconventional piece of "beautiful" music, sensuously romantic in sound, structurally simple, and Donner's *For Emy 2,* for a chamber ensemble, with vocalists and loud speakers, the most discussed of the Finnish "Gesamtkunstwerk," with groups of musicians moving among or behind the public, etc. Both works were written in 1963.

Kenneth Dewey and the activating effect of "happenings" presented in Jyväskylä and Helsinki — also in Stockholm and Lund, the university town of southern Sweden — have had an effect on many younger Scandinavian musicians. Two like-minded and stimulating Swedes have been particularly engaged: Jan Bark (b. 1934) and Folk Rabe (b. 1935).

Both of them are jazz trombonists and both have had a strict technical training at the Academy of Music in Stockholm, where Blomdahl, Ligeti, and Lidholm were among their teachers. One clearly perceives their training in the way they handle form and the tight structure they employ in the original work they wrote together, *Bolos,* for four trombones (1962; ISCM 1964). Of course the means are unusual. And the piece finally dissolves into musical theater. It can best be described as a dynamic and richly faceted investigation into the range and possibilities of the trombone. The instruments are used percussively; sound emerges only from the mouthpiece, and so on. Varèse is brought to mind, but where color and dynamism are concerned the compositional teaching of György Ligeti has been of influence. One may add that the two young composers adopt an extremely critical attitude towards the Darmstadt school of the 'fifties.

These amelodic and arhythmic tendencies came very clearly to light at the school for young composers that the Academy of Music, Radio Sweden, and STIM (the Swedish composers' organization) arranged jointly in the spring of 1963. Though not without frenzied protests from members of the orchestra, six young composers were there allowed to display their works — which included Bark's orchestral piece *Pyknos* (1962), and *Collage* for orchestra (1962) by Arne Mellnäs (b. 1933), who is also a pupil of Blomdahl and Ligeti. The means employed by Mellnäs are more traditional than those of Bark's "sound symphony"; one can hear in *Collage* the earlier influence of Schoenberg on the composer. Probably the title indicates a certain conscious stratifying of different styles.

Two other young composers should be mentioned. They are both pupils of Lidholm, but are very different in temperament: Jan W. Morthenson (b. 1940) and Karl-Erik Welin (b. 1934). Morthenson, a sensitive creator of sound, is a purist. When his orchestral piece *Coloratura II* — which uses a cultivated and "one-dimensional" cluster technique — was given a studio performance, he declared in the program:

For me the sovereignty of music is damaged and transgressed as long as music functions as a reproductive art. I believe that it is foreign to its nature that it should have a social or moralistic function. However, many composers — Nono, for example — use music as if it had, and it is illuminating of their difficulties that in many cases they must have recourse to "concrete" material: text. Personally, every form of illustrative music is wholly alien to me; vocal music, theater and film music, etc.

In the light of Morthenson's esthetic, Welin appears to be an ecstatic, hyperemotional musical interpreter. His few compositions have not as yet allowed his qualities to become as evident as they are in his work as a pianist and organist. He is, meanwhile, the foremost exponent in Scandinavia of musical theater. He has little interest in such an improvised and often "dilettantish" form as "happenings"; always he seems an artist of exclusive tastes who estimates fully his means. As an organist, he has — along with Hambraeus — made a significant contribution to the formation of a radical organ style, one as far from attemptedly neo-Baroque church music as can be imagined. Characteristic works in the style are Hambraeus's *Constellations,* Ligeti's *Volumina,* Maurice Kagel's *Ajoutée,* Morthenson's *Some of These* and *Pour Madame Bovary.* Cluster technique is a trait throughout; the "chord" is always the same, but the form grows forth through changeable registration and a dynamic crescendo.

The esthetic boundary lines lie far apart in music by young Swedish composers, if their attempts at coming to terms with traditional ways of writing and of execution supply a common denominator. Lars Johan Werle (b. 1926) has transferred such attempts to the stage in an arena opera, *Drömmen om Thérèse (The Dream about Thérèse,* 1964, with text by Lars Runsten after Zola's *Thérèse Raquin).* Ake Hermanson (b. 1923) has capsuled the strivings for new form into a structural block of inaccessible expressiveness that leaps heavily forward.

As yet there are few electronic works in Scandinavian music, largely because most productions of the kind have had to be realized abroad: in Cologne (Hambraeus, Bo Nilsson, Morthenson), in Milan (Hambraeus), in Bilthoven (Mellnäs), in Munich (Hambraeus), etc.

Where production at home is concerned, Radio Sweden has temporarily made apparatus and technicians available for the tape-recording of Blomdahl's *Aniara* and Lidholm's *Riter (Rites).* Fylkingen is the concert association of Stockholm most deeply engaged; and its chairman, Knut Wiggen (b. 1927), is the force behind the movement. At the end of the 'fifties a smaller technical studio was set up, with the aid of ABF (the Workers' Educational Organization), the aim being primarily pedagogical. This studio has now been dismantled but the setting up of a modern technical studio at Radio Sweden has now been entrusted to Wiggen and to Tage Westlund, an acoustical expert. It should be ready in 1966.

The difficulties of production have not meant any falling-off in the supply of information about electronic music. Fylkingen — and also the Swedish radio — present yearly a good deal of the work created in other European countries and in Japanese studios. Non-stop concerts given by Fylkingen in the Modern Museum have been an original and valued form of presentation. And in March 1963 a special electronic festival was arranged, in connection with a conference attended by specialists from the whole of Europe (Warsaw, Paris, etc).

During the "Scandinavian Music Days" held in Stockholm in 1960, a number of compositions — from other Scandinavian countries as well as Sweden — were presented; and at the same time *Nutida musik* published a short history and survey of the current situation, *Nordiska klangexperiment (Scandinavian Sound Experiment)*. From this it appeared that in Denmark electronic music could be produced at the Danish radio, as was done by Else Mari Pade (b. 1930), and in a private studio set up by Jørgen Plaetner (b. 1930); in Norway it was necessary to use private means of production (Sönstevold). In Finland, the radio station of Helsinki formerly made apparatus available (for pieces by Bengt Johansson and Jyrkiäinen), but for some years there has been a special studio in an institute of musical science at the university. Erkki Kurreniemi (b. 1941) is in charge.

Cage and the Korean Paik have aroused debate with performances in the Scandinavian capitals. Moreover, a German group, "Fluxus," has performed in Copenhagen. Waves of controversy have rolled high: the attitude to Cage has become more understanding; the reaction to Fluxus is directly negative. Fluxus and Paik reflect an anarchistic element that may have a genuine place in culture generally, but which is so very much on the periphery of musical composition that, comprehensibly, musicians have often been the least interested auditors.

If a greater impression has been made by these figures in Copenhagen, that may be explained by the Danish pleasure in public debate, and also by a certain inflexibility, an absence of joyous discovery, in the Danish tradition. During the 'fifties, many visions of the future formed in the 'twenties had become realities, but at the same time a certain stability hampered development. The rather academic tradition has been so strong that attempts to break out of it have at times seemed desperate. Something of the feeling involved may be found in a composer as eminent as Niels Viggo Bentzon — for example, in his cantata *Bonjour, Max Ernst.*

As, during the latter half of the 'fifties, interest grew in ideas of the avant-garde, certain composers who had hitherto been passed over were "discovered." One of these was Gunnar Berg (b. 1909). He lived for a long time in Paris; while there, he was deeply impressed by Messiaen's techniques — as may be seen from such works of his own as the piano cycle *Gaffky's* (1958-59). Another such composer was Axel Borup-Jörgensen (b. 1924; a Dane, but brought up in Sweden). His *Music for Percussion and Viola* (1955-56) and his orchestral piece *Cretaufoni* (1960-61) bear witness to an expressive talent and an imagination that blasts tradition. Earlier, works by Fleming Weis had been diverting in the classical manner, but later he evidenced an interest in new techniques — for instance, in his piano piece *Tolv monologer* (*Twelve Monologues,* 1958) and *Femdelt form* (*Form Divided in Five,* 1961). But, more particularly, one finds such interest in Bernhard Lewkowitch (b. 1927). After early piano works in the style of Prokofiev and Bentzon, and then, in the middle of the 'fifties, pastorally mild choral pieces, he was inspired by Stravinsky's serial work; one may note this in *Cantata sacra,* for a voice and six instruments (1959; ISCM 1960). Later, he moved into the experimental region with several *a cappella* works, among them *Improperier* (1961; ISCM 1963). Bengt Johnsson wrote: "Spoken choruses are used, with free declamation and an 'open' form; the improvisational character in execution gives a beautiful touch of the ecstatic, the inexplicable, altogether allied with the spirit of the great holiday."

The two composers who can be called pioneers of radicalism are Jan Maegaard (b. 1926) and Per Nørgaard (b. 1932). Both might be said to have "gone the long way round." They began to compose in a style and a spirit close to the Danish tradition. But at a fairly early stage, Maegaard — who is a musicologist with a strong interest in theory and an authoritative knowledge of Schoenberg's works — began to inform the Danish public about stylistic developments on the Continent. Meanwhile, one can follow how these were reflected in his compositions. One finds twelve-tone technique in such works as *Jaevndøgnselegier* (*Equinox-Elegies,* 1955), for soprano, cello, and organ; in certain portions of *Due tempi* (1959) the structure is pointillistically broken to pieces in a manner inspired by Webern; there is experimentation with "open forms" in Maegaard's Second Chamber Concerto (1962), and its instrumentation recalls the Pole Penderecki.

Maegaard has written a book on *Musikalsk modernisme* (*Musical Modernism,* Copenhagen, 1964); this contains an up-to-date description of musical developments; it covers broadly the last decade, and deals with such ideas as "static form," "variable form," "chance music," etc.

During the latter half of the 'fifties, Maegaard was fervently active in *DUT,* which is the Danish association of young composers and virtually identical with the Danish section of ISCM. It is also the Copenhagen equivalent of Fylkingen — with a slight difference. While in Stockholm interest has centered as a rule round certain ideas, *DUT* has directed its energies primarily at giving concerts of modern Danish music.

The other "radical pioneer" mentioned, Per Nørgaard, drew attention when he was still in his twenties. He was then a pupil of Holmboe, and his compositional ideal was closely related to his teacher's. Later, in 1956-57, he studied with Nadia Boulanger. (One may note that she also had Rovsing Olsen as a pupil, and that her *solfège* inspired Jersild's method of listening.) A very typical example of Nørgaard's work is his *Triptychon* for mixed choir and orchestra (without strings, 1957).

Already then, Nørgaard appears to have begun the work that constitutes his first really important attempt at breaking away from tradition: *Konstellationer* for twelve string instruments or string groups (1955-58; ISCM 1959). Rhythmically, but not melodically, this is organized on serial lines. Nørgaard's imagination was further liberated by intensive study of Webern, Boulez, Nono, and others. This liberation caused him to turn in two directions: towards an exclusive sort of music and towards a pedagogical kind.

In the one direction, Nørgaard wrote his poetically beautiful chamber-orchestra songs *Tre nocturner* (1961-62; on Danish translations of Japanese poems) and an orchestral piece, *Fragment VI* (1961; ISCM 1964), so overpowering that some listeners regarded it as more noise than composition. In the other, he has followed closely the conscientious pedagogical ideals for which Jørgen Bentzon and Høffding strove earlier. In a personal way, he revived the matter of putting easily played and easily sung music on a modern stylistic basis. One of the methods by which he arouses his pupils' feeling for improvisation is to give a singer and an instrumentalist some simple musical form; this they are to imbue with pulsing life while preserving the "normal" musical elements. His technique is illustrated in Ex. 5, which derives from the introduction to *Dommen* (*The Judgment,* 1961-62), a version of the Passion for school use, and the most substantial work of those with a pedagogical aim produced thus far in Denmark.

Ex. 5

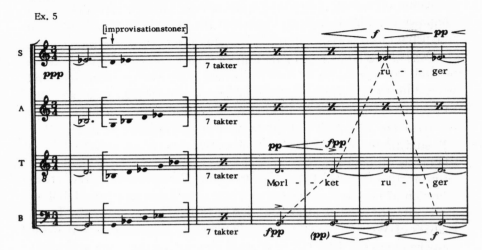

Yet another pair of young composers should be named: Ib Nørholm and Pelle Gudmundsen-Holmgreen — one born in 1931 and the other in 1932.

Nørholm's development recalls Nørgaard's. He, too, is a pupil of Holmboe, and he sought new paths at about the same time. (The ISCM festival of 1959, in Rome, provided much stimulus.) The first important work that followed is *Kenotafium* (*The Cenotaph*, 1960-61), which in parts contains fresh and subtle coloristic experiments. The range is still wider in *Relief I-II* (1961-63; inspired by Asger Jorn's reliefs in Aarhus City Hall). The composer works with structures on different levels — the "relief" idea. But the most noteworthy feature is the orchestration: col legno effects, banking of sound, string glissando, an unusually well-utilized treble register, etc. There is, Nørholm has said in a radio interview, "a cult of instruments that often gets in the way of inventing sound." Certainly, his *Reliefs* belong to the most interesting works in Scandinavian music as far as sound is concerned. Another piece of his — for solo violinist (but not solo violin), presented at a special Danish concert during the ISCM festival of 1964 — shows that he has been in creative contact with the musical theater and with neo-Dada.

As for Gudmundsen-Holmgreen, he has also become a researcher into the possibilities of sound. In 1960, after some student works in traditional style, he composed *Two Improvisations* for ten instruments, for which the closest model is the pointillistic style of the 'fifties in

German and French music. Two years later, there came a *Second Collegium Musicum Concerto;* with only a chamber orchestra, the composer develops a strikingly bold sort of color; there are shrill wind and percussion effects in heavy, brutally accentuated, dissonant blocks of chords. Yet, in spite of all this, there is nothing desperate in the musical expression. As in Varèse's music, one finds a life force that attracts in a positive and desirable way.

What the next step will be in musical development is up to those still studying composition at the Scandinavian academies of music. There, as throughout the musical world of the West, tensions are disturbingly many. Students travel directly from elementary *solfège* collection at home to seminaries of Cologne or Darmstadt where teaching is directed at experiment; or perhaps they leave strictly academic analyses of Webern in order to spend evenings with Cage, Tudor, and Rauschenberg. Of what value, in their situation, is the traditional compositional schooling? And is the teacher who demands a sound understanding of Palestrina's counterpoint and of classical twelve-tone technique helplessly stuck in an out-of-date sort of instruction? Ought he to give up all that and establish himself as an experiment leader?

No answers to these questions hold good in all circumstances. But in Scandinavian composition they have an interest that is not only pedagogical and artistic but also historical. The questions can now be asked as if geographical distance no longer existed; the world-perspective has caused national music to disappear from view. The future will show whether or not it has vanished for good.

SOME REFERENCE MATERIALS

DENMARK

A survey of Danish, and Scandinavian, music will be found in *Vår tids konst och diktning i Skandinavien* (*Contemporary Art and Poetry in Scandinavia*). Here is a selection of other important works: Richard Hove's *Försög på en musikalsk status* (*Attempt at a Musical Status*), in *Nordisk tidskrift för vetenskap, konst och industri,* 1948, Nos. 27, 28; Vagn Holmboe's *Strejflys over nogle problemer i dansk musik* (*Light on Some Problems in Danish Musik*), in the Swedish publication *Prisma,* 1952, No. 2; the Denmark chapter, contributed by Frede Schandorf Petersen, in *Ny musik in Norden* (*New Music in the North*), Stockholm, 1953; the documentary work *Modern nordisk musik,* ed. by Ingmar Bengtsson, Stockholm, 1957; *Modern Music in Scandinavia* by Bo Wallner, in Howard Hartog's *Music in the Twentieth Century,* London, 1957; *Musikkens veje* by Nils Schiørring, Copenhagen, 1959; the collective volume *La Vie musicale au Danemark,* published in Copenhagen, 1962, for *La Commission permanente des expositions à la Maison du Danemark à Paris;* a special Danish number of the Swedish publication *Nutida musik* (1962-63, No. 5); John Horton's *Scandinavian Music: a Short History,* New York, 1963. — The leading reference books for information concerning Danish composition are *Aschehougs musiklexikon* (a two-volume musical dictionary), Copenhagen, 1957; and *Musikkens hvem hvad hvor? (Who's Who in Music),* also in two volumes, Nos. 255 and 256 in Politiken's handbook series, Copenhagen, 1961. This contains full lists of works. Another useful reference book is Jurgen Balzar's *Bibliografi over dansk komponister (Bibliography of Danish Composers),* Copenhagen, 1932. — The most important Danish publication devoted to music is *Dansk musiktidskrift* (founded in 1925). — As for gramophone records, while there was a large production earlier of 78 rpm records, that of LPs is smaller than in the other Scandinavian countries. A selected discography can be found in the number of *Nutida musik* mentioned above. The Danish radio has a relatively large archive of Danish music on tape recordings. A series of music publications was started in 1871 by the society *Samfundet til udgivelse af dansk musik,* and during recent years these publications have been combined with gramophone recordings. There is no large archive containing scores of contemporary Danish music, but information can be obtained through the two associations of composers, *Dansk komponistforening* and that of the younger composers, *DUT* (or *Det unge Tonekunstnerselskab*), also through the music library of the ⟨Danish radio.

FINLAND

The most important archive for the study of modern Finnish music is possessed by the Town Orchestra and the Finnish radio, both in Helsinki. Further material is in the hands of TEOSTO, the office that handles the economic interests of the Finnish composers' society and of the Sibelius Museum at Turku. — The most important recordings are on *Fennica.* — Some surveys are *Suomen säveltaide (Finnish Musical Composition),* Helsinki, 1940; Nils Eric Ringbom's *Skapande tonkonst i dagens Finland (Musical Composition in the Finland of Today),* in *Nordisk tidskrift för vetenskap, konst och industri,* 1948; and Veikko Helasvuo's chapter on Finland in *Ny musik i Norden,* p. 43 ff. (with a short bibliography). He has also written a book on *Sibelius and the Music of Finland,* Helsinki, 1952. — The radio has an archive with tape-recordings of representative works.

NORWAY

The most important archives are the Norwegian music collection of the university libraries of Oslo and Tono, the Norwegian equivalents to KODA, TEOSTO, and STIM. However, as a rule the composers keep their works themselves. Consequently, it is difficult to survey their production. But information about works is given in programs of Oslo's Philharmonic Society. — A representative collection of Norwegian music is recorded as *Classics of Norway* on Philips (A 631 096 — 631 099 L). The sleeves provide relatively full commentaries on the works. A rather extensive archive of tape-recordings is to be found at Norsk Rikskringkasting (the Norwegian Radio) in Oslo. — The most up-to-date surveys are Pauline Hall's contribution on Norwegian music in *Vår tids konst och diktning i Skandinavien;* the Norwegian chapter in *Ny musik i Norden,* p. 69 ff., by Olav Gurvin; Kristian Lange's and Arne Østvedt's *Norwegian*

Music, London, 1958; and Gunnar Rugstad's *Dyrkelse av det genuine* (*Worship of the Genuine*) in the special Norwegian-Finnish number (1963-64, No. 5) of the Swedish publication *Nutida musik*. — One may consult also Guavin's and Anker's musical dictionary *Musikkleksikon*, 2nd ed., Oslo, 1959; and the Swedish reference books *Sohlmans musiklexikon*, Stockholm, 1948-52, and *Tonkonsten*, Stockholm, 1955-57. — The most important publishers are Musikk-huset, Norsk Musikforlag, and Edition Lyche.

SWEDEN

Source material for modern Swedish musical history is in part the same as that for the other Scandinavian countries. Besides Horton's *Scandinavian Music*, *Ny Musik i Norden*, and *Vår tids konst och dikning i Skandinavien*, one should mention Ingmar Bengtsson's *Den nya svenska musikens bakgrund* (*Background to the New Swedish Music*), in *Nordisk tidskrift för vetenskap, konst och industri*, 1951, pp. 297-307, and by the same author and in the same publication, pp. 428-50, *Den nya svenska musiken* (*The New Swedish Music*); still by Ingmar Bengtsson, *Schwedische Musik des 20. Jahrhunderts*, in *Melos*, 1956, pp. 338-42; and special English-language numbers of *Musikrevy: Music in the North*, 1951; *Music in Sweden*, 1954; and *Sweden in Music*, 1960. These contain a number of articles in English translation about composers mentioned here. As sources of information, the two musical dictionaries, *Sohlmans*, Stockholm, 1948-52, and *Tonkonsten*, Stockholm, 1955-57, are invaluable; so also are Åke Davidson's *Svensk musiklitteratur 1800-1945*, Upsala, 1948 (the work lists 5,432 titles), and the yearbooks and newspaper bibliographies of STIM. Since 1956 these have provided annual lists of Swedish music production. — Sweden is better supplied than the other Scandinavian countries with archives of modern music. The most important ones are the Library of the Royal Academy of Music (*Kungl. Musikaliska Akademiens Bibliotek*), the Music Library of Radio Sweden (*Sveriges Radios musikbibliotek*), and the music library of STIM, which contains an almost complete collection of Swedish works from this century not made available by a music publisher. The Museum of Musical History (*Musikhistoriska museet*) has primarily archives of clippings; historical archives of Swedish music are now built up there. Valuable material may be found also in archives of the Stockholm Philharmonic Society (*Stockholms Konsertförening*) and the Royal Theater. All of these are in Stockholm. — Radio Sweden and STIM have representative collections of tape-recordings, and Radio Sweden possesses also a complete collection of Swedish music recorded for the gramophone. — The leading music publishers are *Nordiska musikförlaget* (which publishes works of Rosenberg, Nystroem, Bäck, Bo Nilsson, and Morthenson, among others) and *Gehrmans musikförlag* (which publishes, among others, Larsson and Wirén).

(Translated by W. G. Simpson)

ENTR'ACTE: "FORMAL" OR "INFORMAL" MUSIC?

By DANIEL CHARLES

O NE of the possible criteria by which to characterize the different avant-garde composers in France is their attitude towards John Cage's music.

Xenakis is doubtless the most favorably inclined; in an article published in 1962, he criticized the poetics of the "open work" developed by the "neo-serialists" in recent times. However, he took care to add the following paragraph:

> Still, this meaningless attitude can only be valid in one case. To destroy consciousness and let the deeper strata of the psyche emerge in unreasoned acts is a fascinating thing, which, however, ought to be supplemented by yoga conceptions on the mastery of the reflexes, etc. This path, which John Cage, Earle Brown, and David Tudor have opened up in music, is related to the attempts in certain paintings and poems. It is fraught with promises for a future that will have to produce the integration of conscious and subconscious reason into a harmonious whole that has long been lost.[1]

But this paragraph disappeared when the article was reproduced, and considerably enlarged, in *Musiques formelles*.[2] Apart from Xenakis (and Messiaen, a prudent admirer of the prepared piano), French musicians have reacted to Cage with little more than a mass of indignation, not to say hostility.

Boulez was the first to react, in *Aléa*,[3] against what he called "chance by inadvertence." Since then, his stock of denigration has not run dry; I have seen him lead a riot, at Darmstadt, against a piece by La Monte

[1] In C. Samuel, *Panorama de l'art musical contemporain*, Paris, 1962, pp. 416-25.
[2] *La Revue musicale*, Nos. 253-254, 1963, p. 52.
[3] A famous article published in the *Nouvelle revue française* in 1957.

144

Young.[4] And, in the work he recently published under the title *Penser la musique aujourd'hui,* one may find a little anthology of his recriminations.[5]

In 1958 I went to Brussels, in connection with the Exposition ("the shop window of the universal economy," as Heinz-Klaus Metzger put it[6]), to accompany Pierre Schaeffer in my capacity of member of the Groupe de Musique Expérimentale ("musique concrète") of the French radio and television network. I had been at a Cage concert, after which the Canadian composer Gilles Tremblay and I had the misfortune of manifesting our approval of *Winter Music.* "You must choose," Schaeffer immediately exclaimed, "between Cage and the Studio."

Finally, in a recent polemic that appeared in the *Mercure de France,* Gilbert Amy (who speaks the language of orthodox neo-serialism pretty accurately) and François Mâche (a fugitive from "musique concrète" who nevertheless claims to adhere more or less to Xenakis) were able to agree on one point alone: that the primacy of writing, or "graphisme," as conceived by Cage is unacceptable.[7]

Even if all this mistrust does fluctuate — *Music of Changes* has been given a hearing at the Domaine Musical, and François Bayle has done a great deal to keep Cage's ideas from being ignored in Parisian musical life — the general climate until now has been one of hostility.

It is not my intention to go into the reasons why this ostracism has taken root and, on the whole, maintained itself. I have only mentioned the matter the better to obtain a detached view of recent musical *mores* in France. One may nevertheless say that each man's conception of music history — and of the role he would like to play in it — is the factor that determines his reactions to Cage. The latter's works are only known very imperfectly, but their reputation appears to be established: their composer is thought a visionary, and his productions are considered teratological in that they blindly deny, or seem to deny, all historicity, all relationships to contemporary musical "evolution."

This situation has not escaped Cage himself. No doubt the average avant-garde musician in France resembles his Dutch confrere — at least, if one is to believe this passage from *Silence:*

[4] Played by David Tudor Sept. 6, 1961.

[5] Paris, 1964.

[6] *Hommage à Edgard Varèse,* French transl. in *Lettre ouverte,* No. 3, Oct. 1961, p. 34.

[7] *Le Son et la musique* (F.-B. Mâche, Nov. 1963); *A propos du son et de la musique* (G. Amy, March 1964; with a reply by F.-B. Mâche).

Once in Amsterdam, a Dutch musician said to me, "It must be very difficult for you in America to write music, for you are so far away from the centers of tradition." I had to say, "It must be very difficult for you in Europe to write music, for you are so close to the centers of tradition."[8]

In Boulez, the master of the evolutionary mode of thinking, one finds this concern over loyalty to the Western heritage developed to the highest degree, in the guise of an irrepressible penchant for craftsmanship, for the finely wrought work, for the severity of the finished product. It is as though he had taken an ethical vow, intrinsic to his esthetics; he has often admitted to it.[9] Everything must be structured, everything is finely chiseled in the end: that is why his writings allot so much space to technique and risk being mistaken for catalogues of recipes, if the reader is not on his guard.[10] That is also why, until recently, they manifested such reserve regarding form: before arriving at a renewal of form, it was necessary, after all, to erect a morphology, to build a syntax — so that the forms themselves were craftsmanlike, the direct results of technical manipulations; it is no insult to the composer of *Marteau sans maître* to state that in *Structure 1 a,* for example, form as such does not exist, that it is nothing more than an assemblage of parts, that it is simply the result of a handling of parameters. Similarly, Boulez's writings remained reticent on the question of form — almost in the manner of the most "oriental" of French musicians, Messiaen — up to *Sonate que me veux-tu?*,[11] where one learns that "music is at present in possession of a wide range of means, of a vocabulary that once more attains a universality of conception and of understanding" — which ought to make it possible to tackle "a considerable need: that of thinking through the whole notion of form again."[12]

Progress, for what we may by now refer to as the earlier Boulez, consisted in the attempt to achieve an exact notation; that achievement would signify the regression to the polished, fetishistic object — the concentration of research to a purely stylistic domain. And if this is no longer quite his position today, the reason is not so much that "the essential part of the discoveries has been attained"[13] and one may now look to more comprehensive, if not noble, tasks, as that the work itself

[8] P. 73.

[9] Especially in *L'Esthétique et les fétiches,* in C. Samuel, *op. cit.,* pp. 402-03.

[10] Cf. *Penser la musique aujourd'hui,* p. 166.

[11] Commentary on the Third Sonata, published in *Médiations,* No. 7, Spring 1964, pp. 61-75.

[12] *Ibid.,* pp. 62-63.

[13] *Ibid.,* p. 62.

somehow demands to be articulated in a more supple manner — **like a "labyrinth."**[14]

What about this articulation, whose literary references (Mallarmé, Joyce) must not allow us to forget its strictly musical function?

The Third Sonata, as Metzger has remarked, seems quite the opposite of an "aleatory" work:

They all wrote, and write, particularly the famous senior critics of the leading newspapers, about aleatoric forms, when they are thinking of Stockhausen's eleventh piano piece and Boulez' third piano sonata . . . The forgotten definition is: "Aleatoric processes are those whose course is determined as a whole but whose individual details depend on chance." The formal course of the two works for which they have coined their catchword is, however, the exact opposite: as a whole it is the result of chance, whereas the individual details are determined.[15]

"Aleatoric," here, stands for the opposite of what industrial society produces as semi-finished objects: its finish, on the contrary, is meticulously careful; the point is to exclude "chance by inadvertence" as practiced by amateurs; the craftsmanship must be scrupulously respected. Chance, as it is employed in the Third Sonata, will be "domesticated"; the result, the score (antipodal to the notion of the "ready-made"), will constitute a work that is "open, but a work."[16]

And so, if articulation becomes more fluid, this does not mean that detail is left to improvisation. And the fluidity itself is the token of a stricter control on the part of the creator over his product: far from being weakened, the formal order must find itself reinforced. "Form acquires its autonomy, tends towards an absolute it has never known before; it rejects the intrusion of the purely personal accident."[17]

This is enough to place the protestations of "Orientalism"[18] by a man like Boulez back in their proper perspective: the "rejection of accident" — the search for the essence — looks to us like a typically Western procedure, an avatar of medieval craftsmanship — exactly the opposite of Japanese craftsmanship, for example, which, in producing the humblest object, concerns itself with accident *per se* and is imbued with the respect due to the lines of stress of the material. Again, Boulez's quest, unlike that of a Messiaen, sacrifices "nature" to "culture"; it gives itself up systematically to the delights of the artificial — let this be said without the slightest pejorative intent.

---

[14] *Ibid.*, p. 64.

[15] Heinz-Klaus Metzger, *Abortive Concepts in the Theory and Criticism of Music*, in *Die Reihe*, No. 5: *Reports/Analyses*, Byrn Mawr, 1961, p. 26.

[16] In the words of Umberto Eco.

[17] *Sonate que me veux-tu?*, p. 75.

[18] Which are expressed in a particularly significant fashion *ibid.*, p. 64.

Loyalty to the work as "category" explains the concern with con-
striction and unity in an entity such as *Pli selon pli*. The more a work
is unified, under the very guise of a labyrinth, the more it will be
capable of reflecting the demands and, above all, the hand, the
personal touch, of its creator; artistic craftsmanship, as a result, becomes a de luxe activity. Elegance, for the artist, will certainly consist
in hiding behind a veil of anonymity: with Mallarmé or Joyce, the
text becomes "anonymous," notes Boulez, "since it speaks of itself,
without an author's voice." "If it were necessary," he adds, "to find
a deep motivation for the work I have attempted to describe, it would
be the search for such an 'anonymity.' "[19] But this perfect impersonality
bears an implicit signature.

More generally, the composer will not in the least be prevented
from being irrational; in Boulez's writings one could find a whole
mythology of the imagination.[20] The latter, however, is never synonymous
with relaxation, with letting oneself go; least of all must it be a
"mistress of error." To make a list of the errors that occur in the
transcription of the serial grilles in *Structure 1 a* would therefore not be
a sacrilege at all:[21] the actual work of composing, Stockhausen has said,
begins only *after* that transcription — and what is more, nobody has
ever complained of those errors at a performance. If Boulez's works
have become increasingly "open," therefore, this has been in order
that they might be less "aleatory." The "opening," whatever the literary
pretext, matches in this sense the purely musical discovery of the need
to "animate" the forms — to convert them from their former static
condition to a dynamic one — or again, to breathe a soul into scores
that, like school exercises, seemed unconscious of themselves. Just as
"the novel . . . looks on itself as such, reflects itself, is conscious that it
is a novel," so music "must become conscious of itself, must become
the proper object of its own reflection."[22] The completion of the creative
process demands that the created object be "an object in itself," an
organism and not an assemblage, a *Gestalt* that is moving and at the
same time perfectly controlled — for the author's will is obliterated and
blurred only in appearance. The creator is not really himself unless
he has been able to transmit life.

[19] *Ibid.*, p. 75.
[20] Cf. for example *Penser la musique aujourd'hui*, pp. 166-67. And especially
Nécessité d'une orientation esthétique, in *Mercure de France*, April-May 1964, pp.
624-39 and 110-22.
[21] As it is called in *Penser la musique aujourd'hui*, p. 42.
[22] *Sonate . . .* , p. 62.

In this one sees the fundamental difference that is doubtless at the root of Boulez's mistrust for the procedures of a man like Cage. "The European works present a harmoniousness, a drama, or a poetry which, referring more to their composers than to their hearers, moves in directions not shared by the American ones. Many of the American works envisage each auditor as central . . ."[23] In Boulez's eyes, it would be inconceivable for the creator to descend from his pedestal; to be sure, his mailed fist will not relent with regard to the work, but it will (in a temporary way) with regard to the performer, whose duty it is to convey, as rigorously as before, what has once and for all been decided.

It is hardly surprising, in the circumstances, that Boulez's teachings have become so widely disseminated. Since he proclaims the author's right of property over his own work more loudly than anyone else, he is followed by the great pack of the solipsists. Messiaen's culture and generosity may be fascinating, but they remain inimitable; Boulez's vivacity and sureness, on the other hand, are astonishing, but they earn him a cohort of imitators. Besides, a good many of his polemics reveal — in spite of his most explicit denials — an odd propensity to chastise publicly disciples, epigones, or followers who, for the most part, were never taught or chosen by him. A part of his prestige, to be sure, comes from his organizing talent — he was able, after all, to dispel singlehandedly the silence that reigned in Paris with regard to the Viennese School and all those who followed Webern. The Domaine Musical has propagated a great many unexpected — and unheard — scores; but the main point has been the opinionated affirmation of a veritable ethics of creation, the systematic refusal "to confuse the value of a work, or its immediate novelty, with its eventual power to fertilize."[24]

This is why the most remarkable musical event of the past year in Paris, in our opinion, was the publication — and in a paperback series — of the work we have already mentioned several times, Penser la musique aujourd'hui, a collection of lectures delivered at Darmstadt in 1960, in which we believe the very essence of Boulez's teachings is expressed.

That essence is systematic in spirit: let us skip the partial speculations, in which it is so easy to get entangled (pp. 26-27); what we must view is the totality, the compositional process as a whole.

[23] John Cage, Silence, Middletown, Conn., 1961, p. 53.
[24] Penser la musique aujourd'hui, p. 14.

There is no "natural law" in music, Adorno has said. Boulez's idea is noticeably similar: in music, just as in physics, we find no "laws of nature" to lean on.

"Nature" having been exorcised, what remains, in art, if not tradition? Whether he is for or against tradition, it is nevertheless the creator's function to take a position on the matter. And what is tradition in music, if not one of *techniques* or *forms?* The "content," in the final analysis, does not matter very much: it has only too often led to esthetic misunderstandings. The fundamental premise is: *the history of music is that of its structures*. Does this mean that we must move in the direction of formalism? No, answers Boulez, "in music there is no opposition between form and content" (p. 31).

This conviction is certainly justified, we believe, when it comes to freeing music from the ever-present possibility of confusing technique and esthetics. As Adorno has put it, "discussions of technique pure and simple having nothing whatever to do with art."[25] But, in spite of Boulez's constant precautions, formalism will reappear the very moment tribute is paid to an esthetics of "contents." "I am afraid . . . of being accused [*sic*] of neglecting, by dint of talking 'structures,' the musical content proper of the work that is to be written" (p. 31). Very well: but five lines later we learn that "form and content are of like nature." Formalism never pretended anything else!

In our opinion, to take form for content and content for form is not the best way of escaping formalism. Boulez quotes Levi-Strauss who, speaking of language, has given out that "content derives its reality from its structure, and what is known as form is the structuring [*mise en structure*] of the local structures, which is what content consists of." It is hard to see how such a proposition, which retains its descriptive or explanatory meaning in structural anthropology, can be applied for normative purposes in music — except at the price of an ambiguity (to consider music a language, without further ado) and of a play on words. This rather naive use of Levi-Strauss (and of Rougier, Brillouin, Guillaume), in any case, only brings out what was meant to be blurred.

If we, in turn, did not shrink from approximations, we should qualify this procedure as Kantian. With regard to the above formulation by Levi-Strauss, Boulez goes on to say: "furthermore, these structures must submit to the principles of formal logic we enounced above" (p.

[25] *Musique et technique aujourd'hui,* French transl. in *Arguments,* No. 19 (*L'Art en question*), 3rd *trimestre* 1960, pp. 50-58.

31). Adorno has given a clear characterization of this kind of surrender to "principles of formal logic":

> The idea of absolute unity as it presents itself to the technological work of art is the idea of the unity of a deductive system in a sense that is no longer entirely metaphorical, for it is taken literally: whatever is found in this type of music must be deduced, through a radical elimination of the contingent, beginning with an axiom reduced to the maximum and minimal.[26]

In fact, Boulez's edifice depends on a theory of understanding; and that being so, one is justified in being troubled by its historicism and relativism: music history would be reduced to the history of forms or of the mere use of categories; it would be summed up in a mere history of the mind. In that case, it seems difficult to appeal to "evolution." Let us limit ourselves here to mentioning this difficulty: if the historicistic thesis supported in *Penser la musique aujourd'hui* is coherent, that coherence might well turn out to be metaphorical, illusory; not only that, but it is not even certain there is any coherence in this at all!

It will be remembered that the acquisitions enumerated in the work cannot be considered systematic, or at least well-grounded insofar as they are systematic. Indeed, we shall have to deal with a succession of intuitions that are partial and, at the same time, brilliant. And this is why the book seems important to us.

What is the nature of these intuitions?

Let us not linger too long over what we are told, on p. 37, concerning the primacy of pitch and duration over intensity and timbre. The sequel of the presentation, in fact, will be devoted to qualifying — often very subtly — that privilege. Beginning with pp. 38-39, we find that today it is necessary to transcend the rigidity of the classical twelve-tone series, which limits itself to an "absolute value" of the pitch component, joined to a "fixed density of generation." It is possible, indeed necessary, that there should also exist "relative values" and "mobile densities," and the musician must be able to bring into play the fixed and the mobile, the absolute and the relative.

On p. 42, this flexibility is confirmed and enlarged upon. In contemporary music, what matters is the field, much more than the musical object: each object is "the limiting case of a field."

Boulez's "open," non-aleatory works can give us no idea of a score constructed according to this principle — but Earle Brown's *Available Forms,* for example, can, more precisely; here detail ceases to be organized in an imperative way.

[26] *Ibid.*

Further on, we again find the concern over form, strictly understood. The distinction between sound and noise, says Boulez, reduces itself to that between the possibility and the impossibility of perceiving a structuration. And if it is the structuration that causes the sound to be a sound and the noise a noise, then one may define structure as the *revealer* of the material (p. 45). Similarly, glissandos and clusters should be thought of as the zero point in the scale of structuration, as a vanishing of structuration or a return to the amorphous. — But, ask we, is it not the purpose of the scores thus relegated to the limbo of the "amorphous" (*Métastasis* or *Pithoprakta* by Xenakis, where glissandos are concerned; *Transicion II* by Kagel or Stockhausen's *Klavierstück XI*, with reference to clusters) to demonstrate just the opposite — under the circumstances, the material as revealer of structure? Here we might cite the example chosen by Jacques Guyonnet, the last measure of *Marteau sans maître:*

Boulez considers that the trill on the flute should be covered by the low gong and free itself from it by imperceptible degrees, almost unbeknown to the listener. This is the meaning of that passage, and not one dictated by a sensibility rather than by a "structural" influence.[27]

Why, indeed, should perception necessarily be "conscious" and "analytical"? True, we lack a serious study on the subliminal apprehension of structurations in music; however, many effects would be inexplicable were one to neglect this "synthetic" aspect of our perceptions. Besides, Boulez recognizes that *"noise* represents . . . in the organic state what a *formulated* complex of sounds reproduces at a higher level of elaboration" (p. 45): is this not the same as admitting that, to the listener, the structuration is far from meaning what it does to the composer?

And so, what must in the end be called Boulez's *formalism* answers only a theoretical and rather artificial need, at least on this point. Boulez's music itself almost gives it the lie; but above all, beginning with certain remarks in *Penser la musique aujourd'hui,* one can discern what a music free of everything *a priori* could be — a music that takes care to consider the composer not as the organizer of a technological ritual but, more modestly, as *the first listener.*

Boulez is not particularly fond of the word "informal." "Redoubtable and periodic epidemics: we have had the year of numbered series, the year of timbres re-adopted by current usage, the year of coordinated tempos; we have had the stereophonic year, the year of actions; we

---

[27] J. Guyonnet, *Structures et communication,* in *La Musique et ses problèmes contemporains,* Paris, 1963, p. 272.

France

Right: Pierre Boulez
Below: Olivier Messiaen

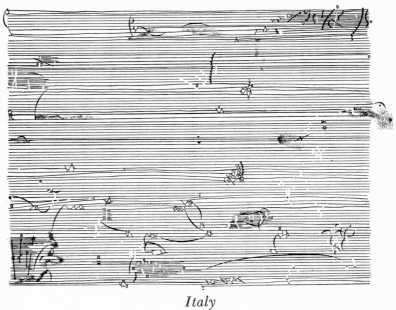

Italy

Top: Bruno Maderna (*left*) and Luciano Berio
in the electronic studio in Milan

Bottom: From Sylvano Bussotti's *Five Piano
Pieces for David Tudor*

Czechoslovakia: Alois Hába at a quarter-tone piano

France: Pierre Henry

Austria: Sketch by Casper Neher for Alban Berg's *Lulu* (Theater an der Wien, 1962, 1963)

Sweden
Ingvar Lidholm

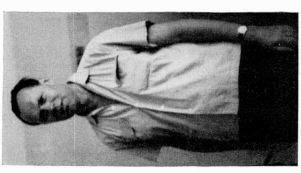

Yugoslavia: Milo Cipra

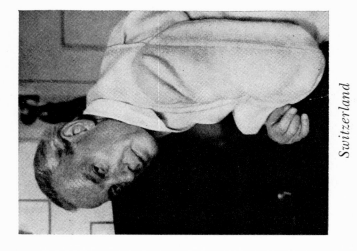

Switzerland
Wladimir Vogel

Holland: Scene from Hendrik Andriessen's opera *Philomela*

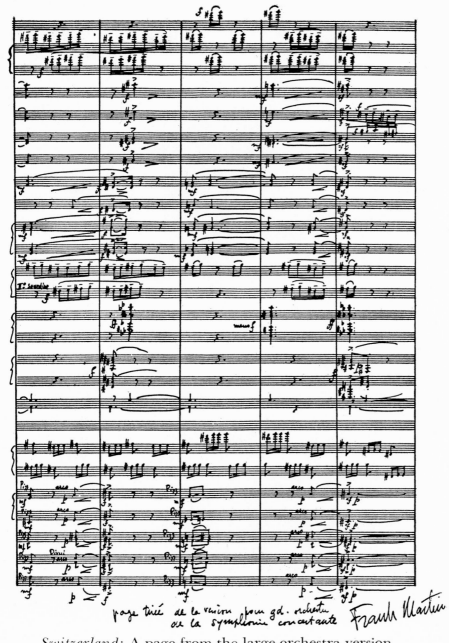

Switzerland: A page from the large-orchestra version
of Frank Martin's *Symphonie concertante,* in the
composer's handwriting

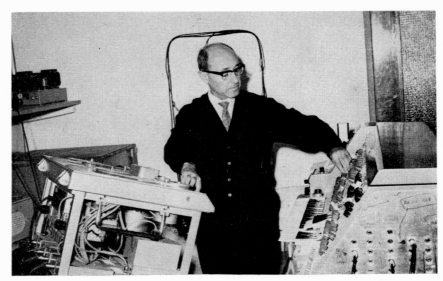

Israel: Josef Tal in the electronic studio in Jerusalem

Spain: *(left to right)* Ramón Barce, Arthur Custer,
Luis de Pablo, Gerardo Gombau

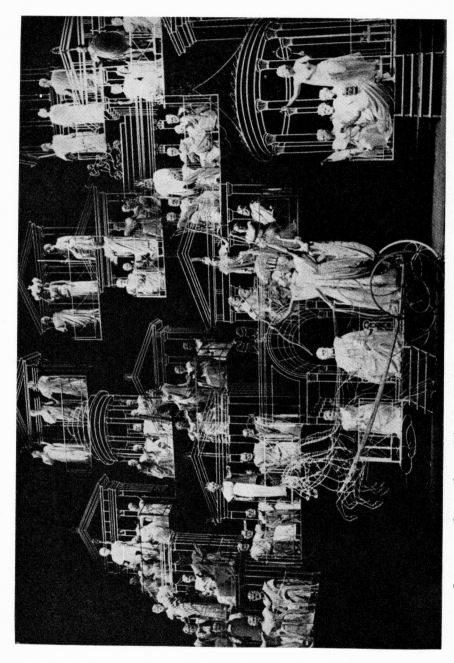

Germany: Scene from Giselher Klebe's opera *Alkmene* (Berlin, Deutsche Oper)

Norway: Scene from Arne Nordheim's ballet
Katharsis, décor by Guy Krogh after Hieronymus
Bosch (Oslo, 1962)

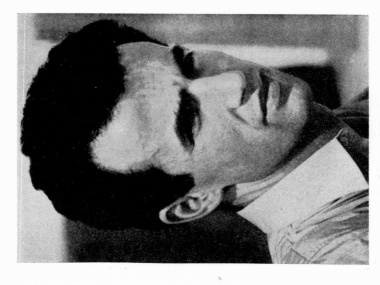

Italy: Luigi Nono

Belgium: Jean Absil

Zygmunt Mycielski

Poland

Boleslaw Woytowicz

Czechoslovakia: Scene from Bohuslav Martinů's *Julietta, or The Key to Dreams* (Prague, 1963)

Greece

Above: Jani Christou
Left: Iannis Xenakis

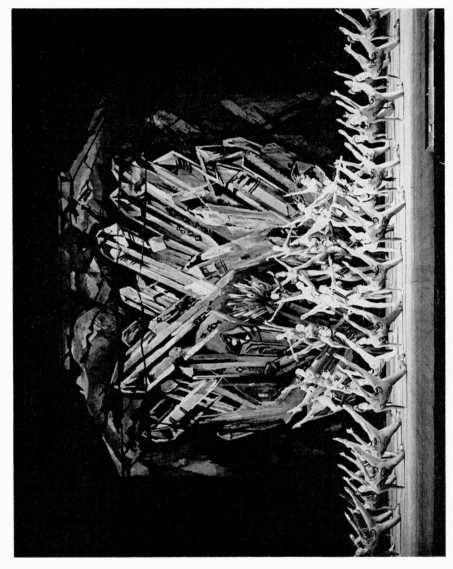

Soviet Union: Scene from Prokofiev's ballet *The Stone Flower* (Bolshoi)

Yugoslavia: Scene from Milko Kelemen's ballet *Appassionata*

have had the year of chance; we can already foresee the year of the informal: that word will have a great career!" (p. 17). And the huge chapter dedicated to "musical technique" in *Penser la musique aujour-d'hui* aims explicitly at preventing this new "epidemic." Describing his own procedures, Boulez observes that "structures, which we have considered as networks of possibilities, are by now abandoning the regions of the non-formed; they are getting realized in figures that are becoming better and better defined and will soon be the direct agents of form" (p. 132).

One might ask if, in order to become conscious of themselves, these structures ought not, on the contrary, to be anchored in those "regions of the non-formed" and somehow contemplate their genesis. "It is thought necessary to impose order on freedom from without, to restrain it, instead of letting it organize itself with no further obedience to any heteronomous criterion that mutilates what demands to develop itself freely": this formulation by Adorno[28] could be directly applied to Boulez's *dirigisme*. The informal music that would ensue would not lead back to the old myths of "inspiration" and "imagination," precisely because certain esthetic systems are dead and done with, not to mention certain esthetic lacunae. But it would surely take into account what Boulez calls "the concrete sonorous object" and its internal requirements — what we have earlier defined as the inclination or the lines of stress of the material (which has no points in common with "natural law" in music!).

This limitation of Boulez's formalism emerges clearly with regard to timbre, for example. While holding the opinion that musicians, in this area, are amateurs by the side of acousticians and psycho-physiologists, Boulez recognizes that serial organization grasps the material only imperfectly here. New instruments alone would be capable of allowing an analysis and synthesis of the sounds on the basis of real works. Thus, serial control is condemned to remain skin-deep: if it is a question of coping with the body of the sounds themselves, there is no further recourse, for the moment, but to *let the sounds be what they are* (Cage). But has this level ever really been left behind? The "concrete sonorous object" remains irritatingly silent here; curiously enough, it refuses to dictate the laws of its own constitution. But did it dictate them at all in what has preceded? We were carefully warned: "it is the very properties of this object that engender the structures of the

[28] *Vers une musique informelle*, in *La Musique et ses problèmes contemporains*, p. 262.

deduced sonorous universe and furnish it with its formal qualities; still, neither the qualities nor the structurations depend on the concrete sonorous object as an accident . . ." (p. 43). But what is an unanalyzed timbre, if not — alas! — an accident?

It becomes necessary, not only in philosophy but also in music, for all formalism to cope with the problem of "accidents." It is the purpose of Boulez's book to show the proliferation of these accidents; the honesty of his systematism emerges in the lucid manner in which that systematism takes note of its own finite character. With *Penser la musique aujourd'hui,* the serial school finds itself placed at the threshold, as it were, of the informal; not to recognize this would be to vacillate in academicism.

We have insisted on timbre because, since Schoenberg's *Harmonielehre,*[29] it has been a sort of touchstone of the success — or failure — of the various attempts at generalizing the serial system. But with the theory that Boulez develops beginning with p. 94 concerning "variable spaces," we find ourselves even more explicitly, perhaps, on the verge of the informal.

Once the continuum has been defined by the possibility of "cutting" a space, of dividing it (p. 95), it will be possible, for example, to differentiate in the space of frequencies those cases in which the cutting is "fixed" (i.e. temperament, which produces "striated" spaces) from those in which the cutting is irregular (giving rise to "smooth" spaces). It is possible to have passages go from the "smooth" to the "striated" without a break (p. 96).

Now the octave — based on the proportion 2:1 to characterize the modulus — had not been banned by the twelve-tone composers except on the same grounds as certain chords that had been "shelved" as a harmonic precaution. What could pass for a simple procedure becomes, for Boulez, a point of departure for a full structuration of sonorous space.

Indeed, if one agrees to call a space with an invariable modulus a "straight" space — in which the octave is only a particular case — one may oppose to that "straight" space a "bent" space, one that depends on variable moduli, whether regularly (in the case of "focalization") or irregularly.

Straight or bent spaces are "striated"; smooth spaces, on the other hand, can provide no topology but only a statistical distribution of the frequencies. Possibilities of joining smooth and striated spaces present

[29] "each day we devote more attention to timbres, and the possibility of describing them and putting them into order seems each day to come closer."

themselves in accordance with the degree of looseness in that distribution. If such a junction were realized, it would produce *non-homogeneous* spaces; in the present state of instrument-making, "non-homogeneous spaces do indeed risk being produced — it is even the likeliest probability! — but least of all will they be controlled" (p. 101) — "there would be no way of taking these accidents of the material or of the interpreter into account!" (p. 103).

What happens, on the other hand, if one transposes all that has just been said to the *temporal* domain? Time can be subdivided in the same way as frequencies; measured time corresponds to striated space, amorphous time to smooth space. In amorphous time there is simply a greater or smaller number of events; in measured time, those events unfold themselves at a certain speed, since everything depends on the relationship between chronometric time and the number of beats. Now, whereas the non-homogeneous can only occur by accident in the domain of frequencies, as we have seen, in the time dimension it is possible to elicit it, to obtain "values in which the proportion of time would become more refined compared with our present concepts" (p. 103). It is towards a qualitative time, therefore, that the musician must orient himself.

The idea of a heterogeneous space has its patents of nobility in philosophy; Bergson defended it under the name of "felt" space (*espace senti*). And it is by its means, we believe, that Boulez's intellectualism — or, at least, his theory of understanding — may acquire some flexibility. Intellectually, we must direct ourselves towards non-intellectual spaces. When the space in question is, in music, that of duration, smooth time is opposed to striated time at the level of the interpreters' actions themselves: "in smooth time, one occupies time without counting it; in striated time, one counts time in order to occupy it" (p. 107). If, as Boulez has it, these are "the fundamental laws of time in music" (p. 108), let us admit that these laws are liberal — and that they authorize the unexpectedness of the informal.

Thus, in *Penser la musique aujourd'hui,* and in a general way in some of Boulez's more recent texts, we have tried to identify some of the acquisitions, but also some of the myths, of the new French music. We have only dwelt on them insofar as these acquisitions and myths are — or will be — those of the current "neo-serialists," particularly in France, where the prestige of the author of *Marteau* is, beyond question, immense. This will save us the task of sketching a "complete" picture — of the sort used for "journalistic reports," "prize-giving," or

"Carte du Tendre"[30] — and particularly of mentioning all those who work in the shadow of Boulez alone.

Need we specify that we have only undertaken to give an account of difficulties of a theoretical nature? The broad outlines of the uncertainties thus extracted — faith in "absolute form," antinomies in the generalized serial organization, the fetishes of "style" and of the continuity of discourse — are nevertheless valid for the works themselves.

And it is not enough, we believe, to discern — as André Hodeir does, reasonably, with reference to these works[31] — a discrepancy between the poetics and the poems, between the aspiration and the realizations in the Boulez of *Marteau* and the works that followed. There is, of course, an element of truth in the thesis according to which a prejudiced position on the discovery and organization of a language risks, "in the long run," becoming an obstacle to "the attainment of the esthetic goals";[32] too much writing and a mannerism exaggerated to the point of rigorously avoiding even the slightest appearance of stylistic repetition from one work to the next can lead to a poetic failure, even if the point of departure was a dazzling technical success. But, on a deeper level, we feel the formalism originates in a conceptualization that has been allowed to drift a little. It is not a question, here, of gratuitously overemphasizing the complexity of thought that has characterized Boulez more than any of his followers or detractors. Rather, we would be inclined to doubt the solidity of Boulez's relationship to tradition. For it is the concern over *rediscovering* tradition systematically that emerges from all the negations or acquisitions. And from this point of view, the theory of the "generalized series" is too well-behaved. Metzger writes:

> The great conceptions of Boulez, Stockhausen and Pousseur draw their strength not only from their quasi-systematic consistency, but equally from the way they "compose out" their historical positional value, and as their act of negation emphasises the concept of what is negated, this concept gives them an exclusive claim to be the legitimate tradition.[33]

There could be no better definition of the way in which the avant-gardists are straggling in the rear.

If history is one's concern, and even more if one appeals to it, how can one not mistrust "legitimisms"? Against these, one must be

---

[30] *Penser la musique aujourd'hui,* p. 11.
[31] Cf. *La Musique depuis Debussy,* Paris, 1961, pp. 106-38.
[32] *Ibid.,* p. 138.
[33] *Abortive Concepts . . . ,* p. 24.

Cartesian — but in the true sense, not merely imagining that one is. Pseudo-Cartesianism has always been a characteristic of French musical intellectualism, which has used it as a stumbling block; and do we not find it again today — *horribile dictu* — in *Nécessité d'une orientation esthétique?*[34] Pseudo-Cartesianism, of all things, whose dangers Boulez himself had clearly outlined when, in a famous article, he denounced those who "love to mingle Descartes and *haute couture.*"[35]

Now, the Cartesian procedure — the true one, we mean — begins with a doubt, which at first rejects tradition; and which later, far from re-creating it, becomes hyperbolic, that is, causes its author to lend no further faith to the truest part of his heritage, to what is evidence itself, to the truth of the mathematical truths. It is in this hyperbolic manner that one ought to proceed in music, simply because that is *the only way of thinking historically* — and that is how Xenakis began, for example: with a radical re-examination of the whole of Western tradition, a re-examination we will now consider, since it seems typical in many respects.

Xenakis's recently published book, which we have already mentioned, contains several articles that had appeared before; but the way in which they have been assembled, recast, and expanded is in itself of considerable interest.[36] Numerous unpublished developments and particularly its over-all direction permit us to ascribe to it an even greater importance. If one compares it with Boulez's work, its originality and power become more palpable, and a more exact idea of the situation of today's living music will be gained.

At the beginning of *Musiques formelles,* Xenakis quotes a manifesto of his, published by the *Gravesaner Blätter* in their first number (July 1955). In that piece, entitled *La Crise de la musique sérielle,* Xenakis took a firm stand regarding the whole history of recent music. Henceforth, he said in effect, the serialists may do anything they please — but within the strict framework of the series conceived as a "linear category of thought" — and within the contradiction "between the linear polyphonic system and the audible result, which is surface, mass" (p. 3). Varèse, "instinctively," has already left both that category and that contradiction behind by using "a plethora of rhythms and timbres, as well as intensities" (p. 4). And it would be short-circuiting the entire recent evolution to decide to start once more from scratch, to

[34] In *Mercure de France, loc. cit.*
[35] *Eventuellement,* in *La Revue musicale,* No. 212, 1952, p. 118.
[36] *Musiques formelles,* in *La Revue musicale,* Nos. 253-54, 1963.

"return to the simple notions of sensation, of message-signals to those sensations, and of thoughts conveyed by those signals" (*ibid.*).

The striking thing about these formulations is their indifference to tradition and to evolutionary dogmas. Further on in *Musiques formelles,* Xenakis resolutely declares that "the problem is not to justify a new adventure historically; quite the contrary, what matters is the enrichment and the leap forward" (p. 139). And concerning an attempt at "symbolic music," he requires that one should make oneself "amnesic," to pave the way for a "setting to music" of purely logical processes borrowed from Boole's algebra (p. 185). To forget all that has gone before and consequently "to track down the mental operations of composition to their sources" in order to "extract general principles that are valid for all music" — this approach, which has a constant demand as its goal, seems infinitely precious to us in that it is "hyperbolic."

From the beginning, then, it is Xenakis's purpose to have recourse to "simple notions" — and, therefore, to place parentheses round a polyphony that has led to a non-receiving, as to both acoustics and principles. These "simple notions" are drowned in the complexity of the serialists' sonorous entanglements: the point of departure, then, must be "independent" sounds (in the statistical sense) — the only way of sparing the listener (for *only the listener matters*) a "linear salon music."[37]

As is evident, Xenakis places himself from the very outset in what Boulez will later characterize as "smooth space" or "amorphous time," which can only be envisioned from the point of view of statistical distribution. But this time, which to Boulez seems "amorphous," is somewhat like Descartes's bit of wax to Xenakis; it is, more precisely, material or matter *par excellence.*[38] Xenakis thus resumes, after many intervening traditions, some very ancient speculations — namely, those of the Greek philosophers on the subject of *hylē,* Aristotle's "matter," or the "materia prima" of the Scholastics. Everything must spring forth from this "primary time"; here, the process of genesis is the opposite of the one we met with in *Penser la musique aujourd'hui,* where it began with the "striated," the structured, to arrive at the "smooth," or with the "measured" to arrive at the "amorphous"; for in Xenakis's view, what is first presented, what first occurs to the mind is the "asymmetrical, non-commutative" character of time; symmetrical or measured, commutative time appears only in second place — "it, too," will serve to

[37] *Lettre à Hermann Scherchen,* Sept. 18, 1956.
[38] Cf. *Musiques formelles,* p. 17.

organize, but it must not be placed first.

And this immediately brings to mind the opposition formulated by a Max Bense between the "physical" and "esthetic" processes.[39] Contemporary physics shows us entropy as being that towards which the phenomena that pass from structure to non-structure tend; on the other hand, esthetics generally reacts against this degradation of order; it aims at the "enhancement of structure, of form, which constitutes the beautiful."[40] If one adopts this classification of Bense's and if one applies it to music, one will perceive the sense in which Xenakis's thought is "physical," in contrast with Boulez's estheticism. Xenakis's problem may be formulated as follows: one must promote an identity between "esthetic sign" and "real sign or signal"; to accomplish this, "it will be necessary to find a structure that will agree with the non-structure of matter, a non-entropy that will agree with entropy."[41]

At once, Boulez's position becomes clear: *his estheticism limits his view of history to the mere history of music.* This is why his goal could at first be characterized in a technical manner; it was a question of filling in the (mainly rhythmical) gaps or "evasions" in the language of the Viennese School and, in a wider sense, of matching the complex treatment of pitch with that of parameters traditionally neglected in the West (durations, dynamics, timbres, spaces): his famous analysis of the *Sacre du printemps* attests to this. Xenakis, on the other hand, takes as his point of departure a view of *the history of civilization as such:* the physical sciences, at the beginning of the 20th century, abandon classical determinism; by breaking the tonal function, "atonal" music opens a parallel way, "but one that is immediately hemmed in by the quasi-absolute determinism of serial music"; the latter, then, cannot help but appear anachronistic from the very outset.[42]

In other words, Xenakis takes his cue from nature — from *physis* — and not from culture. In nature he discovers a "temporal *plastique*" — that of hail, rain, grasshoppers. Messiaen is "inspired" by birds; why not, just as "naturally," emulate the "great politicized throngs"? *The beauty of art is derived from that of nature,* not the other way around, and one must disagree with Hegel and estheticism. In this regard, it is Xenakis, not Boulez, who is closest to Levi-Strauss: to understand art and to create it, one must see a "second natural order" in "the human

[39] In *Aesthetica II, Aesthetische Information,* Krefeld and Baden-Baden, 1956.

[40] §122, devoted to Max Bense, of *L'Esthétique contemporaine* by G. Morpurgo-Tagliabue, Milan, 1960.

[41] *Ibid.*

[42] *Musiques formelles,* p. 16.

order of culture," to paraphrase Merleau-Ponty's comment on Levi-Strauss.

Now, today we can only approach these natural phenomena by taking the laws of probability as our point of departure — those very laws that modern physics, having become statistical physics, brings into play, as well as those that are somehow conveyed by any grasp of "primary time": for, since Greek antiquity, we have been accustomed to thinking in terms of movement; the *Logos* has a hold on Becoming. What is the passage from the "smooth" to the "striated," to return to Boulez's terms, if not a transformation from the continuous into the discontinuous? As early as 1955, in *Métastasis,* Xenakis experimented with this kind of movement: in his string glissandos, he had an extremely general method of modeling space and time: it was applicable to architecture, for example.[43]

How can the laws of probability that afford control over nature's mass movements be put to use? In a way opposite to that of the physicists: according to these laws, the raw elements one adopts at the beginning will be arranged so that the distribution of the sonorous events will correspond to a generally controllable "debit," to over-all fluctuations. The "experimental" attitude adopted by Xenakis does not in the least consist in extracting certain laws from reality, in the manner of the classical physicists — and in the manner attempted by Boulez in connection with what he calls the "concrete sonorous object" — it consists in imposing certain keys that have already been tested in other areas (the consequences of using them not being known beforehand) upon a reality not yet explored in that way. The attitude is quite similar to that of a man like Cage, who is careful, above all, to preserve the unexpected; a confidence that ties in with that which a Descartes used to place in the mathematics, once doubt had been removed.

The result is an extraordinarily fluid, moving, and homogeneous music. If we except *Métastasis,* whose over-all form remains rather too linear, perhaps, considering the complexity of the sonorous means employed, we can say that all of Xenakis's scores realize an astonishing balance between detail and form: the degree of evanescence, so to say, is identical at all levels of the structuration; this is as true of *Pithoprakta,* a relatively harsh work, as it is of Xenakis's most "theatrical" piece, *Diamorphoses.* The fact is that the conception of form is not dissociated from what Xenakis calls "transformations" on the one hand, "micro-

[43] Cf., concerning the Philips Pavilion, *Musiques formelles,* pp. 20-25.

composition" on the other;[44] it is simply their "sequential programming."
The resulting unity is no different from that "unanimity" of a crowd
alluded to in *Musiques formelles* with reference to the idea of "order"
and to the "ataxia" in Markovian music. For "the idea of order
and disorder implies the relationship of effective values to all possible
values the elements of a group can assume, which introduces the idea
of probability into the quantitative evaluation of order or disorder"
(p. 80).

In other words, form can no longer be defined as a formal scheme;
it is directly tied to the entropy or the neg-entropy of the sonorous
events. Or, if one prefers, there is a form (an unforeseeable one) for
every work. And this form is inseparable from the "threads" of detail:
simply put, a "collection," "a notebook of threads, may be expressed
by matrices of probabilities of parametered transitions. They are affected
by a degree of ataxia, by an entropy that is calculable under certain
conditions" (p. 95). It is therefore impossible to isolate the form, to
consider it apart from the material, the content. Contrary to what
happens in Boulez, form according to Xenakis need not then be "re-
considered as a whole".: the language-form dichotomy ceases to exist.
In this sense, it is Xenakis, and not Boulez, who would be entitled to
quote Brillouin: only in a "stochastic" music can one really take into
account the fact that "sonorous discourse is nothing more than a perpetual fluctuation of entropy in all its forms" (p. 94).

But how can the form be renewed for one and the same composition?
How can one deflect the effect of habit that might arise upon hearing
the same work several times? Cage observes that some of his works,
when heard again, start ringing "melodically": how can the "effect of
surprise" be maintained? The answer is found at the end of the
analysis of *Achorripsis* and deserves to be pointed out: the risk of
banality can be avoided if, at the very moment of programming, one
modifies the relative distances of the theoretical statistical frequencies,
and this in a non-significative way. The auditory characteristics will be
preserved as a whole, but what will effectively be perceived beneath
this statistical identity of mass will be capable of differing in the
absolute sense. The problem of unity will thus find itself resolved in
and by mobility: by this means one arrives at a definition of form
in which unity is rigorously blended with uniqueness.

This is the opposite of the "open," anti-aleatory work conceived by
Boulez. When I listen to the Third Sonata, there is, at bottom, no

[44] Cf. *Musiques formelles*, pp. 33-34.

change from one performance to the next; the form is only shattered and reconstituted, as in a kaleidoscope. Here, detail is varied structurally, in and by the form; what does not change and therefore remains a token of unity-uniqueness is the "vector-matrix" (p. 48). "Form," in the sense of "formal scheme," has disappeared; it has turned into function.

One can understand Xenakis's misgivings in the face of the "poetics of indeterminacy," so dear to the "neo-serialists": that poetics is only possible because "serial music has sufficiently banalized itself so that it can be improvised like the music of Chopin, a fact that confirms the general impression" (p. 52); it can be explained theoretically by the fetishisms of "form" in the traditional sense: "in the name of the scheme one betrays the problem of the choice" (*ibid.*).

One might be tempted to object to the programmatic character of Xenakis's music. Why should anything be "set to music" — in the present case, the laws of probability — just as Liszt used to set Lamartine to music? The answer would be that these "laws" do not constitute a program but, at most, the abstract equation (of little concern to the listener) of the material itself. They are strictly functional, they connect this music to the world. Xenakis's music is neither more nor less structured than the physical world: for the myth of composition wound up in itself, for the narcissism of "absolute form," of the work as refuge, and of art for art's sake, Xenakis substitutes the principle of the work as participation with the elements, of the cosmic — not microcosmic — work.

What could be more "closed," in this connection, than the Third Sonata? Even if "developers" are anticipated as additives to the five actual "formants," the structure, from the listener's point of view, will remain just as foreign to the world or the life of that listener; "work in progress," to be sure, but without any reference to Joyce's realism. The music envisaged by Xenakis, basically comparable to the great natural phenomena, does *not,* precisely, give this impression of a "program" or of being rooted in estheticism. Its "openness" might rather consist in its being linked to Rilke's "Open," where a nature and Nature unfold themselves. It is a music of immanence.

There is a second possible objection, derived from the first one, involving any application of mathematical analysis to musical composition: "there is no reason why a musical work, which in fact appears to us as an organic reality, should not have the same properties as any other reality. What remains to be explained is its esthetic interest proper;

now, the theory of groups is incapable of doing so; whether a work is beautiful or ugly, mathematics will always express its internal order."[45]

The answer, at least so far as Xenakis is concerned, would be that the conditions for an "esthetic" perception and creation cannot exist in the prejudice for "pure" form. Rather, there is a sort of spontaneous reflectiveness and a reflective spontaneity at the root of the "esthetic," forbidding it to "will itself" into being esthetic in the face of whatever is declared unesthetic *a priori* in daily life: the distinction between esthetic and unesthetic is not derived from a preliminary decision or division, but emerges from the fall and the folds of the work. As Xenakis puts it, speaking of *Syrmos,* "the sonorous result . . . is not guaranteed *a priori* by the calculation" (p. 98). And Messiaen could confirm this, speaking of *Achorripsis:* "astonishing: the preliminary calculations are quite forgotten as one listens. No brain-work, no intellectual frenzy. The sonorous result is a delicately poetic or violently brutal agitation, depending on the case." In other words, there are no grounds for trying to base an analysis of Xenakis's music on the laws of probability to which it has reference — laws that are merely procedures of articulation or simple "logical frameworks," which, hypothetically, have no bearing on what is heard.

Xenakis thus avoids all ambiguity between the "written" and the "lived." He rejects the "alchemist" conception of the work maintained by men like Schoenberg, careful to conceal the construction as if it were a secret. Such an ideology, in whose name the serialists relegate the work's architectonics to the unheard, to the "subcutaneous," risks sacrificing the creative act to abstraction, the musician to silence: "A silent, imaginative reading of music could make the sonorous performance superfluous, just as reading the written word suppresses the spoken word."[46]

Already in *La Crise de la musique sérielle,* Xenakis was saying that it is impossible to agree with the idea (so dear to Messiaen) of a "mental music lacking material support." And *Les trois paraboles* will later accuse the whole compositional process of the "neo-serialists": their music is theoretically *reversible,* that is to say "it should be possible, under dictation, to reproduce the relationships of all the sound-components of any passage whatever . . ."; in practice, it is *irreversible* by reason of its linear complexity, and this prevents "the reproduction

[45] Jeanne Vial, *De l'être musical,* p. 46.
[46] T. W. Adorno, *Prismen,* Frankfurt, 1955, p. 210.

on paper of a serial work aurally perceived."[47]

What is the exact import of this criticism? Analytical procedures have often been taken for compositional procedures — and that is the danger of formalism: to take the "complete" form as a point of departure in order then to organize the detail as a function of that "completion" is to risk forgetting all about the listener. On the interpretative level, what Schaeffer calls the "causal score," the graphic image or the writing, is favored at the expense of the "score of effects." But "effect" is the only thing that matters to the listener: if it is kept in mind, any division between what is "written" and "lived," between form and detail will be avoided, not merely in practice but also in theory. In prescribing the overstepping of these dualisms, which constitute the basis of "tradition," Xenakis does not hesitate to round the cape of the informal. His works will be "formal" — and this is what justifies the title of his work — in that they will arrange themselves "on the one hand, with the help of probability formulas and of statistics, on the other, with the help of the latest research in the physiology of hearing" (Les trois paraboles, p. 3). They are informal because "after all, instinct and subjective choice are the only guarantors of a work's value. There is no tablature of scientific principles" (ibid.).

And so, with Boulez on the one side and Xenakis on the other, we are dealing with two very distinct conceptions of musical creation. Even if there are certain points of agreement, which certainly prevent us from prejudging the future, the two esthetics diverge profoundly. The formalistic one stresses the autonomy of the work of art and harks back to the Hegelian idea of the primacy of an "artificial" over a "natural" Beautiful; the other, the "informal" one, tends to approach the art of knowing and, in a wider sense, of experiencing, which amounts to a blurring of the classical oppositions between art and nature, art and technique. For the simple "thematic correspondences" that were discernible between the terms of these oppositions, which Boulez, for his part, does not hesitate to cultivate, Xenakis substitutes the principle and practice of a "factorial connection between physical signals and esthetic signs":[48] "physical process and esthetic process become interchangeable factors."[49]

What is being sought, at any rate, is the Beautiful. Rather explicitly with Boulez, in a more veiled manner with Xenakis — but did not the latter choose, as a source of inspiration, "an event that is immensely

[47] An essay written as an introduction to Pithoprakta.

[48] Morpurgo-Tagliabue, op. cit., p. 476.

[49] Ibid., p. 477.

powerful and beautiful in its ferocity,"[50] the breaking-up of the multitude? We have only mentioned the attitude towards Cage, as a criterion by which to classify the avant-garde tendencies, inasmuch as Cage's question — can Art be reduced to the Beautiful? — remains, for the moment, unanswered by both Boulez and Xenakis. We have mentioned Boulez's estheticism; with regard to Xenakis, we might repeat the criticism addressed to Bense's esthetics of informality by G. Morpurgo-Tagliabue:

> There can be no doubt about it: certain natural relationships, especially in microphysics, may contain new esthetic models, that is, "Beauty." It is harder to admit their artistic efficacy if one bears in mind that art cannot be reduced merely to the beautiful.[51]

To paraphrase Adorno: "true informal music" would be one that has rid itself of the difficulties inherent in the division between the *esthetic* and the *artistic*. Until now, living music in France has limited itself to "elementary exchanges" between the two terms. To our knowledge, the only young composer who has taken cognizance of the problem and who alone works independently of the two theoretical orientations we have examined — perhaps of *all* theoretical orientations — is François Bayle; he may be credited with at least one successful score, *Points critiques*. But we have also pointed to a rectification of Xenakis's with regard to Cage, which allows one to assume other developments.

[50] *Musiques formelles,* p. 19.
[51] Morpurgo-Tagliabue, *op. cit.,* pp. 478-79.

THE VARIETY OF TRENDS IN MODERN
GERMAN MUSIC

By WOLF-EBERHARD VON LEWINSKI

THE widening chasm that separates modern music from the listener throughout the world arises in Germany from sources that are not primarily of a sociological, compositional, or technical nature. The problem is deeply rooted in the politics of the "Third Reich" and in the post-war situation. In West Germany, the newly won freedom that came with the end of the war made possible a new beginning for modern music. Composers, at first timidly seeking self-understanding, reached back to the period 1930-1933 and took up the musical language that had developed abroad after 1933. An explosive development began, a development that set out to make up in a few years everything that the Nazi regime had thwarted and strangled. But while in West Germany young composers, particularly those of avant-garde faiths, received a sort of carte blanche, a new curtailment of musical and intellectual freedom took place in East Germany. This choking of creativity seems to be so severe that musical production there lacks sufficient quality to be of more than local importance.

But West German music now plays an important and distinctive part in the international concert. Many composers who were voluntarily or involuntarily silent during the Hitler years made themselves heard again in new and surprising works. Wolfgang Fortner's Symphony of 1947 was a beacon. The composer, who was forty years old in that year, said of it: "It renounces any justification through a compositional system and lives solely from the power of conviction of the artistic assertion." With this symphony Fortner sought a connection with the international world of composition; he was one of the first to do so. But the musical idiom of free atonality that dominates the symphony soon gave way to a new ordering of the musical material through Arnold Schoenberg's row technique. Fortner first used it in his Third String Quartet (1948), though to be sure in a personal modification which distills the so-called *modi* from the row, permits row-free procedure within a *modus,* and which moreover interpolates various transposed segments of the row.

The turn to Schoenberg and the "Vienna School" was no chance event. The music of Hindemith, Bartók, and Stravinsky seemed too personal in style to summon forth a "school." Only the Schoenberg technique — the twelve-tone technique — left open possibilities of personal shaping and handling of musical materials even though it required a decisive turn from tonal formulations. The dominance of this style was clearly demonstrated at the Kranichstein Summer Courses at Darmstadt, which were essential for the development of modern German music. These courses, which soon won international recognition, rapidly satisfied the need to catch up and brought knowledge of the most important works of international modern music to young German composers. In the early Darmstadt years, loan copies of *Pierrot lunaire* or *L'Histoire du soldat* circulated among young composers. The scores were not only studied but often entirely copied. From about 1949 on, the influence of the Schoenberg school became paramount, even obligatory in Kranichstein. The Parisian dodecaphonist, René Leibowitz, brought in a strict twelve-tone regimen and introduced young composers to the secrets of row technique.

Hans Werner Henze (born 1926) was among his listeners. Henze had become Fortner's student when he was twenty and had a period of composition in a motoric and parodistic style behind him. He had just finished a violin concerto in which he had come to grips with twelve-tone technique. Leibowitz's teaching fell on fertile soil; Henze soon became absolute master of the Schoenberg technique. However Henze later acknowledged:

The twelve-tone problem does not play a great part in my music; it was always an exclusively technical means. I have always been concerned with musical substance, particularly with melody. In my early pieces (up to the Second Symphony) the writing was simple and often primitive, but the melodic aspect — and secondly the constant striving to solve the problems of harmony and sound — always dominated. As my scores became more dodecaphonic, sound, melody, and rhythm became more and more dissociated. (*Pas d'action, Der Idiot,* and the String Quartet were the culminating points of this development.)

Henze and a man of nearly the same age, Giselher Klebe, became outsiders at Kranichstein as the Darmstadt courses turned ever more decisively to an uncompromising avant-gardism which now inscribed

Webern rather than Schoenberg on its banners. At the beginning of the
'50s serial, totally determined music was propagated in the Kranichstein
experimental studio. Now not only pitch (as with Schoenberg and his
followers) but also rhythm, register, and dynamics were subjected to
strict, serial ordering and mathematical calculation. The appeal to
Webern's late works — particularly the String Quartet — revealed itself
years later as at least a partial misunderstanding. What in Webern's music
was compression of a discharging *espressivo* gesture — doubly secured,
to be sure, by an ingenious technique — became in the hands of the
post-Webern Kranichsteiners a dry, constricting scheme of row functions
and number manipulations in which there inhered no spiritual or musical
function but only mathematical calculation. However the "fetishizing of
the material," as Theodor W. Adorno called it, was recognized before
too long by the most talented among the young Kranichstein composers.
They fought it by loosening and bursting form and through the introduction of aleatory elements. Finally, through spontaneous interpretation
the performer was supposed to give back to the music, whose text was
no longer unambiguous, the directness that had been taken from it by
the automatism of the serial composition process.

Despite all the errors and false solutions musical avant-gardism,
which became ever more internationalized in Kranichstein, was one of
the most imposing phenomena of musical post-war Germany. Besides
the Italians Bruno Maderna and Luigi Nono, the Frenchman Pierre
Boulez, and the American John Cage, besides Polish and Japanese
composers, it was above all Karlheinz Stockhausen who could offer
new, often sensational, often astonishing compositions or theoretical
results nearly every year.

Stockhausen was born in 1928 and studied at the Musikhochschule
in Cologne with Frank Martin. In Paris he worked with Milhaud and
Messiaen. In 1953 he published *Kontra-Punkte,* a one-movement work
for ten instruments that transforms a plurality of individual tones and
time relationships into a single unity. From the antithesis between
vertical and horizontal tone-relations, Stockhausen procures a two-voiced,
homogeneous counterpoint which is clearly recognizable to the ear. There
is no repetition, no variation, no development, no contrast in the
conventional sense in this piece. "Not the same shape in a changing
light. Rather this: different shapes in the same light that penetrates
everywhere" (Stockhausen). Herbert Eimert — composer, theoretician,
and as broadcaster a decided promoter of young composers — describes
the aural impression as a "free, constantly self-equalizing play of tones

that knows no development whether formal or spiritual, and by its original stasis departs from all traditional music."

Stockhausen was concerned with new problems of musical formulation in each work he published thereafter. He never used a previously found solution in a second work. In *Klavierstück XI* he burst the concept of musical form. Nineteen different groups of notes are irregularly disposed on a single sheet of paper (53 x 93 cm.). Each of these groups can be connected to each of the other eighteen in such a way that each group may be played with any of the six given tempos, basic dynamic levels, and articulations.

In *Zyklus für einen Schlagzeuger* Stockhausen strives for a connection between the "open" form attained in *Klavierstück XI* and the idea of a dynamic, closed form. Sixteen pages are fastened at the side to a spiral. There is no beginning and no end. The player can begin at will with any page; but he must then continue in the given order. While playing he stands within a circle of various percussion instruments. During the performance he moves from one principal station to the next, turning once around clockwise or counterclockwise according to the direction in which he is reading the music.

In two extensive compositions Stockhausen illumined the possibilities of "instrumental music in space." The *Gruppen für drei Orchester,* first performed in 1958 in Cologne, is written for three groups of instruments directed by three conductors and variously disposed about the hall. At times these three orchestras play in different tempos, but they meet now and again in a common rhythm. They call to each other and answer; one echoes the other. It is a modern transformation of the Baroque concertante concept. Each instrumental group is in a position to make it possible for the hearer to experience its own "time-space"; the hearer finds himself in the middle of many such spaces which together then form a new "time-space." "And what the sounding groups bring forth are no longer 'points' — as at first when everything was 'contrapuntal' and cell-like—but 'groups': groups of sounds, noises, and sound-noises as independent entities" (Stockhausen).

The second work on the theme "music in space" — *Carré* for four orchestras and choruses (first performed in 1960 in Hamburg) — simultaneously unfolds again spiritual-expressive possibilities that serial music had previously sought to avoid. Stockhausen wrote this about it:

I found, experienced, and gradually shaped *Carré* in the hours of plane flights that I had to make every day during six weeks in America. I profoundly hope that this music can give a little inner quiet, breadth, and concentration, and a conviction that we can have much time if we take it — that it is better to come to oneself than to get worked into a passion. "For the things that happen need some one to happen to; some one must catch them."

Carré is thus a work of profession or witness — if such worn words may be permitted — a piece that one would like the public not merely to hear passively but to experience in spite of all the boldness and uniqueness of its conception. Again, then, a characteristic "German" work. Voices and instruments were used together to produce a unified, mixed sound; the four orchestras, each with its own chorus, were again placed at the sides of a square hall.

In his latest works Stockhausen continues his approach — on the one hand experimental, on the other based on solitary, pregnant formulations — without however attaining the manysidedness and strength of his earlier solutions. Sound, as the last important "parameter," was subjected to a thoroughgoing compositional and analytical — and most likely, creative — examination, an examination that won new, important (because less rough) territory. Now the most modern music "sounded" again. "Soundstructures" — compositions of the most diverse sorts including pure playings with sound — were the result — and not only in Stockhausen's canon.

In post-war Germany electronic music at first raised a good deal of dust. One of the most valid and long-lasting works in the area is Stockhausen's *Gesang der Jünglinge* (1955-56). Around the Cologne studio for electronic music there were impassioned discussions between modern and traditional musicians, discussions that spilled over into the dining room. But these times are past. The Cologne studio (at which Stockhausen, Herbert Eimert, Mauricio Kagel, and Gottfried Michael Koenig are the principal workers) functions as quietly and with as much freedom from attack as the studio in Munich or the Darmstadt studio headed by Hermann Heiss. There is no longer much trace of the artistic revolution that was hoped for as a result of the emergence of electronic sound possibilities. Electronic music has shown itself to be most fruitful for film and radio-play music; in the concert hall the combination of electronic music with traditional instruments (in works by Stockhausen, Berio, Maderna, and others) has come into prominence.

Besides the Kranichstein summer courses there are a number of important festival weeks and events for contemporary music, for example the *Donaueschinger Musiktage,* which are rich in tradition and which thanks to Heinrich Strobel's and Hans Rosbaud's tolerant arrangement of the programs and interpretations have earned respect and attention.

Other such events to be mentioned are *Musik der Zeit* in Cologne, the *Neue Werk* in Hamburg, the *Musica Viva* in Munich, and the *Tage für neue Kammermusik* in Brunswick. All of these undertakings receive their primary support from broadcasting services.

In general the broadcasting services have worked for modern music in an exemplary fashion. Much new music has been performed but much has also then been forgotten. Young composers have often been generously furthered without however fulfilling their original promise. Some have undoubtedly become famous too soon; their talent could not unfold in peace but was drawn into the wake of commissions and musical management. Heimo Erbse is a case of this sort. This student of Blacher's (born 1925) drew attention to himself through several nicely worked scores ornamented with witty parody. Then followed an opera that miscarried: *Julietta*, first performed in 1959 at the Salzburg Festival. Since then no distinctive score by Erbse has been heard.

But early fame and an unbroken chain of performances have harmed Hans Werner Henze little or not at all. From the early symphonies, ballets, and operas, his agile and personal stamp became more and more solidified and heightened up to *König Hirsch* (first performed in 1956 in Berlin). This opera, which in its original version has half again as many pages as *Die Meistersinger,* shows that in the middle '50s, Henze was on a different road from the avant-gardists. He did not make the new ordering of musical material a goal for itself. Speculative musical thought is always subordinated to the will to expression. Henze's strongly literary and imaginative temperament led him again to the Romantic. The Gozzi fable of *König Hirsch* shimmers and vibrates in multifariously broken coloristic sounds and facets of expression. Finally in the ballet *Undine,* which is based on a classical esthetic, Henze avowedly dedicated himself to carefully made sounds which make no concession to public taste but respond rather to a deep need for a new ease and for beauty in music.

In recent years Henze has frequently been cited as an antipode to Stockhausen. And as a matter of fact his works have scarcely a point of contact with those of the Cologne avant-gardist. Stockhausen held firmly to the principle of serial composition; he was mainly concerned with compositional and stylistic purity and harmonious construction. Henze on the other hand does not fear breaks in style, takes suggestions and ideas where he finds them, and writes passages that could appear indiscriminate and heterogeneous from a style-critical point of view. This "eclectic" trait in Henze's work has been maintained to today. Thus the first act of the opera *Prinz von Homburg* sounds like Alban Berg, the second act like Stravinsky. But every measure of both acts — and this is the main thing — sounds like Henze. Accordingly Henze is the greatest talent among the young German composers.

The first performance of Henze's *König Hirsch* was called "the most important operatic event since the great Strauss premières." Since then success has been true to Henze, the opera composer — in so far as one can speak of success at all with regard to contemporary opera. For the fact is that in Germany many new operas receive first performances but relatively few are subsequently played by many theaters, and scarcely one can maintain itself in the repertory for any length of time. Henze's *Prinz von Homburg*, first performed in Hamburg in 1960, made the rounds of the most important German operatic stages; even smaller houses played it. His *Elegie für junge Liebende* (after a text by Auden and Kallman, the librettists of Stravinsky's *Rake's Progress*), however, makes even greater demands on the performers and for all the composer's sure stage instinct is so complex and unusual in terms of plot that it does not draw the favor of the larger public.

When one speaks of the operas of the post-war period the work of Giselher Klebe must be given a preferred place. Klebe lacks Henze's naturalness and richness of ideas. His operas, beginning with *Die Räuber*, after Schiller, first performed in 1957, continuing with the Balzac setting *Die tödlichen Wünsche*, the Kleist opera *Alkmene,* and the brilliant one-act work *Die Ermordung Cäsars* up to the comic opera *Figaro lässt sich scheiden,* whose contents connects with Rossini and Mozart and musically strives for humor without cheaply parodistic effects — these operas are impressive examples of a lively sense for dramatic and lyric situations, for developments and combinations as the opera stage requires them. Klebe's musical vocabulary is more tart than Henze's. Klebe uses the twelve-tone technique more thoroughly and exclusively. But for him too technique is not the most important thing but — as with Alban Berg — a vehicle for the demands of expression. Klebe, like Henze, is sufficiently vital to remain free from any orthodoxy. "In music," he says, "there are infinite possibilities of statement, possibilities that do not absolutely have to exist in strict separation from each other. On the contrary the musical experience remains vital through mutual penetration and amalgamation of the most varied elements. In my opinion, this is the only way to avoid becoming hardened in sterile pure cultures." In this fashion Klebe has recently loosed himself from dodecaphony and developed his own harmonic system.

Unfortunately Klebe's operas have not yet received the attention they deserve. Fortner had better fortune, with two Lorca settings, *Bluthochzeit* and *In seinem Garten liebt Don Perlimplin Belisa*. Though in *Bluthochzeit* folkloristic formulas were set into the subtle musical texture with all too striking simplicity, the second opera charmed by its renunciation of folklore and through cultivated sound, which was almost perfectly matched to a text as artificial as it was impassioned.

A report on German opera since 1945 would be incomplete without mention of numerous composers of the middle and older generations who do not write as uncompromisingly as Henze, Klebe, or Fortner, but who as solid professionals and excellent masters have a considerably larger audience in their favor, even though, all together, they cannot achieve as many performances in a year as a single work by Lortzing, or Puccini, or the other heroes of public taste.

Carl Orff (born in Munich in 1895) is so original a figure that it is difficult to place him in any scheme of classification. Since after the early *Carmina burana* his style has become even sparer and more artificial, one would almost like to classify him not as a composer but rather as an all-encompassing theatrical genius who has rediscovered and exploited long-forgotten possibilities of the cultic theater. In this sense works like *Antigonae* (1949), *Trionfi di Afrodite* (1953), and *Oedipus der Tyrann* (1959) are new variants of the *Gesamtkunstwerk*.

Werner Egk (born 1901) is related to his fellow Bavarian, Orff, through a sort of Bavarian vitality. He is one of those composers whose simple tonal vocabulary, which uses dissonances only as spices, has always found approving audiences. "Egk's music is direct, sometimes racy, frequently full of charm. It directly touches the listener and is broadly intelligible" (Arthur Honegger). *Abraxas,* which came out in 1947, remains one of the most popular and accessible works of the modern German ballet. The Calderon opera, *Circe,* and even more the buffo work, *Der Revisor,* after Gogol, show Egk as a musician who can write effective ensembles and colorfully and impulsively illustrate dramatic and grotesque situations according to tried and true models.

Since the war things have been quieter around composers like Rudolf Wagner-Régeny, whose *Prometheus,* first performed in 1959 in Kassel, was no more than a *succès d'estime*. In his opera *Don Juan und Faust* (Stuttgart, 1950), Hermann Reutter (born 1900) showed himself to be more brittle than Egk. More important works have been written by Boris Blacher and Rolf Liebermann, a Swiss who has moved to Hamburg (see p. 87).

Blacher (born 1903) is above all a master of terse diction, sketch-like musical characterization, and wittily pointed instrumentation. His spare palette reminds one of Diaghilev's remark about music that is so transparent that one could "see through it with the ear." After the war Blacher brought out an entire series of operas. *Romeo und Julia,* a chamber opera, was written right after the war in Berlin with the same idea in mind that had determined the shape of Stravinsky's *Histoire du soldat* during the First World War: the work should be simple to perform, easy to give again under varying circumstances and as short and free from pathos as possible. In *Preussisches Märchen* irony and gaily fresh desecration of monuments celebrated a triumph. Finally the *Abstrakte Oper Nr. 1* was frankly experimental. Here Blacher renounced plot and tried to represent basic psychological and spiritual situations through a series of phonetic sounds contrived by Werner Egk. *Rosamunde Floris* and the most recent ballet, *Demeter,* are examples of an ingenious and intense esoteric — but not dodecaphonic — personal style of high quality and individuality.

We have not spent so much time on opera in Germany in vain. For the opera composer still finds a stronger response in the press and among the public than the composer of orchestral or chamber music except when the latter is particularly famous. An opera première, as for example most recently the first performance of Ernst Krenek's *Der goldene Bock* in Hamburg, always brings together all the music critics of the nation. Yet in spite of all the publicity that goes out about such events, one must not hide the fact that the opera composer's lot is far harder today than it was formerly. To be sure it is easier to get a first performance, but a new work is hardly ever taken into the repertory. If a composer pays attention to the public taste, if he writes easily accessible, unpretentious scores, he may well have a popular success, but he will not be successful with the press, which has become almost allergic to concessions to the public in opera. Finally, the subscribers will observe that after all, Puccini's cantabiles are more cantabile and that the euphony he has bestowed on them is more euphonious — and they will turn back to *Madame Butterfly.* If the composer opposes the popular taste, if he writes twelve-tone operas, he may have a critical success but he will come up against emphatic resistance from the public and — sometimes worse — of the performers. An opera is a costly and complex undertaking and it must be repeated many times if its production is to be worthwhile to any extent. Because of the German opera subscription system this is generally possible, but when modern operas are performed the box office cash drawer is nevertheless considerably emptier than is otherwise the case. The large number of modern operas to be found on the programs of even the smaller German theaters cannot deceive any one; the fact is that in the opera repertory modern music has not established itself.

One hopeful composer is trying to overcome this in another fashion. He is the Munich composer Wilhelm Killmayer (born 1927). Killmayer is a practical man of the theater and a *Kapellmeister* and he has primarily dedicated himself to a fastidious light muse. Within a few years his *La Buffonata,* a "ballet chanté," has caused a furor at all the important German opera theaters and achieved much success even in the smaller cities. Killmayer, a pupil of Orff's, wrote an effervescent score to an obvious text by Tankred Dorst. We have not yet, however, had a full-length work from him. Killmayer opposed the "literary opera," which, if we examine the concept carefully, plays a considerable role in the work of Henze and Klebe. Killmayer demands a music theater that does not take over classical dramas but creates original operatic material, that does not follow psychological lines but that should be prepared from a purely music-theatrical point of view.

The development of opera in East Germany has been different. This is the explanation of the task of music in an East German music lexicon: "New tasks are given to the composers of our time by the insight that music is a part of the social life of mankind and a reflection of reality. It should be educational and work to form social consciousness."

"Music for the masses" — stirring marches and young people's songs for mass meetings — has great importance in East Germany. The few composers whose fame extended beyond local, East German celebrity have died in the last few years. One of these is Hanns Eisler, formerly a Schoenberg student, who in the '20s turned his back on "modernism" and at the end confined himself to political songs for the masses. In these the fresh, dissonance-spiced style of the early Eisler was replaced by solemnity. In spite of everything, Eisler remained an expert craftsman and a musician who brought pregnant ideas to paper with a light hand.

Paul Dessau's development followed a similar path. Dessau, like Eisler, furnished a series of masterful stage works to Brecht texts and with his Brecht opera *Die Verurteilung des Lukullus* had the only international operatic success scored by a composer from the "German Democratic Republic." Dessau, like Eisler, learned from Weill — he partly watered down his style and partly made it more precise. But in any case, these men have remained Weill's only legitimate German followers.

Originally Ottmar Gerster had a good reputation as an opera composer. His effectively made operas *Enoch Arden* and *Die Hexe von Passau* found many listeners after the war. In 1950 Gerster wrote a *Friedenskantate,* a choral work with the instructive title *Eisenhütten-kombinat Ost,* and a *Thüringischer Symphonie,* all pieces that could bring him only local fame.

The catalogues of the works of the composers of the "GDR," regardless of the generation they belong to, are similar to the point of confusion so far as their production after 1945 is concerned. Each writes songs for young people and songs for the masses, light music and festive processionals. The youngest East German composers, Robert Hanell, Siegfried Kurz, Günter Kochan, all of them about thirty-five years old, remain for the moment in the customary channels of "socialist realism," though sometimes, as in the case of Hanell, they draw attention through vivacious turns of phrase and solid craftsmanship.

Musical life in West Germany is made more varied by foreign composers who come as long-term or even permanent guests because they have found a public interested in their often experimental music in Germany. Thus Mauricio Kagel's surrealist-dadaist show *Sur Scène* amused, thus the Hungarian György Ligeti found approval as a controversial fighter for new notation and a constantly changing musical syntax that is developed anew for each work. The elder statesmen of modern music, for example Paul Hindemith and Ernst Krenek, have been increasingly active in Germany in the last few years, both as composers and as conductors and interpreters of their own works. To be sure Hindemith, who died on December 29, 1963, in a Frankfurt hospital, suffered because he also encountered severe criticism in West Germany. The public greeted him heartily as the beloved master, the already classical composer of *Mathis* even though some reservations about the former shocker of the bourgeoisie remained latent, but young composers wanted nothing to do with Hindemith's *Unterweisung im Tonsatz.*

Ernst Krenek is not, to be sure, a born German. But he had been in Germany for a long time up to 1933 and after 1945 has been there again. Krenek is a tireless stimulus and a constant searcher who in recent years has himself been seeking stimulus in Germany. He has "looked over the shoulders of the young," as he put it in the title of one of his essays, and thereby has himself remained young. He has, however, no more overcome the problem of permanent revolution than his contemporary Winfried Zillig has solved the problem of fidelity to his own stylistic origins. Zillig, who as a writer about music has contributed much to the understanding of contemporary music and as a conductor has brought attention to contemporary works of the most diverse sort, in his own works hews to one line despite all influences for change. Though he was a Schoenberg student, he did not cut himself off completely from tonality. He tried rather to exploit it in his own personal manner. There are no traditional tonal functions in Zillig's music; there is rather a suspension and a wandering among tonalities that — as in Debussy — seems both familiar and strange at the same time. His best pieces, among them the highly personally orchestrated Verlaine songs, are a melancholy Mahler-like echo of late Romanticism. They contain music whose fascination is so strong that it silences the question of the contemporary relevance of the vocabulary.

Karl Amadeus Hartmann (born 1905 in Munich) was in essence similar to Zillig and thus counts as one of the fixed poles of German music. His services to the development of the *Musica Viva* concerts in Munich were themselves sufficient to make him one of the most important personalities of post-war German music. Hartmann gave a hearing to all trends in modern music in this concert series. He furthered everything that seemed original and well-founded. Throughout West Germany, *Musica Viva* enjoyed the reputation of an ideal series of concerts of contemporary music, a series so cleverly organized and so attractively made with regard to both the program and the performers that the public became taken with them; the concerts were not given for a small, esoteric circle, but were held in the largest auditorium in Munich. And the auditorium was always sold out. Hartmann's early death towards the end of 1963, like the deaths of Winfried Zillig and Paul Hindemith a few weeks later, opened a painful gap in the ranks of German composers of stature. Hartmann must be considered one of the last of the great symphonists; he filled the form with Baroque and medieval contrapuntal elements and with an Expressionist pathos. The listener never doubted that he was in the presence of a musician of elemental expressive power. Hartmann's eight symphonies may be counted as the most honest and at the same time most substantial works in German music of the 20th century.

Several German composers of the middle generation are still to be mentioned. There are Günter Bialas, whose music is highly compressed;

Ernst Pepping, who is also important as a church musician; and the splendid contrapuntist Johann Nepomuk David. Siegfried Borris, Karl Höller, Kurt Hassenberg, Harold Genzmer, and Johannes Driessler are among those who practice a moderate modernism with a Hindemithian flavor but also pregnant individual traits. Most of them occupy conservatory posts in addition to their work as composers. Among the younger composers who consciously remain more or less distant from the avant-garde and seek their own ways in a fashion that must be taken seriously, one should mention Jürg Bauer, Reinhold Finkbeiner, Bernd Aloys Zimmermann, Hans Ulrich Engelmann, and Friedrich Voss.

When one realizes that Richard Strauss died in 1949 and that two years later Stockhausen's *Kreuzspiel* was written, that among the young generation the work of Henze and Killmayer is not only possible but can be meaningful alongside Stockhausen's experiments, the variety in German music — insofar as one considers only West Germany — is almost surprising and also encouraging. Today the international musical avant-garde meets in Darmstadt. Tomorrow the modern and serious *Leichte Musik* meets in Stuttgart. The day after tomorrow there is a festival with the works of younger composers who wish to find their own way among Hindemith, Stravinsky, and experimental music. New musical activity and the activity of musical organizations pulsate everywhere. It is impossible to find a single line, a single denominator to which all composers can be brought as one once could do with "neo-Baroque" or "neo-Classical," terms with which historical stages of development could strikingly and comprehensively be characterized. The chronicler may consider that a disadvantage, a failure of music that does not want to bind itself to a unified style for this era. Other observers see here an opportunity and confirmation of the liveliness of the new musical life.

Whereas in the '50s whatever behaved as if it were avant-garde music was often supported onesidedly and without examination — and this attitude was also present in the press and the radio — a certain sobriety has now set in. Today quality again stands in first place. One can find it in the avant-garde camp but also among comparatively conservative composers. The prophets who maintain that one direction and one direction alone has possibilities for the future must realize that there is a broad range of discussable and viable contemporary approaches — alongside, of course, of some genuinely undiscussable absurdities. Everything valid has the right to attentive observation. Thus regarded, the fullness of musical events in the 1960s in West Germany is a happy, positive, and hopeful sign. It can be assumed today that every young composer will have concerned himself with Schoenberg, Webern, Stravinsky, and Bartók. He must then find his own style, and he cannot make it easy for himself by trying to fit himself into a current school, as seemed proper ten years ago. The taboo of the Webern disciples is broken. The avant-gardists are no longer without criticism and competition for the favor of the experts. This may well be to their own advantage. It is certainly to the advantage of tomorrow's musical life.

(Translated by Donald Mintz)

CONTEMPORARY MUSIC IN AUSTRIA

By RUDOLF KLEIN

THE contemporary musical scene in Austria, as far as it is determined by new and creative forces, is distinguished through a number of well-defined, unique personalities, rather than through any soaring genius or even an outstanding talent. This situation, which developed after the First World War, prevailed all through the ensuing cataclysm. Yet, though the typical contemporary Austrian composer stands alone and works alone, there has developed a certain stylistic trend, noticeable, but not strong enough to be defined as a "school." It is therefore important to re-acquaint oneself with the musical currents between the two World Wars before an attempt can be made to judge the present-day situation.

A remarkably large number of composers between the two wars have tried to perpetuate the Romantic past. This group falls into three sections: The first followed the example of German Romanticism: Julius Bittner, Erich Korngold, Wilhelm Kienzl, and other minor luminaries. The second section chose the example of the classicistic, Austrian Romanticism: its last representative is Franz Schmidt, who died in 1939. He gained a certain local reputation through his organ music and especially through the oratorio *Das Buch mit sieben Siegeln*. His four symphonies are appealing to the listener for their classicistic austerity and the seriousness of the counterpoint. In the purity of their procedures they contrast favorably with the pathos and sweeping rhythms of the German neo-Romantics, in the same sense as does Bruckner but without his gigantism in form. *Das Buch mit sieben Siegeln* is still part of the Viennese repertory, while the other compositions are almost forgotten. The third group of this generation comprises those composers who were deeply influenced by Impressionism. One of them, Franz Schreker, wrote a number of operas, none of which is produced any more. The dean of the Austrian composers, Joseph Marx (d. 1964), belonged to the same Impressionistic circle, although he did not compose any operas. He devoted himself, like Hugo Wolf, who was also born in Graz, to the composition of *Lieder,* bringing this genre to its last Impressionistic flowering. They are occasionally still included in concert programs.

The three great masters who are today considered to be the exponents of the modern Viennese School, Arnold Schoenberg, Alban Berg, and Anton Webern, developed in their works the form and expression to which Gustav Mahler aspired but which he was unable to achieve because of his attachment to a highly Romantic style of writing. In applying the term "Viennese School," however, one should not lose sight of the uniqueness and individuality of each of these three masters, qualities that were never lost even though all three men worked along similar lines and in some respects complemented one another.

Arnold Schoenberg's spiritual forces broke through the barriers that seemed to guard the frontiers of musical expression forever. Anton Webern followed Schoenberg's lead into this "terra nova." And since daring and inspiration could not by themselves provide a valid alliance, in the person of Alban Berg a third master had to make his appearance to prove that in the new musical medium, too, nothing would prevail that had not been created by genius.

It is for that reason that Alban Berg's example, being inimitable, has found no successor. After 1945 Austria experienced a marked renaissance of his works, although little of it reached the concert stage. The opera *Wozzeck* was first performed at the Salzburg Festivals, after which it also conquered the stage of the Vienna State Opera. This fact deserves mention because this opera-museum otherwise completely ignores the Austrian music of the 20th century. Even the unfinished opera *Lulu* had a surprising rebirth when it was performed in the Theater an der Wien as part of the Vienna Festival in 1962 and 1963.

Arnold Schoenberg and Anton Webern, however, found a great number of successors, Schoenberg through his clear intellect and great integrity, Webern by setting an example, which was not affected by his early, unfortunate death by a bullet in Mittersill in 1945. There are other masters of the between-wars period who made history, for example Bartók, Stravinsky, Hindemith. Yet Schoenberg and Webern sent out impulses that revolutionized the musical world in an unprecedented way. This revolution has not yet found its classification, but this much is certain: it is world-embracing, it is so profound that every creative musician must come to terms with it, and it has introduced a new epoch in the history of music. Contrary to all theories of historical curves, of the ups and downs of periods of cultural significance, it is obvious that Austria, after having been a leader during the Classic and Romantic periods, has revealed a new peak in the 20th century. The old and antiquated "land of music" has given to the world the longed-for and scarcely expected ferment from which music can strike out in a new direction.

The old "land of music" should perhaps not be blamed for the fact that the prophet was not recognized in his own country. In the period between the wars there was a greater hunger for culture everywhere in the world than in Austria. And so the masters either went abroad or like Webern fled into an "inner exile," into isolation. But even the cultural élite abroad, even the young composers needed time to understand and accept the new. It is in this context that the cultural caesura of the war years seems to be like a rest, the taking of a deep breath for a new beginning. The year 1945 was the year zero of the new music, and not only in Austria but in the whole world.

The first generation, the contemporaries of the masters of the Viennese School, stood of necessity on both sides of the turning-point. These composers were either devoted to the past or headed into the future, depending on their taste and personality. Political developments, too, were responsible for the fact that those composers who looked into the future had to overcome the year zero while in foreign countries. According to their descent and historical nationality, however, they are still to be classified as Austrians. The most important of all is without doubt Ernst Krenek. This composer — now living in America — had never been a direct pupil of Schoenberg's but he had absorbed so much of the Master's ideas and concepts through contact with his Berlin circle that he was for a long time considered to be the most outspoken exponent of Schoenberg's spirit. Moreover Krenek's sharp intellect recognized the great danger of stagnation and inflexibility particularly threatening to this kind of thinking. Thus he was the only one of those composers who formed the first inner circle of the Viennese School who was later in close and continuous contact with the developments of today and tomorrow. This explains, most probably, why Krenek tried to come to grips with all forms of musical expression, including the serial and aleatory experiments. His historical position with respect to the Viennese School seems to be firmly expressed in the two operas *Karl V* and *Pallas Athene weint;* while later experiments disclose an urge to "belong." Krenek's relationship to his homeland was that mixture of hatred and love typical of Austrians living abroad who were not recognized in the country of their birth. Although he has received recognition in the form of awards and prizes, he has not received it in the form of performances of his works.

Egon Wellesz, now living in England, is most probably the one composer of the Viennese School who has moved farthest away from its focus. In him, the eminent scholar, equally important as musicologist and as composer, the spirit of the Austrian Baroque was more deeply alive than in the three grand masters of the Viennese School. Because of this, he could create what the others were unable to conceive of; he filled in the picture of the Viennese School from an aspect that was essential but would have otherwise been missing. His contributions in the fields of the music drama and the symphony were of a remarkable scope and were actually the "missing link" between the Baroque and the Viennese School. Schoenberg's and Berg's attitude towards Romanticism is well known. Wellesz, however, provided the link to a definite Baroque trait within the Austrian that, although subdued at this time, was an essential part of the national character. He therefore succeeded in emphasizing the topological attribute in the concept "Viennese School." This contribution of Wellesz's is of a historical nature. His works, although of remarkable quality, play hardly any part in contemporary musical life, either in international or in Austrian circles.

While Ernst Krenek and Egon Wellesz were successful in blending their individual characteristics with Schoenberg's new ideas, this was not possible for a number of other composers who were drinking from the same fountain but were unable to accomplish anything similar. One could classify these composers as the "second generation" of the Viennese School by not using the term in its chronological sense. The composers so classified followed Schoenberg's ideas but were overtaken and overwhelmed by rapid developments in the world of music during the post-war period. Among them we find first-class musicians. Their failure to keep pace at all times with the newest and most progressive was often due not to inability to adjust but rather to their honesty. And yet since they were unable to create effectively in their own language something new and perceptive, their fate seems to be isolation.

Hans Erich Apostel, who was born in Karlsruhe but has lived in

Vienna since 1919, is widely considered to be the legitimate adminis-
trator of Schoenberg's estate in Austria. Deriving his technique from
an Expressionistic *Lied*-style, Apostel devoted himself more and more
to a fusion of the new musical language, including twelve-tone technique, with the Classical forms, which he found in their purest expression in the works of Joseph Haydn. While Apostel goes about his
work quietly and in isolation and rarely experiences the glamor of an
important performance, Hanns Jelinek enjoys the brighter lights of
publicity, more, however, for his eminence as theoretician and pedagogue
than for his compositions, most of which are mathematically faultless
examples of the twelve-tone technique. Because of his textbook on
that technique and innumerable other writings in which he attempts
to develop a well-defined musical system, he has gained at home as
well as abroad the reputation of being the leading theoretician of
dodecaphony. It is typical of this highly skilled craftsman among
composers that he is capable of writing "light" music in a traditional
manner, and even hit tunes. His teaching activities at the Wiener
Hochschule für Musik are important. There he instructs an international
circle of young composers in the fundamentals of Schoenberg's serial
technique. This circle could be classified as "grandchildren" of the
Viennese School. Their style has often moved a considerable distance
away from that of their predecessors. Jelinek the teacher has adjusted
well to this necessary centrifugal force.

Two other young musicians have been drawn into the circle of the
Viennese School by the personality of Joseph Polnauer, a pupil of
Schoenberg's who has been active only as a theorist. They are Karl
Heinz Füssl and Michael Gielen. Füssl attached himself to Webern;
he disappeared after a short trial period from the concert stage, being
completely absorbed by his interest in musicology. Michael Gielen, son
of Joseph Gielen, the well-known stage director and formerly administrative director of the Burgtheater, is so fully occupied as a conductor
— he is orchestral director of the Stockholm Opera — that he composes
very little. His latest works are attempts to recapture Schoenberg's and
Webern's innovations on another plane. The great mental concentration
expressed in his works brings him close to the style of the serial
experiments.

It is well known how Schoenberg's and Webern's ideas led, after
intermediate stages and transformations occurring on an international
scale, to these new and latest experiments. As manifold and differentiated
as these experiments may be technically, so similar to each other are

the results. While the twelve-tone style of the first and second generations of the Viennese School still left possibilities for individual expression, the conformity of musical language in the latest serial compositions seems to be worldwide and without exception.

International as this language has become, it is scarcely heard in the country in which its foundations were laid. Yet even those alumni of the Viennese School who believe they must fight it must be discussed; ungrateful descendants are still members of the family.

Friedrich Cerha is undoubtedly the most talented and most active member of this third generation. An outstanding violinist, he contributed to the musical scene in Austria by the formation and administration of an ensemble called *die reihe,* a forum through which he brought before the public the latest experiments at home and abroad. The concerts of this ensemble, either in the Wiener Konzerthaus or in the Museum des XX. Jahrhunderts, provide practically the only possibility of information on serial music. Cerha produces, in addition, innumerable compositions that once were avant-garde, from Varèse to Antheil, from Satie to Stravinsky. Austrian composers are rarely represented, except for the works of Schoenberg, Berg, and Webern. Noteworthy is his own composition, *Relazioni fragili* for harpsichord and chamber orchestra. The piece, impossible to follow intellectually, nevertheless gives an impression of logic and coherence. This, together with its unusual sound, creates an effect worthy of comparison with that of some of the finest works of Boulez and Nono.

Kurt Schwertsik, co-founder of *die reihe,* has so far had only a few of his own works performed, none of it very convincing. To the inner circle of serialists belong two "Austrians by choice," György Ligeti and Roman Haubenstock-Ramati, who have gained a certain reputation abroad but are hardly ever performed in Austria.

One other personality, who died in 1959 yet had gained historical significance while still alive, deserves mention in connection with the Viennese School and its successors; less, however, on the basis of his compositions than because of his extraordinary mentality. Abroad, Joseph Matthias Hauer is often grouped with the Viennese School because he also worked with a twelve-tone system. It is true that he had composed his works, at least those he himself regarded as valid, on the basis of a dodecaphony that he had developed even before Schoenberg. But the resemblance of Hauer's style to Schoenberg's is only superficial. His approach to the musical material was at the outset a matter of philosophy and of cosmic proportions, which had only an incidental relationship to music. He could just as well have expressed his numbers game in the form of drawings, or found some other medium for it. Nevertheless his "philosophy in sound," being of a Far-Eastern character, had a unique musical physiognomy: though many notes are used simultaneously, what is heard is transparent, polyphonic, and at the same time monotonous, and as it were "frozen" geometric exercises. After the composer's death they were soon forgotten. Hauer was unquestionably an eccentric and outsider, yet a man who relentlessly pursued his ideas and without seeking for exterior success.

Besides the composers who because of the character of their works belong to the Viennese School or who have a tangential relationship to it, a second group, which displays a certain stylistic unity, deserves mention. It consists of those composers who, despite very different individual styles, are related to each other by the common use of polyphony. This is the first time in two centuries that such a group has appeared in Austria. The country of Classicism and Romanticism has, musically speaking, always been homophonic, which did not, of course, entirely exclude polyphony on a chordal basis. The reason for the appearance of a whole group of composers writing in the polyphonic manner may have its origin in the impetus that this style had gained internationally in the first half of the 20th century, through the models furnished especially by Paul Hindemith. Austria may also consider a model closer to home: Johann Nepomuk David, now living in Stuttgart, who was born in Upper Austria and is probably the most eminent living Austrian composer.

Leipzig and its Bach cult have been of great importance for David: to think in polyphonic terms, as he learned to do from the works of the cantor of the Thomasschule and the music of the Netherlanders, has become his second nature. His long term as teacher at the State Conservatory in Leipzig made him definitely a polyphonic composer in the sense of Bach, yet did not inhibit his Austrian preference for supple melody, flexible rhythm — yes even for a certain melodic opulence. He had gained a secure position in the ranks of internationally acknowledged masters through his choral and organ works and to a lesser degree through his symphonic composition, which had found recognition in the German-speaking countries. His style became in recent years more complicated, reflective, and less popular. Yet it has, for the same reasons, grown in the estimation of the demanding and knowledgeable. Nevertheless, David is one of those introverted natures who pay no attention either to the public or to success. German and

Austrian organists consider his organ works today to hold first place among the compositions of living composers. His choral compositions are seldom missing from programs of any pretentions. The absolute seriousness and concentration of these compositions put them almost into the category of religious music even if the texts are of secular origin. David does not write strictly liturgical music; he prefers to transform the concert hall into a church.

Anton Heiller belongs among the younger Austrian composers who were deeply impressed by David's example. He is one of the most gifted of them and a born dramatist and lyricist in the polyphonic style. In contrast to David, he devotes himself predominantly to religious music; Catholic Masses and choral music on liturgical themes make up the larger part of his work. However he has written some compositions for the concert hall that are stylistically less severe, even though they employ religious texts. A psalm-cantata, a Te Deum, and organ works have aroused considerable admiration and given proof that the composer is developing a personal style.

Paul Angerer, having grown up in the same atmosphere of polyphony, at the very beginning chose Paul Hindemith as his mentor and ideal. While Heiller comes from the organ — he is one of the foremost living organists and improvisers — Angerer is an outstanding violist and chamber-music player. He has gained a good reputation in Vienna, especially by the choice of extraordinary programs, presented with his own chamber orchestra. Unfortunately he lives now in Germany, where his career as a conductor led him. The polyphonic style of his compositions, as time went on, grew from a beginning in diatonic simplicity into chromatic animation and great expressiveness. His real talent seems to be in the field of chamber music, in spite of his remarkable success also in the fields of incidental music for the stage (i.e. for the Burgtheater), for films, radio music, and television operas.

A list of composers who belong stylistically in the group of polyphonists would be rather long. They write primarily music for use in churches and their contrapuntal writing is therefore not too complicated for the listener. Skillfulness in their trade marks the positive side of these composers, lack of distinctiveness in facture their negative side. They play practically no part on the concert stage except for the rare appearance of one or another of their works as part of a choral concert.

A few others should be mentioned: musicians who are basically practitioners and write for practitioners — less, however, in the sense of David than in that of Hindemith; somewhat cool, less vocal, aiming rather at instrumental effects. To this group belongs Robert Schollum, who often composes in the atonal manner and has also established some relationship to the Viennese School through the use of twelve-tone technique. This bond, however, is not as strong as that with polyphonic utilitarianism, which can easily be explained by Schollum's tie to the musical youth movement. Ernst Tittel writes *Gebrauchsmusik* with great skill and knowledge for the church and the concert hall. Karl Schiske, too, teacher of composition at the Musikakademie, comes from this wing. He is a formalist and enjoys refining his phrases with great skill down to the last possible nuance and indulging in polyphonic artificialities somewhat in the manner of the old Netherlanders. His music becomes, as time goes on, more severe, more difficult, asensual, and objective. This is most probably the reason why it is less and less heard. It is, however, of great importance that Schiske's course at the Akademie, like Jelinek's, has become the rallying place of all pupils with an interest in progressive developments. It seems that his reputation as a teacher surpasses that as a composer.

Another group of Austrian composers could be classified as "symphonists"; they write predominantly orchestral works that are influenced by the symphonic tradition. There are of course many and decided differences among this group. They have however one characteristic in common: their language is much more easily understood than that of all the composers mentioned before. The listener subconsciously associates his reminiscences with the style of the new work and, since the idiom of these composers is not too far removed from functional harmony, he seldom has any difficulty in comprehending it. Yet it would be wrong to assume that the composers of this group receive any representation to speak of in Austrian concert programs.

Of those symphonists who consider themselves direct successors to the Romantic tradition, we must mention Bernhard Paumgartner, president of the Salzburg Festival, Franz Salmhofer, and Alfred Uhl. Uhl is the leader of the conservative section at the Akademie. His works — including the oratorio *Gilgamesh* — are occasionally performed on the concert stage, but without achieving more than a *succès d'estime*.

One of the few Austrian composers who play a certain role on the international scene is Gottfried von Einem. His career started with ballet music and was considerably advanced through the Salzburg premières of the two operas *Dantons Tod* and *Der Prozess*. The former, especially, adapted from Büchner's drama, had a triumphal success on most of the European stages. This opera appeared again in the last two years as part of the Vienna Festival weeks at the Theater an der Wien and impressed for its force, the power of its choral scenes, and its thoroughly modern texture. After this work, which had its première in 1947, von Einem's style assumed a definitely Apollonian classicistic cast. In his latest symphonic works, for example in his so-called *Philadelphia Symphony*, he has revealed himself as a pronounced successor of Viennese Classicism; earlier traits of his style — an individual approach to form, emphasis on rhythm, an open texture in the manner of his teacher Boris Blacher — are combined with a return to simple harmony and equally simple melody, often not free of banality. Many consider this style too plain. It is a fact that von Einem has not been able to repeat the impact of his first opera. His work has, nevertheless, undeniable qualities and it is understandable that he alone of the intermediate generation of Austrian composers has risen above purely local recognition.

Theodor Berger, repeatedly heard as a ballet composer and as a "symphonist," was unable to achieve a similar success either in Vienna or abroad. The reason is, first, his severe, often provocative language, which has occasionally led to scandals in the concert hall; secondly, his lack of economy, formal clarity, and lucidity. The composer has now worked for many years in seclusion. Gerhard Wimberger, teacher of a course on conducting at the Salzburg Musikakademie, is one of the younger "symphonists" who has gained a certain recognition, although only in Germany, where his operas, ballets, and concert pieces are occasionally performed. This young composer, who follows the lead of Stravinsky and Bartók, is seldom heard in Vienna.

And herewith we come to the legions of those composers who are industrious, who win prizes, even government prizes, who however are only heard in concerts that are subsidized by the state or other sponsors, because their work is either not good enough to be produced on the basis of free competition on the concert stage or because this is what the concert managers believe. This does not necessarily prove to be the final, unequivocal judgment. Yet the occasional performances in subsidized concerts hardly permit of a revision of this general impression. Of course, contemporary composers all share the opinion that lack of official support of the creative arts in Austria is to be blamed for the catastrophic situation. In fact the state, the most important Maecenas in Austria, does very little for its young composers. Concert managers — with the notable exception, until recently, of the Wiener Konzerthaus and Radio Wien — rarely perform any works by Austrian contemporary composers, so that there is scarcely any opportunity to judge their merits. The older composers get tired and resign, the younger ones know that except in rare cases composing will not provide their livelihood.

Consequently, the musical situation in Austria, as determined by its creative forces, is not a very happy one. After a promising breakthrough in the 'twenties came a period of stagnation, which has today most probably reached its lowest point. Although it was Austria's privilege to be the country where such masters as Schoenberg, Berg, and Webern, who shaped the lineaments of the music of our century, were born, lived, and created, many changes have since taken place. The few Austrian composers of some importance now live abroad, those who stayed at home have put their pens down in disappointment. Austria is gradually becoming a vast music-museum.

Of course, the situation in the rest of Europe is not much better. The public everywhere turns away from the new music. Although it is possible to maintain here and there, with the support of a present-day Maecenas (helped by tax-reduction), ivory towers as a last bastion for contemporary composers, true contact between the general public and modern music does not exist. A real genius will be needed to find the narrow path between experimentation and tradition that may lead to a revival. That this may happen in present-day Austria seems improbable. However, we have not reached the end yet, and the old "land of music" has surprised the world before. As Hofmannsthal says in Strauss's *Arabella:* "But the right one, if there is one for me in this world, he will stand there one day . . ."

(Translated by Helen Lange)

PROBLEMS OF STYLE IN
20TH-CENTURY CZECH MUSIC

By JAŇ RACEK and JIŘÍ VYSLOUŽIL

THE connection between contemporary Czech music and the native
traditions was perhaps at its strongest at the turn of the 19th
century. In the tendency of Czech music to maintain this connection
there was expressed not only its healthy, elemental, centuries-old talent
and strength, but also to a certain extent its disinclination to take the
measure of the new and bold creations of contemporary international
music. For this reason Czech music after 1900 did not present to the
artistic culture of Europe such vigorous features as for example did
Czech painting, even though great creative personalities developed
among Czech composers. This was the case even after the First World
War, when Czech music, too, unavoidably came into direct contact with
avant-garde international music. As late even as 1924, at the time of
the hundredth anniversary of the birth of Bedřich Smetana, founder
of modern Czech music, this great composer was still presented as the
leader of Czech musical culture, as the only possible signpost to the
future. The emphasis on the road laid out by Smetana was made with
deliberate thoroughness and was even intended to have the effect of a
healthy national corrective against all the universalizing tendencies, a
corrective that was the social and political consequence of the struggles
of the Czech nation for self-government and national independence
during the First World War and immediately after, and which, with
its clear-sighted nationalism, humanism, and democratic feeling to a
great extent renewed in contemporary Czech music the ideas and
artistic principles of Smetana's day. This dependence on Smetana
appeared once more in Czech music, and with great intensity, though
from the musical point of view more or less as an anachronism, after

1945 or 1948 in the work of the younger and middle generation of
modern, present-day Czech composers, although here the social and
ideological background was different.

An exceptional artistic personality in the post-Smetana generation
was undoubtedly Vítězslav Novák (1870-1949), without whom the
picture of contemporary Czech music would be incomplete. In his
symphonic cantatas (*Bouře — The Storm*, 1910), his operas and ballets
(*Zvíkovský rarášek — The Imp of Zvíkov*, 1914; *Lucerna — The
Lantern*, 1922; *Signorina Gioventú*, 1928), choral songs, symphonic
poems (*V Tatrách — In the Tatra Mountains*, 1902; *O věčné touze —
Eternal Longing*, 1904; *Toman a lesní panna — Toman and the Wood
Nymph*, 1907), and chamber compositions he broadly approached the
structural type of Smetana, but on the other hand was one of the first
composers who created — we may say with some slight exaggeration
— the conditions for the development of Czech musical Impressionism.
This, unlike the Impressionism of Debussy, was distinguished by an
exceptional feeling for melody and rhythm not infrequently of folk
origin. After Dvořák (and also after Janáček), Novák once more
discovered the significance of folk music for artistic creation.

Also in the post-Smetana generation a highly individual and important place was filled by Josef Suk (1874-1935), whose emotional nature
was close to the musical type of Dvořák. Gradually he freed himself from
the weight of Czech musical tradition, attaining a remarkable creative
upsurge of melodic and harmonic thought. He was also in vital contact
with international music, being influenced by Debussy, Reger, and perhaps too by the young Schoenberg. Suk's artistic growth led from Czech
traditionalism towards modern Czech music. This development of Suk
can be traced too in the intellectual organic structure of his works.
He gradually freed himself from a too fragile lyricism and in his
culminating piano cycles (*Životem a snem — Things Lived and
Dreamed*, 1909; *O přátelství — Friendship*, 1920), in the symphonic
poem *Zrání* (*Harvest-Tide*, 1917) and the symphonic cantata *Epilogue*
(1933), he seized artistically on ideas of great, timeless, and comprehensive human significance.

Otakar Ostrčil (1879-1935), for many years the notable head of
the Opera of the National Theater in Prague, in his operas (*Vlasty
skon — The Death of Vlast*, 1903), symphonic and choral compositions,
originally set out from the foundations laid by Smetana and Fibich,
but later a decisive influence on his work was that of Mahler. He was
a thorough musical craftsman, with a feeling for a firm, structural line

(the symphonic variations *Křížová cesta — Calvary,* 1928; and the opera *Honzovo království — Johnny's Kingdom,* 1932). The musicologist and composer Otakar Zich (1879-1934) followed a development similar to that of Ostrčil, early overcoming the one-sided influence of the Czech national and folk musical tradition and through the study of the last works of Beethoven and the compositions of Mahler attaining a highly personal polyphonic style.

The post-Smetana generation created with its finest compositions a further significant stage of Czech music. It meant that the proverbial spontaneous Czech musicality could claim yet another artistic victory, even although this new generation was destined to an increasing degree to hold the balance against Romantic hypersensitivity by means of a more concrete creative attitude on a rational basis. The artistic example of Novák was especially characteristic from this point of view. If we consider Czech music of the first decades of the century as a whole, it is no mere chance that the final word in the artistic growth of several new generations of composers fell to him.

We do of course find in the circle of Novák's immediate pupils artistic personalities that, from the point of view of quantity and the generation they belong to, are contradictory and varied. (Alois Hába, for instance, and numerous Slovak composers, including Alexandr Moyzes, Eugen Suchoň and Ján Cikker, were also pupils of Novák.) The main body of Novák's pupils however eventually took the road of their master, accepting formally and intellectually his compositional constructivism and folklore trend, revitalizing a somewhat stiff inventiveness with the refreshing waters of folksong. Many of Novák's pupils did not succeed in resisting the influence of their teacher and did not find sufficient strength to make original additions to his legacy. Others, especially the earliest, and thus the oldest of his pupils, were well prepared by Novák for their further musical vocation. This is particularly true of Ladislav Vycpálek (b. 1882), whose not very numerous but stylistically unusually well-balanced works represent a rare and decidedly intellectual type. In his songs, cantatas (*O posledních věcech člověka — Of the Last Things of Man,* 1921; *Blahoslavený ten člověk — Blessed is the Man,* 1933; *Czech Requiem,* 1940) and instrumental compositions (suites for solo violin and viola), he showed a distinct sense of strict structural order, models for which he found in Bach, Brahms, and also in Novák, who in addition showed him the way to the sources of folk music, from which Vycpálek drew. The bold sound effects and promising beginnings of a further pupil of Novák,

Boleslav Vomáčka (b. 1887) were expressed in his early vocal, choral, and piano compositions. This latter composer, who also wrote for the press, did not however find the strength to keep up with the development in music and expression that was thrusting so strongly ahead, and later sank into a sober traditionalism. Obviously happier, even if less vigorous, was the artistic development of another composer belonging to Novák's circle, Jaroslav Křička (b. 1887), who while he remained within the sphere of Novák's musical expression and sound, nevertheless acquired a fresh musical utterance with a folk coloring and considerable individuality. Křička is one of the masters of Czech chamber and children's song and is also the author of many stage and choral works. Many composers from Moravia attended Novák's class in composition at the Prague Conservatory, certainly because of the master's lasting tie with the folksong of that song-loving countryside. Outstanding Moravian pupils of Novák's were Jan Kunc (b. 1883), to whom the organization of musical education in Brno owes much, and who composed choral songs, songs, and instrumental works with a tinge of Dvořák in them; Vilém Petrželka (b. 1889), a great teacher of composition and composer of the remarkable Fifth String Quartet (1947); and Václav Kaprál (1889-1947), whose songs and choruses are among the outstanding expressions of Czech musical lyricism in the small forms. All these composers came to Novák from Janáček's school of composition in Brno. Another Moravian, Emil Axman (1887-1949), studied directly under Novák. In his cantatas, choruses, and symphonic compositions he attained a personal musical expression distinguished by the balladic and rhapsodic character typical of Moravia.

It was its tendency towards folk music that perhaps distinguished Novák's school most from the rest of modern European music and secured for it in the context of contemporary Czech music of the first decades of the 20th century a firm and conspicuous place. In that respect Novák and his pupils clearly stood apart from those of their own Czech generation who either organically carried on the Romantic-Classic tradition of Smetana (such as Otakar Jeremiáš, 1892-1962, the author of the astonishing soul-probing music drama *The Brothers Karamazov,* 1927); or found their own characteristic reaction to post-Wagnerian German music, such as Karel Boleslav Jirák (b. 1891), since 1947 active in Chicago, and Jaroslav Kvapil (1892-1958), a highly cultivated and intellectually inclined composer of the Mahler-Strauss type, with Dvořákian directness; or those who learned much from the Impressionism of Debussy, such as fertile opera and instrumental composer Osvald Chlubna (b. 1893).

The field of Czech music in the first decades of the 20th century is undoubtedly a rich one; in all sections of musical composition the leading members of the post-Smetana generation composed works that indicated a fruitful continuance of the Czech tradition of musicianship. This traditional character had its disadvantages, however. At those moments when the leading phenomena of the international musical avant-garde were demonstrating reliable new ways of sound and expression for the development of European music, the mainstream of contemporary Czech music was arrested somewhere at the level of late Romanticism and Impressionism. And this — taking the widest view — was not only the somewhat ungrateful fate of such great masters as Novák and Foerster, who, we may say, long outlived their day (let us recall here too Strauss and Pfitzner), but also the unenviable destiny of many of the pupils of those masters.

From this stylistically outdated and narrowly conceived artistic outlook Czech music was liberated by Leoš Janáček (1854-1928), a composer who was long condemned to linger with his creative work on the very periphery of the Czech musical life of Brno, but who, no sooner had he attained international recognition (the Vienna première of *Jenufa,* 1918), at once took his place as one of the leading world composers of the 20th century.

It is certainly paradoxical that this member of the generation of Dvořák and Fibich is today accounted the most advanced composer of Czech contemporary music. Nor can it be denied that even he did not completely succeed in freeing himself from the dynamic Czech musical tradition. This traditional element, however, does not affect his work disturbingly, but on the contrary has an attractive and suggestive effect, since he was able to fit it organically into the context of 20th-century music, as did Bartók and Stravinsky. He was also the only Czech composer of his generation who succeeded immediately after the First World War in making close contacts with the avant-garde in current international music, above all at the festivals of the International Society for Contemporary Music in Salzburg (1923), Prague (1924), Venice (1925), and Frankfurt (1927).

The graph of development of Janáček's musical style went through several stages from the late neo-Romantic period almost up to the Expressionism of the so-called Second Viennese School. In his first creative period (from about 1873 to 1895), Janáček based his work on the monumental Czech national art, especially on the Classic-

Romantic synthesis of Smetana and Dvořák (the opera *Šárka*, 1888, the orchestral *Lašské tance — Lachian Dances,* 1889). But even at that time he bade farewell to the neo-Romanticism of Wagner and decisively refused Wagner's musico-dramatic principle, thus attaining his own personal style, founded on the melodic basis of Czech folksong and the intonation of colloquial Czech. In his second creative period, which began with *Její pastorkyně (Jenufa,* 1894-1903) and ended roughly about 1918, he created a new functional form for musical drama. Thus Janáček passed from folklore raised to a higher power by realism, to a psychological realism in which he rid himself of direct dependence on folksong and created on the basis of a prose libretto a new, freely and rhapsodically constructed type of vocal dramatic melody that denied the dualism of aria and recitative traditional for opera. This determined Janáček's historical importance for the further development of Czech and international opera, in which he already occupied an entirely exceptional place alongside Debussy and Strauss. The further operas of this period (such as *Výlety pana Broučka — The Excursions of Mr. Brouček,* 1918) are based on the same stylistic principle as *Jenufa,* as are the choral songs (*Kantor Halfar — Schoolmaster Halfar,* 1906; *Maryčka Magdonova,* 1907; and *Sedmdesát tisíc — Seventy Thousand,* 1909), and the overwhelming chamber cantata for tenor, female chorus, and piano, *Zápisník zmizelého (The Diary of a Young Man Who Vanished,* 1919).

The third creative period of Janáček belongs roughly to the years 1918-28. During it Janáček thought out to its conclusion the realistic style of *Jenufa* and created one of the supreme works of Slavonic psychological and musically realistic drama, the opera *Káta Kabanová* (1921). In his next opera, *Příhody lišky Bystroušky (The Cunning Little Vixen,* 1923), Janáček almost approached the sensuously affecting Impressionism of Debussy, preserving of course considerable musical independence thanks to the fact that he continually drew on the melodiousness and rhythm of colloquial Czech and of folksong. This basis of sound and expression assured Janáček's independence even when in his last works he approached the avant-garde music of Schoenberg and Stravinsky, namely in chamber music (the Piano Concertino, 1925, and the Capriccio, 1926), orchestral music (the Sinfonietta, 1926), choral music (*Glagolitic Mass,* 1926) and operas (*Věc Makropulos — The Makropulos Case,* 1925; *Z mrtvého domu — The House of the Dead,* 1928). It is true that his musical expression and sound, especially in *The House of the Dead,* attained remarkably expressive dramatic conviction, not unlike the Expressionistic utterance of Berg's *Wozzeck*, but nevertheless Janáček, by virtue of the fact that not even now did he forsake his firm tonal basis and his Slavonic folk melody, remained true to himself.

In comparison with the most vigorous streams of sound and expression in the avant-garde of international music, Janáček even in his culminating works preserved much of tradition. He also consistently endeavored to attain music that would have a programmatic content, differing in this diametrically from that part of the international musical avant-garde of the inter-war period which stressed only the so-called pure, absolutely artistic interplay of musical forms dependent solely on pure sound phenomena.

For long Janáček was denied his exceptional position in the development of modern Czech and international music, and because of his apparent isolation he was removed from its context as a musical phenomenon who could be followed only with difficulty. Owing to his highly individual musical language and headstrong vigor he found little comprehension among his immediate pupils. The most promising of them was Pavel Haas (1899-1944), a concentration camp victim of the Second World War, who composed daring avant-garde chamber music (three String Quartets, 1920, 1925, 1938; a Wind Quintet, 1929; a Piano Suite, 1935); an opera, *The Charlatan*, 1937; and songs (the cycle *Vyvolená — The Chosen One*, 1926; *V lidovém tónu — In a Folk Key*, 1940; and *Songs to Words from Chinese Poetry*, 1944). It was not until some distance of time, however, that it was possible to recognize how Janáček, mainly by the work of the last decades of his life, showed the way to that section of the Czech generation of composers after the First World War who took part in the current struggles for a new outlook on art and whose work proved a fruitful continuation of the artistic endeavors of the musical avant-garde of Schoenberg and Stravinsky.

The artistic endeavor and work of one of the most characteristic figures of Czech and European music of the last fifty years, namely Alois Hába (b. 1893), are particularly symptomatic of this. A daring musical thinker and artist, he was bound to Janáček by family background and also by his intrinsic relationship to the Czech tradition of folk and art music, to which he proclaimed his theoretical allegiance and on which he also drew in his compositions. The melodic and rhythmic substance of Hába's musical expression is based on the

archaic melodic types of East Moravian folk music, in which he discovered microtonal interval relationships and sequences and a free
(athematic) method of composition. The melodic and rhythmic elements from the songs of his native countryside, along with those of
oriental music, whose inner genetic connections he also studied theoretically, became one of the basic points of departure of his musical
style. Without these we could scarcely succeed in imagining the microtonal (mainly quarter-tone) compositions of Hába. The freely conceived
modality of the half-tone compositions can also be considered a result
of the fruitful influence of Moravian folksong on the musical thought
of Hába. The study of the masters of vocal and instrumental polyphony
and acquaintance with the "atonal" music of Schoenberg then
strengthened Hába in his determination to develop microtonal and
chromatic sounds at the level of the structurally most difficult forms of
European music. Hába thus became one of the most daring composers
in respect of sound and one of the artistically most individual experimenters in Czech and international modern music. In harmony he got
as far as using eighteen voices, in melody he began to use still more
varied shades of interval and expression than did for example Schoenberg in his twelve-tone chromatic composition.

The initial stages of Hába's microtonal composition were indissolubly
bound up with string instruments (the first mature microtonal composition in athematic style was the Third String Quartet in the quarter-
tone system, 1922). Hába required a certain length of time in order
to create, by constructing new quarter-tone instruments (piano, har-
monium, clarinet, trumpet), the conditions necessary for the further
development of microtonal composition. Thus gradually Hába's
microtonal composing developed for the piano, voice, and
chamber combinations, and at length in a mature work of artistic
synthesis, the opera *Matka* (*The Mother*, 1929-30, to the composer's
own libretto). Besides soloists, choir, and dancers Hába used in this, his
masterpiece, a chamber orchestra with quarter-tone instruments
and thus attained in sound and expression entirely new musico-dramatic
values. The style of Hába in *The Mother* follows the musico-dramatic
type of Janáček and consistently sticks to athematicism.

In recent years Hába has written further quarter-tone compositions
(the Sixth, Twelfth, Fourteenth String Quartets, 1950, 1960, 1963)
and sixth-tone compositions (the Tenth and Eleventh String Quartets,
1952, 1959) and is also the composer of an unperformed sixth-tone opera
Přijd království Tvé (*Thy Kingdom Come*, 1942).

In Hába's extensive work half-tone compositions occupy as significant a place as his microtonal pieces. The remarkable half-tone quartets (the Seventh, Eighth, Ninth, 1951-52), orchestral pieces (Overture, 1921; Symphonic Fantasy, *Cesta života* — *The Way of Life*, 1934; *Wallachian Suite*, 1952), the opera *Nová země* (*New Land*) based on the novel by the Soviet Russian writer Gladkov (1936), and piano compositions (Piano Pieces, 1921; Symphonic Fantasy, 1921) show us Hába as the representative of the chromaticism of the Second Vienna School and of a freely conceived modality whose origin lies in folk music.

Hába succeeded with obstinate consistency in carrying out his artistic conceptions, but any one-sided consistency was always contrary to his free conception of creative art. Hence all these half-tone compositions are also the expression of Hába's freely growing artistic nature, which was never willing to be bound by *a priori* compositional rules and schemes. This rare quality also distinguished his very considerable teaching activity at the Prague Conservatory, where he founded and developed the Department of Quarter-Tone Music (1923) and educated a generation of Czech and foreign composers to a free and conscious recognition of all compositional techniques and styles. Hába's class produced a vigorous group of Czech composers who followed his artistic example in microtonal and athematic compositions. Outstanding among them was Miroslav Ponc (b. 1902), the prominent adherent of quarter-tone music in Germany (at one time member of the avant-garde group Sturm), composer of remarkable stage music, interesting microtonal miniatures, and a quarter-tone *Overture to an Antique Tragedy* for ochestra (1930), which aroused interest at the Festival of the International Society for Contemporary Music in Vienna (1923). Alois Hába's brother Karel (b. 1898) is not only the creator of compositions written microtonally and with modal technique, but at the same time was for many years a distinguished interpreter of violin and viola quarter-tone works. So too another pupil of Hába's, Karel Reiner (b. 1910), devoted himself to the interpretation of quarter-tone music on the piano. In composition, however, he inclined more to athematic and "atonal" half-tone composition. Still another talented pupil of Hába's, Václav Kašlík (b. 1919), belongs to the leading avant-garde opera producers and composers of the present day.

A number of other pupils of Hába began their artistic career with promising and vigorous compositions, but during the period of the renaissance of Smetana's artistic legacy, which took place after 1945, they also adopted uncritically the sound and expression of Smetana's music and thus could not find for the new content they wished to express an adequate form. In this unequal relation of intended content and of actual sound lie for example the contradictions of the symphonic cycle *Ostrava* (1953) by Rudolf Kubín (b. 1909), who intended in this work to write a kind of modern equivalent to Smetana's *My Country*, or even the contradictions of the cantata *The Czech Polka* (1950) by Václav Dobiáš (b. 1909), which owes its musical language to Smetana's polkas.

Hába's contemporary Bohuslav Martinů (1890-1959), decidedly, after Dvořák and Janáček, the most internationally significant Czech composer, was in his artistic temperament the very antithesis of Hába. If we place alongside each other the two leading figures of modern Czech music, we cannot help calling to mind the parallel, at the level of international music, with the names of Schoenberg and Stravinsky. Nevertheless we shall not take as axiomatic any inner or stylistic bond between the Czech master and the suggestive artistic personality of Stravinsky. It is true that Martinů became acquainted with *The Rite of Spring* and *The Wedding* at decisive moments of his artistic development, and was carried away by his enthusiasm for the linear constructivism and polytonal modality of these great scores, but what Stravinsky led Martinů to was a highly personal reshaping and development of the compositional principles he had recognized, and the discovery of the vital values of traditional Czech musicality, which could be organically welded into the context of contemporary international music.

This dual aspect runs through the entire creative striving of Martinů as a composer from the very beginning of his artistic development. In the first years of his stay in Paris he wrote not only the orchestral pieces *Half-Time* (1924) and *La Bagarre* (1926), marked by the civilism of Satie, but also the *Three Czech Dances* (1926) and the *Seven Czech Dances* (1929) for the piano. Martinů's compositions even of this period show that he consciously inclined towards the Czech folk lyric quality. This penetrated ever more markedly into his numerous neo-Classic scores, which in their melody and rhythm bear witness to the Czech nationality of the composer. Martinů's orientation towards folksong culminated in several extensive stage and choral works, in which he made considerable use of folk ballad models: in the ballet *Špaliček* (1931), in the operas *Hry o Marii* (*Games about Mary*, 1935) and *Divadlo za branou* (*The Suburban Theater*, 1936), and in the cantata *Kytice* (*Bouquet of Flowers*, 1937). In many vocal miniatures of the war and post-war periods on the texts of folksongs and on verses in the folksong mode, Martinů returned once more to the sources of art in folk music (songs, choral songs, chamber cantatas). He moved in the sphere of folksong invention with the certainty of a unique connoisseur and sensitive artist, and this permitted him to formulate his musical thoughts in the simplest artistic terms.

In spite of all this, folksong composition did not become part of the artistic synthesis of Martinů. This Czech composer of spontaneous musical gift soon realized the possibilities and the limitations of musical expression based solely on folk sources. This is shown not only by his extensive concertos and chamber compositions, but above all by the series of great programmatic works that he wrote in the last twenty years of his life. The lyric opera in three acts *Julietta, neboli Snář* (*Juliette, or The Key to Dreams,* 1937) must be considered the first great work of his maturity: Czech melody is mingled in it with a delicate compositional culture of French origin. In the Double Concerto for two string orchestras, piano, and drums (1938) Martinů composed a work whose dramatic content far surpassed the pure estheticism of his early and fresh neo-Classic works. In the time of grave and fateful clashes the artistic conceptions of Martinů were clearly acquiring a new profundity of content. In the group of six symphonies (1942, 1943, 1944, 1945, 1946, 1955), he created a counterpart, of equal artistic worth, to the symphonies of Honegger. The development of Martinů's operatic work was also remarkable. *Ženitba* (*The Marriage,* 1952), *Mirandolina* (1953), *Řecké pašije* (*The Greek Passiontide,* 1958), and *Ariadne* (1958) signified a further step both musically and in subject matter on the way towards a modern type of opera, renewing the continuity with the Classic and pre-Classic opera. The full-length cantata *Gilgameš* (1955) was the climax of the composer's development in the field of vocal music.

Martinů spent by far the greatest part of his life abroad. His personal contact with Czech composers and direct influence as a teacher could thus only be slight. Only two Czech composers of the younger generation had the good fortune to study under him directly: the prematurely deceased Vítězslava Kaprálová (1915-40), who, in her songs, her Sinfonietta (1937) and Partita (1939) attained a remarkable maturity, and Jan Novák (b. 1921). The artistic tendencies that Martinů followed first of the Czech modern composers did however attain a sufficiently wide hearing in the creative efforts of his contemporaries and of the younger generation of composers. This was undoubtedly due to the efforts of the distinguished composer and

teacher Pavel Bořkovec (b. 1894), whose artistic development, recalling
in many ways that of Martinů, has presented modern Czech music with
valuable elements of style formation. The creative field of Bořkovec
lies in chamber and instrumental compositions of a neo-Classic trend
(five String Quartets, a Concerto Grosso, 1942). His class produced
a number of talented members of the present-day generation of young
composers: Jiří Pauer (b. 1919), Viktor Kalabis (b. 1923), Petr Eben
(b. 1929), and others. Among Bořkovec's contemporaries, who remained
true to the neo-Classic trend, the highly individual Iša Krejčí (b. 1904)
is outstanding with his three remarkable symphonies (1955, 1958, 1963)
and his successful comic opera *Pozdvižení v Efesu* (*The Revolt at
Ephesus,* 1943). Another of Bořkovec's contemporaries, Jaroslav Řídký
(1897-1956), made use in his orchestral and chamber music of a
spontaneous Dvořák-like musicality. Musically refreshing artistic expression appeared in the work of other composers of the middle generation whose trend was traditional, namely Václav Trojan (b. 1907),
Jan Kapr (b. 1914), and Jan Hanuš (b. 1915).

At this moment, when we can scarcely yet see our way reliably
through the music of the immediate present, it is not possible to come
to final conclusions about the main trends of development in modern
Czech music. It seems however that in the work of a certain section of
contemporary Czech composers there is crystallizing a new, interesting
current of style, which on a different and stylistically far more vigorous
basis is renewing the structural tectonism of Novák's school with a
fierceness of expression comparable to that of Janáček. Those who take
an active part in the shaping of this trend are once more reaching out
to folk music of Eastern European origin, but are not relinquishing
either the advantages or the difficulties that come from the use of
rational techniques in music. It is a process just beginning in Czech
music at the present day, but it has already produced fruitful results.
In speaking of this process we must not forget that at least indirectly
it was participated in also by those who helped to renew and develop
in modern Czech music a continuity with the work of Janáček, Novák,
and Hába. This can be said of Emil František Burian (1904-59), the
composer of the remarkable music drama based on folk music *Maryša*
(1938), of Jaroslav Doubrava (1909-60), the composer of three symphonies (1938, 1944, 1958) and stage works, of Zdeněk Blažek (b.
1905), who drew upon folk melody in his chamber cycles, of Theodor
Schaeffer (b. 1903), whose Symphony (1963) is worthy of notice, of
Clement Slavický (b. 1910), of the prematurely deceased Milan

Harašta (1919-46), and others. A significant place in contemporary Czech music is held today by Miloslav Kabeláč (b. 1908), thanks to his wealth of creative experience and production (the cantata *Neustupujte* [*Do Not Give Way*, 1938], the six symphonies 1942, 1946, 1957, 1958, 1960, 1961) and also to his boldness in seizing on new musical patterns and making them his own. Much too was promised by the rapid creative development of Jan Rychlík (1916-64). Among the young generation of composers it will undoubtedly be above all Vladimír Sommer (b. 1921), Svatopluk Havelka (b. 1925), Miloš Ištvan (b. 1928), Josef Berg (b. 1927), along with some of the composers already mentioned, who will play their part in the decisive creative struggles for the new stylistic trend of Czech music in our time. We have already good reason to express the opinion today that this will be in the spirit of the best traditions of Czech music, which never rejected the fertilizing influences of international art, but which always drew from the native wells of cultivated and folk music.

(*Translated by Jessie Kocmanová*)

Selected Bibliography

Albert Soubies, *Histoire de la musique en Bohême,* Paris, 1898; Otakar Hostinský, *Hudba v Čechách* (*Music in Bohemia*), Prague, 1900; Zdeněk Nejedlý, *Zdeněk Fibich,* Prague, 1901; the same, *Dějiny české hudby* (*A History of Czech Music*), Prague, 1903; Otakar Hostinský, *Česká hudba 1864-1904* (*Czech Music, 1864-1904*), Prague, 1904; Richard Batka, *Die Musik in Böhmen,* Berlin, 1906; Jaromír Borecký, *Stručný přehled dějin české hudby* (*A Short Survey of the History of Czech Music*), Prague 1906, 2nd ed. 1928; Max Brod, *Leoš Janáček, život a dílo* (*Life and Work*), Prague, 1924, Vienna, 1925, 2nd ed. 1956; Henri Hantich, *La Musique tchèque,* Paris 1907; Otakar Šourek, *Život a dílo Antonína Dvořáka* (*Life and Work*), Prague 1922-33, 4 vols., 3rd ed. Prague, 1954-57; Zdeněk Nejedlý, *Bedřich Smetana,* Prague, 1924, new ed. 1962; the same, *Bedřich Smetana,* Prague 1922-33, 4 vols., 2nd ed. Prague 1950-54; Dobroslav Orel, in Adler's *Handbuch der Musikgeschichte,* Berlin 1930; Antonín Srba, ed., *Vítězslav Novák, studie a vzpomínky* (*Studies and Memoirs*), Prague, 1932, with additions 1935, 1940; the same, *Ceskoslovenská vlastivěda* (*Czechoslovak Homeland*) VIII, *Umění* (*Art*), Prague, 1935; Alois Hnilička, *Kontury vývoje hudby poklasické v Čechách* (*The Contours of Development of Post-Classical Music in Bohemia,* Prague, 1935; J. M. Květ, ed., *Josef Suk, život a dílo* (*Life and Work*), Prague 1935; Vladimír Helfert, *Česká moderní hudba* (*Modern Czech Music*), Olomouc, 1936; Vladimír Helfert - Erich Steinhard, *Geschichte der Musik in der Tschechoslowakischen Republik,* Prague, 1936, 2nd ed. 1938 (in French, Prague, 1936); Vladimír Helfert, *Půlstoletí české hudby před válkou v evropské perspektivě a Moderní Česká hudba na světovém foru — Co doly naše země Evropě a lidstvu*

(Fifty years of Czech Music Before the War in European Perspective, and Modern Czech Music in the International Field — What Our Land Gave to Europe and Mankind) Prague, 2nd ed. 1940; Vladimír Helfert, *Leoš Janáček, Obraz životního a uměleckého boje (The Picture of a Fight for Life and Art)*, I, Brno, 1939; Jan Racek, *Leoš Janáček a současní moravští skladatelé (L. Janáček and Contemporary Moravian Composers)*, Brno, 1940; Rosa Newmarch, *The Music of Czechoslovakia*, Oxford, 1943; Miloš Šafránek, *Bohuslav Martinů, The Man and His Music*, New York, 1944, London, 2nd ed. 1946, Prague 1961; Igor Belza, *Ocherku razvitiya cheshskoy muzikalnoy klassiki (A Sketch of the Development of Czech Musical Classicism)*, Moscow, 1951; Václav Štěpán, *Novák a Suk*, Prague, 1945; Z. Nejedlý, *Otakar Ostrčil*, Prague, 1949; the same, *J. B. Foerster, jeho životní pout a tvorba 1859-1949 (His Lifetime's Pilgrimage and Creative Work)*, Prague, 1949; Karel Hoffmeister, *Tvorba Vítězslava Nováka z let 1941-1948 (His Creative Work from 1941-48)*, Prague, 1949; *Musik der Zeit, Heft VIII*, Bonn, 1954; J. Matějček, *Tschechische Komponisten von Heute*, Prague, 1957; Jan Racek, *Grundlinien tschechischer Musikentwicklung*, in *Musica* XI, Vol. 9-10, Kassel, 1957, 488-97; Jan Racek, *Česká hudba (Czech Music)*, Prague, 1958; Bohumír Štědroň, *Dílo Leoše Janáčka, abecední seznam (An Alphabetical List of Works by Janáček)*, Prague, 1959, in Czech, German, English, Russian; Igor Belza, *Česká klasická hudba (Czech Classical Music)*, Prague, 1961; Jan Racek, *L. Janáček*, Leipzig, 1962; Jiří Vysloužil, ed., *L. Janáček a soudobá hudba (Janáček and Contemporary Music)*, in Report of International Musical Scientific Congress, Brno, 1958; J. Vysloužil, *Nad dílem Aloise Háby (On the Work of A. Hába)*, in *Hudební rozhledy (Musical Survey)*, XVI-1963, 522-24, Prague, 1963; Jan Racek, *L. Janáček národní a světový (Janáček National and International)*, in *Ročenka Dvacaté století (Twentieth-Century Annual)*, Prague, 1964; Jiří Vysloužil, *Skladatelia 20. století (Composers of the 20th Century)*, Bratislava, 1964; Václav Holzknecht, *Profil Pavla Bořkovece (A Profile of P. Bořkovec)*, in *Hudební rozhledy*, XVII-1964, 451-53; the same, *Nad životem a dílem Iši Krejčího (Life and Work of I. Krejčí)*, in *Hudební rozhledy* XVII-1964, 493-95; Jiří Vysloužil, *Hábova čtvrttónová opera Matka (Hába's Quarter-Tone Opera "The Mother")*, in *Hudební rozhledy*, XVII-1964, 556-57.

MODERN HUNGARIAN MUSIC

By IMRE FABIAN

O NLY forty years ago, Zoltán Kodály, in a newspaper article, had to come to the defense of his pupils who, following in the footsteps of their master, had attempted a fusion of European tradition with Hungarian folk music in their works. "We are still far from having a homogeneous musical public which, brought up in Hungarian culture, combines exact knowledge of Hungarian tradition with musical education," Kodály wrote. Looking at the development of the past decades and particularly of the last twenty years, we come to the conclusion that such a public, the public desired by Kodály, has now come into existence. This is mainly due to the work of Bartók and Kodály, the two masters who fulfilled the task of several generations in the history of Hungarian music. To analyze here the musicological significance of these two masters cannot be attempted. But in order to appreciate fully the present situation of music in Hungary we have to realize that prior to their appearance the country — to use Kodály's words — had been a German province without a genuine musical tradition. In spite of heroic efforts, the Hungarian composers of the Romantic era did not succeed in giving real Hungarian character to their music. Franz Liszt was too much of a cosmopolite to become a source of national musical tradition for ensuing generations. Bartók and Kodály had, so to speak, to create a continuity of tradition to fashion a synthesis between age-old folk music and European art music on its highest level.

They found the sources for a Hungarian musical language with its individual characteristics in Hungarian folk music, unknown until the turn of the century. For decades they had to fight tenaciously to prove the high artistic values and profoundly Hungarian character of this music to a public whose idol was the superficial Romantic Magyarism of

Gypsy music. It is easy to understand that the pupils of Kodály considered the continuation of this struggle their most important task. Kodály, the grand old man of Hungarian music, is still today the active leader in the musical life of the nation. He is the head of the Folk Music Research Group of the Academy of Science, played a leading part at the International Society for Musical Education conference and at last year's meeting of the International Folk Music Conference in Budapest. As composer he proclaimed his artistic ideas a few years ago in his First Symphony. Without Kodály the composer, the teacher, the musicologist, today's musical life in Hungary could scarcely be imagined.

His students, whom he had to defend four decades ago, belong today to the older generation of composers. Those who did not develop their talent abroad — as did for instance Antal Dorati, Tibor Serly, the late Mátyás Seiber, Sándor Veress, Géza Frid, or Miklós Rózsa — are today the heads of important musical institutions or professors at the Academy of Music. Of the composers who were contemporaries of Bartók and Kodály, Leo Weiner (1885-1960) and László Lajtha (1892-1963) showed individual profiles. Weiner, a composer leaning towards Romantic lyricism, was a virtuoso of the orchestra and an ardent admirer of Classical ideals. His chamber music shows, convincingly, a cultivated personality and an outstanding craftsman. But Weiner was more a dreamer about past ideals of beauty than a mapper of new roads for the future. He gained deserved recognition as the teacher of many outstanding musicians at the Academy.

László Lajtha, who died only two years ago, was a very different personality. His music has perhaps more admirers in France, his second home, than in Hungary. Lajtha, a devoted admirer of French culture and at the same time an enthusiastic explorer of Hungarian folk music, was fond of surprising twists, of playful, sparkling ideas, reminding one of Eric Satie.

Ernst von Dohnányi (1877-1960), an older contemporary of Bartók and Kodály and a brilliant piano virtuoso, continued in his music the Brahmsian tradition. He rather preferred in his works the type of Magyarism that was considered superficial by Kodály. The same applies to Jenö von Hubay, a great violinist and teacher. The work of these two composers found no following in the next generation. Among the musicians who made their appearance earlier than did the pupils of Kodály we must also mention Alexander Jemnitz (1890-1963), who was frequently heard — mainly in the 'twenties — on the international musical scene as the representative of German Expressionism in Hungary.

A connecting link between the two generations is György Kósa, born in 1897.

This leads us directly to the pupils of Kodály, most of whom have developed after the Second World War. Their main aim was the continuation of Kodály's ideas. This explains why we must think of every composer of this generation as a pupil of Kodály even if he, in a technical sense, was not a student in Kodály's class at the Academy of Music. All those who now have reached the age between forty and sixty will undoubtedly find their place in the history of Hungarian music under the collective title "Kodály School." The fact that this collective title can be applied to all composers of this generation should not mean, however, that they were not able to develop their own personality under the influence of their master. Ferenc Szabó (b. 1902), for example, at present head of the Music Academy in Budapest, has embraced the principle of tonality in his music after having started out in the 'thirties, in an atonal, Expressionistic style. He is a master of large-scale oratorios as well as of spontaneous, intimate lyricism. A personality of a different kind is Pál Kadosa (b. 1903), whose name used to appear frequently on the programs of the ISCM festivals before the war. His works, published by Schott in Mainz, have been made available internationally and it is regrettable that, nevertheless, he has not achieved international recognition. During recent years his Fourth Symphony has earned well-deserved attention. It is a highly cultivated score with the meticulous workmanship and seriousness of a Honegger.

Lajos Bárdos (b. 1899) has been recognized as a choral composer outside of Hungary as well as within. The beginnings of Endre Szervánszky (b. 1911) as a composer were strongly influenced by folklore. But this contemplative artist, a man who constantly struggles with himself, has now been attracted by more recent developments of new music and has tried — at the age of over fifty — to find a new language in which to express himself. His *Six Orchestral Pieces,* written in 1959, are the first indication of these new tendencies in Szervánszky's work. Without doubt one can find in these pieces the significant influence of Webern. But Szervánszky tries, in a manner not to be underrated, to combine the influence of the Viennese School with the traditions of Hungarian music created by Bartók. Ferenc Farkas (b. 1905) is not a struggling personality in conflict with itself: he writes his music with the facility and craftsmanship of a Hindemith. His development has been favorably influenced by Ottorino Respighi's master class in Rome. Farkas is a composer of amazingly different facets: his work comprises almost every

genre from operetta to opera, from the chanson to symphonic and
movie music. What he does, however, is always done with taste and
convincing workmanship. His style flows from many sources and the
diversified elements in his scores reach from folklore to dodecaphony,
from German Romanticism to Impressionism. The music of this generation finds still another expression in the somewhat coarse, sometimes
grotesque humor of György Ránki (b. 1907), in the operas of Jenö
Kenessey (b. 1906), which grow from Puccinian soil, in the highly
cultivated symphonic and chamber music of János Viski (1906-61)
and Rezsö Kókai (1906-62), and in the music of Tibor Sárai (b. 1919),
András Mihály (b. 1917), Gyula Dávid (b. 1913), and Béla Tardos
(b. 1910). Rezsö Sugár (b. 1919) and Pál Járdányi (b. 1920) remain
direct pupils of Kodály.

The cultural and political seclusion of the 'fifties had an unfavorable
influence on the development of this generation of composers. Musical
life was threatened by provincialism. After 1956, however, contacts with
the world abroad became more pronounced and musicians could obtain
more intimate knowledge of the development of new music. Closer
contact with the outside world and the resulting rejuvenation of the
bloodstream of cultural life produced favorable effects. We have to say
frankly that for some artists this development brought about particularly
positive results, for others very questionable ones. It was especially those
who were belatedly exposed to these influences who became insecure.
It seems always difficult for an already fully developed personality to
re-evaluate established values and to scrutinize again what had been
accepted as success. To other composers whose artistic gift was not
strong enough for them to maintain a critical distance, the unquestion-
ing acceptance of new stylistic and technical developments, the aim to
compose "up-to-date," posed a different kind of danger. However, this
upheaval had very healthy consequences. It was necessary, after Hungarian musical life had been separated from the outside world for many
years. Only meretricious values faded in these tests. What had real significance lost nothing of its convincing strength. Béla Bartók could serve
the young generation as the great example, he who had found a supreme
synthesis of the most diversified influences from atonality to folklore.

This breakthrough in Hungarian musical life began four or five
years ago, when the new music of our time began increasingly to be
known. We have already mentioned the first sign of it: the *Six
Orchestral Pieces* by Szervánszky. The new language of the Hungarian
avant-garde made itself heard in the Etudes for Orchestra by Rudolf

Maros (b. 1917), who had been a pupil of Kodály. Much talent came to the fore as the young generation, men between twenty and forty, joined in. Emil Petrovics (b. 1930) wrote the most successful opera of recent years, *C'est la guerre*. In its musical language *Bluebeard* influences as well as repercussions of the Expressionistic style of the Viennese School can be heard, but also Stravinsky's influence. Petrovics has not yet developed his own style. Carl Orff has been godfather, for example, to his comic opera *Lysistrata*. By contrast, György Kurtág (b. 1926) is definitely going his own way, following the path of the Webern school without being epigonal. The musical world will certainly hear of him. His String Quartet was a great success at the ISCM festival in Copenhagen in 1964. In the works of Sándor Szokolay (b. 1931) one senses great tensions. Contrary to Kurtág, he is fond of great dramatic climaxes and monumental developments, not of brief, concise statements. We can also include András Szöllösy (b. 1921) in the avant-garde. He even succeeded in being heard in Darmstadt. Attila Bozay (b. 1939) has written refreshing, talented works under the helpful influence of late Stravinsky. There is also the expressive style of Lajos Papp (b. 1932) and the very different language of Zsolt Durkó (b. 1934), a Petrassi pupil whose music promises much for his future.

As we look at these many facets of Hungarian music in our times, the daring, healthy dynamism of the young generation offers much hope. True, Hungarian composers have not yet conquered the international world of music to the extent of their Polish colleagues. But there is no lack of talent. Free, healthy contacts with the world abroad can help its development. As for the experimental wing, it is particularly significant that last year composers and electronic experts met to discuss problems of electronic music. The founding of a studio for electronic music was declared an immediate necessity. It will not be long in coming into being.

Hungarian musicology staked its claim internationally with the epochal explorations in the field of folksong by Bartók and Kodály. Their work is being continued by the Folk Music Research Group at the Academy of Science in Budapest under the leadership of Kodály. This group of musicologists prepares and brings out the most ambitious publications of Hungarian folk music so far, the volumes of *Magyar Népzene Tára*. Hungarian musicologists also take active part in the work of the IFMC, and their working methods created general interest at the conference of the IFMC. Pál Járdányi, László Vikár, Bálint Sárosi, author of a book on Hungarian folk instruments that will be published in Berlin as the first volume in a series of books on folk instruments, Lajos Vargyas, and György Kerényi are well known in musicological circles through their publications. Benjamin Rajeczky has won recognition through his publication on the Gregorian tradition in Hungarian music. His volume of Hungarian dirges is published and must be considered the foremost musicological achievement of the Folk Music Research Group.

The Bartók Archive of the Academy of Science has become a focal point of musicological activity. The Archive was founded at the suggestion of Bence Szabolcsi to preserve the legacy of Béla Bartók, to edit it scientifically, and to become the central point for musicological research. Bence Szabolcsi was appointed director, Denijs Dille, the Belgian Bartók researcher, chief musicologist. In *Documenta Bartókiana* the Archive published hitherto unknown works, letters, and other documents. The series will be continued. The Institute and Dille personally have made a significant contribution to Bartók research through the publication of early works: the Scherzo for piano and orchestra, the symphonic poem *Kossuth,* and songs. The Bartók Archive is also at work on a thematic catalogue of his works. The magazine *Studia musicologica,* published by the Archive since 1961 in several languages, gives twice a year a survey of achievements of musicological research in Hungary.

Bence Szabolcsi and Dénes Bartha, two musicologists of international standing, are in the center of these manifold, very active efforts. Szabolcsi laid the foundations for research into Hungarian musical history. His publications on the general history of music are likewise well known. His scientific work opened new vistas for research on Liszt and Bartók. His books *History of Melody, Franz Liszt in the Last Years of His Life,* and *Béla Bartók* show the finest results of Hungarian musicology. Dénes Bartha in 1964 taught at Smith College and Harvard University. His Haydn research (he published a book *Haydn as Operatic Conductor* together with his former pupil Lászlo Somfai), his publications on Bach, Debussy, and Bartók, and his *History of Hungarian Music,* published in collaboration with Kodály, have put him in the front ranks of musicologists in his field. Bartha and Szabolcsi are also the teachers of a younger generation of musicologists who have published several important papers during the past few years. The most important task to be fulfilled is that of the Hungarian Bartók research. Here, after the pioneering labors of Kodály, Szabolcsi, and Antal Molnár, the names of József Ujfalussy (*Bartók Breviary,* a Bartók book in preparation), Ernö Lendvai (*About the Style of Bartók*), János

Demény (*Letters and Documents*), György Kroó (*The Stage Works*),
Lajos Lesznai (a Bartók book in German) have to be mentioned and
among the biographers of Kodály besides the basic work by Antal
Molnár the publications of András Szöllösy and László Eösze, the latter
work also published in German and English. The music of the 20th
century has been treated extensively in musicological publications of the
past few years. Of special importance are a comprehensive volume *Music
of Our Century* by Rezsö Kókai and Imre Fábián, a valuable book on
Schoenberg by János Kárpáti, a book on Honegger by András Szöllösy,
and a volume on Stravinsky by László Fábián. Ferenc Bónis has published valuable contributions in the field of Hungarian music. The
Hungarian National Museum has invaluable manuscripts in the music
division of the Széchényi Library through the purchase of the Esterházy
library. Scientific editorial work on these treasures is carried out by a
group of young musicologists under the guidance of Jenö Vécsey, head
of the library. The first publications resulting from these studies were
manuscripts by Süssmayr and J. J. Fux, edited by István Kecskeméti.
Zoltán Falvy makes valuable contributions in the field of Hungarian
musical history, particularly through the publication of unknown
medieval and Renaissance documents. József Ujfalussy is also the author
of a basic work on Marxist musical esthetics, and János Maróthy has
made a heroic attempt to write a history of folksong along Marxist
ideological lines. The magazine *Magyar Zene* provides a forum for
Hungarian musicology. It is published six times each year. A more
popular magazine, *Muzsika,* is a monthly.

Hungarian musicology has gained measurably in status since the
Haydn conference in Budapest in 1959. But concert life in Hungary
has also been invigorated by the events of the Haydn year. During that
year the Budapest Music Weeks were organized for the first time. Since
then, the musical season is opened every year with these music weeks.
The artistic and musical level of these events is rising steadily and in
the past few years Budapest has reconquered its place among the
musical capitals of Europe. Igor Stravinsky, Goffredo Petrassi, Benjamin
Britten, Dimitri Shostakovich came to visit and to appear as guest
artists during the last two years.

Concerts in Hungary are arranged by a single organization, the
Országos Filharmónia. This makes it possible for Hungarian composers
and generally masters of the 20th century to find their appropriate place
on the programs. Here are a few figures from the recent past: During
the season 1959-60, 25 Hungarian composers (not including Bartók,

Kodály, and Weiner) were heard in 38 different compositions. During the next season 23 composers were presented by 32 works. A similar situation prevailed during the last two years, an indication that every work of significance will get a public hearing. Concerts, as a rule, are well attended. The more than 5000 subscriptions for this year's Music Weeks were sold out within two days. This is due to low prices as well as good programming. Ticket prices are one fifth of the prices in Western Europe.

One of the most important — and best frequented — concert series of the last year was the cycle *Chamber Music of Our Century.* Here one could hear Hungarian first performances of works by Webern, Hindemith, Schoenberg, Malipiero — but also Nono, Boulez's *Improvisations sur Mallarmé,* Stockhausen's *Gesang der Jünglinge,* Maderna's *Notturno,* works by Penderecki, Kotonski, Lutoslawski, Haubenstock-Ramati, and by young Hungarian composers. Another cycle offered all the string quartets by Haydn. The contacts with abroad have obviously had their favorable effect on our concert life.

Its conservative policies have frequently made the National Opera House the center of sharp criticism. Indeed, the theater where Gustav Mahler, Arthur Nikisch and, after the Second World War, Otto Klemperer worked has lost much of its prestige. Recently, however, it has been struggling, with marked success, to gain back its lost glory. The repertory has been invigorated. A beautiful performance of *Pelléas* during the Debussy year, the first, highly successful performance of *Wozzeck* (with Alban Berg's widow, Helene, in the audience), performances of works by Benjamin Britten, Carl Orff, Gian Carlo Menotti have helped to bring about a new, more contemporary style of operatic production. The most pronounced successes were — as mentioned before — the opera *C'est la guerre* by Emil Petrovics and the ballet *Maria and the Magician* by István Láng, based on a short story by Thomas Mann. The music of our century has also reached the operatic stages in the provinces. Britten's *Midsummer Night's Dream* had its first Hungarian performance in Debrecen, *Dantons Tod* by Gottfried von Einem in Szeged. The National Theater in Pécs made quite an impression with performances of Milhaud's *Opéras minutes* and Menotti's *Medium.* This theater has a young ballet master, Imre Eck, who, while influenced by the work of Maurice Béjart, has his own personal style and has encouraged the creation and given the first performances of several new works by Hungarian composers. He has created a modern style of ballet production in marked contrast to the style of the ballet of the

Budapest Opera, which is oriented after the Bolshoi Ballet and whose dancers appear in many of the capitals of the world.

As all over Europe, radio and television play an important part in the musical life of Hungary. Radio, the generous commissioner of new compositions, has also done valuable work in acquainting the public with contemporary music, including works of the experimental school. In the month of November 1964, for example, the Hungarian Radio presented 13 complete operatic performances, among them five works of the 20th century. Television, with almost 700,000 subscribers, has the same importance in Hungary as in other European countries. Musical programs are steadily increasing in number. Two television operas in original productions had substantial success: Dallapiccola's *Volo di notte* and Emil Petrovics's *C'est la guerre.*

The Hungarian recording industry has not yet obtained sufficient importance. There is no lack of successful beginnings, however; by joint productions with Deutsche Grammophon and by a number of their own Bartók recordings, the firm of Qualiton has already obtained a certain success in the international market. Mention should be made of the recording of Bartók's *Mikrokosmos* by Ditta Pásztory and of the six string quartets by the Tátrai Quartet. The company now plans to record some of Bartók's earlier works.

Hungarian music publishing has made itself known internationally by a joint publishing venture with Schott in Mainz. This series should help to fill in the rather sketchy impressions of Hungarian musical life by the publication of new Hungarian music and by the series *Thesaurus Musicus,* which already includes works by Albrechtsberger, Dittersdorf, and Michael Haydn. Important books on music are being published by the Gondolat publishing house.

This report would not be complete if no mention were made of the celebrated system of musical education in Hungary. Kodály considered it his most important task to create such a system on a broad basis and the title of his book *Music Belongs to Everybody* should be considered the motto for the attitude behind these efforts. Such outstanding musicians as Yehudi Menuhin, Pablo Casals, and many other experts have expressed the highest praise and admiration for Hungarian musical education. The Congress of the ISME that took place in Budapest in the summer of 1964 has further encouraged this successful development. One of the results of the sustained attempt to provide widespread musical education has been the high level of choral performances, which Kodály considers the very base of all general musical education. During the past few years, there was no lack of recognition. Hungarian choral groups won first prizes in Llangollen and Arezzo and the artistic level of oratorio and other choral performances in the country is very high.

This survey could only give a bird's-eye view of musical life in Hungary. It is hoped, however, that it will provide some general information and will show how a small people, which has given the world so many outstanding musicians, tries to administer its great values.

MUSIC IN YUGOSLAVIA

By EVERETT HELM

W E CANNOT properly speak of Yugoslav music, but rather of music in Yugoslavia. As in few other countries of the world, the various cultures, languages, and ethnic groups that comprise present-day Yugoslavia are more heterogeneous than homogeneous. Not only the musical life but to a certain extent the creative products of Yugoslavia reflect this fact.

The musical life is decentralized to a degree, representing in this respect the polar opposite of such countries as France, in which "everything" happens in Paris, and England, where "nearly everything" happens in London. The decentralization that is so striking in Yugoslavia, however, is of a different sort from Western Germany's, where there are numerous important centers, each "competing" with the others and each having a "direct line" to the others — a line that keeps all parties informed in detail as to what is going on throughout the country.

Yugoslavia's musical decentralization often approaches isolation of the various centers. Ljubljana, for example, knows in a general sort of way what is going on in Belgrade (and vice versa), but contact between the two is amazingly loose, considering the relatively small size of the country. And contact between some of the other centers is even looser.

The centers in question are the capitals of the six People's Republics that constitute the Yugoslav federation: Ljubljana (Slovenia), Zagreb (Croatia), Sarajevo (Bosnia and Herzegovina), Skopje (Macedonia), Titograd (Montenegro), and Belgrade (Serbia). By far the most important are Ljubljana, Zagreb, and Belgrade (not necessarily in that order). In recent years, a distinct effort has been made by the central government to raise standards in the other three centers and in various provincial cities as well. This effort has been remarkably successful, particularly in Sarajevo, Skopie, Maribor, Rijeka (Fiume), Novi Sad,

215

and several other smaller cities.

The fact that music in Yugoslavia is only now beginning to reach a European level is, of course, a reflection of this country's history — or lack of history.[1] Before World War I (and even thereafter) this history was one of wars, invasions, occupations by Turks, Austrians, Hungarians, and Italians, mutual distrust and bitter struggles on the part of the various ethnic groups to maintain their identities. Yugoslavia as a country came into being only after the Treaty of Versailles. Even today, under a strong federal government, the component republics maintain a large measure of "states rights" and present striking contrasts with one another.

This system of organization along federal principles has its parallel in the musical set-up as well. The radio stations, which play an important role in furthering contemporary music, function independently, as do the opera houses, orchestras, music schools, and the like. In each of the six republics there is a local Association of Composers which belongs to the national Union of Yugoslav Composers (Savez kompozitora Jugoslavije), whose offices are in Belgrade. This organization has been of primary importance in effecting closer cooperation among the member groups, furthering international exchange, and sponsoring the cause of contemporary music at home and, to a limited extent, abroad.

At the risk of over-simplification but in the interests of clarity, it is possible to divide musical composition in Yugoslavia into three categories: works based on or reflecting folk music; works reflecting the neo-Classical esthetic; and works reflecting, to varying extents, more "modern" practices, such as twelve-tone and serial. The first two categories mentioned are often seen in conjunction.

One might expect to find here a "chronological" stylistic progression, corresponding to age groups. Such a progression does, by and large, exist, but there are so many exceptions that the rule is valid only to a qualified extent.

---

[1] We are speaking here of music in "modern" — i.e. post-Baroque, times. In earlier periods there were, to be sure, some centers of musical activity worthy of note. But as Cvetko states in *MGG* (col. 307), "musical life in Slovenia could not develop to the same extent [as in Western Europe] because of unfavorable circumstances." These circumstances induced gifted musicians, such as Gallus, to leave their own country and take positions elsewhere. Speaking of Croatia, Andreis states (*MGG*, col. 315): "During the great musical epochs of Western Europe, from the 15th century to the 18th, art music could not develop in Croatia"; he cites the centuries-long battle with the Turks as the principal reason. And Djurić-Klajn says of Serbia (*MGG*, col. 323): "Serbian art music is not old. For centuries the political-national circumstances of the Serbian folk permitted no free development."

Among the "elder statesmen," to be sure, neo-Romanticism is prevalent. It forms the stylistic basis of the works of Jakov Gotovac (b. 1895), whose *Symphonic Kolo* has had an international success and is representative of a whole series of similar works. This Croatian composer incorporates elements of folk music into an otherwise "normal," thoroughly traditional style, much as Liszt and Brahms employed Hungarian melodies.

The works of the late Stevan Hristić (1885-1958) reflect the same basic procedures. His best-known composition is *The Legend of Ohrid,* a "ballet from folk life."

Although born a generation later than the composers just mentioned, the Croatian Stjepan Šulek (b. 1914) cultivates an equally conservative neo-Romantic, markedly eclectic style, but without reference to folk music. His works, which are frequently performed in Yugoslavia, include four symphonies, the opera *Coriolanus,* three orchestral concertos, two piano concertos, and various other concertos in Classical form.

The Serb Mihajlo Vukdragović (b. 1900), whose influence as conductor, critic, and organizer has been enormous, is also in his creative work an outspoken neo-Romanticist, who has made frequent use of folk material. His best work, such as the Second String Quartet, is marked by a highly personal, typically Slavic quality, which is related to but does not cite Serbian folk music.

Among the composers of the elder generation mention should also be made of Matija Bravničar (b. 1897), whose style might be described as late Romantic with Expressionist tendencies. His compositions, a number of which employ the folk music of his native Slovenia, include operas, symphonies, and various orchestral works.

Many composers of the middle generation completed their studies during the 1930s, and their earlier works not unnaturally reflect the neo-Classical "wave" of that time. One of the leaders of this generation is the Serb Milan Ristić (b. 1908). Like many of his contemporaries, Ristić studied in Prague and was exposed to the more radical tendencies of the time. And like many others, he has in the course of time "retreated" to a more traditional style. In his frequently performed *Symphonic Variations* Ristić uses tonality in an extended sense, which combines consonance and dissonance freely. The work displays considerable originality and a sure command of technique — an asset more frequently found in this "middle" generation than in the preceding one. In one of his recent works, Seven Bagatelles for Orchestra, Ristić writes in a brittle, parodistic style recalling (as do many Yugoslav works of recent date) the Stravinsky of *L'Histoire du soldat*. His Third Symphony (1961) is a remarkably well-written and effective work, based in tonality but making free use of dissonance. The constantly shifting textures reveal a fine feeling for sound. Although it contains no "tunes," the symphony is permeated by a typically Slavic kind of melody.

Stanojlo Rajičič (b. 1910) followed a similar pattern, studying first in Belgrade, then in Prague with Karel and Suk. He too began as something of a radical and modified his style subsequently. Some of his instrumental works (four symphonies, three piano concertos, two violin concertos, a cello concerto, many piano pieces) are in the neo-Classic vein. Among his more recent works one of the most interesting is the cycle *Na Liparu* (*In Lipar*) for solo voice and orchestra — a composition that is in many respects typical of the best qualities of Yugoslav music. Attention is focussed from start to finish in the highly expressive and elastic melodic line, which reminds one occasionally of Janáček's "Sprechmelodie." The vocal writing is extremely expert and effective, but the effects are there not for their own sake but in the interest of expression.

The most attractive feature of this five-movement cycle, however, is the natural and uninhibited quality of the musical expression, which contains nothing cramped or artificial. In the works of less gifted composers, this lack of musical inhibitions can lead at times to a rather embarrassing kind of naïveté — or even to outright banality. Here, however, it produces a welcome freshness and spontaneity which are often characteristic of Slavic music and are all too rare in the more sophisticated music of Western countries.

Neo-Classicism forms the basis of the more recent style of the Croatian Milo Cipra (b. 1906), whose most important contribution is in the field of chamber music. His four string quartets, piano trio, sonatas for various instruments, and numerous piano pieces are among the best Yugoslav chamber works — a genre, incidentally, that is somewhat neglected today. Cipra's recent work, *The Path of the Sun* for chamber orchestra, is an extraordinarily attractive piece; concise, to the point, very well written, and full of interesting sound combinations.

Whereas the works of Ristić, Cipra, and many others show the influence of the neo-Classical Stravinsky, certain pieces by the Slovenian composer Danilo Švara (b. 1902) betray the fact that he studied in Frankfurt am Main and came strongly under the influence of Hindemith — an exception in Yugoslavia, where the Hindemith influence has been minimal.

One or two composers of the middle generation successfully evade stylistic classification — which is all to their credit. One of these is Ljubica Marić, Yugoslavia's leading female composer (b. 1909). After studying in Belgrade, Marić, like many of her colleagues, went on to Prague, where she worked with Suk and came under the strong influence of Hába, writing quarter-tone music. In more recent years she has developed a style of considerable individuality, which combines the experience she gained in twelve-tone technique with a freely tonal approach. Her cantata *Pesme Prostora* (*Songs of Space*) is a thoroughly impressive work of large dimensions.

This cantata is imbued with the spirit of Serbian folk music, although no direct quotations occur; Marić has here approached that ideal synthesis of folk spirit and personal expression that marks the compositions of Bartók. The cantata's seven sections are settings of simple and naively touching inscriptions from tombstones of the 13th century. The texts are treated at times polyphonically, at times homophonically but always with appropriate sobriety. The expert choral writing is kept relatively simple, while the orchestra part is often very complex. Marić displays great sensitivity in the orchestral and harmonic coloring.

Her *Musica octoicha* (1958) for orchestra, employing the modes of Orthodox church music, is an outstanding composition. *On the Threshold of Dreams,* cantata for two voices, speaker, and instrumental ensemble (1961), is also a remarkable, highly original work, combining strong emotional expression with classical clarity of form and texture.

The gifted Croatian composer Natko Devčić (b. 1914) has made telling use of folk material in his excellent *Istrian Suite* (1948) and in his opera *The Witch of Labin* (1957). In his more recent works, such as the attractive, slightly neo-Classic Concertino for Violin and Chamber Orchestra, folk music plays a relatively unimportant role.

Equally difficult to pigeonhole is the gifted Slovenian composer Primož Ramovš (b. 1921). He got off to an unconventional start as the pupil of Hába's pupil Slavko Osterc, whose death in 1941 deprived Yugoslavia of an outstanding talent. Ramovš continued his study in Rome and developed a personal style which in its fine feeling for form has certain neo-Classic attributes but which incorporates elements of polytonality and atonality. He has written three symphonies, several concertos, and a number of orchestral, chamber, and piano works. His recent Chorale and Toccata for Orchestra is an impressive composition of great vitality, making telling use of bitonal effects and displaying a remarkable command of technique.

Before turning to the younger generation, mention should be made of the Serb Mihovil Logar (b. 1902), also a pupil of Suk in Prague, whose point of departure is neo-Romanticism and who possesses a considerable lyric gift; the Croatian Natko Devčič (b. 1914), whose powers of dramatic expression are evident in his opera *The Witch of Labin;* and Boris Papandopulo (b. 1906), a prolific composer in all forms, whose easily accessible style, combining neo-Romantic and neo-Classic elements, often produces music of distinct charm and interest. All three of these middle-generation composers make occasional use of folk music.

The acceptance or rejection of folk music as a basis for composition has been a primary question for many years in Yugoslavia — and in a way that is for Western composers perhaps hard to understand. Folk music was a factor in the nationalist and pan-Slavic movements of the 19th century, in which the regions of today's Yugoslavia participated, and whose influence is still felt in many Eastern European countries. Over and above this, composers of the territories that constitute present-day Yugoslavia saw (and in some cases still see) in folk music a means of arriving at a "national form of expression." Like other countries (including notably the Latin American) that are on the fringe of or far removed from the centers of musical happenings, Yugoslavia has produced music of "influences and followings." In this situation Yugoslavia's rich tradition of folk music has seemed to many to offer a way of establishing the special identity of Yugoslav music.

The fallacies in this thesis are too obvious to demand recounting and are made the clearer by the quantities of "folksy" compositions that are little more than routine potpourris with local color. The use of folk music is in itself neither "good" nor "bad." In most contemporary styles, however, it is inhibiting.

From the end of World War II until 1948, when Tito broke out of the Stalinist camp, there was considerable pressure on Yugoslav composers to adhere to the esthetic party line established by Moscow. Since 1948, Yugoslavia has gone its own artistic way, free of all dogma and restriction.

Practically, this has meant a gradual lessening of folk-music-based composition; a determined effort to "catch up" with the Western musical world; a trend towards the adoption of more "advanced" techniques and styles of composition; and, in consequence, the emergence of a more European and cosmopolitan (as opposed to nationalistic) attitude towards music and musical creation.

In Yugoslavia there has been no avant-garde movement comparable to that of Poland, where the use of "advanced" styles and techniques is practically *de rigueur* for young composers wishing to make a name for themselves. This continence is perhaps a good thing for Yugoslav music in the long run; for the organic development that is taking place in Yugoslavia may well lead to more healthy results than an attempt to digest the newest trends in one gulp — which might cause musical indigestion. Yugoslav music was, at the beginning of this development, quite out of touch with the main currents of Western music, and a natural evolution is preferable to a forced stylistic revolution.

This evolution has not taken place without protests, which still continue but grow constantly fainter, from musical conservatives on one hand and political "party liners" on the other. And the evolution, which is still continuing, has been contained within moderate stylistic bounds not through duress but by the nature of the Yugoslavs themselves, whose strong propensity for melody stands in a certain opposition to serial techniques and fragmented melodic styles.

Such an opposition is felt even in the works of Yugoslavia's *enfant terrible,* Milko Kelemen (b. 1924), who represents the most "radical" trends of younger Yugoslav composers and who is responsible, it should be added, for the important biennial festival of modern music in Zagreb, which has done much to make Yugoslav musicians acquainted with recent developments in other countries. But the fact that his music has a special quality is attributable, I believe, to his inherited Croatian feeling for traditional melody.

His earlier work (Symphony 1951, Piano Concerto 1952, Violin Concerto 1953, Concerto for Bassoon and Strings 1956, etc.) is strongly Romantic, although cast in Classical forms. From around 1958, when he studied with Wolfgang Fortner and attended the Darmstadt Holiday Courses, his style developed rapidly towards twelve-tone and serial practices. His *Skolion* (composed in 1958) for orchestra received the Beethoven Prize of the City of Bonn in 1963. Among his more recent works are: *Constellations* for chamber orchestra (1958); *Equilibri* for two orchestras (1961); *Transfigurations* for piano and orchestra (1961); the ballet *Der Doppelgänger; Epitaph* for mezzo-soprano and chamber orchestra (1961); and the opera *The New Tenant* (1963). His most recent works, the thirty-minute ballet *Appassionato* (1964), based on Garcia Lorca's play *Bernarda Alba's House,* is an impressive piece with strong dramatic impact, combining pointillistic technique with somewhat more conventional Expressionist procedures.

It is interesting to observe that the majority of young Yugoslav composers are presently at a stage of "stylistic audacity" that was reached by a small number of "radicals" some thirty or more years ago — notably Josip Slavenski (1896-1955), Slavko Osterc (1895-1941), and Marjus Kogoj (1895-1956). In this connection mention should be made of the Croatian Krešimir Fribec (b. 1908), a pioneer of twelve-tone technique in Yugoslavia whose works include the opera *Blood Wedding* (1957) and *Metamorphoses* (1953) for chamber orchestra.

In recent years, however, young Yugoslav composers have shown a growing interest in twelve-tone and serial techniques, although with the exception of Kelemen in his recent works none has followed them exclusively, and very few have pursued consistently the pointillist manner stemming from Webern. Schoenberg and Berg, to a greater extent than Boulez and Stockhausen, seem to be the point of departure for most Yugoslav twelve-tone composers.

An exception, as regards both technique and musical quality, is the Slovene Aloiz Srebotnjak (b. 1931), whose early works — *Fantasia Notturna* for three violins, clarinet, and harp (1956); *Sinfonietta in due tempi* (1958) — are strikingly Expressionist. Among his more recent serial works in the pointillistic manner are the cantata *Ecstasy of Death* for baritone, French horn, and orchestra (1961); *The Mother* for chorus and orchestra; *Invenzione variata* for piano (1961); and *Monologues* for flute, oboe, French horn, timpani, and strings (1963).

Ruben Radica (b. 1931 in Dalmatia) is among the promising young composers employing an advanced idiom. His style reveals that he was a pupil of Kelemen. His principal works include: *Concerto abbreviato* for cello and orchestra (1960); *Lyrical Variations* for strings (1961); and *Choreographic Music* (1962). Mention should also be made in this connection of the Slovene Milan Stibilj (b. 1929), among whose works are the symphony *The Nightingale and the Rose* (1961) and a suite for percussion instruments. Also a pupil of Kelemen, he bids fair to surpass his teacher in his search for new means of expression.

Electronic music is still in its initial stages of development in Yugoslavia and has as yet produced no significant results. In the Parisian Studio for Musique Concrète, the Croat Ivo Malec (b. 1925) has produced interesting works. Janez Matičič (b. 1926), a Slovene composer who also lives in Paris, has worked in the same studio of the Radiodiffusion Française.

Apart from the more "advanced" trends mentioned, the works of young Yugoslav composers display all the colors of the stylistic spectrum. The highly gifted Serbian Aleksandar Obradović (b. 1927) is a true Slav in his unabashed use of highly charged melody and expressive harmony that have their roots deep in tradition and that are conceived along late Romantic lines. One of his most impressive works is the cycle *Wind of Fire* (1955) for baritone and orchestra, in which Obradović appears as a follower of Mahler on the one hand and Mussorgsky on the other. For the expression of emotion in music Obradović employs all means, including the most conventional. A dangerous procedure, perhaps, which runs the risk of banality. But *Wind of Fire* is not banal; on the contrary it possesses an intensity of expression that is rare today. His recent works include *Through the Atmosphere,* an orchestral suite employing traditional harmony, and, surprisingly enough, *Scherzo dodecafonico* for orchestra (1962). This work, the composer relates, employs a technique based on the principle of the organ "mixture" stop: the fundamental tone is heard simultaneously with its upper partials.

Obradović together with the majority of young Yugoslav composers represent the first generation to receive their entire musical training in their own country. This applies as well to Dušan Radić (b. 1929), who like Obradović studied at the Belgrade Academy of Music but developed an entirely different style. Radić's work on the whole shows a strong bent towards neo-Classicism. In his Divertimento for orchestra this leads to a curious situation. In its formal clarity, in the abstract nature of its material, which avoids the illustrative and subjective, in its motoric, somewhat brittle rhythmic patterns, in its melodic structure, which is composed of short motifs rather than long melodic lines, and in its thoroughly non-Romantic harmony, this work is neo-Classic in spirit and technique. But the power and uninhibited quality of the expression, reminding one of the *fauve* works of Stravinsky (*Sacre du printemps* and *Les Noces,* especially), threaten to break through the neo-Classical framework. It is precisely this uninhibited kind of expression that gives this work, and many other Yugoslav compositions, their special character.

In his amusing suite bearing the title *Spisak* (*The List*) Radić has written thirteen sketches for small chorus and chamber orchestra of an almost surrealistic nature, in which every trace of Romanticism is excluded. Each of the pieces is short, concentrated, and in sharp contrast to the others. Radić makes a valiant attempt at melodic compression and conciseness — not entirely successfully, for his native instinct for melody prevails, and the melodic element emerges as the primary one. In this work, as in others, it is clear that Radić has learned from the scores of Stravinsky, Prokofiev, and Bartók. Each movement bears a title: *Horse, Duck, Moss, Chair, Paper, Donkey, Cactus,* etc., but there is practically no literal illustration in this strange score. Radić's most recent work, *Symphonic Picture No. 2* (1964) for violin, women's chorus, and orchestra, is a curious and interesting piece in which traditional harmonic practices are combined with effective use of bitonality and polytonality in a kaleidoscopic manner, with constant changes in mood, rhythm, tempo, and musical material.

Uninhibited expression marks the fascinating Variations for Chamber Orchestra by the young Croatian composer Pavle Dešpali (b. 1934). Written while he was still a student at the Zagreb Conservatory, this work displays extraordinary talent and technical ability. Within the framework of extended tonality, Dešpali succeeds in creating a series of sharply contrasting variations that bears his personal imprint and holds the attention from start to finish. Again one is struck by the naturalness of this typically Slavic expression, which avoids banality while employing fairly conventional means. Among his other works are a Violin Concerto and Variations for Orchestra.

Among younger composers, one of the most gifted appears to be Petar Bergamo. This thirty-four-year-old Dalmatian, who has lived for fifteen years in Belgrade, has written a twelve-minute work called *Musica concertante* that consists of a series of "studies" for orchestra in one movement. The amount of variety packed into this short piece is astonishing. It contains modern Impressionism à la Bartók's "night music," some enormously vigorous, powerful, highly dissonant passages, bits of diatonic melody, and a great variety of rhythmic patterns. The piece is entirely free of systems or schematicism, yet it gives a thoroughly unified impression.

NEW MUSIC IN GREECE

By NICOLAS SLONIMSKY

IN MODERN Greece Orpheus tunes his lyre atonally. This scordatura was initiated by Nikos Skalkottas, a Greek disciple of Schoenberg, who died in 1949, at the age of forty-five. He left a large number of manuscripts, and a special Skalkottas Committee was organized in Athens to prepare his music for publication.

Skalkottas makes use of Schoenberg's method in an almost rhapsodic manner. His little piece for cello and piano, written shortly before his death and published under the title *Tender Melody,* is instructive in this respect. The cello part consists of fourteen consecutive statements of a songful theme of twelve different notes: F♯, E, D, C♯, C, B, G♯, A, F, G, E♭, and B♭. The rhythm varies radically, and the register shifts freely from one octave to another. Individual notes of the basic series, and even sizable thematic fragments, are repeated, but the denominations of the tone-row never change. There is no transposition, no inversion, no retrograde motion. The piano accompaniment traces a twelve-tone row of three mutually exclusive diminished seventh chords formed by symmetrically diverging and converging minor thirds. An incidental tone-row in the piano accompaniment is represented by three arpeggiated four-note figurations, and its elements enter an explicit tonal coda with a double pedalpoint on the tonic and dominant. *Tender Melody* is an example of a dodecaphonic way of writing a Romantic piece of music. On its pages Schumann seems to meet Grieg in a fine mist of chromatic vapors. But Schoenberg himself never demanded orthodoxy from his students, and he spoke warmly of Skalkottas as one of his most gifted students.

The image of Schoenberg is much more clearly visible in another score of Skalkottas, his *Little Suite* for strings, written in 1942. In it he applies the method of composition with twelve tones to melodic forma-

225

tions that suggest modern Greek melorhythms, with their serpentine melismas and angular intervallic structures. Time and again, in the midst of this folksong atmosphere, there suddenly rises a Schoenbergian outcry, an eighth note paired with a quarter note of the same pitch, and followed by a despairing sigh escaping to a high note in decrescendo.

It is only natural that dodecaphony, being a Greek word and a Greek numerical concept, should have special fascination for modern Greek composers. Yet one of the most remarkable composers of modern Greece, Jani Christou, is not a follower of Schoenbergian precepts. He describes his *Metatropes* for orchestra (its English title is *Patterns and Permutations*) as written in a "meta-serial" idiom. "The music expresses the endless formation of patterns through various levels of experience," Christou writes, "while at the same time it reveals the urge to break up this merciless process."

Christou submitted *Metatropes* to the National Radio of Athens for a competition in 1962. It was selected for the finals, and after eleven rehearsals was recorded on tape. But the work was disqualified when the rumor spread that it had already been performed in America, thus breaking the *jus primae noctis* for the competition. The rumor was false. There was no American performance, but Christou's name was inadvertently (or maliciously, as Christou claims) disclosed, and since anonymity was essential, the score had to be withdrawn.

Patterns and Permutations finally was performed in Athens on March 11, 1963, and created a riot, a rare phenomenon in the annals of musical events in modern Greece. The reasons for displeasure on the part of the audience and some critics were familiar: the harshness of the music and the annoying abundance of percussive rhythms.

Quite different from *Patterns and Permutations* is Christou's set of six songs to poems of T. S. Eliot, composed for voice and piano in 1955, and arranged for mezzo-soprano and orchestra in 1957. This is a haunting score, partaking of cosmopolitan Romanticism and Viennese Expressionism, somewhere on the geodesic line between Mahler and Berg.

Christou's earlier work, a symphony, was first performed in London on April 29, 1951 under the direction of Alec Sherman, while the rest of the program was taken up by Tchaikovsky. One newspaper review was headlined: "New Greek Work — a Protest against everything Tchaikovsky stands for."

A still earlier work, *Phoenix Music* for orchestra, should be mentioned. It had a performance in London in 1950, one at the Maggio

Fiorentino in 1951 conducted by Willy Ferrero, and several performances in Athens. The music is programmatic and "freely atonal," but
lacks discipline. Christou is "no longer fond of it," and regards it as a
"souvenir" of his early moods.

Among Christou's current interests is theater music. His score for
the *Prometheus Bound* of Aeschylus was performed at the Epidaurus
Festival in the spring of 1963. In the same year he wrote background
music for a television program sponsored by Esso Petroleum Co. and
shown internationally on the home screen, with the poet Robert Graves
as narrator. The television scenes were filmed at Delphi, and for its
music Christou went back, as he puts it, to his "ancestral memories."
Some of this music is almost operatic in style, for Christou believes that
"music and dancing were quite as important as the spoken parts" in
ancient Greek tragedy. But, he carefully adds, he "did not attempt to
imitate what might have been valid 2,500 years ago."

Jani Christou was born in Heliopolis, Egypt, on January 9, 1926.
His father was a Greek businessman, who did a lot of traveling with
his family. Christou attended a British school in Alexandria. In 1945
he entered King's College in Cambridge, where he studied philosophy.
At the same time he took private music lessons with Hans Redlich in
Letchworth. He obtained his M.A. Cantabriensis in philosophy (known
in Cambridge as Moral Sciences). He is convinced that philosophical
disciplines, especially logic (not Aristotelean logic, but symbolic logic
of Bertrand Russell and linguistic logic of Ludwig Wittgenstein) helped
him form his own musical style. In order to be "validly non-logical"
he had to master the techniques of logic.

For a brief period Christou studied orchestration with Lavagnino
in Italy; he also spent some time in Zurich, where he became interested
in the psychological theories of Dr. Jung, mainly through his brother,
a brilliant student of Jung, whose book *The Logos of the Soul* was
published posthumously, after he was killed in an automobile accident.

Like Ulysses, Christou eventually returned to Greece, married, and
settled on his father's estate on the island of Chios. It was in Chios,
Christou says, that he found himself in music, working in his own
creative laboratory "like some medieval alchemist." He continued to
maintain a studio in Athens, and frequently traveled to Italy and
Switzerland. "I have never held an official position in my life," Christou
writes, "and I never attended a conservatory. I have no degrees in music,
never had any orthodox musical training, and I consider myself mainly
self-taught. I did try to attend music classes in Cambridge, but I could

not stand the academic method of instruction."

Christou's personal idiom is unlike any other composer's even though it is not absolutely original. The rhythmic canons, the ingenious displacement of natural accent, the subtle hammering on repeated notes, the fusion of incompatible instrumental colors, the complex but widely dispersed harmonies, the curiously meandering melodies gliding along an imaginary tangent, the sudden eruption of fanfare-like proclamations, all these traits of Christou's music look and sound familiar, but their ensemble is unique. Perhaps his "medieval alchemy" led him inadvertently to the philosopher's stone that transmutes the base metals of common devices into musical gold.

The name of Yorgo Sicilianos is known to American audiences through a performance of his First Symphony by Dimitri Mitropoulos with the New York Philharmonic on March 1, 1958. He was born in Athens on August 29, 1922 and studied music at the Athens Conservatory, graduating in 1951. He subsequently entered the Santa Cecilia Academy in Rome, where he was a student of Pizzetti. In 1955 he received a Fulbright Scholarship, which enabled him to study composition with Walter Piston at Harvard University, with Boris Blacher in Tanglewood, and with Vincent Persichetti at the Juilliard School of Music in New York. He then returned to Athens, where he became active at the Hellenic Broadcasting Institute. There are parallel developments between his early music and that of Jani Christou; both experienced the spell of expansive rhapsodic forms. But Sicilianos adopted a more severe neo-Classical idiom than Christou, and made a transition to more orthodox serial techniques. Chamber music is a natural form of expression for Sicilianos, but not for Christou. If Christou is the Greek Ives, then Sicilianos is the Greek Bartók. Sicilianos writes music of solid substance and polyphonic lucidity. His predilection for works of limited sonorities with an autonomous percussion section is a Bartókian trait. In this respect, his ballet *Tanagra,* for two pianos and percussion, is characteristic. After a performance in 1958, he arranged it for full orchestra, a version that was first performed in Athens on February 5, 1962. This was followed by an extensive work in the same general style, *Synthesis,* scored for double string orchestra and percussion. It was successfully performed in Athens on November 26, 1962.

The list of works composed by Sicilianos during the fifteen years of his creative maturity is impressive. His first significant work, *The Revelation of the Fifth Seal,* a symphonic poem in a grand rhetorical, oratorical manner, was brought out in Athens on May 11, 1952. A performance of his Concerto for Orchestra took place in Athens in 1954. His three string quartets demonstrate his ability in modern polyphonic writing.

Sicilianos writes this about himself, using third person singular: "Sicilianos belongs to that group of musicians who believe in a renovation of Greek music and who, having freed themselves from the narrow folkloric tradition created by the former generation of Greek composers, are following contemporary musical trends with the conviction that the music of our time, as an artistic manifestation, has abandoned the framework of the so-called national school, and has acquired a more universal and more human character."

The "former generation of Greek composers," to which Sicilianos alludes, was bound to the Italian tradition. Its most outspoken representative was Manolis Kalomiris, the grand old man of Greek music, who wrote operas and symphonies in a fine Italian style. He died in 1962, and with him died the Greek dependence on Italian operatic models.

If the oldest generation of Greek composers gravitated towards Italy, their immediate successors turned their sights on Paris. Georges Poniridis, who was born in Constantinople in 1892, went to Paris to study with Vincent d'Indy, became completely Parisianized, and even published a collection of erotic poems in French. His music presents a fusion of Greek modalities with Impressionistic harmonies. Particularly interesting are his works of the latest period, in which he makes use of dodecaphonic structures in a tonal or bitonal context.

Petro Petridis, born in Asia Minor in 1892, had a brief moment of modified glory in the 1920s when some of his symphonic pieces had scattered performances in Europe. He studied with Albert Roussel in Paris and adopted a neo-Classical style of strong polyphonic texture. After he returned to Greece, he wrote a powerful oratorio and pieces in Greek folk modes. A man of cosmopolitan culture, a linguist (he can recite Homer in the original for hours), Petridis finds himself unjustly suspended between two musical worlds, that of traditional Classicism and obsolescent modernism. But with a favorable shift in world esthetics, his music may yet enjoy a revival. It is good music, and there is no reason why it should not become more widely known.

Dimitri Levidis (1886-1951) lived most of his life in Paris, and was naturalized as a French citizen, esthetically as well as legally, for his music assimilated the technique of French Impressionism to the full. Also French-oriented was Emil Riadis (1890-1935), who had some lessons with Ravel, and wrote a number of pieces reflecting Ravel's influence.

Greek composers of the middle generation, chronologically encompassed within the 20th century, should be mentioned. Antiochos Evanghelatos, born in 1904, is a distinguished pedagogue, as well as composer of a number of effective works in various genres. Theodore Karyotakis, born in 1903, was a student of Mitropoulos; he wrote music for the theater, some symphonic pieces, and choral works. Finally, the name of Dimitri Mitropoulos himself ought to be included among modern Greek composers, for he wrote a fine Debussyan opera and many sensitive songs.

With Skalkottas, the needle of the Hellenic musical compass shifted to the north, to Vienna. Several Greek composers of his generation experienced a similar change of orientation, starting out with stylized Greek dances and later adopting, integrally or partially, the dodecaphonic credo. Such was the case of Yiannis Papaioannou. He was born in Kavala on January 5, 1910. He studied at the Conservatory of Athens, and subsequently took lessons with Honegger in Paris. His early programmatic symphonic works — *Poem of the Forest* (1942), *Pygmalion* (1951), *Hellas* (1956) — followed the golden mean of acceptable modern music, but in his Fourth Symphony, composed in 1962, and in his Quartet for flute, clarinet, guitar, and cello, written in the same year, he asserts himself as a serial composer. In this music the intervallic scheme becomes angular, tonal connotations disappear, rhythmic figures branch out in asymmetrical patterns, and the instrumentation assumes a spastic character. Indeed, orthodox dodecaphony is here superseded by serialism rooted in the music of Webern.

A very active group of Greek composers born in the 1930s, to whom dodecaphony is pre-natal, and even obsolescent, is represented by the names of Yannis Ioannidis, Theodor Antoniou, and Stephanos Gazouleas. Yannis Ioannidis was born in Athens on June 8, 1930. He studied organ and composition in Vienna. His early works — Piano Sonata (1959), String Quartet (1961), *Triptych* for orchestra (1962) — adhere to a greater or lesser extent to Schoenberg's practices. But his Duo for violin and piano, written in 1962, veers away from strict dodecaphony to free atonality, thus reversing the historical course of modern music. He explains this retreat by his conviction that "atonality, as a system of absolute equality and independence of all twelve tones, insuring an unlimited number of harmonic combinations, is self-sufficient."

Theodor Antoniou was born in Athens in 1935. He studied violin and composition there; in 1961 he went to Munich, where he continued his study at the Staatliche Hochschule für Musik. His music is serial but not necessarily atonal. In this respect, his Concertino for piano, strings, marimba, vibraphone, kettledrums, and other percussion instruments, is most unusual. It starts out with a supremely tonal interplay of the tonic, supertonic, and dominant in unison, in the plainest G major. The basic tone-row grows out of this figure by a simple additive process. The rhythm is organized serially at a different rate of distribution of stresses from that of the cumulative tone-row, so that each individual note of the theme is stressed as the tone-row is gradually integrated. There are three movements; in the second movement the process of serialization is intervallic, and in the third movement the rhythmic parameter is the prime thematic impulse. In his orchestral *Antitheses,* Antoniou applies a different technique to each of its three movements, and their titles suggest these contrasting styles: *Pedal-Melos, Lines-Spaces, Planes-Points.*

His *Epilogue,* written in 1963, is serially organized in most of its elements, and the score contains an aleatory episode in which the conductor gives only entrance cues, and the players improvise along prescribed notes, with the rhythms and octave positions free. The piece, to a text from *The Odyssey,* is scored for mezzo-soprano, speaker, oboe, horn, guitar, piano, double bass, and percussion.

Stephanos Gazouleas, born in Larissa in 1931, studied with Hanns Jelinek in Vienna, and acquired from him a thorough technique of twelve-tone composition. Esthetically, his main influence is the music of Anton Webern. His *Six Lyric Pieces* for flute and piano, written in 1962, are congenial imitations of Webern's poetic miniatures. His other works reflect an affinity with Skalkottas; of these, his *11 Aphorisms* for piano are modern evocations of Romantic moods.

An interesting attempt to organize ancient Greek melos according to modern serial ideas is made by Arghyris Kounadis in his orchestral work *Chorikon.* Kounadis was born of Greek parents in Constantinople on February 14, 1924. Having completed his primary musical education in Athens, he received a fellowship from the Greek government to continue his studies in Germany, where he became a student of Wolfgang Fortner. It was Fortner who conducted the first performance of *Chorikon,* with the Berlin Philharmonic Orchestra, on May 15, 1962. The work is in four movements, with characteristic titles: *Melos, Strophe, Antistrophe,* and *Epilogue.* The thematic elements of the score are derived from a dodecaphonic series, which is articulated into two quasi-symmetrical tropes, covering, in its original form, the range of an augmented octave. The inner notes of each trope are permutated, generating two subsidiary tone-rows. The series appears in inversion and retrograde motion, and is integrated into the harmonic structure. In contrapuntal development Kounadis applies the principles of heterophony, which, according to his observation, underlies the melodic formations of modern Greek folksongs. Furthermore, he distinguishes three types of heterophony: canonic, i.e. diagonal; monophonic, i.e. linear; and harmonic, i.e. vertical.

Kounadis is a versatile composer. He writes theater music for performances of ancient Greek tragedies, using archaic modes, and instrumental works in an ultra-modern idiom. Of the latter, his *Triptychon* for flute and chamber orchestra (1964) is of importance. He also experiments in Webern-like instrumental sonorities, as exemplified by a trio for flute, viola, and guitar composed in 1958.

Among Greek modernists, the curious figure of Manos Hadzidakis stands apart. Curious, because he started out as a composer of witty modernistic piano pieces, but achieved fame as the author of the theme song for the Greek film, *The Children of Pireus*, released in France under the title *Jamais le dimanche*, and in America as *Never on Sunday*. Hadzidakis was born in Xanthi, Macedonia, on October 23, 1925, received academic education in Greece, and published, as his Op. 1, a piano suite, under the title *For a Little White Seashell*. The second movement of this suite is named *Conversation with Serge Prokofiev*, and it catches the spirit of Prokofiev's polymodality very nicely.

It was inevitable that Greek music should have taken an Icarus-like flight into the ultimate dimension of space-time, proceeding on a stochastic course. Stochastic is the key word in the hyper-sophisticated circles of musical innovators of the second half of the century. It denotes a variable function determined by random phenomena in time. In other words, stochastic music is aleatory. The prime apostle and protagonist of stochastic composition is Ianis Xenakis. He was born, of Greek parentage, in Braila, Rumania, on May 22, 1922, and studied engineering in Athens. Upon graduation, he joined the studio of Le Corbusier in Paris, and worked with him on architectural projects for twelve years. It was not until Xenakis was nearly thirty years old that he undertook serious musical studies. He enrolled in the class of Messiaen at the Paris Conservatory, and also took lessons with Honegger and Milhaud. Bypassing Schoenbergian dodecaphony and Webernian serialism, Xenakis began writing music according to the mathematical theories of sets and calculus of probability. The titles of his works indicate his preoccupation with scientific concepts. Thus, *Pithoprakta* for orchestra connotes the idea of "probable realization" (the first half of the word means probable in modern Greek, and the second half is obviously cognate with the word practical). *Pithoprakta* was first performed in Munich on March 8, 1957, and had an American performance at one of Leonard Bernstein's avant-garde programs with the New York Philharmonic. The title of another work by Xenakis, *Achorripsis,* scored for twenty-one instruments, is derived from the word for sound in modern Greek and the plural of the word for jet. The music is then, according to Xenakis, a spray of sounds, a sonorous radiation, a stream of musical electrons.

In 1962 Xenakis wrote two pieces for the IBM 7090 electronic computer. He programmed the music specifying duration and density of "sound events," leaving the parameters of pitch, velocity, and dynamics to the computer. The first piece is entitled *Morsima-Amorsima,* with an affix ST/4-1, 030762, which is deciphered as Stochastic Music for 4 performers, No. 1, completed on the 3rd day of the 7th month of the year No. 62 in the present century. Its duration is calculated to be in the vicinity of ten minutes, but it can be stochastically expanded or contracted. The second piece is *Amorsima-Morsima,* and its affix is ST/10-2, 080262, which signifies Stochastic Music for 10 Performers, No. 2. According to the symbol, it was completed on the 8th day of the 2nd month of 1962, that is, earlier than No. 1. Both pieces were played for the first time at a rather memorable concert given at the Technological Institute of Athens on December 16, 1962, sponsored and financed by, of all people, Manos Hadzidakis, the composer of *Never on Sunday.* And it was conducted by Lukas Foss, no mean aleatorist himself. For future archivists it should be noted that the official Greek program carries the wrong date, December 16, 1961, on its title page. Since the program states that the concert took place on the Day of the Lord (*kyriaki*) and since December 16, 1962 was a *Sunday,* and since many of the works played at this concert were composed in 1962, the error of the date of this computerized concert is patent.

For the 1963 Festival of Contemporary Music in Venice, Xenakis contributed a piece for two orchestras and two conductors, entitled *Stratégie.* The strategy consists in antiphonal wrestling. The conductors are given "parameters" of duration and intensity; strategic meetings are held at cadential fermatas, at the end of each of the nineteen divisions of the piece. The audience decides by acclamation which conductor and which orchestra overwhelmed which. The degree of vociferation of individual members of the audience enters as a stochastic factor. At its first performance on April 23, 1963, Bruno Maderna was an easy winner against his less known rival.

Stochastic music requires special symbolic notation, in which curves of probability point to the occurrence or non-occurrence of a sound event, and the thickness of terraced lines corresponds to the optimum loudness. This type of "optical notation" is now employed by probabilistic composers all over the world.

Several composers of the Greek avant-garde have settled, more or less permanently, in Germany. Of these, the name of Nikos Mamangakis is beginning to be known. He was born in Rethymnon, Crete, on March 3, 1929, and studied with Carl Orff and Harald Genzmer. In his music he adopts numerical sets as thematic complexes which determine the parameters of the entire composition. Because an arithmetical series can be infinitely varied, one such composition is unlike any other that has a different numerical matrix. *Monologue* for unaccompanied cello, which Mamangakis wrote in 1962, is based on the set of numbers 7, 5, 8, 9, 2, which determines the principal parameters, making the music unique.

George Tsouyopoulos was born in Athens on October 11, 1930. He studied with Hindemith in Zurich. In 1957 he settled in Munich, and joined the cosmopolitan avant-garde there. He strives to achieve a total organization of serializable elements, but he is circumspect about free improvisation. His *Music for Percussion*, composed in 1959, is serialized according to seven parameters: 1) spatial placement of sound, that is, pitch; 2) time structure of sound, that is, rhythm; 3) instrumental timbre; 4) dynamics in three levels, corresponding to forte, mezzo-forte, and piano; 5) sound density; 6) duration of pauses; 7) dodecaphonic linearity. The serial rows of these factors are not synchronous, so that multiple interpenetrations result. Tsouyopoulos emphasizes that the unfolding of each row may continue ad infinitum, and that there is therefore no concrete end of the work; nor, he adds as an afterthought, can there be any beginning, for the whole composition represents an event placed between two asymptotes. *Music for Percussion* contains 95 measures in all, but Tsouyopoulos puts the word "end" in quotation marks over measure 95, thus suggesting an open end and an indefinite continuation.

Music for Percussion represents the latest stage in the development of Tsouyopoulos. His earlier works are still safely neo-Classical, according to the tenets of Hindemith. In this style he wrote two string quartets, a Sinfonietta for eight instruments, and some vocal music. His *Serenata* for voice, flute, viola, and guitar (1957) discloses Webernian traits.

Anestis Logothetis came to music through painting. He was born in Burgas, Bulgaria, of Greek parents, on October 27, 1921. He studied art in Greece and in Vienna, exhibited a series of "polymorphic graphs" in art galleries, and then used these drawings as symbolic musical notation. He states: "As a result of research, I came to the conclusion that appropriate graphic representations of sound can be used as psychological associations between the visual impression and its rendering in sound. Such graphs then become catalyses that release multiple transformations and combinations of actual sounds, providing a stimulus to performers to produce music." He points out that, given such latitude of interpretation of his polymorphic graphs, there exists an infinity of possible integrations of the differential points and curves in "graphic music."

The titles of his graphs are significant: Cycloid, Culmination, Co-ordination, Expansion-Contraction, Impulse (quantitative), Impulse (qualitative), Interpolation, Catalyzation, Parallax, Texture-Structure, Concatenation, Centrifugal.

George Leotsakos, born in Athens in 1935, studied oriental languages, and became interested in expressing the poetic brevity of Japanese Haiku verses in atonal music. His cycle of songs to the texts of Haiku poems, each of which has three lines and 17 syllables, is written in dissonant counterpoint, but the melorhythmic outline is as precise as the Japanese form itself.

The parallelism between the trends of new Greek music and modernistic developments elsewhere in the world is obvious, and parallel lines do meet in global geometry. But Greek composers strive to relate the abstract concepts of modern music to the modalities and the ethos of ancient Hellas. It is to be hoped that their stochastic asymptotes will lead them towards a fruitful synthesis of the new and the old, of the national and the cosmopolitan.

MODERN COMPOSITION
IN RUMANIA

By NICOLAS SLONIMSKY

T HE spirit of Georges Enescu dominates the minds and the art of
musical Rumania today. International Enescu Festivals are celebrated every other year in Bucharest, attended by numerous delegations
from the countries of the socialist bloc as well as from the West. Prizes
of great prestige value are distributed at an international contest held
in connection with the Enescu Festivals. A series of postage stamps with
Enescu's portraits as a child prodigy playing the violin, and as a famous
artist and conductor, has been issued by the Rumanian Post Office.
The Moldavian village where he was born on August 7, 1881, has been
renamed Enescu. There are "Enescu Conservatories" in virtually every
Rumanian city or town. An Enescu Museum has been established in his
former residence in Bucharest, housing his manuscripts, photographs, and
family mementoes. There exists already an impressive collection of mono-
graphs on Enescu's individual works, and his detailed illustrated biography, containing a complete chronology of his life and works, day by
day, year by year, has been published in five languages — Rumanian,
Russian, German, French, and English. How precious every item connected with Enescu's works is considered in Rumania, is illustrated by
the fact that the Enescu Museum paid $2,500 to a New York dealer for
the manuscript of Enescu's orchestral arrangement of a piano piece by
Albéniz.

All these honors have an element of nostalgic irony, for Enescu died
in Paris in 1955, after a long and debilitating illness, almost in poverty.
Paris was his second home, for it was there that he started his prodigious
career as a violinist, composer, and conductor. He also achieved a remarkable proficiency as a pianist. When an obscure Rumanian violinist

named Sandu Albu gave a concert in Paris in 1920, he persuaded
Enescu to accompany him at the piano. It so happened that the great
Alfred Cortot volunteered to turn the pages for Enescu, which moved
a Paris critic to write: "The man who played the piano should have
played the violin; the man who turned the pages should have played
the piano; and the man who played the violin should have been the
page turner."

As a patron saint of contemporary Rumanian music, Enescu had
much to offer. He was a cosmopolitan Parisian and a Rumanian nationalist. He was a Romantic traditionalist and a modernistic experimenter.
He turned the orientalistic Rumanian scale patterns to atonal uses, and
the asymmetric Balkan meters to primitivistic polyrhythmics. In his
opera *Roi Oedipe* he injected a few quarter-tone progressions to suggest
the Greek enharmonic mode in a modernistic context. Rumanian composers of the new school are free, therefore, to select any aspect of
Enescu's musical personality, to write traditional Romantic music, strongly national music, or even serial music.

The proliferation of Rumanian composition in the last twenty years
is staggering. Symphonies and operas, concertos and chamber music,
piano pieces and songs are produced in quantity, and almost instantane-
ously published. The time lag between composition and publication is
much smaller than elsewhere, with the exception of Russia. Music
dictionaries have caught up with only an elder crust of Rumanian
musical creativity, but even in the entries already incorporated in lexi-
cographical volumes, the reports are far behind the actual production.
Dimitrie Cuclin, for instance, has already written eighteen symphonies
and is rapidly progressing towards equality with the champion symphonist of the 20th century, Miaskovsky, who wrote twenty-seven. It
is beside the point to observe that Cuclin's symphonies are not exactly
world-shaking, for he himself has declared that music ended in 1890,
with the death of César Franck. But his symphonies are being dutifully
performed in Bucharest, and some are published. One stands in silent
awe before this accumulation of playable notes. But even Cuclin was
driven to experimentation in essaying a quintet for piccolo, English horn,
trombone, contrabassoon, and piano, a unique combination in chamber
music.

Unrestrained musical productivity does not necessarily imply artistic
inferiority. Alfred Mendelson, who was born in Bucharest in 1910, has
written nine symphonies since 1945 and as many string quartets since
1930, as well as concertos, oratorios, overtures, and symphonic poems.

All these works testify not only to his mastery of the craft but also to his ingenuity in the application of esthetically meaningful technical devices. Particularly interesting in this respect is his Sixth String Quartet, derived from an atonal motif of four notes, permutated, but invariably reverting to the central keynote, and in fact designated as being in C major despite numerous bitonal excursions. Mendelson is also a master of illustrative music. In his oratorio entitled *1907*, the year of a rural Rumanian uprising, the marching steps are projected in appropriately dissonant counterpoint onto the solid tonal background. Thus, Mendelson's music is both modernistic and tonal, a perfect compromise to satisfy both sides of the barricade separating the traditionalism of the socialist bloc and the adventurism of the unguided West.

A whole group of Rumanian composers of the older generation devoted themselves primarily to collecting native folksongs. In their own works, they used these materials either by direct quotation or by way of stylized re-creation. The dean of these composers is Tiberiu Brediceanu, born in Banat in 1877. He studied law in Italy, and occupied administrative posts in Rumanian opera houses. He published a volume of 1000 popular melodies of Transylvania and other valuable anthologies. He composed an "ethnographic" symphonic poem, ballet music, and numerous dances in the Rumanian manner for piano, as well as many arrangements of Rumanian melodies for voice and instruments.

Constantin Brailoiu (1893-1958) is known primarily as a musical ethnographer and founder of the International Archive for Folk Music in Geneva, but he maintained contact with Rumania, and his few original compositions are derived mostly from Rumanian folksongs.

To the same group of composers who are primarily folklorists belongs Theodor Rogalski (1901-54). He is one of the few Rumanian composers, after Enescu, who succeeded in writing a work in the native manner that has had repeated performances abroad, an orchestral suite of three Rumanian dances, composed in 1951. This score possesses a degree of variety and universality that makes it both authentic and accessible to popular taste.

The name of Martian Negrea, born in Kronstadt on January 29, 1893, ought to be mentioned. His symphonic suites are programmatically designed to portray colorful regions of Rumania. In the process of composition, he incorporates allusions to popular melodies and rhythms. Negrea is greatly esteemed as a pedagogue and the author of several manuals for music students.

Among Rumanian composers of cosmopolitan persuasion, the name of Alfred Alessandrescu (1893-1959) imposes itself. He was a student of Vincent d'Indy in Paris, and acquired from him an elegance of harmonic procedure and instrumental gesture that lends distinction to his essentially traditional music. With the exception of his *Rumanian Fantasy* for orchestra, Alessandrescu did not follow the national line in his concepts of composition.

Much less known than Alessandrescu but meriting mention is his close contemporary, Mihail Andricu. He was born in Bucharest on December 22, 1894 and studied with Vincent d'Indy and Gabriel Fauré in Paris. In Rumania he was for many years a composition teacher at the Bucharest Conservatory. During the last twenty years he has written nine symphonies, eight symphoniettas, and much chamber music. But he is best known to the outside world as the piano accompanist of Georges Enescu.

Mihail Jora commands respect as composer of fine *Lieder*. He was born in Roman, on August 2, 1891, and studied in Leipzig with Max Reger. His symphonic and chamber music reveals indeed some Reger-like traits, but his talent is sufficiently plastic to forfend the oversaturation with Germanic polyphony. The poetic fragrance that his songs exhale creates an atmosphere of melodious consistency pleasing to the senses. Apart from his compositions, Jora played an important role as an educator. A whole generation of Rumanian musicians passed through his composition classes at the Bucharest Conservatory. Among them was Dinu Lipatti, who rose to fame as a pianist, but who was also a composer of brilliant gifts. Lipatti's early death in 1950, at the age of thirty-three, deprived Rumania not only of its greatest pianist but quite possibly of a minor Chopin in composition.

One of the most enlightened composers of the Rumanian modern school is Zeno Vancea. He was born in Banat on October 8, 1900, and studied in Rumania, before taking a course of composition with Ernst Kanitz in Vienna. He excels in chamber music, and his predilection is for strong and smooth polyphony. In his symphonic works Vancea allows himself to relax in broad rhapsodic sonorities. His *Symphonic Triptych* (1958) is a fine study in contrasts; there is a suggestion of programmatic content. Vancea is also active in the field of musical folklore, and is editor-in-chief of the informative Rumanian magazine *Muzica*.

Sigismund Toduta is one of the most eloquent symphonists of Rumania. His music possesses a fine rhetorical quality which is all the more impressive because of the maintenance of classical equilibrium in his melodic, contrapuntal, and harmonic components. Toduta was born in Simeria on May 17, 1908. For some years he studied at the Santa Cecilia Academy in Rome, where he was a student of Casella in piano and of Pizzetti in composition. Returning to Rumania, he became director of the Conservatory in Cluj. He composed three symphonies in three years (1954-56) and a number of sonatas for various instruments with piano.

The music of Tudor Ciortea adheres to the French tradition. This may be explained by the fact that his first teacher, Ion Nonna Otescu (1888-1940), was himself a product of the Parisian school of composition. Ciortea was born in Kronstadt on November 15, 1903, and after a course of studies at the Bucharest Conservatory under Otescu, went to Paris, where he took lessons with Paul Dukas and Nadia Boulanger. He is one of the few Rumanian composers who devotes himself almost entirely to chamber music. What is remarkable is the contrapuntal complexity of his writing, as demonstrated by one of his best productions, a piano quintet (1958). Among his other works are two string quartets, a violin sonata, a cello sonata, and a flute sonata.

Paul Constantinescu (1909-1963) was a Romantic Classicist. He liked to attach imaginative subtitles to his symphonic scores in the manner of Smetana and other central European nationalists. Thus his Ballade for cello and orchestra (1950) bears the subtitle *Haiduc,* descriptive of a disfranchised peasant of the feudal period. But he wrote a number of concertos, among them one for harp and orchestra (1960), which are entirely classical in concept and form. His harmony barely transcends the borderline of tonality, and his instrumentation is orthodox. Constantinescu also wrote an opera, *A Stormy Night,* in the robust manner of musical horror tales, enlivened by a characteristic grotesquerie. A later opera, *The Mermaid* (1955), utilizes a subject familiar to Romantic composers, but since it is a fairy tale in the context of native folklore, he incorporates in its score a wealth of Balkan melodies, with their asymmetrical meters and orientalistic inflections.

In the field of opera, the most successful Rumanian composer of modern times is Sabin V. Dragoi. He was born in Banat on June 6, 1894, and studied in Prague with Vitězslav Novák. He became an ardent collector of folksongs, and was appointed director of the Folklore Institute in Bucharest. An extremely prolific composer, he wrote music in all genres, but it is in his operas that he achieved lasting success. One of them, *Napasta,* to a characteristic libretto involving adultery, murder, and natural disaster, which he wrote in 1928, became a permanent favorite on the Rumanian operatic stage.

Two brothers, Ion and Gheorghe Dumitrescu, born in the village of Otesani, respectively on May 20, 1913 and December 15, 1914, both studied at the Bucharest Conservatory with Mihail Jora, but chose different creative paths. Ion Dumitrescu turned towards symphonic composition with undertones of Rumanian folk music, while his younger brother took the more ambitious course in writing grand national oratorios. Ion Dumitrescu wrote several orchestral suites, a symphony, and an interesting Sinfonietta (1957) in which quasi-atonal and polymetric Rumanian melodic patterns are set in sharp bitonal harmonies. The acknowledged masterwork of Gheorghe Dumitrescu is his trilogy, consisting of the oratorio *Tudor Vladimirescu* (1952), to a subject dealing with a national hero of the Rumanian struggle for independence from the Ottoman Empire, the opera *Ion Voda the Terrible* (1955), and the musical tragedy *Decebal* (1957).

Ovidiu Varga, who was born in Jassy on October 5, 1913, is at his best in handling choral masses. In his music he aims at direct communication with the audience through a stirring patriotic or revolutionary text and sonorous harmonic formations. Among his works is an oratorio on the liberation of Rumania, several cantatas, and some chamber music.

Rumanian composers born in the 1920s follow divergent roads towards the establishment of a style of composition that would be national in essence and cosmopolitan in modern technique. Of these, Dumitru Bughici, born in Jassy on November 14, 1921, studied at the Leningrad Conservatory, and acquired a style reflecting the moods, both tragic and optimistic, that pervade the symphonic scores of Shostakovich. Characteristic of these influences are Bughici's *Youth Symphonietta, Spring Poem* for violin and orchestra, and *Poem of Joy* for chorus and orchestra. The inherent Romanticism of Bughici's concepts does not prevent him from making use of the most acrid dissonances at his disposal. Thus the Scherzo in his *Symphonie-Poème* ends on a chord composed of a G minor triad with a superstructure containing the discordant notes C♯, F♯, and F.

Laurentiu Profeta, born in Bucharest on January 14, 1925, studied at the Bucharest Conservatory, and after the end of the war went to Moscow for further study. He wrote several symphonic poems and cantatas in a highly effective style, with a thin veneer of modernity which imparts a certain brilliance to the music. Profeta was for many years active in Rumanian cultural organizations and on the Bucharest Radio.

Profeta's younger contemporary, Tiberiu Olah, born in Arpasel on January 2, 1928, also studied in Moscow during the post-war years. In his music he combines modern Romanticism with energetic neo-Primitivism. His Symphony, composed in 1955, is designated as being in D major, but it departs widely from its tonal centers and establishes a melorhythmic disequilibrium that is stimulating. His resources are found in Balkanized scales and asymmetrical meters; the development is cumulative, reaching considerable tension, before the symphony concludes with a sonorously optimistic and eminently tonal finale. His oratorio *The Galaxy of Man,* to words by Vladimir Mayakovsky, generates an enormous amount of kinetic energy. In his chamber music he experiments with novel combinations of instruments, as in his *Song of the Cosmos,* scored for tenor, clarinet, and piano (1957).

Undoubtedly the most original Rumanian composer of the generation that came to maturity at the end of the war is Anatol Vieru. He was born in Jassy on June 8, 1926. He studied in Bucharest, and began his musical career as an opera conductor. In 1952 he went to Moscow, where he became a student of Aram Khatchaturian at the Moscow Conservatory. After his return to Rumania, he was appointed instructor at the Bucharest Conservatory. In 1956 he wrote two string quartets, and in the following year he began the composition of his first work of major importance, a folk oratorio *Miorita,* to texts collected from popular verses, and dealing with a lost sheep. The entire score is based on two six-note tropes, mutually exclusive and aggregating to a twelve-tone series: 1) C, D, F♯, G, B, and C♯ and 2) E♭, E, F, A♭, A, and B♭. Both tropes are mirror formations, the first being symmetrically built around the central interval of the semitone, and the second around the central interval of a minor third. The interplay of these two tropes creates a fruitful engagement of melodic elements, with ingenious allusions to authentic Rumanian modes that contain intervals involved in the series. *Miorita* was performed for the first time in Bucharest on March 27, 1958, with excellent success.

Among Vieru's other works are two Concertos for Orchestra (1955 and 1961), a quintet for clarinet and strings (1958), a flute concerto (1958), *Cantata Anilor Lumina (Cantata of Luminous Years;* 1960), and a set of children's pieces for piano. In 1962 he wrote a Cello Concerto for the International Competition in Geneva, and it received the first prize. This was a great victory for Vieru, and established him as a composer of international reputation.

Rumania is fertile in talent. The youngest generation of Rumanian composers produces a number of interesting works, making use of modern techniques of composition but instinctively retaining the basic intervallic and rhythmic formations of native melodies. The biennial Enescu Festivals promise to reveal new Rumanian music of charm and significance.

POLISH MUSIC AFTER WORLD WAR II

By STEFAN JAROCINSKI

THE two factors that have had the greatest impact on modern Polish music are neo-Classicism and the works of Szymanowski. If any historian of music tried to draw a logical curve of evolution of Polish music in the first three decades of the 20th century omitting Szymanowski's work, he would be amazed at the inexplicable gap that would yawn between the works of Paderewski, Karlowicz, or Rózycki and the works of those composers whose talents matured in the years between the two World Wars. It is precisely and only Szymanowski's work that fills the gap, supplying the link between the two periods. We must remember that strictly speaking there was neither Impressionsim nor "fauvism" nor Expressionism in our music. Its Romantic desert was not thoroughly irrigated by such works as *The Rite of Spring, The Miraculous Mandarin,* or *Scythian Suite,* to say nothing of the works of Schoenberg's school; and the consciously cynical and defiant esthetics of the Group of Six and the *Neue Sachlichkeit* came down to us in a modified, tempered version, modelled on Stravinsky, in the shape of neo-Classicism.

Since in Poland all this revolution acted solely and exclusively on Szymanowski's music, and genuinely took place only in him — it was he alone who made up nearly half a century of our cultural lag — the new composers came, as it were, to a tilled field. They missed the *Sturm und Drang* period of new music, because they had inherited it all through the experience of Szymanowski in his music. This fact explains the amazing attitude of acceptance and lack of any polemical attitude towards the basic categories and problems of sound, technique, and form in the younger generation of composers. They had no need to fight for what already had been acquired by new music in the West, and by Szymanowski in Poland. Thus their only concern was to concentrate

244

on the problems of their own style, and to follow the new music in its development; this was not difficult because of its temporary stagnation (Schoenberg's school had not yet acquired the meaning and importance it enjoyed later).

Kazimierz Sikorski (b. 1895), a composer of great experience, professing neo-Classical views, was for a long time the spiritual leader and patron of young musicians. He educated many gifted composers, among others Bacewicz, Krenz, Malawski, Palester, Panufnik, Serocki, Spisak, Szalowski.

It became a kind of tradition that nearly all these composers after taking their diplomas went abroad, in most cases to Paris, to continue their musical studies, and to deepen their knowledge under the direction of such masters and pedagogues as Nadia Boulanger, Paul Dukas, Albert Roussel, or Charles Koechlin. A particularly prominent role must be allowed here to Nadia Boulanger, whose help and direction shaped two generations of Polish composers, including Szeligowski, Perkowski, Woytowicz, Kondracki, Mycielski, Szalowski, Spisak, Bacewicz, Rudzinski, Zulawski, Serocki, and Skrowaczewski. This distinct domination of the *Ecole de Paris* and its neo-Classic esthetics in the musical education of our youth has of course influenced the shaping of artistic ideas in our music, especially since the times in which our youth had its start in music seemed to favor the spreading of neo-Classic ideas.

The infiltration of the neo-Classic trend into Poland can be traced back to about 1926 — that is to say, to about the same time when it spread in the West. Yet neo-Classicism, transplanted into Polish ground, took on a peculiar coloring. As is well known, Szymanowski in his last period found inspiration in folklore. A great number of composers aspiring to modernity followed and imitated him. They also tried their hand at the risky blending of artistically refined art with the folk-primitive, and, like Szymanowski, looked for inspiration not only in the kinds of rhythm and melody characteristic of folklore, but also in the folk manner of executing music.

Józef Koffler (1896-1943), murdered by the Nazis, had a unique and isolated position in Polish music of the period between the wars. He was Schoenberg's pupil, and in that period the first and only dodecaphonist in the country. He did not, however, succeed in transplanting his master's method of composition to Polish soil. His twelve-tone works (Variations for String Orchestra, Op. 19, Third Symphony, Op. 21, and others) were oftener performed abroad than in Poland, where they met with no response, except among a small group of friends and musical experts. It is remarkable, however, that even Koffler's compositions bear a stamp of neo-Classic style. No wonder that this current, so decidedly dominating in Polish music before World War II, managed to maintain its key position for many post-war years.

In the period immediately after World War II and in quite new political and social conditions Polish music first of all tried to get rid of the burden of the martyrdom of the Occupation. This explains the great number of works that were full of pent-up emotion (such as Palester's Violin Concerto and Second Symphony or Malawski's Symphony) as well as compositions in which the tone of dramatic rhetoric prevailed, as in the Second Symphony by Woytowicz or in the much slighter *Grünwald* by J. A. Maklakiewicz (1899-1954).

Both the Requiem by Roman Palester (b. 1907) — much more reserved in expression and in which the composer has recourse to an ingenious vocal polyphony, with widely flung arches of melody — and the sombre, tonally dark *Olympic Symphony* by Zbigniew Turski (b. 1908) may be included in this "martyrological" trend.

None of these works, however, can match in artistic ripeness and power of expression the short *Tragic Overture* composed by Andrzej Panufnik (b. 1914). Written in 1942, two years before the Warsaw Uprising, it now seems to us a musical foreboding of that shattering event. The composition is based on a motif of four notes which emerges persistently in an ever-changing harmonic atmosphere, often accompanied by sharp polytonal chords resulting from contrapuntal intricacies. It is an admirable example of powerful music achieved with extremely economical and simple means. This economy, and at the same time judicious selection of means, could be already noted earlier in Panufnik's colorful *Five Folk Songs,* where the composer achieves effects of singular charm by juxtaposing the simple unison singing and the chromatic accompaniment of five woodwinds.

Neo-Classicism was undoubtedly the trend that had a shaping influence on the development of Polish music quite apart from the weaker or stronger national features or the degree of expressiveness of particular works. Thus, in the vocal music composed during the Occupation by Stanislaw Wiechowicz (1893-1963), for example, though still closely connected with Polish folklore and masterly in its choral technique, we hear echoes of Stravinsky of the period of *Les Noces.* I refer in particular to the *Harvest Cantata* with its chorus of characteristic "barking" staccatos, as one of the critics put it.

The first works by Grazyna Bacewicz (b. 1913), her most eminent composition being undoubtedly the Concerto for Strings, were closely related to the neo-Classicism towards which all her later works tended. Witold Rudzinski's (b. 1913) Nonet, too, was closely connected with neo-Classicism, but this composer's attention turned later to larger forms (the opera), and to a more conservative musical language. The *Symphonic Studies* by Artur Malawski (1904-57) as well as the Toccata of Boleslaw Szabelski (b. 1896) could also be classed with the neo-Classic trend if we did not regard these works as intermediary stages in these composers' artistic development. Neo-Classicism, however, has taken its purest shape in the works of two Polish composers living in Paris, i.e. Antoni Szalowski (b. 1907) and Michal Spisak. Their compositions met with a very good reception in Polish musical circles when they were performed in Poland.

The former came to the fore nearly at once with his brilliant Overture for orchestra (1936). It is a work, masterly in instrumentation, that has kept its freshness to the present day. It has captivated listeners with its dynamic motion and piquant details. Other works by Szalowski, most of them chamber compositions (four string quartets, a woodwind trio, a wind quintet, etc.), are faultless in construction, and always fresh in their harmonic ideas, though generally faithful to tonality.

The vicissitudes of Michal Spisak (b. 1914) were of quite a different kind. He remained in obscurity during the years of the Occupation, and it is only after World War II that he emerged on the international scene. He became known first as the author of a Toccata, a Suite for Strings, and a Bassoon Concerto. These compositions, notable for their excellent craftsmanship and kinship to the neo-Classic manner of Stravinsky, are endowed with individual features, especially in their melody (the lyrical nature of their themes in the slow movements), and their rhythm, which is sometimes, as in the Suite for Strings, quite Polish in its briskness and cockiness. These features are striking both in Spisak's early Serenade for Orchestra (1939) and in one of his latest works, the *Concerto giocoso*. But perhaps the most original work of Spisak thus far is his seldom-performed first *Symphonie concertante* of 1948, scored for an almost normal orchestral ensemble (with piano and four trumpets). The Intermezzo stands out among the five movements of this Symphony, in which groups rather than individual instruments play concertante parts. Here all the strings hold the pedal all the time, producing the effect of a sonorous web against which the slow chords of piano, four hands, thread a thematic yarn strange in its simple deployment of several notes, creating a unique atmosphere of an almost mystic tension.

The earliest and most evident symptoms of overcoming the neo-Classical tendency appeared in the works of composers of such different personalities as Lutoslawski, Panufnik, Szabelski, and Malawski. They had, however, one common feature: the persistent search for their own individual artistic media expressed in a new, modern musical language. Witold Lutoslawski (b. 1913), for example, in the *Folk Melodies* (1945) combined tonal melody with atonal harmony. In his Symphony (1941-47), one of the most eminent works of this period, he used Classical form but infused it with musical contents that have much more in common with "fauvism" than with neo-Classicism or neo-Romanticism. The composition, however, bears above all the mark of the composer's great individuality, transcending the stylistic categories of neo-Classicism. The universal aspirations of Polish post-war music, which sought a synthesis between a contemporary musical language and elements of native tradition within the frame of individual stylistic categories, are very clearly reflected in this work.

But Lutoslawski's Symphony has acquired an almost symbolic meaning because it became the first eminent musical composition to be accused of being "formalistic," and subsequently it was for many years removed from the concert hall repertory.

In spite of lavish material help and cultural patronage by the state, the years 1949-1955 were beyond any doubt exceptionally difficult for Polish composers. The highest commandment, that music must be distinctly national, directed all cultural policy. And national meant "connected with folklore" — it could not be otherwise. The proposal that composers seek their inspiration in folklore was neither new nor harmful in itself but it began to grow absurd when it was coupled with the demand that composers return to functional harmony and to the major-minor system — in a word, to the musical language of Moniuszko. Composers recognized their duty towards the new listener, and fulfilled it or fulfilled the demands that were imposed on them, for example in mass songs, cantatas, and other forms of vocal music, as the kind of music that is most accessible to popular audiences. But at the same time they defended the acquisition of modern musical techniques. The attitude of the leading composers — such as Lutoslawski, Malawski, Szabelski, and others — who would not compromise on the fundamental questions of art, was of great importance in this crisis. By their example they favorably influenced young musicians, who grew up under new conditions.

Thanks to this, Polish music developed fairly well, though at a slackened pace. Many eminent works were written in this period. We shall mention here first those that were in one degree or another connected with folk music — *Little Suite, Silesian Triptych,* and *Bucolics* by Lutoslawski; *Lullaby* and *Sinfonia rustica* by Panufnik; the ballet-cantata *Wierchy* (*The Mountain Tops*) of Malawski (based on highland folklore), *Old Town Concerto* and *Kasia* (*Kitty*), a suite by Wiechowicz.

Works that would be difficult to classify as taking inspiration from folklore formed a separate group. To it belonged the Second Symphony and Piano Trio of Malawski, Overture for Strings of Lutoslawski, Nocturne of Panufnik, Third Symphony and Concerto grosso of Szabelski, Violin Concerto of Turski, and String Quartet No. 4 and Fourth Violin Concerto of Bacewicz. The works of composers of the young generation who made their début in those years should also be included in this group, among them the suite *Colas Breugnon* and Concerto for Orchestra of Tadeusz Baird (b. 1928), First Symphony of Kazimierz Serocki (b. 1922), Symphony and Rhapsody for Orchestra of Jan Krenz (b. 1926), Prelude and Passacaglia for Orchestra of Wlodzimierz Kotonski (b. 1925), Symphony for Strings of Stanislaw Skrowaczewski (b. 1923).[1]

Undoubtedly the highest artistic achievement of those years, however, was Lutoslawski's Concerto for Orchestra (1954), a summit of invention, of a composer's self-knowledge and originality. While it was inspired by folk motifs (both genuine and imaginary), it is worked out in a way that distinctly avoids stylization. Folk motifs are used as raw material completely subjected to the larger pattern of the work, and not as a form-determining factor. The Concerto unites two aspects of musical evolution: one has its sources in the development of a modern musical language, and the other in the incorporation of patterns suggested by native folklore.

The indifference of Polish composers to the experiments in the field of new sound structures and of new organization of musical material, so vital then in the West, is the most striking feature of Polish music of that time. These experiments were, as we know, stimulated as much by Messiaen's modal technique as by Schoenberg's school and its twelve-tone technique, which after World War II was developed by the post-Webern school in so-called "pointillism." The reason for this indifference is quite clear if we remember that Polish music was cut off from Western

[1] Skrowaczewski is at present conductor of the Minneapolis Symphony Orchestra.

musical centers. Its chief effort was to keep up and develop those achievements of the contemporary musical language that had been within its reach up to 1949, to draw the maximum profit for composing technique from the example of folk music, and finally to focus on the problem of style and synthesis. Hence came the worship of Bartók, whose masterpieces represented to many the highest artistic incarnation of those few hopes and desires that pervaded Polish music of that time. Therefore we can notice but few discoveries and little search for novelty in Polish music, except in the field of meter and rhythm (Lutoslawski). Hence too, in spite of individual differences, there arose a stylistic homogeneity. This became evident in the common features of numerous works. Such features included a rich melodic invention, often inspired by folk music; a strong emotional element, having its counterpart in the sense for construction, a highly developed harmonic sensibility, and a propensity for a rich color palette in the orchestra.

In 1956 and 1957 contact with the chief centers of avant-garde music in the West was resumed, and the long-awaited creative freedom became a reality. Musical scores and recordings began to flow into the country, and an almost normal exchange of cultural goods between East and West was achieved. Poland was assigned the honorable role of an intermediary in this exchange. This role of Poland has found expression in the international festivals of contemporary music in Warsaw (the so-called "Warsaw Musical Autumns") whose aim has been to present each year all the eminent musical achievements of both the capitalist and the socialist countries, and to foster exchange of experiences and ideas through personal contacts, between composers and critics of the entire world.

After the first shock that Polish composers experienced when they became acquainted for the first time with the less known works of Schoenberg, Berg, Messiaen, and particularly of Webern — the last-named had been quite unknown in Poland before — and with the avant-garde pursuits of Boulez, Nono, Stockhausen, and electronic music, the artistic milieu was greatly revived and stimulated. A useful and blessed process of fermentation was begun in those minds imbued with conformist esthetics, the elements of traditional musical thought were brought into sharp encounter with the elements of the modern musical mind.

The late Arthur Malawski's premature death did not allow him to express his attitude towards technical innovations. His last work, the dramatic and stormy *Hungaria* (1956), written under the impression of the tragic events in Hungary, adheres to the stylistic tendencies of his earlier compositions.

The last triumphs of neo-Classical tendencies in rhythm, structure, and melodic character were scored during the festivals of modern music in the works of M. Spisak, G. Bacewicz (Music for Strings, Trumpets and Percussion, 1958), and in the Sinfonietta for Two String Orchestras (1956) by K. Serocki. Soon, however, Bacewicz and Serocki were caught in the wave of new music. Neo-Classicism was rapidly becoming an outdated ideology followed only by older composers who, like Szeligowski and Perkowski, had a skeptical attitude towards the change, or, like Sikorski and Woytowicz, felt no need to renew their technique of composing. The only exception here is perhaps B. Szabelski's serialism with interesting coloristic and harmonic effects in his three lyrical *Sonnets for Orchestra* (1958); he confirmed his unexpected arrival at serialism in his *Improvisations* for mixed chorus and chamber orchestra (1959) and above all in his excellent *Verses* for piano and orchestra (1961).

We should be wrong, however, if we assumed that new composing techniques and new esthetics were accepted spontaneously and without discussion. There have been cases of slavish imitation of the scarcely adopted new patterns, but much oftener we can see them gradually absorbed into the store of technical devices, without encroaching upon the confines of the composer's own style.

The music of the most eminent Polish composer, Witold Lutoslawski, is a striking instance of such a case. Neither those who look for emotional experiences in music nor those who find particular pleasure in an intellectual adventure, in detecting the logical development of a composition, can remain indifferent to Lutoslawski's *Funeral Music* for string orchestra (1958), dedicated to the memory of Béla Bartók. Its construction is extremely simple and purposeful in its final effect. Its basis is a twelve-tone row of a peculiar arrangement of intervals (a tritone and a descending minor second). This suggestion of a basic series, often repeated in the course of the work, assumes a somewhat altered shape every time it recurs, though preserving throughout the same rhythmic form. The *Funeral Music* in particular strikes a perfect balance between technical fluency and inspiration. Here Lutoslawski's insistent search for a technique of his own has finally led him to true artistic independence.

In *Jeux vénitiens* for orchestra, written for the Venice Festival of April 1961, he has even explored the possibility of random music, allowing the performers to play with a certain rhythmic freedom. This "controlled" aleatorism was given a yet maturer shape by the composer in the *Trois Poèmes d'Henri Michaux* for mixed chorus and orchestra (1963). Here the bold, new choral and orchestral technique is matched by lofty inspiration, producing in effect one of the most eminent works of contemporary music. Let us only note the inventiveness and ingeniousness developed by the composer in handling the chorus in this fragment of the second part, entitled *Le grand combat* (see Ex. 1).[2]

But other composers too are careful not to obliterate their personalities by adapting mechanically new techniques. And so, for example, Tadeusz Baird, one of the most gifted younger composers, while at the same time nurturing an attachment to such models as Berg, submitted the intense emotional values of his music to the severe rules of twelve-tone technique in works like Cassation for Orchestra (1956), String Quartet (1957), *Four Essays* for orchestra (1958), and *Expressions* for violin and orchestra (1959). But Baird's submission to the rules of twelve-tone technique has never been dogmatic and rigid. The melodic factor (motifs, phrases) and its expressive values have always been prominent. Kazimierz Serocki also used the twelve-tone technique in an original, unconventional way in a cycle of songs for baritone and piano, *The Heart of Night* (1956), to the words of K. I. Galczynski, before he decided to attempt total serialization in a cyclic symphonic form — *Musica concertante* (1958). Wlodzimierz Kotonski distinguished himself in his *Chamber Music* (1958) by his clever adaptation of pointillism, which he used in an advanced manner in his *Musique en relief* (1959) for six instrumental groups.

Grazyna Bacewicz, the remarkable woman-composer, also remained true to her former technique and stylistic manner, but she enriched the long list of her works with her *Meditations in the Night* for chamber orchestra (1961), written in serial technique, like her earlier Sixth String Quartet (1960).

Zygmunt Mycielski (b. 1907), a composer combining musical and literary abilities (he is the present editor-in-chief of the fortnightly periodical *Ruch Muzyczny*), remained for a long time under the spell of Szymanowski. Lately, inspired by the ideas of Xenakis, he attempted in his Second Symphony, and not without success, to construct a classical form upon mathematics-derived tone material.

The youngest generation of Polish composers has plunged into the new, present-day world of music much more naturally and easily; they had no need to change their mode of thinking and feeling and to overcome any emotional and rational barriers within themselves. They

[2] Example copyright 1964 Polskie Wydawnictwo Muzyczne.

Ex. 1

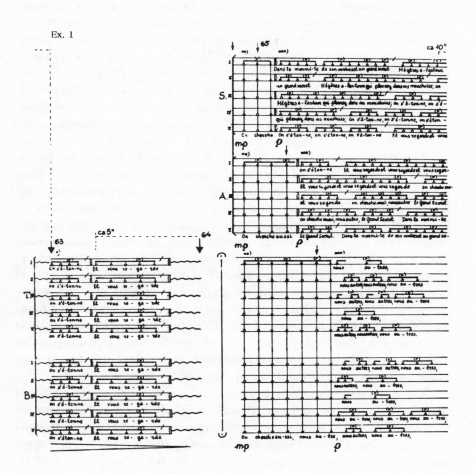

*) Au signe du chef de chœur, chacun des exécutants récite jusqu'à la césure la plus proche, et ensuite passe aux paroles «on s'étonne»; cet endroit est atteint à des moments différents par chacun des chanteurs. Par conséquent les chanteurs passent, aussi à des moments différents, aux paroles «Et vous regarde» qu'ils répètent jusqu'au signe que leur donne le chef au n° 64. Après ce signe chaque exécutant va au bout de la phrase «...et vous regarde...». Le diminuendo entre les n°s 63 et 64 est à considérer comme le passage au chuchotement

**) à battuta
***) ad libitum

did not experience the period of isolation in the years 1949-1955, and
they imbibed the present time in a perfectly natural way, simply by
living it. All the products of present-day culture — printed music, films,
books, paintings of the most avant-garde artists — were open to them
without limitations. The festivals of contemporary music called the
Warsaw Autumn and the recently gained ability to travel abroad played
an important part in forming their artistic attitude and their esthetics.
They made their débuts as composers mostly during the festivals of the
Warsaw Autumn and soon they scored successes abroad.

The Experimental Studio of Polish Radio and Television, set up in
1958 and headed by Józef Patkowski, a young musicologist, has also
played an important part in the general process of rejuvenating the
minds of artists and listeners and teaching them to appreciate the new
present-day music. It is enough to state that this studio encouraged many
composers to do their own experimental work (Dobrowolski, Kotonski,
Markowski, Penderecki, Wiszniewski) and enlisted them in its service
preparing among other things musical accompaniments for about a
hundred films and more than thirty plays; in the course of a few years
it organized a wide exchange of tape recordings of experimental music
with similar studios in Milan, Paris, Cologne, and elsewhere; finally,
it secured a regular weekly program on the air (in the Third Program),
and an annual show of topical achievements in the field of experimental
music at the festival of the Warsaw Autumn.

The numerous composers belonging to the youngest generation include an eminent theoretician, Boguslaw Schäffer (b. 1929), who is
the author of many studies on composing technique that have aroused
lively discussion. His compositions, such as *Quattro movimenti* for piano
and orchestra (1958), *Monosonate* for 24 string instruments (1959),
Topofonica for 40 instruments (1960), and *Musica ipsa* for orchestra
(1962), constitute a kind of compendium of the problems prominent
in the Polish music of today. They exhibit, perhaps, a not too powerful
individuality, they are sometimes too erudite and coquettishly estheticiz-
ing, but they show a complete mastery of the new composing technique
and a remarkable sensitivity to sounds.

Witold Szalonek (b. 1927) earned fame with his highly artistic
stylization of folklore in his *Suite from the Kurpie District* (1955) for
alto and nine instruments. Then he surprised his listeners with his ecstatic
Confessions (1959) for a speaker, mixed chorus, and chamber orchestra
— a work that has its origin in the early and somewhat naive Expressionism kept by Szalonek within the framework of twelve-tone technique.

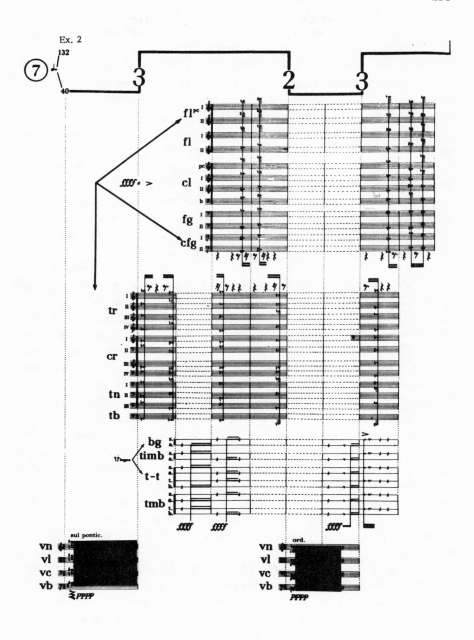

It seems, however, that this composer has not yet had his last say, and we can expect to hear more interesting works of his.

Wojciech Kilar (b. 1932), who did not appeal to the musical public in his early works, evoked vivid interest and hopes for a promising development of his talent by two brilliant compositions for large orchestra: *Riff 62* and *Générique* (1963).

The greatest achievement, however, and successes extending far abroad were scored by two composers, united by the year of their birth (1933) but divided by different artistic tempers: Henryk Górecki and Krzysztof Penderecki.

Górecki showed genuine and brilliant talent in his miniature cantata *Epitafium* (1958), which bears an affinity to Webern's *Das Augenlicht*, though it is composed in a freer pointillistic technique. Górecki's *Symphony 1959*, which shows some influence of Luigi Nono's *Composi-tione per orchestra* (for example in the role assigned to percussion in the finale), confirmed the general opinion that enormous power is latent in this unusually vital and sensitive composer. It is with great spiritual tension that we listen to his music, which is imbued with profound emotion and "metaphysical" unrest. His talent was voiced yet more remarkably in the original *Scontri* for orchestra (1960), where he operated with blocks and bands of tones not individualized into separate instruments (tone-clusters of strings and winds), thus adding an interesting feature to the total serialization of the material (see Ex. 2).[3]

Górecki's way of filling the tone space with broad, distinctly contrasted bands — discharging in sharp, sometimes consciously brutal, forceful explosions — recalls an *al-fresco* technique. On the other hand Krzysztof Penderecki was recognized as a master of delicate color-combinations already in his first composition, presented at the Third Festival of the Warsaw Autumn in 1959, *Strophes* (to texts of Menander, Sophocles, Isaiah, Jeremiah, and Avicenna). He is fond of drawing the most extraordinary and unexpected effects from the traditional instruments and the human voice as well. In *The Dimensions of Time and Silence* for chorus and orchestra (1960) varicolored lines and structures (among others: vibrating "tone areas") are joined by means of permeation; the mixed chorus of forty persons takes over the function of percussion and also serves to produce rustling effects by an appropriate combination of whistling and sibilants (see Ex. 3).[4] Penderecki developed an equal inventiveness as regards the problem of color and

[3] Example copyright 1962 Polskie Wyndawnictwo Muzyczne.
[4] Example copyright 1961 by Hermann Moeck Verlag, Celle.

Ex. 3

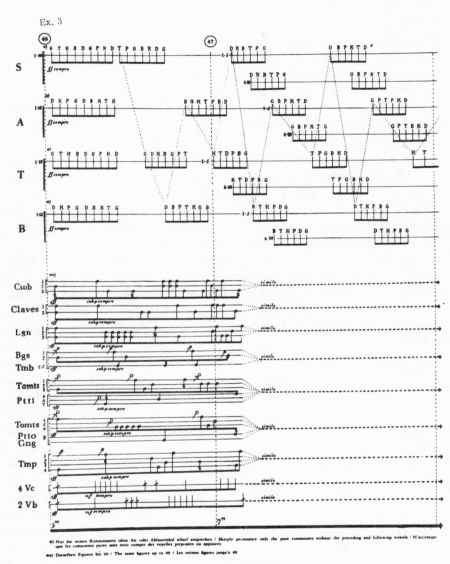

S

A

T

B

Cwb

Claves

Lgn

Bgs
Tmb

Tomts
Ptti

Tomts
Ptto
Gng

Tmp

4 Vc

2 Vb

*) Nur die reinen Konsonanten ohne An- oder Ablautvokal scharf ansprechen / Sharply pronounce only the pure consonants without the preceding and following vowels / N'accentuer
que les consonnes pures sans tenir compte des voyelles préposées ou apposées

**) Dieselben Figuren bis 49 / The same figures up to 49 / Les mêmes figures jusqu'à 49

Edition Moeck Nr. 5005

dynamics, in his *Anaklasis* for strings and percussion (1960), in the String Quartet (1960), and in *Fluorescences* (1961). Articulation and dynamics are the two chief shaping factors in the two earlier of the above-mentioned compositions. The *Threnody Dedicated to the Victims of Hiroshima* (1960) for 52 stringed instruments has a middle part composed in a technique of strict imitation. This composition opens a list of works in which the amazing tonal imagination of the composer began to look for inspiration in polyphonic forms and techniques. Here belong especially the *Canon* for 52 stringed instruments (1962), which is composed in three layers and constructed stereophonically, and the *Stabat Mater* for *a cappella* chorus (1962).

Other composers of the same generation — A. Bloch, R. Twardowski, K. Meyer, A. Rudzinski, L. Ciuciura, Bujarski, Bogustawski — deserve at least mention. Their talents are not yet so clearly crystallized and decided in their tendencies as those of the two composers just mentioned but we can hope to get remarkable works from them as well.

The works of many young composers, together with those of their older colleagues, such as Lutoslawski, Baird, Serocki, Kotonski, and several others, are now performed at various festivals abroad, and this shows the vitality of Polish music and the growing recognition of its creative contribution to the common cultural treasure of European nations.

SOVIET MUSIC SINCE THE
SECOND WORLD WAR

By BORIS SCHWARZ

MUSICAL life in the Soviet Union continued throughout the Second World War. Many composers were evacuated to the interior of the country, where they could pursue their creative work. Significant symphonies, such as Prokofiev's Fifth or Shostakovich's Seventh (the *Leningrad*) and Eighth, were written during the war years and bear the imprint of the titanic struggle. Once victory was won, the Soviet people proceeded to restore their cultural life at the same time as they rebuilt the physical destruction wrought by the war. The recovery was remarkably swift and testified to the resilience and determination of the entire nation.

Problems soon arose, however, in the field of cultural restoration. During the war, ideological feuds were set aside in a surge of patriotism. Now, in peace, old animosities were rekindled. The party dogmatists led by Andrei Zhdanov, Stalin's cultural commissar, resumed the struggle to suppress "formalism" and to reaffirm control in artistic matters. In the fall of 1946, literature, theater, and film were subjected to severe public criticism. On February 10, 1948, Soviet music was dealt a staggering blow in a document that accused the leading composers of "formalistic distortions and anti-democratic tendencies." Named were Shostakovich, Prokofiev, Miaskovsky, Khachaturian, Shebalin, Popov, and Muradeli. Also condemned were music critics for being "adherents of decadent formalistic music." The reorganization of the Composers Union carried the thirty-eight-year-old composer Tikhon Khrennikov into a powerful position, which he still holds today.

For some five years the events of 1948 cast a dark shadow over Soviet music. True, after a temporary eclipse, the leading composers regained a measure of public stature. Yet, this was not accomplished

259

without apologetic recantations and artistic concessions that must have embittered the last years of Miaskovsky and Prokofiev. The bolder spirits among composers and critics were silenced. Prokofiev's works virtually disappeared from the stage or were deliberately delayed. Shebalin lost his post as director of the Moscow Conservatory, Popov slipped into oblivion. Shostakovich withheld his Violin Concerto, completed in 1948, until 1955. Musicologists and critics avoided discussions of the contemporary scene and chose "safe" classical topics instead. The atmosphere reflected scared uncertainty. Stalin's death in March 1953 brought slight relief from immediate pressures, and a gradual, almost imperceptible, relaxation set in. But not until the XXth Party Congress in 1956 was official sanction given to cleanse Soviet cultural life from the oppression of the "cult of personality." In 1957, the Second All-Union Congress of Composers spoke up for increased liberalization. Finally, in 1958, a public document rescinded the unjustified personal criticisms contained in the 1948 decree, though the principle of "socialist realism" was reaffirmed. Since 1962, we have seen the "thaw" yield to a cold wave when Khrushchev declared in his speech of March 8, 1963, "We are opposed to peaceful co-existence in matters of ideology." What the implications of this statement are remains to be seen, though with Krushchev's removal from power we may be faced with a new set of directives.

After the musico-political feud of 1948, the Union of Soviet Composers — originally established in 1932 to supersede all other professional organizations — assumed a more active role. There were yearly plenums, at which ideological discussions were stressed. Regional chapters were organized; at present, forty-two nationalities are represented in these associations. Fall festivals of contemporary Soviet music were initiated; lately they are limited to composers under thirty-five years of age. During these ten-day events, talented young composers from the entire country meet in Moscow to hear their works performed by the best professional groups before a metropolitan audience. Thus, the Composers Union exerts firm control over the destinies of its members. Commissions, publications, performances, positions, assignments to trips at home and abroad — in short, the entire career of a composer depends, to a large extent, on his standing within the Union and on the support of the directorate. There are a few potential young "rebels," and they are carefully watched; but the majority seems well satisfied. The composer Rodion Shchedrin, thirty-two and a leader of the younger generation, has this to say: "With us musicians, there is absolutely no reason for the generations to oppose each other. There is no cleavage between the generations within the composers' organization . . . Music of the young does not exist separately. We have our Soviet socialist musical culture, powerful in the unity of ideas and strong ethical aims . . ." Shchedrin assures us that the young composers have nothing but the warmest regard for their "musical fathers" — Prokofiev and Miaskovsky, Shostakovich and Khachaturian, and the others. Cautiously, he admits also to other influences; he speaks of the "artificial isolation" imposed on Soviet musicians which was lifted after the decree of 1958. "Such figures as Hindemith, Bartók, Stravinsky, Britten, Honegger, Poulenc, Milhaud, Orff, and others not only entered the horizon of composers but were made the object of creative absorption. All this could not fail to enrich the musical language of young composers."[1]

This list, while seemingly broad, deliberately excludes Western composers connected with twelve-tone music and the latest trends.

Despite dogmatic harassment, the post-war period brought significant achievements to Soviet music. The years immediately following the war saw the culmination of the creative careers of Miaskovsky (died 1950) and Prokofiev (died 1953), the two leading masters of the older generation. The middle generation — Shebalin, Kabalevsky, Khachaturian, Khrennikov, and above all Shostakovich — also made important contributions. To that group a new name should be added — Georgii Sviridov (born 1915), who achieved somewhat belated recognition in the 1950s. Finally, there is a long list of young composers, mostly born between 1920 and 1940, whose works have attracted national attention. While the largest group comes from the Russian Federal Republic, there are also composers from the Ukraine, from the Baltic (especially Estonia), from Azerbaidzhan, Armenia, and Georgia, from Byelorussia and Moldavia; there are Tatar, Kirghiz, Uzbek, Kazakh composers. The most striking aspect of this list is its vast geographic distribution. Obviously, the multi-national approach has borne fruit. It is unavoidable that there should be different levels of achievement: the sophisticated composers of Leningrad or of Estonia cannot be judged in the same manner as the emerging compositional school of an outlying region which, until some decades ago, may have been without a system of musical notation.

Soon after the doctrine of Socialist Realism was formulated in 1934,

[1]*Sovietskaya Muzyka,* 1963, No. 6, p. 10.

composers began to favor genres that were able to convey "concrete images" — opera, song, oratorio and cantata, and instrumental program music. The latter was stressed again in 1948 when Zhdanov proclaimed that "Russian classical music was, as a rule, program music."

The opera received particular attention. In January of 1936 — shortly before Shostakovich's *Lady Macbeth of Mtzensk* was blasted by *Pravda* — Stalin formulated three criteria for the Soviet opera: 1) socialist subjects, 2) realistic musical language, and 3) the new, positive hero as representative of the new socialist age. Basically, these guide lines are still valid today. However, the choice of subjects has been widened to include the historical national drama (e.g. Prokofiev's *War and Peace,* Shaporin's *Decembrists*); the revolutionary events of 1905 and 1917 (Khrennikov's *The Mother,* Kabalevsky's *Nikita Vershinin*); and episodes dealing with the last war, stressing the heroism and the suffering of the people (Prokofiev's *The Story of a Real Man,* Kabalevsky's *The Family Taras,* Dzerzhinsky's *The Fate of a Man*). Occasionally, freedom fights in other countries are depicted (Spadavecchia's *The Gadfly,* Molchanov's *Del Corno Street*). All these librettos serve the aim of either national or socialist glorification. Comic operas are rare; in fact, only two successful examples can be named — Prokofiev's *Duenna* and Shebalin's *The Taming of the Shrew.*

Little need be said here about Prokofiev's achievements — he is, in the words of Arthur Honegger, "one of the greatest figures of contemporary music." From 1933 — the year he returned to Moscow after fifteen years abroad — until his death in 1953, he dominated the Soviet musical scene despite setbacks and criticisms. In recent years, Soviet evaluation of Prokofiev has moved from selective approval (still reflected in Nestiev's biography)[2] to an almost total acceptance as a "modern classic."

Between 1939 and 1948 Prokofiev wrote four operas — the epic *War and Peace* (1941-52), the comic *Duenna* (1940-46), and two on Soviet topics, *Semyon Kotko* (1939-40) and *The Story of a Real Man* (1947-48). Both his Soviet operas were considered failures. For *Semyon Kotko* he devised a "new kind of simplicity" which avoided the oversimplification of the conventional "song opera" of the day. "New life, new subject matter demand new forms of expression, and the listener must not complain if he has to exert a little effort to grasp these forms."[3] Neither

[2] I. Nestiev, *Sergei Prokofiev,* Moscow, 1957. English transl. by Florence Jonas, Stanford, 1960.

[3] S. Prokofiev, *Autobiography, Articles, Reminiscences,* Moscow, n.d., p. 119 f.

listeners nor critics were willing to "exert" themselves, and *Semyon Kotko* was withdrawn soon after its première in 1940. Revived in 1957 at the opera house in Perm (Ural), the work is now recognized as a bold new departure in Soviet opera.

The outright rejection of *The Story of a Real Man* after a closed trial performance in 1948 was a major disappointment of Prokofiev's last years. The exchange of letters between the composer and his "judges" has a pathetic ring. In an attempt to make his forthcoming opera more acceptable, he wrote to the directorate of the Composers Union in February 1948, shortly after he had been publicly denounced, "I will make use of some interesting Northern Russian folk songs. Lucid melody, and as far as possible, a simple harmonic language are elements which I intend to use in my opera . . ."[4] The December 1948 issue of *Sovietskaya Muzyka* — the organ of the Composers Union — brought a vitriolic denunciation of the new opera and foreshadowed its rejection. Trying to save his work, Prokofiev wrote again, "In depicting my heroes I was concerned, first of all, with revealing the inner world of the Soviet man, love of his country, Soviet patriotism . . ."[5] The official answer, over Khrennikov's signature, was swift and uncompromising: "Formalism still lives in the music of Soviet composers. This is demonstrated by the new opera of Prokofiev . . . In the modernistic, anti-melodic music of his opera, in the treatment of the Soviet people, the composer remains on his old positions, condemned by the Party and by Soviet society."[6]

This judgment must be seen in the light of the harsh mood of 1948; yet it shows a complete misunderstanding of the score. Actually, the music is melodious and appealing, rather simple but skillful, and avoids pseudo-heroism. The four acts are organized into short scenes or numbers connected by orchestral interludes. The version presented at the Bolshoi Theater in 1960 condensed the work into three acts and made dramaturgical changes, which are summarized in the printed piano score. The idea of beginning and ending the opera with a chorus from Act I, *A Young Oak Grew,* is a definite improvement, for it eliminates the undistinguished overture and the awkward ending of the original version. Judging by the piano score, the last opera of Prokofiev is an attractive but not overly characteristic work.

[4] Quoted in N. Slonimsky, *Music since 1900,* 3rd ed., New York, 1949, p. 706.

[5] Dec. 28, 1948. Printed in the Preface to the piano score of the opera.

[6] Dec. 29, 1948. Quoted in Slonimsky, *op. cit.,* p. 625. See also the same author's *The Changing Styles of Soviet Music,* in *Journal of the American Musicological Society,* Fall 1950, p. 253.

While *The Story of a Real Man* may not be "exportable," *War and Peace* certainly is. The coolness of Western opera houses towards this monumental masterpiece is hard to understand.[7] The present production at the Bolshoi Theater, first shown in 1959, is a stirring experience, both musically and theatrically. It is a virtually uncut version, consisting of thirteen scenes in three acts, with a choral epigraph. The history of *War and Peace* is a history of its revisions. After completing the first version in 1942, Prokofiev added material, which made a division into two evenings advisable. The first part (eight scenes) was staged in 1946, the second part (scenes 9-13) at a closed preview in 1947. Dissatisfied, Prokofiev began the task of reintegrating and condensing the score to make a one-evening performance possible. Many of his cuts were found too drastic when the opera was given in Leningrad in 1955, two years after the composer's death. Ultimately, a return to the thirteen-scene version, but staged in one evening, was found to be the best possible solution. Prokofiev's score shows some stylistic inconsistencies caused by the many years of revision during which his approach underwent certain changes. The final result is, in a way, a compromise between his innate spirit of innovation and the classical tradition of Russian opera. The minor flaws are swept aside by the grandeur of the concept.

Prokofiev's *Betrothal in a Monastery* shows the versatility of his talent. This is a modern *opera buffa* of sparkling sophistication. The orchestration is so transparent as to make every word intelligible. Based on Sheridan's 18th-century comedy *The Duenna,* the opera was completed in 1940 but had to wait until 1946 for its first performance. Writing in *Pravda,* Shostakovich called it "a real masterpiece of this genre" and "one of the composer's most perfect operatic works."[8]

Another comic opera on a classical play is *The Taming of the Shrew* by Vissarion Shebalin (1902-63), which was first given in 1955. It is elegant, light-hearted music, somewhat stylized without being archaic.

Yuri Shaporin, a master of the old generation (born 1887), has worked for decades on his opera *The Decembrists,* which deals with the unsuccessful uprising of 1825. An early version was ready in the 1930s, a final one was presented in 1953. An opera in the great Russian tradition, it has a score that Gerald Abraham aptly describes as "a curiously satisfactory synthesis of the seeming incompatibles, Mussorgsky and

[7] A television version by the NBC Opera Theater, in a translation by Joseph Machlis, had merits but was cut too drastically.

[8] Quoted in Information Bulletin 1960, No. 1, p. 18, Soviet Composers Union, Moscow.

Tchaikovsky."[9] Despite many fine details, I find the work rather static and too much like an oratorio.

Contemporary topics dominate the operas of the younger generation. Kabalevsky's *The Family Taras* (1947-50) has a libretto based on events of the Second World War, demonstrating the trend towards subjects of actuality. The score reflects the immediacy of personal experience. To add realism to the musical idiom, the composer interspersed actual songs of workers, peasants, and young people — a procedure referred to by Soviet critics as "historical concreteness." Kabalevsky's next opera, *Nikita Vershinin* (1954), on a libretto dealing with the Civil War in Russia's Far East, was planned on a larger scale but proved less successful.

Tikhon Khrennikov's most important post-war opera is *The Mother* (1957), based on Gorky's novel of the 1905 Revolution. It is an effective though uneven work. There are lyrical sections of appealing "folkishness" while others (like the flag-waving finale) appear stereotyped. With innate theater sense, the composer draws on urban revolutionary songs of the period and uses a similar idiom for some of his own tunes. The grandiose setting at the Bolshoi somewhat overwhelms the attractive intimate qualities of the work. Khrennikov's *Frol Skobeyev* (1950), a comedy based on a 17th-century satirical Russian story, foundered on dramaturgical weaknesses of the libretto. His early opera *Into the Storm* (1939) is still a successful repertory piece.

How an essentially good libretto can be ruined by an inadequate musical score is demonstrated in Ivan Dzerzhinsky's *The Fate of a Man* (1960), on a story by M. Sholokhov. The book is simple and affecting, the score is primitive and static. Lack of inventiveness, a routine use of leitmotif technique, and thin orchestration hamper the unfolding of the drama to a point of utter dullness. It must be on the strength of the libretto that the work ever reached the Bolshoi. Soviet musicians, incidentally, are well aware of Dzerzhinsky's "creative irresponsibility," which is all the more disappointing since he started his career back in 1935 with a successful opera, *And Quiet Flows the Don*. It was the first of the so-called "song operas" and attracted Stalin's personal attention.

A recent addition to the repertory of the Bolshoi is *Not Love Alone* (1961) by Rodion Shchedrin (born 1932), whose career has been meteoric. The libretto describes life on a collective farm. To draw a realistic picture of post-war Soviet youth, Shchedrin inserts so-called *chastushki* — ditties or folk verses, some lyrical, some humorous. The

[9] Gerald Abraham, *Eight Soviet Composers*, London, 1943, p. 98.

young composer has a good sense of theater, an engaging melodic gift, and a youthful exuberance tempered by intelligence and craftsmanship.

Two recent operas are based on Italian subjects. *The Gadfly* by Antonio Spadavecchia (born 1907) treats the revolutionary struggle of the Italian people against Austrian oppression during the 1830s and '40s. *Del Corno Street* by Kyril Molchanov (born 1922) is based on the bloody events of one night of Fascist terror. Both works are praised as dynamic, theatrically effective, and as making good use of advanced stage techniques.

An event of historic significance took place on December 26, 1962, when Shostakovich's *Lady Macbeth*, renamed *Katerina Ismailova*, was revived in Moscow after twenty-six years of banishment. It is a piece of superb theater: the cruelly strong libretto is intensified by a score of blazing passion and cutting satire. Western Expressionism of the 1920s stands side by side with unmistakable Russianism. For the revival, the composer made certain revisions, the extent of which can only be ascertained after the new version is published; he himself said that the changes were limited to some details of vocal line and orchestration, as well as two new orchestral interludes. Obviously, all earlier ideological objections to the work have been dropped, for it has just been announced that *Katerina Ismailova* will be made into a film.[10]

There is considerable domestic criticism of the state of Soviet opera. The critics find fault with the dramaturgy of the librettos, with the repertory of the Bolshoi Theater, with the stodginess of the staging, with the slowness of new productions, with the absence of an experimental theater. However, rarely — if ever — is anything said about the crucial fact that so many Soviet operatic composers treat 20th-century topics in a 19th-century musical language. No "historical concreteness" can disguise the faded, epigonal idiom that is perhaps one of the reasons why Soviet opera is none too popular in its own country. The following statistics are revealing: out of 120 operas composed in the Soviet Union between 1948 and 1957, only five or six were ever performed in more than one theater. The need for a "breath of fresh air" was stated by Shostakovich in 1957. Perhaps he will provide it in his newly announced operatic project, *And Quiet Flows the Don*.

Traditionally, the ballet in Russia is accorded the same artistic stand-

---

[10] See also Boris Schwarz, *Soviet Music since Stalin*, in *Saturday Review*, New York, March 30, 1963, p. 69.

ing as the opera, and both art forms share the physical facilities of the great theaters. This permits the ballet to approach its new productions with the same costly leisureliness as the operatic wing. While the excellence of Russian-trained dancers is generally recognized, criticism has been expressed concerning Soviet choreography and staging, which to Western tastes often seem rather conventional. To attempt a comparative evaluation of Russian vs. Western conception of ballet would lead too far. Let us concentrate instead on the music written for the dance.

In the history of Soviet ballet, Prokofiev occupies a dominant position. His "trilogy" — *Romeo and Juliet* (1936-40), *Cinderella* (1945), and *The Stone Flower* (completed 1950, first performed in 1954) — was a challenge to Soviet choreographic art and led to a new plateau of achievement. His pre-Soviet ballets (of which there are five, including *Pas d'acier* and *The Prodigal Son*) are rarely, if ever, mentioned. This is what Leonid Lavrovsky, the choreographer closest to Prokofiev, has to say:

Prokofiev carried on where Tchaikovsky left off. He developed and elaborated the principles of symphonism in ballet music . . . The boldness of his musical treatment, the clear-cut characterizations, the diversity and intricacy of the rhythms, the unorthodoxy of the harmonies — all these elements of his music, and primarily his *Romeo and Juliet,* serve to create the dramatic development of the performance . . .[11]

Of the "trilogy," *Romeo* is the most interesting score—characteristic of the composer's bold and vital style after his return, seeking an artistic reconciliation between the West and Soviet reality. *Cinderella* is somewhat pallid and had only a moderate success. *The Stone Flower* occupies a special place in the affection of the Soviet people, for it is Prokofiev's only ballet on a Russian topic, continuing the folk-tale tradition of *Ruslan and Ludmilla,* of Mussorgsky, of Rimsky-Korsakov. It is a score of mellow retrospection and limpid charm — like its sister piece, the Seventh Symphony. Prokofiev incorporated a few lovely folksongs from the Urals and shaped his idiom in a Russian style; he also used some of his own older themes. Though dealing with a fairy tale, he was well aware of certain social implications when he described the *Stone Flower* as a ballet "about the joy of creative work for the good of he people . . ."[12] In fact, Soviet choreographers endeavor to stress the social roots of folk tales, their humanism, their close-to-life realistic base.

Prokofiev did not live to see *The Stone Flower;* after a delay of

[11] S. Prokofiev, *Autobiography* . . . , p. 275.
[12] *Ibid.,* p. 137.

three years, rehearsals finally started on March 1, 1953. On the morning of March 5, the choreographer Lavrovsky visited the ailing composer and found him working on the ballet score, "seemingly quite well and absorbed in his work." He called that evening to report about the progress of the staging. "Madame Prokofieva answered the phone and in a barely recognizable voice told me that Sergei Sergeyevich was dead."[13]

In 1954, Aram Khachaturian completed the ballet *Spartacus,* that "true representative of the proletariat of antiquity" (Marx). Describing the uprising of Roman slaves, it is a lavish spectacle — more pantomime with interspersed dances than ballet. Soviet commentators were not un-critical of the romanticized treatment of antiquity "in the style of Sinkiewicz." As for the music, it is ancient Rome seen through Armenian eyes: full-blooded rhythms, post-Romantic lushness, and unabashed sentimentality. The musical idiom of *Spartacus* is not much different from that of *Gayaneh,* the Armenian *kolkhoz* ballet that, in 1942, made Khachaturian's name famous. As produced at Leningrad's Kirov Theater in 1956 by the young choreographer L. Yakobson, with effective mass dances and sculptured "tableaux-vivants," *Spartacus* is a lusty entertain-ment (though it got a memorably bad reception in New York). Barely recognizable is the ideological meaning of the "struggle of the enslaved colonial people rising . . . against imperialist tyranny."[14]

A more convincing picture of the "colonial revolt" is the ballet *Path of Thunder* by the Azerbaidzhan composer Kara Karayev (born 1918). Set in modern South Africa, the scenario is based on a novel by the South African writer Peter Abrahams. In preparing the score, Karayev made a thorough study of African music, which (as he says) took him more time than the composition of the score itself. He used not only tribal music of South African natives but also themes from North Africa, from urban centers, and even some Afro-American rhythms and tunes. Far from being an ethnomusicological exploit, the material is developed in a contemporary, almost symphonic, manner. Karayev's handling of the orchestra — particularly a battery of percussive instruments — lends color and excitement to the score. He has a preference for strong rhythms and ostinato basses. His musical "ancestors" are Prokofiev (to whose memory the score is dedicated), Khachaturian, Ravel, and occasionally Gershwin. *Path of Thunder* was first presented in Leningrad in 1958 and is considered one of the best contributions to contemporary Soviet

[13] *Ibid.,* p. 281.
[14] *Sovietskaya Muzyka,* 1953, No. 1, p. 20.

ballet. In his earlier ballet *Seven Beauties* (1952), Karayev used effectively the songs and dances of his native Azerbaidzhan. Shostakovich (who was Karayev's teacher at the Moscow Conservatory) called this score "genuinely symphonic music with scope and breadth."[15]

A few other ballets may be mentioned briefly. From neighboring Georgia comes Alexei Machavariani (born 1913), whose ballet *Othello*, first performed in Tbilisi in 1957, continued the Shakespearean tradition of Prokofiev's *Romeo and Juliet*. Machavariani's score is fiery, dramatic, and national in the Georgian manner, using certain ancient forms and rhythms of Georgian tribal traditions. Surprisingly, the exotic, "barbaric" colors are not detrimental to the story line, which, of course, is treated with considerable freedom.

It should be noted that the initiator of all this "historical concreteness" is Boris Asafiev (1884-1949), Soviet Russia's most eminent musicographer and a somewhat less eminent composer. His best-known ballets, still in the active repertory, are *The Flame of Paris* (1932) and *The Fountain of Bakhchisarai* (1934). He worked on the ballets, as he said, "not only as a dramatist and composer, but as a musical scholar, historian, and theoretician . . ."[16] *The Flame of Paris* is virtually a musical history of the French Revolution, from Grétry to *Ça ira*. Musically, it is a pastiche.

The veteran composer Reinhold Glière (1875-1956), best known for his ballet *Red Poppy* (1927), composed several ballets in the last years of his life. Most successful was *The Bronze Horseman*, given in 1949 in celebration of Pushkin's 150th birthday.

A return to the Russian fairy-tale is *The Little Hump-backed Horse* (*Koniók-Gorbunók*) by young Rodion Shchedrin. The music, originally an orchestral suite (1955), was expanded into a ballet and entered the repertory of the Bolshoi in 1960. It enjoys great success and is considered by Soviet critics a "partial continuation of the tradition of Rimsky-Korsakov's satirical fairy-tale operas."[17]

The vocal-symphonic genre, a modified kind of secular oratorio or cantata, enjoys remarkable popularity in the USSR. This is mainly due to the official policy, reiterated since the 1930s, that Soviet music should convey concrete images. Soviet composers complied en masse and produced odes to Stalin, to peace, to victory, reforestation, the moon

[15] *Pravda,* Dec. 18, 1952.
[16] Quoted in Ludmilla Polyakova, *Soviet Music,* Moscow, n.d., p. 132.
[17] *Istoria Russkoi Sovietskoi Muzyki,* Vol. IV, Part 2, Moscow, 1963, p. 24

rocket, and other praiseworthy enterprises. Most of this music is dutiful and dull. Another method, somewhat more successful, is to shape film scores into cantata-like works; the most notable example, of course, is *Alexander Nevsky* by Prokofiev. An attempt by the conductor Stassevich to fashion a similar work out of Prokofiev's score to the film *Ivan the Terrible* was unconvincing. Shostakovich and Khachaturian, among others, have reworked their film scores in a similar manner.

The most significant contribution in the vocal-symphonic genre was made by Georgii Sviridov (born 1915). After years of comparative obscurity, Sviridov was catapulted into the front rank of Soviet composers by two oratorio-like works: the *Poem in Memory of Sergei Yesenin* (1956) and the *Pathetic Oratorio* on words by Mayakovsky (1959). The latter brought him the 1960 Lenin Prize. Yesenin's poems are intensely Russian, and so is Sviridov's music. The poet speaks about the Russian countryside with nostalgia and sensitivity, and the composer captures the elegiac mood in a musical idiom of utter simplicity and sincerity. His language is close to that of Mussorgsky; in fact, Sviridov's musical means are entirely traditional and retrospective. Far more extrovert and assertive is Mayakovsky's revolutionary poetry, and Sviridov's music follows suit. The narration of the male soloist is partly sung, partly recited in the style of a melodrama, set against a musical background. Some sections — like the opening March or the closing *The Sun and the Poet* — are noisily obvious. But several of the center movements (there are altogether seven) are introspective and deeply moving. The most interesting part, perhaps, is the sixth movement — *Dialogue with Comrade Lenin* — where song, recitative, and speech are ingeniously combined. The chorus is an active participant — sometimes divided into male or female choirs, then again combined in massive outbursts. Sviridov's music creates an intense rapport between stage and audience. He captures the inflections of Mayakovsky's free-flowing lines so well that one is willing to accept the basic conventionality of the musical idiom. Robert Craft, though, is not — he calls Sviridov's music "steady, solid, unhurried (all euphemisms for 'boring' . . .); it does not venture beyond a primitive triadic scheme . . ."[18] But Craft overlooks the fusion of words and music that is Sviridov's essential accomplishment.

The oratorio-poem *Twelve* (1957) by Vadim Salmanov (born 1912) is a setting of a text by Alexander Blok. The poet wrote his impassioned lines in 1918 under the impact of the October Revolution. Salmanov's

---

[18] Robert Craft, *Stravinsky's Return, a Russian Diary*, in *Encounter* (London), June 1963, p. 44.

musical orientation is quite modern; in fact, some of his chamber music is "avant-garde" — in Soviet terms.

War and its senseless cruelty is almost an obsession with Soviet composers, old and young. For example, Alfred Shnitke (born 1936) chose *Nagasaki* as the subject of a six-part oratorio, dedicated to the victims of the atom bomb; it was first given in 1958. Arvo Piart (born 1935) wrote a *Necrologue* dedicated to the victims of fascism (1960). The list could be extended. Coming from the very young who had no personal involvement in the war, all these laments sound somewhat less than convincing.

Much more appropriate to youth is a work like the *Four Ukrainian Songs* by Leonid Grabovsky (born 1935), which received a first prize in 1962. It is a vocal-symphonic cycle in which the traditional folk melodies are retained almost unchanged in a choral setting while the orchestra's task consists of variation and elaboration. At times, the orchestral complexity almost overwhelms the simplicity of the themes; but the strong talent of this young Ukrainian is beyond doubt.

It is in the field of purely orchestral music that Soviet composers have achieved the most decisive international recognition.

Among Soviet symphonists, Nicolai Miaskovsky (1881-1950) must be mentioned first for sheer quantity of output. His symphonies number twenty-seven, of which the last three were written after the war. Miaskovsky was a complex personality of great integrity who struggled all his life to reconcile his inner self with the world around him. In Moscow he is remembered with affection but rarely played; in fact, his former student Khachaturian complained in 1961 that "his works have completely disappeared from concert programs." Miaskovsky's 27th Symphony, first played in 1950 a few months after the composer's death, was received with praise. Soviet critics noted its greater "optimism" in contrast to the "cheerless subjectivism" found in previous works. To me, the "optimism," as exemplified in the march theme of the Finale, seems somewhat artificial — an effort, perhaps, to reverse the public criticism of 1948.

To the post-war period belong Prokofiev's Sixth and Seventh Symphonies. Neither achieved the popularity of the Fifth, which was a "war" symphony. The Sixth Symphony was roundly denounced as a reversion to the composer's old Expressionistic tendencies. After the première in 1947, it soon disappeared from the repertory, to be resurrected after the composer's death. Even abroad, the somber, austere score did not find much favor — "it lacks impulse but not interest," was a wry English comment. Perhaps it is this dichotomy in the score, the struggle between the "old" and the "new" Prokofiev, that makes the work an interesting but not entirely satisfying experience. Lately, Soviet critics have begun a rehabilitation of the Sixth, trying to explain away the "outbursts of unrestrained expressionism utterly incomprehensible to the listener."[19]

In contrast, the Seventh Symphony is unproblematic, limpid, and serene. Originally planned as a "symphony for children," it grew into a score of lyricism and nostalgia — an older man looking back on youth. The themes are ingratiating, almost too suave, and they are developed without dramatic conflict. Yet, the master's touch is evident in every measure. Prokofiev lived to witness the triumph of his last symphony when it was first performed on October 11, 1952.

In the creative life of Prokofiev, the symphonic genre played only a peripheral role. In the case of Shostakovich, however, the symphony is the center of his creativity. His thirteen symphonies are the documents of a composer's evolution that in its climaxes and crises recalls Gustav Mahler. From the First Symphony in 1926, which propelled the nineteen-year-old Shostakovich into fame, to the 13th Symphony in 1962, which was withdrawn under pressure, we witness the development of a highly sensitive, searching musical intellect.

After the war, following the "war" symphonies No. 7 (the *Leningrad*) and No. 8, Shostakovich surprised (and disappointed) many of his friends and followers by writing, not a symphony of "victory," but a merry, light-hearted scherzo — "probably the least symphonic music ever written."[20] The cool reception given to his Ninth Symphony (1945) may have induced the composer to delay his Tenth until 1953. But there may have been other reasons: the witch-hunting atmosphere of 1948 was not propitious for large-scale, abstract works. Thus, in the years 1947-51, we see Shostakovich devoting himself mainly to film music, where problems of style were less acute.

The Tenth Symphony was begun in the summer of 1953, a few months after Stalin's death, and first performed in December 1953. The new work became the focal point of an intense discussion;[21] its foes branded it as a step back into "formalism," its adherents sensed the

[19] Nestiev, *op. cit.*, p. 398.
[20] Neville Cardus in *The [Manchester] Guardian,* Jan. 28, 1961.
[21] See *Sovietskaya Muzyka,* 1954, Nos. 3, 4, 6; 1955, No. 5; 1956, No. 5; 1957, No. 4.

coming of a new dawn. But the comparative freedom of discussion was in itself a sign of approaching liberalization. The Tenth Symphony became a symbol beyond its musical significance, for it is not a flawless masterpiece. But it carries an "intensely personal message, full of anxiety, but also of cheerful dynamism."[22] Clearly, it was a new departure for the composer who struggled to come to terms with problems of form and musical idiom.

In his next two symphonies, Shostakovich abandoned his essentially abstract approach to the genre. The 11th and 12th Symphonies are programmatic works — a diptych of the Revolutions of 1905 and 1917. It is useful to recall the composer's youthful attempts in a similar vein: his Second Symphony of 1927 was dedicated to the "October Revolution," his Third of 1929 to the "First of May" — both works are now disavowed by the composer.

The 11th and 12th Symphonies were designed for mass appeal, and they achieved that goal in their homeland. In the West, the reception was rather cool and disappointing. Of course, the Western listener cannot be expected to react to the revolutionary subject with the same emotional fervor as the Soviet audience; the question is whether these symphonies, apart from the underlying program, have sufficient musical strength to radiate universal appeal. This test has not been met to everyone's satisfaction: "the program rather than the music has gained the upper hand."[23] The excessively pictorial character of these scores, a drawback in Western estimation, appears an asset to Soviet critics, as one can judge by the following comment: "The problem of 'mass appeal' in the symphonic genre was solved by Shostakovich in a brilliant and original manner by means of . . . the penetration of the symphony by elements of other mass genres . . . One can say that the symphonism of Shostakovich has been subjected to the influence of *film music*."[24] On the other hand, a British critic remarks in his review of the 12th Symphony: "To the Western ear, its alternatively drab and garish colors, and obsessive repetition of commonplace musical ideas are intolerable, while the naive ideological program suggests that perhaps the work's true home might be the *cinema*."[25]

Perhaps Western critics have overstressed the "programmatic" mean-

[22] Marcel Frémiot in *Twentieth Century Music,* ed. Rollo Myers, London, 1960, p. 213.

[23] Donald Mitchell in *Daily Telegraph* (London), Sept. 5, 1962.

[24] *Istoria* . . . , Vol. IV, Part 2, p. 163 (italics added).

[25] Martin Cooper in *Daily Telegraph* (London), Nov. 29, 1962 (italics added).

ing of the titles heading each of the four movements of the 11th and 12th Symphonies: they are more suggestive than descriptive. Yet Shostakovich does not dismiss the technique of "historical concreteness": in the 11th Symphony (subtitled "The Year 1905"), he uses five authentic revolutionary songs of that period and shapes some of his own themes in a similar musical idiom. Both symphonies achieve unification of the cyclic form: the movements follow each other without break, and they are related by thematic cross-references and dominating leitmotifs. There is much thought and skill in the fusing of all musical and extra-musical elements. Ultimately, however, the length of these symphonies (especially the Eleventh) is not sustained by commensurate musical content. One is reminded of a rather *méchant* witticism of Ernest Newman: the position of a Shostakovich symphony on the musical map of the future will be located "between so many degrees longitude and so many degrees platitude."

The 13th (and, to date, last) Symphony is actually a symphonic cantata, based on texts by the young Soviet poet Yevgenii Yevtushenko. Each of the five movements is a musical setting of a poem for baritone, male chorus, and orchestra. The poems were not planned as a "cycle" by the poet, though they are somewhat related to each other by an oblique criticism of the Stalinist past. The titles are — 1) *Babii Yar* (the poet's outcry against anti-Semitism), 2) *Humor* (not to be imprisoned by despotism), 3) *Women* (a tribute to Russia's women who "mixed concrete, ploughed and reaped" and stand in a queue), 4) *Fear* ("fears are dying in Russia like the ghost of past years"), 5) *Career* (a good-humored tribute to the non-conformist . . . "forgotten are those who cursed, remembered are those accursed"). Shostakovich's musical setting — alternating between solo voice, choral recitations, and orchestral comments — underlines and intensifies every inflection of the words, giving wings to the humor and impact to the drama.

I attended the first performance of the 13th Symphony in Moscow on December 18, 1962, and it proved an unforgettable experience. It was more than a musical event: in a symbolic gesture, two generations of Soviet artists — the composer near sixty, the poet near thirty — had joined hands to reassert the liberty of the spirit. The triumph was short-lived: the symphony had to be withdrawn for revisions of text and music, and no foreign performances have as yet been given, as far as I know.[26]

In the shadow of such accomplishments, it does not seem

[26] See B. Schwarz, *loc. cit.*, p. 56.

easy for a young Soviet composer to approach the symphonic genre. There are many talented attempts, but as yet no major personality has emerged. The Sinfonietta No. 2 (1960) by Moissei Vainberg (born 1919) is a serious, beautifully wrought work. The Concerto for strings by the Estonian Jan Riaats (born 1932) was recently introduced to New York by the Moscow Chamber Orchestra under Rudolph Barshai but received unfavorable comments. The same composer's *Cosmic Symphony* caused apprehension in Moscow. A fellow Estonian, Arvo Piart (b. 1935), was severely scolded in Moscow for his *Necrologue* (1960), which was termed "ultra-expressionist" and a "twelve-tone experiment." Symphonies in the traditional manner, yet with a certain appealing freshness, were written by Alexei Nikolayev (b. 1931), Andrei Eshpai (b. 1925), and Lucian Prigozhin (b. 1926). A major success was the Symphony for strings and timpani (1961) by the Armenian Edward Mirzoyan (b. 1921). It is a work of infectious vitality that skirts the commonplace. In fact, many of the nationally tinged compositions coming from Russia's remote regions have limited meaning for Western listeners who are unfamiliar with the (often obscure) folkloristic roots. Yet, these compositions are important stepping stones towards an indigenous symphonic school. For example, Fikret Amirov's *Symphonic Mugams* (based on extemporized folk materials of Azerbaidhan) have brought orchestral music to many unsophisticated listeners of that region; but the same effect cannot be expected at Carnegie Hall, where in 1959 the work failed to produce any impression. Many of the symphonic poems with programmatic content now being composed in the USSR fill the needs of the Soviet concert repertory, but they will hardly penetrate beyond the borders.

In contrast, the Soviet solo concerto — with its flair for virtuosity and colorful orchestration — is acclaimed the world over. Most of them are so well known that mere mention will suffice. To his five piano concertos and two violin concertos, Prokofiev added (as one of his last works) the impressive Symphony-Concerto Op. 125 for cello, actually an expanded and revised version of his early Cello Concerto Op. 58 (1933-38). In the late 1940s Kabalevsky — always concerned with good music for young people — began writing several "youth" concertos: a violin concerto (1948), a cello concerto (1949), and the Third Piano Concerto (1952); all have charm and vitality. Another concerto for youth is the Second Piano Concerto (1957) by Shostakovich, written for his son Maxim. Shostakovich's major contributions, however, are his Violin Concerto (composed 1948) and the Cello Concerto (1959).

The Violin Concerto was not heard until 1955, and it is more than probable that the composer preferred to withhold the work rather than to expose it to the intolerant mood of 1948. It is a composition of considerable depth and complexity, and novel in many of its formal aspects. The Cello Concerto is more extrovert, less involved, but equally interesting from the formal point of view. Though the technical demands in both concertos are extreme, neither is a virtuoso piece in the accepted sense of the word: soloist and orchestra are juxtaposed on equal musical terms.

More widespread, however, are the uninhibited display pieces. Such is the melodious Violin Concerto (1959) by Tikhon Khrennikov, which has much brio. Khachaturian's Rhapsody for violin and orchestra (1962) lacks the vitality of his early Violin Concerto. Andrei Eshpai has an attractive Piano Concerto (1955-56) dedicated — not without reason — to the memory of Ravel. A remarkable talent is the twenty-two-year-old Boris Tishchenko, who played his Piano Concerto for me in 1962; it is a piece of immense vitality, somewhat in the style of young Prokofiev. In 1963 the composer (still a graduate student of Shostakovich at the Leningrad Conservatory) introduced his work to Moscow, where it received high praise. He is a talent to be watched.

Chamber music seems to be less congenial to the Soviet composer than other musical genres.[27] Perhaps the prevailing style of Soviet music — colorful, nationalistic, and "realistic" — does not lend itself easily to chamber music, where the classical heritage leads us to expect abstract and lofty utterances. At one time Soviet chamber music underwent a deliberate process of "democratization" to make its language understandable to broad audiences.

This objective was achieved in the First String Quartet (1938) of Shostakovich, where charm borders on triteness. A second quartet followed in 1944, and six more were added between 1946 and 1960. None, in my opinion, reaches the mastery of his Piano Quintet of 1940. Shostakovich, like many pianist-composers, seems more at ease when the piano is a participant. In contrast, his string quartets waver between pseudo-naive gaiety and cerebral profundity without striking a satisfying balance. Nor are the technical problems of quartet writing solved convincingly: frequently one instrument leads while the others merely accompany. Problems of form seem uppermost in the composer's

[27] Ivan Martynov's essay in *Cobbett's Cyclopedic Survey of Chamber Music* (2nd ed., Vol. 3, 1963) is informative but tends to overpraise.

mind; thus, his trend towards thematic unification within a work (already demonstrated in his late symphonies and concertos) is brought to ultimate concentration in his Seventh Quartet (1960). His Eighth and, to date, last quartet (also 1960) is unified by the leitmotif D-S-C-H (D-E♭-C-B — Shostakovich's own initials). In addition, he interweaves thematic fragments from his earlier works — the First Symphony, the Trio, *Lady Macbeth,* and others. Thus it becomes an "autobiographical" quartet.[28] The mood is, once again, dominated by the thought of the victims of war, and it veers, as one English critic remarked, "between sad rumination, anger, and a kind of nervous obsession."[29]

Some younger composers deserve attention. Moissei Vainberg (b. 1919) has written nine string quartets, a piano quintet, a half-dozen violin and cello sonatas. The last three quartets are particularly impressive though at times too academic. More experimental is Vadim Salmanov (b. 1912), who is influenced by Bartók; his Third String Quartet (1960) seems to be an attempt to fit certain twelve-tone techniques into a modal framework — a queer combination of two incompatibles. Also strongly modernistic is Galina Ustvolskaya (b. 1919), whose Violin Sonata (c. 1960) was described by Roy Harris as "dissonant from beginning to end" and "kind of ugly";[30] nevertheless the work, which shows considerable talent, won acclaim at a recent Warsaw Festival. A young "rebel" is Andrei Volkonsky, who was born in 1933 as an émigré but returned to Moscow to study at the Conservatory. Expelled in his second year because of infractions of rules (more likely because he was a "difficult" student), he succeeded in having a Piano Quintet published in Moscow, with a dedication to his former teacher, the venerable Shaporin. The work was denounced and defended in two successive issues of *Sovietskaya Muzyka* (1956, Nos. 5 and 6). The controversy is puzzling, for the Quintet — showing talent though immature — is prevailingly conservative, except in the third movement, a more adventurous Passacaglia. Volkonsky's Viola Sonata (1960) is described as an example of his "pseudo-innovatory 'avant-gardiste'

[28] See Yuri Keldysh, *An Autobiographical Quartet,* in *Musical Times* (London), Apr. 1961. A version for string orchestra and timpani (*Sinfonietta,* arr. by Stassevich) was played in Moscow in December 1962.

[29] Felix Aprahamian in *Sunday Times,* London, Nov. 19, 1961.

[30] Roy Harris, *The State of Music in the Soviet Union,* in *American Music Lover* (*American Record Guide*), interview with Herman Neuman, May 1959, pp. 576-79. Ustvolskaya is not named but merely identified as a "woman composer from Leningrad."

inclinations."[31] His future within the circumscribed orbit of Soviet music bears watching.

One well-tried approach to "popular" chamber music is the use of folk or pseudo-folk material — a technique favored by composers of regions where "classical" music is still in a state of evolution. The string quartets by the Georgian Sulkhan Tzindzadze (b. 1925), by Karayev of Azerbaidzhan, by Mirzoyan of Armenia are suffused with folk-like themes and native rhythms, but the development of this material is predominantly conventional. Belonging in the same "nationalist" category are Shebalin's Slavic Quartet No. 5 (1942), Lyatoshinsky's Ukrainian Piano Quintet (1942-45), and Miaskovsky's Seventh Quartet (1941). A masterpiece of its kind is Prokofiev's Second String Quartet (1941), which uses Caucasian themes; it is, as Martynov rightly says, "an object lesson in the creative transmutation of original folk material."[32]

The Soviet Union has the world's most elaborate system of music education: there is a national network of 1966 children's music schools, 187 specialized secondary schools, 23 conservatories for college-age students. Especially gifted children are educated in 22 so-called Central Music Schools (usually attached to a conservatory) with an integrated curriculum of elementary-plus-high school and music.[33] The possibilities are immense, the results are impressive. Yet, there is a certain imbalance: while Soviet virtuosos are admired everywhere, Soviet composers have not achieved comparable international recognition. True, Prokofiev and Shostakovich are known in every civilized country, Khachaturian and Kabalevsky enjoy a certain reputation; but the last three named are sixty years old, or close to it. It is the younger generation that is virtually unknown in the West, despite the useful efforts of cultural exchanges. How strange it is to read that the only Soviet work announced for the 1964 Warsaw Festival (which specializes in "modernism") is Shostakovich's *The Nose,* a youthful work dating back to 1930 and still considered "ultra-left," hence unacceptable, in the USSR!

The British critic Colin Mason, returning from a brief visit to Moscow, analyzed the Soviet musical scene in two sharply worded articles.[34] After stating that, apparently, "in all the Soviet Union not a

[31] L. Raaben, *Sovietskaya kamerno-instrumentalnaya muzyka,* Moscow, 1963, p. 182.

[32] In Cobbett, *op. cit.,* III, p. 139.

[33] Figures as of November 1962, given to me by the USSR Ministry of Culture.

[34] Colin Mason, *Russia's Young Conservatives* and *Anti-music in Russia,* in *The Guardian,* March 21 and 30, 1963.

single interesting composer has emerged since 1930," he blames the outmoded idiom, the ideological chauvinism, the intrusion of non-musical criteria, and — ultimately — Socialist Realism. "Music is not made with ideas, but with notes." How right is Mason? How right is Craft, who terms Soviet "musical logic at least a light year away"? Or Stravinsky, who admits, "This is the real Iron Curtain"?[35] There are no simple answers.

Stalin's cultural policy or enforced isolation is undoubtedly one of the reasons for a "lost generation" of Soviet composers. Those musicians whose formative years fell roughly in the period 1935-1955 were cut off from the mainstream of Western music and became totally estranged from contemporary musical thought. "The danger of becoming provincial is unfortunately a very real one for modern Soviet composers," said Prokofiev in 1934.[36] This danger has not subsided. For while Soviet composers now have the opportunity of hearing many types of Western music, they are constantly exhorted not to succumb to alien experimentations. "Our young 'experimenters' should realize that there is a difference between freedom of creative searchings and lack of principles," said Khrennikov in 1961.[37] Despite a united front of Shostakovich, Kabalevsky, and Khachaturian against dodecaphony, it is not unknown to the young generation. Khrennikov admits, "We all know that certain Soviet composers (true, there are very few) show a heightened interest in the twelve-tone gimmicks. Influences of avant-garde music have wormed their way into the music of some socialist countries . . ."[38] Specific information about these "rebels" is provided by the West German critic Fred Prieberg; he describes their work, the models and textbooks they use.[39] Here, on the next page, is a brief twelve-tone essay (from a Piano Suite) by the young Ukrainian Valentin Silvestrov, composed in 1961, when he was a conservatory student at Kiev.

The focal point in all these discussions is that of musical idiom. No idiom can be "imported"; it must grow from within. The natural evolution of the Russian musical idiom towards non-tonality was cut short by the death of Scriabin in 1915, and by the silencing of Nicolai

[35] Robert Craft, *loc. cit.,* p. 44.

[36] Prokofiev, *op. cit.,* p. 99.

[37] Information Bulletin, USSR Union of Composers, 1962, No. 1, p. 11.

[38] *Ibid.,* 1963, No. 2, p. 11.

[39] F. Prieberg, *Die Neue Musik in der Sowjet-Union,* in *Die Zeit,* Hamburg, April 12, 1963.

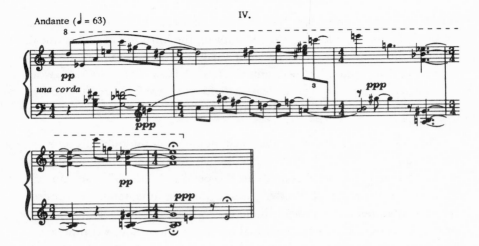

Roslavetz[40] in the 1920s. For young Soviet composers now to explore
the Schoenberg of 1925 (as Prieberg reports in isolated cases) would
seem quite logical. As for Webern, we have the word of an expert,
Robert Craft, "To the custodians of this outward growing society,
Webern's music can only seem like the nervous tick of a moribund
culture. I feel no need for it here . . . or correspondence between it and
what I have seen of Soviet life . . ."[41]

It is not serialism that is threatening Soviet music; the true threat,
as I see it, is the colossal inbreeding, the constant reference to the great
models of Russian musical classicism, the complacent acceptance of a
past idiom for the present day while talking about "contemporaneous-
ness." Asafiev once ridiculed the prerevolutionary "Petersburgian-bureau-
cratic estheticism and chauvinistic academicism which perverted a good
harmony book into a 'symbol of faith' . . ."[42] Today we witness the
arbitrary division of musical systems into "bourgeois-decadent" and
"socialist-realist." Fortunately, the dividing line is not immutable; we
have seen it happen that some work, "decadent" one day, became quite
acceptable the following day. The leaders of Soviet music are too intelligent not to realize the danger of stale conservatism. "We are not
ascetics or reactionaries in our attitude to modern musical idiom,"[43]
Khrennikov declared recently. Obviously, the goal is a combination of

[40] The Third String Quartet by Roslavetz (1920) was played at an ISCM
concert in New York on March 13, 1964. On the same program was a Suite for Piano
(1961) by an anonymous Soviet twelve-tone composer.

[41] Robert Craft, *loc. cit.*, p. 46.

[42] Boris Asafiev, *Kniga o Stravinskom*, Leningrad, 1929, p. 7.

[43] Information Bulletin, USSR Union of Composers, 1962, No. 1, p. 14.

tradition and innovation; the question is only which of the two will prevail.

In the meantime, one must in all fairness acknowledge the tangible accomplishments of Soviet music. It has strengthened its ties with the life of the country and its people. It has brought enjoyment and musical literacy to millions. It has preserved its musical past and explored the wellsprings of folk music. It has educated (perhaps too stringently) a generation of composers to be mindful of the cultural needs of the broad masses. Once the excessive tutelage will subside, once the young composers are given freer rein to search for themselves, Soviet music will undoubtedly experience a new period of efflorescence.

MUSICAL COMPOSITION IN
MODERN ISRAEL*

By ALEXANDER L. RINGER

IN THE process of composing his 1964 Israel Festival cantata *Abraham and Isaac,* Igor Stravinsky made the unexpected discovery of "certain musical potentialities" of modern Hebrew, which, he claimed, in turn revitalized his "musical enzymes."[1] The sense of exhilaration and artistic stimulation that Stravinsky derived from his first contact with Hebrew as a spoken language has been a common experience among Israeli composers for well over a generation. They have, moreover, profited from an intimate acquaintance with ancient types of Hebrew cantillation as well as the modal system of Arabic music with its peculiar motivic and structural procedures based on the *maqam* principle.

Many of the composers who arrived prior to World War II as refugees from Central Europe spoke little or no Hebrew. Then, too, their solid academic training in the Western harmonic tradition inevitably outbalanced any possible impact of the monophonic, at most heterophonic, music of the East. But at the same time, they were deeply affected by their encounter with a way of life that was novel not only because of the absence of racial persecution but also because it opposed a Levantine, often rural existence to the overwrought sophistication of the European city. And so, accepting the ideological tutelage of Max Brod, the writer and former Prague music critic, men like Paul Ben-Haim, Karel Salomon, Marc Lavry, and Menahem Avidom decided to renounce expressive dissonance and structural experimentation in favor of a pastoral lyricism inspired by the songs of the pioneers turning disease-

---

* The author is indebted to Mr. Yohanan Boehm, music critic of the *Jerusalem Post,* for certain biographical data and other favors in connection with this article.

[1] Cf. *Stravinsky at Home,* in *Musical America,* January 1963, p. 11.

breeding swamps into rich agricultural soil and the sounds of the shepherds' pipes echoing through the green hills overlooking the Sea of Galilee. As if to seal their conscious rejection of an urban, for the most part German, past, the members of this "Mediterranean School" turned to French, post-Impressionistic methods of composition. Their melodies reflected the modality of the prevailing folk idiom, and the harmonic style relied a good deal on parallel motion of perfect intervals, as well as combinations of fourth chords. Rhythmic patterns were often derived from Arabic dances and the modern Palestinian *Hora,* while texts and descriptive titles drew heavily upon the lyrical poetry of the Psalms. Freed of the tensions that had beset diaspora Jewry for centuries, the Mediterranean School turned to David, the "Sweet Psalmist of Israel" (to quote the title of one of Ben-Haim's best-known compositions), the shepherd-musician turned king, who danced in ecstasy before the Holy Ark, as its guiding spirit.

By the same token, their compositions were in no way specifically religious, let alone liturgically conceived. As far as that goes, the orthodox hierarchy that rules every aspect of the country's religious life to this very day has never admitted anything beyond the post-Mendelssohnian *a cappella* style into the Western-type synagogue. Instead, the attitudes of Israeli composers, both old and young, reflect the conviction shared by the majority of their countrymen that Judaism represents in essence more of a civilization than a religion, since it has always dealt with the totality of social existence, not excluding aspects associated elsewhere with secular culture. Thus, the fact that few Israeli composers would admit to being religious in the traditional sense is by no means irreconcilable with their dedication to the monumental concepts of the Old Testament and the spiritual wisdom of post-biblical literature, or, for that matter, their fascination with musical motifs and procedures that survived the ages exclusively through prayer and scriptural cantillation. Nothing is more symptomatic of the very special cultural climate of modern Israel than this unique interpenetration of religious, socio-political, and artistic values, which is reflected in the work of the youngest group of composers somewhat differently, to be sure, but hardly less intensively than a generation ago.

Ben-Haim (born 1897 in Munich) remains the most representative of the earlier eclectics who attempted to capture the oriental flavor of their new environment within the framework of Western musical tradition. His output is prolific and his technical command impressive. A superb orchestrator, he prefers the symphonic medium, seemingly unimpressed by the venturesome chamber combinations of his younger colleagues. Presumably because his music is well written for orchestra and appeals to a broader public, he is better known in the United States than any other Israeli composer. Leonard Bernstein, Izler Solomon, and Robert Whitney have been among his most dedicated champions in the concert hall as well as on records, affording American music-lovers the rare opportunity to judge for themselves. Those who heard the Indianapolis performance of the First Symphony (completed in 1940) and subsequently listened to the Louisville recording of *To the Chief Musician,* written eighteen years later, were no doubt struck by Ben-Haim's remarkable stylistic consistency. The orchestration may sound a bit more Ravellian now than previously, but for the rest Mahler, Hindemith, and Prokofiev still compete with French composers like Honegger and Ravel as the principal patron saints of his eclectic conservatism. As far as indigenous elements are concerned, his frequent reliance on pastoral, march, or dance movements leaves relatively little room for passages in cantillation style or similar musical Hebraisms.

Quite the opposite holds true for Oedoen Partos, unquestionably Israel's leading composer for conventional media today. Significantly, Partos is not only ten years younger than Ben-Haim; born in 1907 in Budapest, he also differs greatly in educational and general cultural background. Whereas Ben-Haim's studies in Munich were dominated by the Bruckner tradition, Partos reached musical maturity under the aegis of Hubay, Bartók, and Kodály. The first turned him into an outstanding violinist and viola player; the two latter left their imprints on much of his creative output. Partos came to Israel in 1938 as principal violist of the Palestine Philharmonic Orchestra, founded by Bronislaw Huberman only a short time before. As a newcomer he perhaps inevitably succumbed at first to the lure of the "Mediterranean" ideology. But he apparently realized the ultimate futility of an artificially contrived orientalism and soon decided to come to terms with the underlying *principles* of Middle Eastern music instead. Or, to put it differently, he gradually switched allegiance from his teacher Kodály to Bartók and eventually Bartók *cum* Schoenberg. For obvious reasons Partos has always favored string instruments. One of his earliest international successes involved the performance of his Concertino for Strings at the 1941 Festival of the ISCM in New York. And his *Yiskor* (*In Memoriam*) for viola and strings made a particularly strong emotional impact shortly after the war.

The spirit of Kodály still pervades Partos's symphonic fantasy *Ein*

Gev, which won him the Israel Prize in 1954. This rousing piece was written for the opening of the huge concert hall erected with the financial support of the American ESCO Foundation in the kibbutz *Ein Gev* on the Sea of Galilee, only a short distance from hills occupied by hostile Syrians. In keeping with the occasion the composer wished to pay tribute to the perseverance and heroism of the embattled settlers in a truly "big" piece. Only recently in his *Dmuyot (Visions)* has he returned to orchestral virtuosity on a similar grand scale. As a rule, he reserves virtuosity for soloists. In fact, if Ben-Haim may claim un-challenged leadership in the symphonic field, Partos is without question Israel's foremost concerto composer. William Primrose has played his first viola concerto, subtitled *Song of Praise,* and Yehudi Menuhin performed the successful première of the violin concerto commissioned by the Fromm Foundation. Two years ago in London Partos himself gave the first performance of a *Sinfonia concertante* for viola and orchestra.

As late as 1959 Partos voiced his opposition to dodecaphony as a method of composition, whatever its stylistic guise. It is typical of the man that he unblushingly and literally "changed his tune" once his own organic musical evolution reached the stage where some form of identification with serial procedures became inevitable. Characteristically, Partos, like many a younger Israeli, found his way to serialism through the study of Eastern musical systems, specifically the *maqam* principle with its emphasis on gradual motivic expansion and continuous varia-tion. In the end it was this Eastern principle that provided the link between the Bartókian and Schoenbergian procedures typical of his current work. Surely, in historical perspective Schoenberg's descent from a people who, locked behind ghetto walls for a thousand years, had preserved Eastern monophony in the very heart of Europe, largely unaffected by the conquests of harmony and counterpoint that shaped the musical destinies of their "hosts," was no more accidental than Bartók's birth in Hungary, a country where East and West so often struggled for supremacy. Be this as it may, however, in the case of Partos and similarly oriented composers the *maqam* principle not only made possible the fusion of certain procedures typical of 20th-century Western music; it also served as the catalytic agent permitting the outright adoption of Eastern structural schemes, such as the pairing of a *taqsim,* a rhythmically free initial solo improvisation, and a strictly metrical ensemble section. An outstanding non-dodecaphonic example of this rather typical arrangement is the opening of Partos's very

effective *Maqamat* for flute and strings, completed in 1960. Here an
extended, rhythmically irregular flute solo leads to the metrically
organized Andantino sostenuto, in which string pizzicatos are used to
suggest the drum beats that would mark the corresponding portion of
an Arabic piece. Oriental *fioriture* permeate the entire work, but
microtones as such are avoided. Instead, the combination of a highly
chromatic melos with a strongly dissonant harmonic idiom creates at
times the illusion of unstable intonation. Subsequent works, especially
the string quartet entitled *Tehilim* (*Psalms*), unquestionably Partos's
finest piece to date, and *Agada* (*Legend*) for viola, piano, and percussion, pursue the same stylistic line further in the direction of dodecaphony.

In its consistent juxtaposition of an admirably controlled rhapsodic
style incorporating numerous *fioriture* and sophisticated structures featuring elements of Bartók's motivic serialism as well as a harmonic language
often reminiscent of Schoenberg, Partos's recent output somehow brings
to mind the work of Leon Kirchner, an American of Jewish extraction,
who, moreover, favors a similar unleashing of musical energies. Thus,
it may be said without the slightest implication of actual imitation or
even indirect influence, that Partos's *Dmuyot* shares many a stylistic
and formal characteristic with a piece like Kirchner's Toccata for
orchestra. Like Kirchner, Partos is an eclectic of great originality and
artistic maturity, who owes his truly international stature to both unerring
musical instincts and the steadfast determination to reject all momentary
fads and fashions in the interest of an organically evolving personal style
that is as unique as it is solid.

Born the same year, the late Alexander Boscovich (1907-64) also
hailed from Hungary. Yet he reached his ultimate post-Webernian
position in an entirely different manner. After leaving the Budapest
Academy as a very young man, he went to Vienna and finally to Paris,
where he attended the Schola Cantorum as well as the École Normale.
Under the tutelage of Nadia Boulanger and Paul Dukas, Boscovich
developed a neo-Classicist *stile secco* which continued to prevail even
in such "Mediterranean" works as the *Semitic Suite,* a relatively early
piano piece that has become very popular in Israel in a later orchestral
version. Shortly after the war Boscovich, always a seeker religiously,
intellectually, and artistically, stopped composing altogether, firmly resolved not to write another note until he had completely found himself.
For fifteen years he made a considerable impact on the Israeli musical
scene as a critic, teacher, and translator of Hindemith's theoretical
writings, until he suddenly re-emerged creatively with a small number

of compositions that represent a complete stylistic, though not necessarily esthetic, change of heart. In line with the general trend in Israeli music, the "new" Boscovich, too, attempted a synthesis of dodecaphonic and oriental Jewish elements. But in contrast to Partos, who embraced the Schoenbergian tradition, Boscovich leaned in the direction of Webern, whose dispassionate lyricism conflicts little with the "dry" neo-Classicism of his own earlier period. Thus, Boscovich's road to dodecaphony rather resembles that chosen by Stravinsky.

The first decisive composition in this vein, *Shir Hama'alot* (*Song of Degrees*), commissioned by the Israel Philharmonic Orchestra on the occasion of its twenty-fifth anniversary season (1960/61), relies more explicitly on the rhythmic-melodic formulas of Hebrew chant than the subsequent *Concerto da camera* (1962). The motivation for this emphasis on liturgical resources follows from the title, a characteristic psalm beginning. The eighteen-minute Concerto for violin solo and ten instruments (including four percussion players), on the other hand, has no such liturgical connotations. Instead, its three movements reflect the composer's mystic concern with the seasonal cycles of nature. Though definitely logo-genic, the motivic material is therefore freely treated in ever-changing combinations producing — in Boscovich's own words — "a flowing prose-like texture." The colorful first movement consists of three "toccatas" representing three seasonal types of rain in Israel, early (fall), winter, and spring. The toccatas are separated in turn by two "ricercares," symbolic prayers for rain. If the two remaining movements, entitled *Song of the Spring Month* and *Song of the Summer Month*, sound somewhat redundant, it is because Boscovich, like so many of his European and American colleagues, has succumbed to the temptation of employing a highly refined idiom developed originally within a formal context of utter conciseness on a temporal scale that requires a far more varied and robust approach to sustain the listener's attention. On the whole, the sound as well as certain structural features suggest a thorough familiarity with Boulez's *Marteau sans maître*. But Boscovich certainly added individual touches. The very imaginative duet for violin and vibraphone in the second ricercare is but one successful case in point. Needless to say, Boulez himself has long since recognized that the persistent use of utterly transparent yet highly saturated, gamelan-like sonorities in conjunction with a mosaic-like texture is not without its dangers. But whatever Boscovich's specific structural problems, it is largely thanks to this devoted and greatly lamented man that Israel may now claim a substantial stake in the "wide-open spaces" of post-Webernian music.

Israel's foremost electronic composer, Joseph Tal, was born near Poznan in 1910 but came to Berlin as an infant, and it was in the capital of the Weimar Republic, buzzing with musical ventures of all kinds, that he received his musical training and general orientation. A graduate of the Berlin Hochschule in both composition and musical pedagogy, Tal is also an excellent pianist, plays the harp, and has a solid background as a conductor. It was this thorough academic training, as well as his notable creative achievement, that moved the Hebrew University of Jerusalem in 1951 to give him an appointment as Israel's first, and until a year ago only, university lecturer in music. Tal arrived in Palestine in 1934, a year after Ben-Haim. But instead of seeking to pursue a musical career at once, he decided to do his share in the physical rebuilding of the land by joining a rural settlement, kibbutz *Gesher*. Somehow, this initial gesture characterizes the whole man, whose entire career mirrors an uncompromising singlemindedness and dedication to principle. After a year and a half of kibbutz labor he was invited to join the faculty of the Jerusalem conservatory and later became director of the Israel Academy of Music, a post he held until 1954. Since then Tal, perhaps the least academic of Israel's older composers, has steered clear of anything that might involve him in the petty struggles for position characteristic of musical politics anywhere, and especially in a very small country. Aside from part-time teaching at the University and at Oranim, a teachers' institute near Haifa, he has devoted himself with singular energy to the Center for Electronic Music in Israel, an institution now located on the campus of the Hebrew University, but which he built from scratch, beginning with a single tape recorder in his own home.

Tal's numerous works for traditional media defy classification as part of any "school." No doubt Schoenberg had an early influence on the Berlin composition student. But neither his widely played First Symphony (1952) nor his exceedingly well-wrought String Quartet in one movement, nor, for that matter, his subsequent Cello Concerto is in any structural sense dodecaphonically conceived. While row materials are freely used, the method of composing with twelve tones is nowhere strictly applied, not even in as recent and completely atonal a piece as the *Structure* for solo harp. Similarly, oriental materials are employed sparingly and with the greatest caution. Whereas the Symphony is actually based on a Persian-Jewish lament as notated by A. Z. Idelsohn, the Quartet no longer goes beyond the use of a few characteristic motifs. And if the Symphony still features a dance section in accordance with the then prevailing tenets of the Mediterranean School, such sacrifices to popular taste, however subtle, have been conspicuously missing in recent years. Tal continues to draw much inspiration from the Bible. But the references are almost entirely of a textual nature. This holds true not only for the short operas *Saul at Endor* and *Amnon and Tamar* but for the electronic music as well. His first work for the new medium was called *Exodus II* (an earlier ballet, *Exodus,* originated during the immediate post-war years); an electronic opera deals with *The Tower of Babel.* Even his seemingly "abstract" Concerto for Piano and Tape Recorder reaches its climax with the dramatically whispered mention of "the One who is in the heavens and the earth."

It takes a man of Tal's persistence and integrity to overcome the enormous material handicaps and outright suspicion facing the new and expensive field of electronic music in a small, economically struggling, musically conservative country like Israel. With the exception of a token government subsidy, his Center depends entirely on private funds, secured for the most part by an enthusiastic and equally tenacious young physicist, Shalhevet Freier. Mr. Freier's mother, in turn, founded the Israel Composers Fund, a private agency that issues numerous commissions every year to the most deserving of Israeli composers. Without the selfless help of such dedicated individuals Israel's discovery of "the new music" could hardly have proceeded as rapidly as it did.

As might be expected from a man of his candor, Tal is completely undoctrinaire about electronic music and broaches its problems with the same healthy skepticism that has marked his approach to the twelve-tone method or the issue of a "national" Israeli style. Thus, he declared several years ago: "We can make a religion of the purity of the sine-tone, we can use white noise as a counterpart, but we cannot shut our ears to the fact that compared with conventional tone material, as the bearer of sound content, electronic tone material is inherently narrower and more rigid; indeed it has the characteristics of the synthetic . . ." He then proceeded to condemn originality *à tout prix* and concluded with an appeal for concentration on "the possibility of controlling the individual components with financially feasible and aesthetically satisfying projects."[2] Imbued with the kind of realism found only in the true idealist, Tal is indeed a liberal in a realm of artistic endeavor where extremism often goes on a rampage. Combining a

[2] *The Modern Composer and His World,* ed. by John Beckwith and Udo Kasemets, Toronto, 1961, p. 119.

good deal of modesty with a strong sense of personal value, he impresses even those who find his music rather forbidding and exerts a far more powerful influence on the younger generation than some of his more "successful" colleagues who intoxicate a gullible public with their facile "Mediterranean" orientalism.

A somewhat younger man of similar esthetic and ethical firmness is Russian-born Mordecai Seter, best known abroad for *The Legend of Judith,* a ballet commissioned by Martha Graham in 1962. Seter was brought to Palestine in 1926, when he was ten years old. He later spent several years in Paris studying at the École Normale. There can be no question but that intensive preoccupation with Gregorian chant and Renaissance polyphony left a profound imprint upon his basic musical attitudes even after one of Israel's musical pioneers, Joachim Stutchevsky, induced him to examine Idelsohn's *Thesaurus of Hebrew-Oriental Music* with at least equal care. As a result, he is prone to give precedence to purely melodic considerations in contrast to those who, like Partos, draw upon Eastern models for much of their rhythmic inspiration. Characteristically, Seter devoted himself at first entirely to vocal music, a field strangely neglected by the composers of this "singing nation." Like his three well-written motets dating back to 1951, the more recent *Four Festive Songs* employ imitative techniques in an often clashingly dissonant harmonic context. In 1962 his expert handling of large vocal forces earned him the Prix d'Italia for a radio work, *Midnight Vigil,* a concert version of which was performed during the 1963 Israel Festival. The libretto of this often fascinating forty-minute oratorio combines biblical, talmudic, and late medieval mystic texts in an ambitious effort to re-create the experiences of a solitary worshipper confronting his God at midnight, when according to the cabbalistic tradition the Divine spirit bewails the destruction of the Temple. But whereas the original midnight service, compiled by Rabbi Isaac Lurie in the 16th century, consists almost exclusively of lamentations and prayers for redemption, Seter and his librettist, Mordecai Tabib, added a rousing Hallelujah in praise of modern Israel as the beginning of national redemption.

Seter uses a large orchestra, including four percussion players in addition to harp and piano. A tenor sings and at times speaks the part of the worshipper. A small mixed choir represents the heavenly voice in a lyric polyphonic style, while a group of boys' and men's voices recounts the legend in the manner of a liturgical recitation. The people's case is taken up by a large mixed choir homophonically, or even in unison, frequently employing Yemenite folk intonations. This massive apparatus requires expert handling, if the danger of a certain monotony inherent in the stylistic limitations the composer chose to impose upon himself is to be avoided. But then, so do the far more primitivistic neo-medievalisms of a Carl Orff. Whatever the case, Seter has produced some stunningly evocative moments, by simple means like the alternation of recitative and choral dance in the *Love of Hadassah* section as well as through calculated effects like the successive flageolet entrances of the strings *divisi* shortly before the pianissimo ending lets the piece recede into the quiet of the night.

Seter's instrumental music carries the stamp of both his experience in vocal writing and the influence of oriental monophony and heterophony. His solo Violin Sonata, for example, consistently avoids wide melodic skips in favor of *fioritura* motifs, often little more than chromatically embellished whole-tone progressions. The resulting affinity with Bartók is particularly striking in the Ricercare for string quartet, a nineteen-minute composition based entirely on a small number of closely knit motivic nuclei.

Akin to Seter's instrumental procedures are those employed in the *Bashrav* for solo violin by Abel Ehrlich (born in Germany 1915). The title refers to a varied rondo form popular with Arabic musicians, and Ehrlich goes much farther than Seter in the use of microtones, as well as specific rhythmic patterns directly derived from Arabic models. The composer explains that in pieces of this kind "the rhythm follows only the dictation of the player's mood." He has tried to distinguish also between different types of rhythmic sonorities, such as the ringing and muffled percussion sounds of the Arab drummers. Melodically, *Bashrav* has much in common with Seter's Sonata for Two Violins, composed in the same year, 1953. Ehrlich, too, favors the narrow motivic ranges coupled with the kind of "creeping chromaticism" that marks, for example, the opening of Bartók's *Music for Strings, Percussion, and Celesta.* The comparative table of typical Israeli motifs (Ex. 1) selected more or less at random may serve to show that these

Ex. 1a)   Ehrlich, *Bashrav*

b)   Seter, *Sonata for Two Violins* I

c)   Seter, *Midnight Vigil* mm. 196-8

d)   Seter, *Ricercare*

e)   Partos, *Magamat*

f)   Partos, *Tehilim* (II) mm. 242-6

g)   Sheriff, *Ashrei* mm. 9-10

h)   Lakner, *Sextet* mm. 24-25

melodicles derived from Eastern sources have by now become a common stylistic characteristic of numerous composers whose artistic outlooks may differ greatly in other respects. The same may well be said for the related *fioriture* (see Ex. 2) and to a lesser degree for the functional

Ex. 2*a)*   Sheriff, *Music for Woodwinds, Trombone, Piano and Bass* mm. 2-5

b)   *Taqsim* printed in Erlanger, *La musique arabe*, V, p. 333

c)   Seter, *Sonata for Two Violins* IV

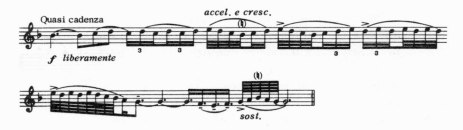

significance of such materials in continuously unfolding **structural patterns.**

The unusual interest in compositions for solo string instruments results, of course, from the obvious fascination exerted upon the Israelis by Near-Eastern monophonic and heterophonic music. Then, too, there is the authority of Partos, the violist-composer, ever ready to promote the cause of a younger man in whom he believes. Thus, Yehoshua Lakner (born 1924 in Czechoslovakia) wrote an effective *Improvisation* and Ben-Zion Orgad (born 1926 in Germany) a *Monologue* for viola solo. Lakner has more recently turned to electronic and strict serial techniques. Orgad, on the other hand, continues to explore avenues suggested by cantillation and the prosody of the Hebrew language. Example 3 juxtaposes a passage from his *Monologue* and the

Ex. 3*a*)   *Yemenite Mah Nishtana,* transcribed by A. Herzog in *R'nanot,* V–VI, p. 2

b)   Orgad, *Monologue*

Yemenite version of the "Four Questions" recited at the Seder ceremony on Passover. Orgad's piece eventually reaches a rhythmic climax through a process of diminution, which in turn produces an increase in ornamental figuration. But the close interval texture persists throughout; there is hardly a motivically significant skip in the entire piece.

Orgad employed this technique as early as 1950 in his two-movement symphony for baritone and orchestra, *Hatsvi Yisrael,* first performed in Israel under Leonard Bernstein, to whose own *Jeremiah Symphony* it is somewhat related. He continued to compose in the same vein for at least a decade until he came to the United States to study at Tanglewood and Brandeis University. *Seven Variations on C,* a piano piece dedicated to his teacher, the late Irving Fine, clearly shows the **drastic** effects of this sudden contact with advanced Western idioms **rarely** heard in Israel. Even so, after a beginning dominated by unusually

wide intervals, the range gradually narrows, and before it is all finished
the magnetic power of middle C, on which the entire piece is centered,
manages to eliminate most of the earlier octave transpositions, thus
reducing the range to typical Orgadian proportions. Like the other
Israelis groping towards serialism, Orgad is aware, of course, of the
tenuous nature of his country's musical culture. Hence, anxious to
preserve a modicum of historical continuity, he has insisted that this
piece, too, "brings to mind the melodic patterns of Bible cantillation."

While a mere listing of the disproportionately large number of able
composers active among the less than one million Israelis of Western
descent could serve no possible useful purpose, except to mollify the
many who have not been mentioned, this brief survey of trends and
attitudes would hardly be complete without some indications as to what
the future may have in store. Clearly, any such indications will have
to come from the creative output of the men now about thirty years
of age. A *sabra* (native Israeli) of considerable promise is Noam Sheriff.
He first drew attention with a *Festival Prelude,* which was given its
première by the Israel Philharmonic Orchestra under Leonard Bernstein in 1957, when the composer was only twenty-two years old. Since
then the "Mediterranean" influence of Ben-Haim, his Israeli teacher,
has been counterbalanced by studies with Boris Blacher in Germany.
As a result, more recent pieces like the *Music for Woodwinds, Trombone,
Piano, and Bass,* and especially his delicately scored *Ashrei* (Psalm I)
for contralto, flute, two harps, and two tom-toms, combine the melodic
characteristics of the *fioritura* style with a highly variable metrical
organization, to the point where on page 20 of the printed score of
Ashrei each of the ten measures carries a different time signature.

Yitzhak Sadai's (born 1930) admittedly somewhat tentative *Ricercar
symphonique* reveals a certain affinity with the broad rhetorical gestures
of the earlier Schoenberg as well as the lyrical flow and basic idiom
of Alban Berg. His *Impressions of a Chorale* for harpsichord, on the
other hand, is a symmetrically conceived serial structure based on a
hexachord and a pentachord, each formed by the transposed notes
of the initial line of *O Haupt voll Blut und Wunden.* The chorale itself
appears precisely at midpoint. In keeping with his choice of a Protestant
melody, Sadai excludes musical Hebraisms of any kind.

The same can be said of Sergui Natra (born 1934), though for
entirely different reasons. The extraordinarily gifted Natra is a relatively
recent immigrant from Rumania, where he was held in the highest
official esteem and accordingly rewarded even as a very young man.

His *March and Chorale* received the Enesco Prize when he was barely seventeen years old. But while he was writing in the "realistic" folk style expected of him, he also studied Schoenberg and Stravinsky. And his ultimate decision to renounce a comfortable life in Rumania for an uncertain future in Israel was motivated as much by the urge to leave the narrow artistic confines of the Communist world as by the ardent desire to live in dignity as a Jew. To him, therefore, Israel represented above all the bridge between East and West, politically as well as culturally. Since his arrival in 1961 Natra has written relatively little. But a comparison of the well-wrought *Sinfonia per archi,* composed shortly before he left Rumania, with the Toccata for orchestra, commissioned for the 1963 Israel Festival, while revealing a common reliance on polyphonic structural patterns such as passacaglia and fugue, also shows that the secure conservatism of the earlier work has given way to new expressive means, specifically in the realms of rhythm and harmony. Near-Eastern elements, on the other hand, are missing altogether, no doubt because Natra became part of the country's musical scene just as Israeli composers were beginning to look for more cosmopolitan stylistic pastures themselves.

Finally, there is the unique figure of Habib Touma, an Arab pupil of Boscovich. Born into a community that holds the professional musician in thorough social contempt, Touma explains that he risked "studying Western music in order to write good oriental music that can be performed and appreciated by artists who so far may have regarded Arabic music as primitive and monotonous." In his *Samai* for oboe and piano, Touma has indeed tried to capture the flavor of Arabic music within a context of Western sonorities. He observes the division into alternating *Taslim* and *Khana* sections characteristic of the traditional *Samai* and employs typical meters, such as 10/4, 5/8, and 9/8. The piano often assumes the part of the drummer, above whose ostinato patterns the oriental soloist weaves his florid improvisations. As one might expect, it is precisely in aleatory terms that Touma's ornamental heterophony connects with the latest Western developments. Both the oboist and the pianist have solo passages in which groups of notes may be repeated "with slight variations, starting from higher or lower notes." Elsewhere they are urged to insert free cadenzas and eventually to improvise together "on melodic material from any or all preceding 'Khana' sections for no less than twenty-five seconds and no more than fifty seconds."

With Touma, it would seem, Israeli music has come full circle. If the Mediterranean School attempted to write oriental music with the inevitable bias of the Western musician, Touma, his somewhat naive rationalizations notwithstanding, composes what amounts in fact to Western music in an Eastern idiom. The future clearly lies somewhere between these essentially post-Romantic extremes. With history on her side — if only in view of the growing importance of composers, from Debussy to Boulez, inspired by Eastern musical esthetics — Israel with her enormous reservoir of talent is bound to find a secure place within the very mainstream of the world's music, away from the periphery onto which she has often been forced in the past either by circumstances beyond anyone's control or by some well-intentioned but artistically misplaced ideology. Provided she is granted the lasting peace for which all her citizens pray, that time will be reached *bimhera b'jamaynu,* "soon in our day."

NOTE

The examples by Ehrlich, Partos (*Maqamat*), and Orgad are copyright by Israel Music Publications (U.S. agent: Leeds Music Corp.). Those by Seter, Partos (*Tehilim*), Sheriff, and Lakner are copyright by Israel Music Institute (U.S. agent: Boosey & Hawkes).

INDEX

Abraham, Gerald 264
Abril, Antón Garcia 59
Absil, Jean 94
Adorno, T. W. 10, 150f, 165, 168
Albu, Sandu 237
Alcazar, El 44
aleatory music
30-34, 73, 144-65, 168, 251
Alessandrescu, Alfred 239
Almeida, F.A.A. 39
Alpaerts, Flor 93
American ESCO Foundation 285
Amirov, Fikret 275
Amy, Gilbert 25, 31f, 145
Anderberg, Carl-Olof 125
Andersen, Alf 127
Andricu, Mihail 239
Andriessen, Hendrik · 101f
Andriessen, Louis 110
Antoniou, Theodor 230f
Apostel, Hans Erich 183f
Arp, Hans 83f
Asafiev, Boris 269, 280
Ateneo de Madrid 44f, 55, 57
Aula de Música 44f
Auric, Georges 34
Avidom, Menahem 282
Axman, Emil 194
Baaren, Kees van 104, 106-08
Bacewicz, Grazyna 246, 249, 251f
Bäck, Sven-Erik 117-22
Badings, Henk 103f
Baekkelund, Kjell 126f
Baird, Tadeusz 249, 252
Barce, Ramón 45, 52-54
Bárdos, Lajos 207
Bark, Jan 135
Barraqué, Jean 25, 27
Barraud, Henri 34

Barrault, Jean-Louis **28**
Barshai, Rudolph 275
Bartha, Dénes 210
Bartók Archive of the Academy of
  Science (Hungary) 210
Bartók, Béla, *passim,* but see espe-
  cially 205-14
Bayle, François 165
Beck, Conrad 85
Béjart, Maurice 212
Bengtsson, Ingmar 117
Benguerel, Xavier 58
Ben-Haim, Paul 282-85, 288
Bennett, Richard Rodney 13, 18
Benoit, Peter 92f
Bense, Max 159, 165
Bentzon, Niels Viggo 111, 114-17
Berg, Alban, *passim,* but see espe-
  cially 180-90
Berg, Gunnar 138
Berg, Josef 203
Bergamo, Petar 224
Berger, Theodore 189
Bergman, Erik 125, 129-31
Berio, Luciano 13-15, 63f, 110
Berkeley, Lennox 13, 19f
Berlin Hochschule 13, 16
Berlioz, Hector 13
Bernaola, Carmelo Alonso 59
Bernstein, Leonard 233, 284, 294f
Bialas, Gunter 177
Birtwistle, Harrison 13, 16, 18
Bittner, Julius 180
Blacher, Boris 173
Blancafort, Alberto 59f
Blazěk, Zdeněk 202
Bloch, A. 258
Blok, Alexander 270
Blomdahl, Karl-Birger 117-22

Blum, Robert   85
Bondeville, Emmanuel   35
Bónis, Ferenc   211
Borba, Tomás   40
Bořkovec, Pavel   202
Borris, Siegfried   178
Borup-Jörgensen, Axel   138
Boscovich, Alexander   286f
Boulanger, Nadia
        19f, 42, 60, 240, 245, 286
Boulez, Pierre, *passim,* but see
    especially   5f, 8, 22-25, 28-33, 37,
                    144-65, 168, 237
Bozay, Attila   209
Bradshaw, Susan   14, 19n
Braein, Edvard Fliflet   127
Brailoiu, Constantin   238
Branco, Joao   41
Branco, Luís de Freitas   40f
Branco, Pedro   41
Bravničar, Matija   217
Brecht, Bertolt   175
Brediceanu, Tiberiu   238
Brian, Havergal   20
broadcasting systems:
    B.B.C.   13-15
    Belgium   95
    Bucharest Radio   254
    Cadena Azul de Radio Difusion   60
    Germany   171
    Hungary   213
    National Radio of Athens   241
    Radio Nacional (Spain)   54, 57
    Radio Sweden   118, 136f
    Radio Wien   190
    Polish Radio   254
    Yugoslavia   214
Broch, Hermann   27
Brod, Max   282
Broman, Sten   125
Bruckner, Anton   12f
Brunner, Adolf   85
Bucht, Gunnar   125
Bughici, Dumitru   241
Bull, Edvard Hagerup   128
Burian, Emil František   202
Bussotti, Sylvano   72-75

Cage, John   5f, 30, 67, 72-75, 137,
        144f, 149, 153-54, 160f, 165, 168
Cantar y Tañer   58
Cardew, Cornelius   18f
Carlid, Göte   119
Carlstedt, Jan   124
Carnegie Hall   275
Carneyro, Claudio   41
Carra, Manuel   45, 54f
Carter, Elliott   13
Casanova, André   27
Casanovas, José   59
Cassuto, Alvaro   43
Castiglioni, Niccolò   64-67
Castillo, Manuel   59
Cerha, Friedrich   185
Cercós, José   58
Char, René   29f, 33
Charles, Daniel   5
Chase, Gilbert   66
Cheltenham Festival   17
Chevreuille, Raymond   94
Chlubna, Osvald   194f
Christou, Jani   226-28
Ciortea, Tudor   240
Cipra, Milo   218
Círculo de Cultura Musical
    (Lisbon)   40
Círculo Manuel de Falla   59
Clementi, Aldo   69-72
Cluytens, André   96
Cochofel, Joao José   40
Coelho, Ruy   39-41
Collaer, Paul   95
Companhia Portuguesa de Opera   39
concert series:
    Budapest Music Weeks   21f
    Cantar y Tañer (Madrid)   58
    Chamber Music of Our Century
        (Hungary)   212
    Concerts de Midi   94f
    Concerts Marigny   28
    die reihe   125
    Domaine Musical   28f, 32, 109, 149
    Fylkingen   118, 126, 137
    Jeunesses Musicales   95
    Juventudes Musicales   58f

Música Abierta 58
Musica Viva 177
Nutida musik 118, 126
Országos Filharmónia 211f
Sociedad de Música de Camara 58
Thursday Invitation Concerts
(B.B.C.) 14f
Tiempo y Música 58
Concerts de Midi 94f
Concerts Marigny 28
Constantinescu, Paul 240
Coria, Miguel Angel 59
Cortot, Alfred 237
Craft, Robert 279f
Cruz, Ivo 41f
Cuclin, Dimitrie 237
Cunningham, Merce 118
Dallapiccola, Luigi 61, 213
Darmstadt 14f, 18, 21, 167f, 170
Darmstadt Festival 51f
Dávid, Gyula 208
David, Johann Nepomuk 178, 186-88
Davies, Peter Maxwell 16-18
De Boeck, Auguste 92f
de Freitas, Frederico. See Freitas,
Frederico de
De Greef, Arthur 95
de Leeuw, Ton. See Leeuw, Ton de
de Pablo, Luis. See Pablo, Luis de
de Vasconcelos, Jorge Croner. See
Vasconcelos, Jorge de
Debussy, Claude
22-24, 28, 64, 67, 94, 192, 196
Delcroix, Léon 92
Delius, Frederick 12
Delvincourt, Claude .24
Demény, János 211
Denijn, Jef 95
Despali, Pavle 224
Dessau, Paul 175
Deutsch, Max 19
Deutsche Grammophon 213
Devčič, Natko 219f
Dewey, Kenneth 133f
Diepenbrock, Alphons 97f
Dille, Denijs 210
d'Indy, Vincent 239

Dobiáš, Václov 200
Documentu Bartókiana 210
dodecaphony. See serial composi-
tion
Dohnányi, Ernst von 206
Domaine Musical 28f, 32, 109, 149
Donatoni, Franco 75-77
Donaueschingen 14
Donaueschingen Festival 48, 109
Donner, Henrik Otto 133f
Dorati, Antal 206
Doubrava, Jaroslav 202
Dragoi, Sabin V. 240f
Dresden, Sem 99
Drew, David 14
Driessler, Johannes 178
du Pin, Patrice de la Tour. See
Pin, Patrice de la Tour du
Duhamel, Antoine 27
Dukas, Paul 27, 240
Dumitrescu, Gheorghe 241
Dumitrescu, Ion 241
Durkó, Zsolt 209
Dutilleux, Henri 34
Dvořák, Antonín 17, 192, 194, 196, 202
Dzerzhinsky, Ivan 262, 265
East Berlin Radio 33
Eben, Petr 202
Eck, Imre 212
Edlund, Hans 124
Egge, Klaus 111
Egk, Werner 173
Ehrlich, Abel 291
Ehrling, Sixten 117
Eimert, Herbert 168, 170
Einem, Gottfried von 188f, 212
Eisler, Hanns 175
electronic music 8f, 14f, 21, 36-38,
45, 68, 93, 104, 127,
136, 222, 250, 288f
Elgar, Edward 13
Eloy, Jean-Claude 32
Eluard, Paul 104
Enescu, Georges 236f
Engelmann, Hans Ulrich 178
Englund, Einar 129
Eösze, László 211

Erbse, Heimo 171
Ericson, Eric 117
Escher, Rudolf 104
Eshpai, Andrei 275
Evangelisti, Franco 68
Evanghelatos, Antiochos 230
Fábián, Imre 211
Fabian, László 211
Falvy, Zoltán 211
Fano, Michel 25, 31
Farkas, Ferenc 207f
festivals:
   Concours International Reine
     Elisabeth 95
   Cheltenham 17
   Darmstadt 51f
   Donaueschingen Musiktage 170
   Enescu Festivals 236
   ISCM 17, 117, 195, 199, 209, 284
   in Israel 282, 290, 296
   Leeds 17
   Moscow 260
   Musica Viva 171, 177
   Muzik der Zeit 171
   Neue Werk 171
   Scandinavian Conservatory
     Festivals 126
   Tage für neue Kammermusik 171
   Venice 52, 251
   Vienna 189
   Warsaw Musical Autumns
     250, 254, 256
Fine, Irving 294
Finkbeiner, Reinhold 178
Flothuis, Marius 106
Flyckt, Yngve 119
Folk Music Research Group of the
   Academy of Science (Hungary) 206
Folklore Institute of Bucharest 240
Fortner, Wolfgang 166f, 173
Foss, Lukas 232
Fougstedt, Nils-Eric 128f
Franco, Enrique 45, 56f
Freier, Shalhevet 289
Freitas, Frederico de 42
Fribec, Krešimir 222
Fricker, Peter Racine 20n

Frid, Géza **206**
Froidebise, Pierre **94**
Fromm Foundation 285
Füssl, Heinz 184
Fylkingen 118, 126, 137
Gaudeamus Foundation 109
Gazouleas, Stephanos 230f
Gedda, Nicolai 117
Geiser, Walther **84**
Genzmer, Harold 178
Gerhard, Roberto 58
Gershwin, George **40**
Gerster, Ottmar 176
Gewerder, Alexander Xaver **91**
Gielen, Michael 184
Gilson, Paul 92f
Glière, Reinhold 269
Glock, William 13-15, 21
Goehr, Alexander 12-14, 16-18
Goehr, Walter **16**
Goléa, Antoine 7, 63
Gombau, Gerardo 45, 55f
Goossens, Eugene 19
Górecki, Henryk 256
Gotovac, Jakov 217
Grabovsky, Leonid 271
Graça, Fernando Lopes **39, 42**
Graham, Martha **290**
Graves, Robert 227
Grovlez, Gabriel **40**
Grumiaux, Arthur 95
Grupo Nuevo Música 57
Gudmundsen-Holmgreen, Pelle 140f
Guillaume, Eugène 92
Haas, Pavel 197
Hába, Alois 197-200, 202
Hába, Karel 199
Hadzidakis, Manos 232f
Halffter, Cristóbal 45-49
Halffter, Ernesto **46**
Halffter, Rudolfo **46**
Hall, Pauline 126
Hambraeus, Bengt 122-24
Hamilton, Iain 20n
Hanuš, Jan 202
Harašta, Milan 203
Harris, Roy 277

Hartmann, Karl Amadeus   177
Hassenberg, Kurt   178
Haubenstock-Romati, Roman   185
Hauer, Joseph Matthias   185f
Haug, Hans   85
Havelka, Svatopluk   203
Heiller, Anton   187
Heinninen, Paavo   134
Hemel, Oscar van   104f
Henderson, Robert   17n, 17n
Henkemans, Hans   104-06
Henry, Pierre   9
Henze, Hans Werner   12, 167, 171f, 178
Hermanson, Ake   136
Hidalgo, Juan   58
Hindemith, Paul
              38, 42, 116, 167, 176, 178
Hodeir, André   25, 156
Holewa, Hans   125
Höller, Karl   178
Holliger, Heinz   90
Holmboe, Vagn   111-14, 116
Holmquist, Bengt   119
Homs, Joaquin   58
Honegger, Arthur   79, 173
Hovland, Egil   127f
Hristić, Stevan   217
Hubay, Jenö von   206
Huber, Klaus   89
Huberman, Bronislaw   284
Idelsohn, A. Z.   288, 290
Instituto de Alta Cultura   41
International Archive for Folk
    Music   238
International Folk Music
    Conference   206
International Society for Contem-
    porary Music (ISCM)
        17, 109, 117, 195, 199, 209
International Society for Music
    Education   206
Ioannidis, Yannis   230
Israel Academy of Music   288
Israel Composers Fund   289
Israel Philharmonic Orchestra 287,295
Ištvan, Miloš   203
Janáček, Leoš   192, 194-98, 202

Jaques-Dalcroze, Emile   80
Járdányi, Pál   208f
Jelinek, Hanns   184
Jemnitz, Alexander   206
Jeremiáš, Otakar   194
Jersild, Jörgen   116
Jeunesses Musicales   95
Jirák, Karel Boleslav   194
Johnson, Bengt   138
Jolivet, André   35f
Jongen, Joseph   92
Jora, Mihail   239
Juventudes Musicales   58f
Jyrkiäinen, Reijo   133
Kabalevsky, Dmitri   261f, 265, 275
Kabeláč, Miloslav   203
Kadosa, Pál   207
Kagel, Mauricio   176
Kalabis, Viktor   202
Kalomiris, Manolis   229
Kapr, Jan   202
Kaprál, Václav   194
Kaprálová, Vítězslava   201
Karayev, Kara   268f
Karkoff, Maurice   124f
Kárpáti, János   211
Karyotakis, Theodore   230
Kašlík, Václav   197
Kecskeméti, István   211
Kelemen, Milko   221
Keller, Hans   14
Kelterborn, Rudolf   90
Kenessey, Jenö   208
Kerényi, György   210
Ketting, Otto   109f
Khatchaturian, Aram   259-61, 268, 276
Khrennikov, Tikhon
            261-63, 265, 276, 279f
Khrushchev, Nikita   260
Kienzl, Wilhelm   180
Kilar, Wojciech   256
Killmayer, Wilhelm   175, 178
Kirchner, Leon   286
Kirov Theater   268
Klami, Uuno   129
Klebe, Giselher   167, 172f
Kodály, Zoltán   205-07, 209, 284

Koffler, József	245f
Kogoj, Marjus	222
Kókai, Rezsö	208, 211
Kokkonen, Joonas	132
Koppel, Herman D.	111f
Korngold, Erich	180
Kotonski, Wlodzimierz	249, 252
Kounadis, Arghyris	231f
Kox, Hans	108f
Krejčí, Iša	202
Krenek, Ernst	174, 176f, 182f
Krenz, Jan	249
Křička, Jaroslav	194
Kroó, György	211
Kubin, Rudolf	200
Kulm, Walter Müller von	85
Kunc, Jan	194
Kurtág, György	209
Kuusisto, Ilkka	133f
Kvapil, Jaroslav	194
Lajtha, László	206
Lakner, Yehoshua	294
Landowski, Marcel	34
Landré, Guillaume	102f
Láng, István	212
Laurosky, Leonid	267f
Lavry, Marc	282
Le Roux, Maurice	25, 27-29
Leeds Festival (1961)	17
Leeuw, Ton de	108f
Legley, Victor	94
Leibowitz, René	24, 27, 32, 167
Lendvai, Ernö	210
Leotsakos, George	235
Lesnai, Lajos	211
Levidis, Dimitri	229
Lewkowitch, Bernhard	116, 138
Leygraf, Hans	117, 119-23
Lidholm, Ingvar	117
Liebermann, Rolf	87f, 173
Lier, Bertus van	100
Ligeti, Gyorgy	45, 176, 185
Lipatti, Dinu	239
Lisbon Philharmonic	41
Logar, Milhovil	220
Logothetis, Anestis	235
Loriod, Yvonne	16
Lutoslawski, Witold	248f, 251-53
Lutyens, Elisabeth	19f
Machavariani, Alexei	269
Mâche, François	145
Maderna, Bruno	13, 61, 168, 234
Madrid New Music Group	60
Maegaard, Jan	138f
Mahler, Gustav	12
Maklakiewicz, J. A.	246
Malawski, Artur	247, 249-51
Malec, Ivo	222
Mamangakis, Nikos	234
"Manchester Group"	16, 18
Marescotti, André-François	86
Marić, Ljubica	219
Maros, Rudolf	208f
Maróthy, János	211
Marsick, Armand	92
Martin, Frank	79-82
Martinet, Jean-Louis	25, 32-34
Martinů, Bohuslav	200-02
Marx, Joseph	181
Mason, Colin	278f
Matičič, Janez	222
Maw, Nicholas	13, 18n, 19
Meijer, Bernard van den Sigtenhorst	98
Mellers, Wilfrid	20
Mellnäs, Arne	135
Mendelson, Alfred	237f
Mengelberg, Willem	97
Menotti, Gian Carlo	212
Menuhin, Yehudi	285
Meriläinen, Usko	134
Messiaen, Olivier	16, 22-29, 32-36
Mestres, José Maria	58
Metzger, Heinz-Klaus	145, 147, 156
Meyer, Kerstin	117
Miaskovsky, Nicolai	259f, 271
Michaux, Henri	27, 31
microtonality	198-200
Mieg, Peter	86
Mihály, András	208
Milhaud, Darius	31, 34, 93
Mirzoyan, Edward	275
Moeschinger, Albert	84
Molchanov, Kyril	262, 266

Molnár, Antal   210f
Morpurgo-Tagliabue, G.   165
Mortelmans, Lodewijk   93
Mortensen, Finn   127f
Morthenson, Jan W.   135f
Moscow Chamber Orchestra   275
Müller, Paul   84
Musgrave, Thea   13, 15, 19
music education:
  Hungary   213
  Soviet Union   278
music publishing in Hungary   213
Musica Viva   177
musicological research:
  Belgium   95
  Hungary   209-11
musique concrète   9, 21, 36f, 145, 222
Mycielski, Zygmunt   252
National Symphony of Mexico   48
Natra, Sergui   295f
Negrea, Martian   238
New York Philharmonic   233
Newman, Ernest   274
Nielsen, Carl   112, 114
Nigg, Serge   25, 32f
Nikolayev, Alexei   275
Nilsson, Bo   124
Nystroem, Gosta   119
Nono, Luigi   13-15, 61-63, 168
Nordheim, Arne   125, 127f
Nørgaard, Per   138-40
Nørholm, Ib   140
Novák, Jan   201f
Novák, Vítězslav   192-94
Ny Musikk   126
Nykymusiikki   129
O Seculo   41
Obradović, Aleksandar   223
Ogdon, John   16
Ohana, Maurice   34
Olah, Tiberiu   242
Oliveira, Fernando Correia   43
Olsen, Paul Rovsing   116
Ondes Martinot   36
opera:
  British   19f
  Czech   196

French   35
Hungarian   212f
Portuguese   39f
Russian   262-66
Orff, Carl   4, 173, 175
Orgad, Ben-Zion   294f
Osterc, Slavko   222
Ostrčil, Otakar   192
Oswald, Gösta   124
Pablo, Luis de   45, 49-52, 58
Palermo Festival   50
Palester, Roman   246
Palestine Philharmonic Orchestra   284
Panni, Marcello   77
Panufnik, Andrzej   246, 248
Papp, Lajos   209
Partos, Oedoen   284-86, 290, 294
Pásztory, Ditta   213
Pauer, Jiří   202
Paumgartner, Bernhard   188
Pedroso, Elisa de Sousa   40
Peeters, Flor   95
Peixinho, Jorge   43
Penderecki, Krzysztof   256-58
Pepping, Ernst   178
Pereira, Joaquím de Silva   39
Perkowski, Piotr   251
Petrassi, Goffredo   14, 59, 209
Petridis, Petro   229
Petrovics, Emil   209, 212f
Petrželka, Vilim   194
Pettersson, Allan   125
Piart, Arvo   271, 275
Pijper, Willem   97, 99-106
Pin, Patrice de la Tour du   27
Pinto, Victor Macedo   43
Pires, Filipe   43
Piston, Walter   228
Polnauer, Joseph   184
Ponc, Miroslav   199
Poniridis, Georges   229
Poot, Marcel   94
Popov, G. N.   259f
Portugal, Marcos   39
Poulenc, Francis   34
Pousseur, Henri   94
Prigozhyn, Lucian   275

Primrose, William 295
Pro Arte Quartet 95
Profeta, Laurentiu 241
Prokofiev, Sergei, *passim,* but see
　especially　259-64, 267-72, 275, 278
Pylkkänen, Tauno 128
Quinet, Marcel 94
Rabe, Folk 135
Rachmaninov, Sergei 3
Radić, Dušan 223f
Radica, Ruben 222
Radio Française 36
Rajeczky, Benjamin 210
Rajičič, Stanojlo 218
Ramovš, Primož 219
Ránki, György 208
Rautavaara, Einojuhani 130
Rawsthorne, Alan 13f, 20
Reeser, Eduard 97f
Regamey, Constantin 88f
Reiner, Karel 199
Riaats, Jan 275
Riadis, Emil 229f
Řídký, Jaroslav 202
Riisager, Knudage 116
Rilke, Rainer Maria 80
Ristić, Milan 217
Rivier, Jean 34f
Rodgers, Richard 19
Rogalski, Theodor 238
Rogister, Jean 92
Rosenberg, Hilding 114, 116, 119
Rosenthal, Manuel 35
Roslavetz, Nicolai 279f
Rostand, Claude 49
Roussel, Albert 34
Royal Academy of Music, London 18
Rózsa, Miklós 206
Rubbra, Edmund 14, 20
Rudzinski, Witold 247
Ruetter, Hermann 173
Ruiz Coca, Fernando 44f, 57
Ruyneman, Daniël 98
Rychlík, Jan 203
Rydman, Kari 133f
Ryelandt, Joseph 93
Sadai, Yitzhak 295

Saedén, Eric 117
Saeverud, Harald 111
Sallinen, Aulis 134
Salmanov, Vadim 270
Salmenhaara, Erkki 132f
Salmhofer, Franz 188
Salomon, Karel 282
Santa Cecilia Academy 228
Santos, Joly Braga 39, 42f
Sárai, Tibor 208
Sárosi, Bálint 209
Sauguet, Henri 34
Schaeffer, Pierre 9, 36f, 164
Schaeffer, Theodor 202
Schaffer, Boguslaw 254
Schat, Peter 109
Schibler, Armin 88
Schiske, Karl 188
Schmidt, Franz 180
Schoeck, Othmar 79
Schoenberg, Arnold, *passim,* but
　see especially　13, 22, 27, 29, 38,
　　　44, 54, 58, 61f, 69, 82f, 88, 94,
　　114f, 119, 167, 179, 181-85, 200,
　　　　222, 250, 285, 287-88
Schollum, Robert 188
Schreker, Franz 181
Schuller, Gunther 15
Schweizerische Musikgesellschaft 79
Schwertsik, Kurt 185
Searle, Humphrey 20
Seiber, Mátyás 206
serial composition:
　Austria 184f, 188
　Belgium 94
　France 24f, 27-34, 37
　Germany 167, 171
　Great Britain 19-21
　Greece 225f, 231f
　Holland 107f
　Italy 61f
　Poland 245, 249, 251-57
　Portugal 38
　Scandinavia 115, 119f, 129, 138f
　Soviet Union 279f
　Spain 46, 50, 58f
　Switzerland 82-84

Yugoslavia 221f
Serly, Tibor 206
Serocki, Kazimierz 249, 251f
Seter, Mordecai 290f
Shaporin, Yuri 264
Shchedrin, Rodion 260f, 265, 269
Shebalin, Vissarion 259-62, 264
Sheriff, Noam 295
Shnitke, Alfred 271
Shostakovich, Dmitri
13, 259-62, 266, 269, 272-77
Sibelius, Jan 12
Sicilianos, Yorgo 228f
Sikorski, Kazimierz 245, 251
Sindicato Español Universitario 58
Skalkottas, Nikos 225f, 230
Skrowaczewski, Stanislaw 249
Slavenski, Josip 222
Slavicky, Clement 202
Smalley, Roger 20
Smetana, Bedřich 191-96
Smijers, Albert 99
Socialist Realism, doctrine of 261f
Société Belge de Musicologie 95
Söderström, Elisabeth 117
Solomon, Izler 284
Sommer, Vladimir 203
Sonninin, Ahti 128
Sopeña, Federico 52, 54
Souris, André 94
Spadavecchia, Antonio 262, 266
Spisak, Michal 247, 251
Srebotnjak, Aloiz 222
Stalin, Josef 259f, 262, 279
Stein, Erwin 19
Stibilj, Milan 222
stochastic music. See Xenakis, Ianis
Stockhausen, Karlheinz, passim,
but see especially 14f, 30, 36, 43,
51, 123, 152, 156, 168-71, 178, 250
Strasbourg Festival of 1964 33
Stravinsky, Igor, passim, but see
especially 24, 38, 63, 88, 94, 116,
122, 130, 167, 178f, 195,
206, 218, 224, 282
Stutchevsky, Joachim 290
Sugár, Rezsö 208

Suk, Josef 192, 218
Šulek, Stjepan 217
Suter, Robert 89
Sutermeister, Heinrich 86f
Sydney Conservatorium 19
Švara, Danilo 218
Sviridov, Georgii 261, 270
Szabelski, Boleslaw 247, 249, 251
Szabó, Ferenc 207
Szabolcsi, Bence 210
Szalonek, Witold 254
Szalowski, Antoni 247
Szeligowski, Tadeusz 251
Szervánszky, Endre 207f
Szokolay, Sándor 209
Szöllösy, András 209, 211
Szymanowski, Karol 244f
Tal, Joseph 288f
Tardos, Béla 208
Tawaststjerna, Erik 133
Teatro de San Carlo 37
Theater an der Wien 187
Thursday Invitation Concerts 14f
Tippett, Michael 13, 30
Tishchenko, Boris 276
Tittel, Ernst 188
Toduta, Sigismund 239f
Togni, Camillo 61, 72
Tomasi, Henri 35
Touma, Habib 296f
Trojan, Václav 202
Tsouyopoulos, George 234f
Turski, Zbigniew 246
Twardowski, R. 258
Tzindzadze, Sulkhan 278
Uhu, Alfred 188
Ujfalussy, József 211
Union of Soviet Composers 260
Union of Yugoslav Composers 216
Ustvolskaya, Galina 277
Vainberg, Moissei 275, 277
Valen, Fartein 111
Valls, Manuel 59
van Baaren, Kees. See Baaren,
Kees van

Van den Borren, Charles 95
van Hemel, Oscar. *See* Hemel,
  Oscar van
Van Hoof, Jef 93
van Vlijmen, Jan. *See* Vlijmen,
  Jan van
Vancea, Zeno 239
Vandor, Ivan 77
Varèse, Edgard 157
Varga, Ovidiu 241
Vargyos, Lajos 210
Vasconcelos, Jorge Croner de 42
Vaughan Williams, Ralph 12
Vécsy, Jenö 211
Veress, Sándor 206
Vermeulen, Matthijs 98
Viana da Mota, José 40f
Viennese School 116, 180-90, 207, 209
Vieru, Anatol 242
Vikár, László 209
Viski, János 208
Vlijmen, Jan van 110
Vogel, Wladimir 82-84
Volkonsky, Andrei 277f
Vomáčka, Boleslav 194
von Einem, Gottfried. *See* Einem,
  Gottfried von
von Kulm, Walter Müller. *See*
  Kulm, Walter Müller von
Voormolen, Alexander 102
Voss, Friedrich 178
Vreuls, Victor 92
Vuataz, Roger 84

Vukdragović, Mihajlo 217
Vycpálek, Ladislav 193
Wagner-Régeny, Rudolf 173
Walton, William 13, 17, 20
Warsaw Uprising 246
Webern, Anton von, *passim,* but
  see especially 14, 49, 61f, 67, 71,
    89, 109, 114, 119, 123, 138f,
    179, 181f, 184f, 222, 250, 280
Weis, Fleming 138
Welin, Karl-Erik 135
Wellesz, Egon 183
Werle, Johan 136
Whitney, Robert 284
Wiechowicz, Stanislaw 246, 249
Wiele, Aimée van de 95
Wiener Konzerthaus 190
Wiggen, Knut 118
Wildberger, Jacques 89
Williamson, Malcolm 13, 19f
Wimberger, Gerhard 189
Wöldike, Mogens 117
Wolff, Christian 77
Wolpe, Stefan 13
Woytowicz, Boleslaw 251
Xenakis, Yannis 144, 157-65, 232f, 252
Yakobson, L. 268
Yevtushenko, Yevgenii 274
Ysaye, Théo 92
"Zak Incident" 14f
Zhdanov, Andrei 259
Zich, Otakar 193
Zillig, Winfried 177